DISLOCALISM

The Crisis of Globalization and the
Remobilizing of Americanism

SARIKA CHANDRA

THE OHIO STATE UNIVERSITY PRESS • COLUMBUS

Library of Congress Cataloging-in-Publication Data

Chandra, Sarika, 1969–
  Dislocalism : the crisis of globalization and the remobilizing of Americanism / Sarika
Chandra.
      p. cm.
  Includes bibliographical references and index.
  ISBN 978-0-8142-1166-3 (cloth : alk. paper)—ISBN 978-0-8142-9269-3 (cd)
  1. Literature and globalization. 2. Nation-state and globalization. 3. Americanization.
I. Title.
  PN56.G55C47 2011
  809'.93355—dc23
                              2011020797

Cover design by Larry Nozik.
Type set in Adobe Sabon.
Printed by Thomson-Shore, Inc.

9 8 7 6 5 4 3 2 1

CONTENTS

ACKNOWLEDGMENTS

I am indebted to numerous people who have provided much-needed intellectual engagement and sustenance during the time that I have worked on this project. First and foremost is Susan Hegeman, whose support and enthusiasm have been constant. I have been most fortunate to have her intellectual presence, her example, and her patience. Tace Hedrick, Stephanie Smith, Maxine Margolis, and Robert Hatch offered valuable advice in the early stages of this project. Phil Wegner, Sid Dobrin, Amitava Kumar, and Robert Thomson helped me articulate my initial thinking as I struggled to think about intellectual work and critique.

I have been privileged to find support among friends and colleagues at Wayne State University and elsewhere. Conversations filled with wit, humor, irony, and sarcasm proved to be most fruitful for my work. For that, I thank Richard Grusin, Ross Pudaloff, Lisa Ze Winters, Jonathan Flatley, Kirsten Thompson, Steven Shaviro, Danielle Aubert, Lara Cohen, Alex Day, Anne Duggan, Robert Diaz, John Pat Leary, Bill Harris, Dana Seitler, Cannon Schmitt, Jaime Goodrich, Kathryne Lindberg, Donna Landry, and Gerald MacLean.

Many others have given their time in reading this book at various stages and have saved me from countless errors. In particular, I thank Trish Ventura and Jeff Rice for their comments on earlier drafts; Jonathan Flatley, Jeff Geiger, Richard Grusin, Bill Mullen, Chris Connery, Dick Terdiman, and Imre Szeman for their insights and steadfast encouragement; Neil Larsen for helping me think through various conceptual problems and for offering the most unflinching criticism of my work; Rachel Buff for her generous help with crucial problems; Anne Duggan, who probably grew tired of reading parts of this work numerous times but offered her help most graciously; and Matthew Guterl not only for helping me with many important questions but also for taking seriously the smallest of my concerns.

I am appreciative of my students for their curiosity and the energy they bring to the classroom. I especially thank my students in the graduate seminars "Fordism/Postfordism," "Theorizing America in a Global Economy," and "Globalization in Crisis." And the enthusiasm of my students in the undergraduate seminars "Im/migration," "Theories of Globalization," "Food Politics," and "Global Literature" was extremely infectious. In particular, I thank Katrina Newsom, John Conner, Joe Paszek, Ana Gavrilovska, Diana Daghlas, Kyle Walivaara, and Steven Remenapp for engaging in a prolonged intellectual inquiry that continues to be a source of inspiration for me.

Wayne State University has provided material assistance in the form of a sabbatical award; publication funds; the Humanities Center faculty fellowship award; and the Josephine Nevins Keal Faculty Fellowship from the English department. Martha Ratliff and Ellen Barton have supported the completion of this book. Walter Edwards made it possible for me to present my work in progress at the humanities forum.

Carla Freccero facilitated my time at the Center for Cultural Studies, University of California Santa Cruz. This book is better for the feedback I received from the participants of the Cultural Studies Colloquium Series.

Parts of this work were presented at the American Studies Association and have benefited enormously from the advice, comments, and response that I have received over the years.

The staff members at the various institutions that I have been affiliated with have made it much easier for me to finish my project. In particular, I thank Kathy Zamora, Margaret Maday, Myrtle Hamilton, Kay Stone, Rhonda Agnew, Diara Prather, Royanne Smith, Brian Shields, Kathy Williams, Carla Blount, Stephanie Casher, and Shan Ritchie.

Sustaining this project would have been difficult without the rich conversations with many friends, including Dennis Childs, Marcy Newman, E. Taranasis, J. J. Melendez, Gaea Honeycutt, Sandeep Ray, Daniel LaForest, Luis Martín-Cabrera, Joe Voiles, and Akash Kumar. Akash has taught me the most useful conceptions of his own—the "existential multiplier" and the "mui" (shorthand for Michigan left turns). And of course this book would still be incomplete without the help of Lorenzo and B. Jamoli.

Most of all, I am deeply indebted to those, perhaps the only people, who have the potential to make me forget about work—Jai, Priya, Sejal, Esha, Khalil, and Etua. It has been especially great to work on this book while living in close proximity to Jai and Priya for some of the time.

The opportunity to work with The Ohio State University Press has been very rewarding. I am grateful to Sandy Crooms, who has been the best and most encouraging editor; to Maggie Diehl for her attention to all of the necessary details; and to Malcolm Litchfield for his support of intellectual production. Martin Boyne was extremely helpful with his work on the index.

Sections of this project have been previously published as essays. A section of chapter 1 was published as "From Fictional Capital to Capital as Fiction: Globalization and the Intellectual Convergence of Business and the Humanities," in *Cultural Critique* no. 76 (Fall 2010). A section of chapter 2 was published as "Reproducing a Nationalist Literature in the Age of Globalization: Reading (Im)migration in Julia Alvarez's *How the García Girls Lost Their Accents*" in *American Quarterly* 60, no. 3 (September 2008). These essays have been extensively revised for this book.

INTRODUCTION

I. GLOBALIZATION AS OBJECT . . . AND SUBJECT

Globalization, according to what has for some time become the conventional wisdom, refers to a radically new social, economic, and cultural reality in which all preexisting, locally constituted practices and ideas have ceased to be viable. Whether, as once proclaimed from the standpoint of "New Economy" Realpolitik by a Robert Reich[1] or championed outright by, say, a Thomas Friedman,[2] globalization's proponents say there has been no choice but to line up and keep pace with this new reality or be left behind by history. Globalization, in this hegemonic and vernacular sense, has taken on the form of a rhetoric of obsolescence, threatening virtually all existing practices and life-ways with eventual extinction should they fail to adapt. The perceived choice has been to globalize or to become what Evan Watkins has termed a "throwaway," a term that describes the coding of "isolated groups of the population" as those "who haven't moved with the times" (3). As Watkins explains in his book of the same name (*Throwaways: Work Culture and Consumer Education*, 1993), people and practices don't simply become obsolete with the advent of "new" technologies and economic or cultural conditions. The concept of the "obsolete" is itself already posited and rendered necessary by the discourse of the "new." "Obsolescence," writes Watkins, "involves conditions of both cultural and economic production in the present, not what has survived uselessly" (7). It is in the form of such a ubiquitous rhetoric of obsolescence that globalization—beginning as early as the first waves of financialization in the 1970s in the wake of the crisis of Fordism, well before the jargon itself became widespread—forced its way into virtually all spheres of mainstream opinion and secular-intellectual discourse as though it were a new categorical imperative. Largely ever since, the response on the part of a widening range of social practices, institutional, intellectual, cultural, and otherwise, has been to jettison— or *appear* to jettison—existing local, regional or even national models and methodologies and embrace purportedly more global paradigms, however the latter were to be understood. My objective in this work is to analyze and critique globalization in academic, intellectual, and cultural spheres as an *ideological* discourse that took hold post-1980s and generated this rhetoric of obsolescence.

None of this is to deny that profound, far-reaching, and, undoubtedly, *global* transformations *have* radically altered capitalist society since the crisis of Fordism took hold in the 1970s and 1980s[3]—roughly the same time frame during which globalization became a fixture of quotidian discourse in the Western metropolis and beyond. Recall David Harvey's observation that the popularizing of the term itself can be traced back to an American Express Card advertising campaign in the mid-1970s[4] and Harvey's (self-critical) rebuke to the left for its own rush to adopt a language in which a subtle apology for economic and social policies and outcomes just as easily associated with much less savory terms (e.g., neoliberalism) was already detectable.

As regards the historical *reality* of the world ushered in by the end of Fordism and of the post–World War II capitalist "Golden Age," whether or not one literally refers to it as "globalized," there exists a rich body of theoretical and critical literature from which to draw critiques of mainstream globalization's brave new world. This includes the work of well-known radical scholars including Harvey, Samir Amin, Immanuel Wallerstein, Mike Davis, Saskia Sassen, Fredric Jameson, Slavoj Žižek, and journals such as *New Left Review, Monthly Review,* or *Public Culture,* as well as that of many other critics and activists within (and outside) the left academy.[5] A systematic assessment of this collective historicizing and critical demystification of globalization—upon much of which I myself rely, explicitly and implicitly, throughout *Dislocalism*—would require at least as much space and time as I've allotted to the present study. But here at least we have a critical-theoretical foothold from which it has become possible to challenge globalization's rhetoric of obsolescence and its metanarrative of free-market, high-tech driven universalisms in their mythical power to enthrall and coerce.

I intend the present work as, in the most general sense, a contribution to this larger, collective theory and critique of globalization. *Dislocalism,* however, although it too concerns itself with social and economic changes associated with the period of globalization, also differs from this trend of critical scholarship.[6] For it is on the ideology of globalization—the latter's "common sense" as an imperative in which the threat of obsolescence appears as if fatefully coterminous with the local itself—and even more specifically on what I understand here as the rhetorical, discursive, metanarrative dimension of such ideology that I will focus my critical analysis throughout the four chapters that comprise the main body of the book. I address the peculiar collective anxiety generated by globalization as various institutional and cultural sites answer the call to produce new work in keeping with the global "Zeitgeist." Regarding globalization as, simultaneously, a discourse *and* a historical process, I examine closely the symptomatic inversion resulting from the anxiety of the global: while presenting their work as if it were a response to globalization, intellectuals, writers, academics and corporate managers are in fact working simultaneously to *produce* globalization itself *as* discourse—the very discourse that then produces the imperative to adapt to the new, to escape obsolescence.

Methodologically grounded in literary and cultural studies, the chapters that make up the body of *Dislocalism,* which I will preview shortly in more detail in order to explain the thinking that has gone into the selection and sequencing of their fundamental subject matter, take up the transformations produced by the above-mentioned ideology and the discursive effects of globalization, beginning in the 1980s, in four, outwardly quite diverse American cultural/intellectual objects. The first of these is management theory, especially as concerns its methods of training future corporate managers and its rethinking of the very structure of American business organizations in a fully globalized marketplace. There follows a discussion of the field of U.S. immigrant and ethnic literary narrative, and in particular the globalization of critical and interpretive scholarship centered on two immigrant novels, Julia Alvarez's *How the García Girls Lost Their Accents* and Diana Abu-Jaber's *Crescent,* and the process of their canonization within a transnational U.S. immigrant literature. The third chapter focuses on U.S. travel-writing and the efforts, as traced in three particular works by Robert Kaplan, Mary Morris, and Paul Theroux, to find ways to reinvent that genre itself, given what appears to be the "end" of travel in any traditional sense in the wake of globalization. The final chapter takes up the relationship between food and tourism in American popular media narratives (here magazines and broadcast television) where the response to globalization becomes a recoding of tourism itself as culinary and the seeking out of specifically American food–based experiences in places that can be (re)constructed, at least as far as eating is concerned, as nationally "other."

II. DISLOCALISM
Its Meaning and Conceptual Necessity

In focusing my critique of globalization along such rhetorical/ideological-discursive lines, I necessarily distinguish between globalization as such a discourse and as a term referring to a real historical process. In making this distinction I argue that various intellectual and cultural sites, in responding to the call to globalize, are in fact engaging in a profoundly ambiguous and contradictory strategy through which to promote global or transnationalized practices. In so doing, however, they consolidate existing national, institutional, and local forms of intellectual and cultural methodologies. I refer to this strategy as dislocalism—a concept of my own that doubles as the title of my book and as a conceptual synthesis, a kind of theoretical miniature, of its contents.

In order to explain fully what is meant by dislocalism and how it can help to analyze more precisely these rhetorical and ideological dimensions of globalization,[7] I will begin on the most fundamental and abstract level, focusing on the logic of the term itself. Then I will add to its critical-theoretical mediations by considering it in relation to the two categories most clearly central to any ideology–critical understanding of globalization, the *nation* as such, and, as a special, perhaps unique subset of the former, globalization's unmistakable national-ideological center of gravity: America and American*ism*. I use the term America here cognizant of what is already the ideology conveyed by the word itself, making it into what might almost be considered the semantic derivative rather than the root of words such as Americanism and Americanization and also as a way of pointing to the blatantly ideologizing content of the word when, forgetting the existence of the America(s) south of the Rio Grande, it is used as though synonymous with the national entity called the United States.

That "globalization" can be made as theoretically precise and diverse in meaning as the context demands is clear.[8] But the same is true of its ambiguities in popular conceptions, and not the least of these is its seemingly indifferent capacity to take on utopian (as well as dystopian) meanings, whether on the right or the left. Conjuring images of the "blue planet" itself as seen from outer space, "globalization" and cognates such as the "global," and so forth, become, from a purely rhetorical point of view, the perfect word: as frictionless as the world imagined to be the result if all local barriers to mobility, whether of capital or simply of ideas and cultures, really were possible to clear away through the lifting of all forms of protectionism or the introduction of new communications technologies. Indeed, for globalization in this sense the local per se verges on becoming nothing but a barrier, the flipside of the pure abstraction of, to return to Justin Rosenberg's expression, "the process of becoming worldwide."

A moment's thought is sufficient to detect the logical fallacy of simply superimposing a "mobility/stasis" onto a "global/local" binarism—as if a space divided into ten thousand mutually incommunicable localities were any less a world or a globe than one in which ten thousand were reduced to one. That, to reiterate an observation often returned to in Marx's writings, that the world itself does not become a truly global reality in the active, historical sense before the creation of the world market in early Western modernity, does nothing to corroborate the ideology of globalization. That same world market also lays the groundwork for the most extreme reassertion of barricaded localisms: the ever more destructive and more *global* wars that are the result of globalizing markets themselves. The very same historical forces of "bourgeois civilization" that, as the *Manifesto* already had it, give us "in place of the old local and national seclusion and self-sufficiency . . . intercourse in every direction, universal inter-dependence of nations" also create the conditions for the reassertion of the "old local and national seclusion" in new, more universal, more—the world is unavoidable—*global* forms. Globalization, here, regardless of whether we date it back to 1972 or to 1492, works so as to overcome the local, and, without doubt, steadily reduces the historical hold of localism as a dominant form of social organization and experience. But this is a relative process. In the very process of doing so, globalization, insofar as it names an irresistible secular tendency of capitalism, likewise creates new localisms, even to the point, as recent history in particular demonstrates in multiple ways, of exacerbating the grip of the local precisely as an effect of transformations undergone on a world scale.[9]

In what has come to be its dominant understanding since globalization entered the mainstream of public and popular discourse in the 1980s, this very necessity that it manifests itself *in and as new forms of the local* has undergone a kind of erasure. The ideology of globalization, its rhetorical sleight of hand—what Justin Rosenberg terms its "folly"[10]—is, in a word, *to make it appear as though this erasure of the local were itself the meaning and content of "globalization."* It is to convey this overdetermining resistance to the local as the obsolete that I have devised the term "dislocalism" as, initially, a simplified means of reference to this specific ideological and rhetorical effect. Dislocalism provides me here with a means of referring, on the level of abstract generality, to an ideological and rhetorical phenomenon that continues to refer to itself with a signifier—globalization—that it shares with a perfectly legitimate and meaningful theoretical concept. I intend to capture by means of dislocalism what is historically specific to the rhetoric of globalization dominant since the 1980s. To that end, dislocalism self-consciously deviates from more familiar, cognate terms within the "globalization" discursive field—e.g., "displacement" or "dislocation"—through an ideological ambivalence built into the new term itself. The drive to "dislocalize" is thus, in the broadest and most immediate sense, a drive to displace the local in order to engage with the global—that is, placing the stress on the prefix, a form of *dis*localism. But it is my contention—to be demonstrated at length and in multiple contexts throughout this work—that, in many instances, intellectual and cultural spheres for which "globalization" serves as a means of *dis*localizing are no less invested in *remaining* localized. In this, then, they may be said to adhere to a dis*localism* (here stressing the root noun, a neologism itself)—precisely so that older intellectual-cultural and institutional practices are not *entirely* displaced or dislocated, and thereby rendered obsolete. Dislocalism, in other words, describes a dislocation, a move to supersede the local that is at the same time a form of stasis, a movement whose aim is also to remain in place.

III. THE NATION AND AMERICANISM

Any attempt to analyze and critique the ideology embedded in the imperative to globalize inevitably raises the question of the local in its form as the nation and what has been, according to certain theoretical perspectives, its purported obsolescence in the wake of globalization. There is simply too little space in this book to do real justice to this question and the sheer mass of theoretical literature devoted to debating it. What can and should be said here, especially as concerns the matter of how *Dislocalism* situates itself in relation to theories of the nation as globalization has reframed them, is that the question of its obsolescence cannot be correctly posed at all without first recognizing that the nation as a general category can often be too abstract for *any* answer to be made. Thus when Appadurai openly questioned, in 1996, whether the "nation-state" might be "on its last legs," notwithstanding the care he took to qualify this claim, it was and is hard if not impossible to know what it would mean to uphold or disprove it.[11] It seems almost too obvious a point to be made, and yet one that all too readily disappears from view, that the respective relationships to globalization of China and, say, of Slovenia—both unquestionably nations from a juridical standpoint—are so radically different as to put into question what sort of meaning the concept of the nation could have in this context. That said, however, there remains a wide range of work, both theoretically and historically centered, that has informed the present study as concerns the question of the nation and the changes it undergoes with the onset of globalization beginning in the 1970s and 1980s. Along with now virtually classic studies by scholars such as Benedict Anderson, Ernest Gellner, and Eric Hobsbawm, these sources also include, inter alia, work by Samir Amin, Michael Mann, Roberto Schwarz, Aijaz Ahmad, and Pepe Escobar.[12]

But I do want to offer two further general observations here on the nation that bear in essential ways on the general theory and critique of dislocalism as well as on its various concrete instances, in the chapters that follow. The first is that *any* argument regarding the much-debated "decline of the nation-state" at the hands of globalization, whatever the position argued, is certain to encounter serious problems if it does not pose the underlying structural question of changes in the *historical* relation of the *form* of the nation to capital itself. I argue explicitly in chapter 1, and implicitly throughout *Dislocalism*, that this relation has changed in fundamental ways as capitalism has increasingly broken free of the limits of national markets and local and state regulation of capitalist enterprises, driven closer and closer toward the asymptotic (that is, never fully attainable) point of reproducing itself directly on a global plane—with the correspondingly increased potential to collapse in on itself in a crisis of likewise ever more global proportions. But this is *not* to argue—a point others have made as well—that the nation has therefore become obsolete in any sense, or that it exerts any less of a shaping, decisive influence on political, cultural, or intellectual developments. One could with equal and perhaps greater justification argue that, in certain ways, globalization has *increased* this shaping influence, even as it has also, in my terms, dislocalized it, that is, produced forms of ultra-nationalism precisely so as to counteract and correct for increasing cosmopolitanism. The globalization of capital may indeed negate what had previously been the more or less spontaneous historical identity of capital and nation during earlier phases of capitalist development, but it does not put anything positive in place of the nation as nation-*state,* that is, as a political/territorial entity evolved for the purpose of regulating the *social* effects of commodity production and "self-valorizing value" outside the sphere of value itself. (Take, as one example of this absence or sheer impossibility of nationally based regulation under the regime of globalization, the case of global warming and catastrophic environmental damage to the planet as a whole.) The nation is, so to speak, hollowed out—the more precise concept I propose in chapter 2 is denationalization—but globalization does not fill it in with any positive, transnational substance.[13] The concept of dislocalism here is, if nothing else, one way to try to place a conceptual marker on this negative persistence of the nation even after the ground has shifted, sometimes beyond the point of disintegration, underneath its foundations.

When the nation and nationalism in question are, respectively, the U.S. and Americanism, then the need to grasp the changed historical relation between global capital and the nation-state as form becomes even greater and, correspondingly, more difficult to meet.[14] This is because, as successive, global economic crises are making increasingly clear, the U.S. as national economic formation occupies—or has occupied since at least the end of World War II—a position of combined military and financial dominance and in this sense a unique position in the global capitalist system.[15] The highly ideological, mystified projection of America as exceptional, as a "nation of nations," to the extent that the U.S. has continued to be the leading force behind globalization, can thus claim a certain degree of historical truth. In the case of America as nation, the contradictions of globalization will therefore appear—once again objectively, if only up to a point—to have become *internalized*. (Take, for example, the decision by the U.S. Treasury Department and the Federal Reserve not to come to the rescue of Lehman Brothers in 2008, which was certain to have enormous international as well as national implications.) The result of this—and this brings up my second observation—is that the effort to globalize or transnationalize American intellectual, cultural, or disciplinary formations itself becomes a uniquely paradoxical one. The effects of globalization, due to the leading U.S. role in its institution, are themselves identified as Americanization. Dislocalism in an Americanist context—that is, as an effort to globalize that is at the same time a move to consolidate Americanism—revolves around this ambivalence. If globalization appears as somehow internal to Americanism, what does it then mean to speak of nationally, regionally, ethnically, and racially distinctive *American* cultures, practices, identities, and so forth?

Indeed, a number of scholars and critics in American studies—among them, John Carlos Rowe, Melanie McAlister, Robyn Wiegman, Donald Pease, and Amy Kaplan—have addressed the latter question in a variety of ways. In a 2009 article,[16] Pease, although utilizing a terminology quite different from my own, analyzes precisely the above paradox. While defending the advances made by a transnationalizing, "post-exceptionalist" American studies and its "abandonment of the discourse of exceptionalism as wholly identical with Cold War imperatives that had been rendered obsolete by global realities" Pease now wonders "whether this renunciation of American exceptionalism did not produce still another structure of disavowal" (22), that is, another, paradoxically *globalized* form of exceptionalism.

> Does not the representation of the US as altogether embedded in economic and global processes turn a blind eye to the exceptions to market regulations that US policy makers have constructed to give the US an economic edge in the global economy? Does not post-exceptionalist American studies also simply ignore the ways in which two of the core tenets of the discourse of American exceptionalism—the rule of law and neoliberal market ideology—have saturated the global processes in which America is embedded? (ibid.)

One must observe great caution, warns Pease, lest the result of a globalized American studies turn out to be a "disavowal" of the already Americanized dimensions of globalization itself. I will examine some of these same difficulties in the context of American ethnic and immigrant studies in chapter 2 of *Dislocalism*.

Consider, as further illustration of what I mean by dislocalism in this more mediated context, what has been, coeval with the turn to globalization, the widespread currency in cultural as well as American studies of ideas and terms such as "transnationalized" forms of border crossing and migrancy. These terms replace more familiar ones such as immigration and travel, forms of mobility in which the crossing of more or less fixed national boundaries has been tacitly understood. And, to be sure, immigration and travel, as concepts, do now seem inadequate to fully describing the new patterns of mobility of peoples across the globe. But, as I argue in detail in chapter 2, the (relatively) new, globalized paradigms nevertheless continue, in subtle ways, to reproduce the American- and nation-centered perspective they are meant to supersede. Their ideological effect is often to discount the reality of *non-U.S.* national specificities and histories, forgetting that a border becomes a very different thing depending on whether one is crossing it out (or outside) of rather than into the United States. Because the uneven and contradictory reality of globalization is transitive and directs the movement of migration *toward* global centers of wealth and capital accumulation such as the U.S., merely proclaiming the borderless condition of migrancy or the transnational can readily become a way of *preserving* a U.S.-centered, nationalist perspective. Throughout *Dislocalism* I show how, whatever else they do, the very categories of transnational mobility, designed to reflect more accurately a globalized sensibility, can also work—in the instance of dislocalism analyzed in chapter 2, via *domestic* notions of race, gender, ethnicity, and class—to consolidate existing institutional, disciplinary, and generic boundaries drawn along national and local lines. In the process they redefine and shore up American identity *through* the affirmation of its global others, positing the U.S. as *both* a global and a local place. This particular strategy of defining American identity is not new in itself, but I will show throughout the various chapters of *Dislocalism* that it has taken on new dimensions as a result of changes in social relations specific to the globalization-driven period from the 1980s forward.

IV. DISLOCALISM
Constants and Variables

I have already touched, very briefly, on the specific objects of analysis and research around which I have articulated and assembled the following chapters. But now that I have offered a brief introduction to dislocalism as their common theoretical and conceptual framework, I want to remark on the thinking that has governed the selection of the objects themselves—especially given what may seem, at first glance, their considerable heterogeneity. My claim here is that American management theory, literary critiques of immigration narrative, and travel- and food/tourism-writing produced under the aegis of the post-1980s globalization imperative are each, in fact, especially illuminating as ideological strategies for positing the U.S. as *both* a global and a local place, that is, as instantiations of the particular adaptive response to globalization I term dislocalism. Yet this still leaves the appearance of a gap between dislocalism as theoretical abstraction and its mediation in this particular set of cultural-intellectual phenomena. Let me then try to explain how I have sought to provide a mediating link. To do that, I want to show how the specific objects of analysis in the work as a whole represent variations on the specific *cultural and social logic* of dislocalism.

But there is, of course, at least one thing that does *not* vary in the four chapters that make up *Dislocalism,* and that is their Americanist focus. The objects or phenomena at the center of each chapter are, whether consciously or not on their own part, inseparably tied to the society, culture, and politics of the U.S. This Americanist focus, the connection of

America and Americanism to dislocalism as concept, is neither accidental nor simply normative, and thus no less in need of theoretical grounding in a book that analyzes and critiques globalization than the transition, qua dislocalism, from management theory to critical readings of Julia Alvarez, or from there to travel writing and narratives about food tourism. Recall the observation made previously, in the context of a general remark on the nation and dislocalism:

> The highly ideological, mystified projection of America as "exceptional," as a "nation of nations," to the extent that the U.S. has continued to be the leading force behind globalization, can thus claim a certain degree of historical truth. In the case of America as nation, the contradictions of globalization will therefore appear—once again objectively, if only up to a point—to have become *internalized.*

If we turn to mainstream, sanctioned public opinion as voiced in the *New York Times* or the *Wall Street Journal,* the purported internal identity of globalization with Americanization becomes the most blatant form of apology for U.S. national/imperial interests, themselves understood as inseparable from the global spread of neoliberal economic policies. Or in those and other media it becomes the mere flip side of such apologetics, which substitutes anti-Americanism for the critique of capitalism as such. Either way, what is missed is the apparent spatial anomaly in which, to be more precise, the transformations of capital that begin to make themselves felt following the collapse of the Fordist boom in the 1970s presuppose the continued domination of the U.S. over a capitalist world system in which, thanks mainly to increasingly rapid financialization, such transformations can no longer be contained within *any* national economic matrix and are *global before* they are national. But on the more immediate, manifest plane of the intellectual and the cultural, the deepest structural contradictions of globalization, insofar as they describe a space *both* internal and external to the U.S.—a condition that is *not,* it should be stressed, synonymous with globalization per se across its entire range of possible articulations and effects—will be experienced either as already American or as virtually, inescapably vulnerable to Americanization. Here we have the form of dislocalism to be specifically examined in this work: dislocalism as a form of spatializing of intellectual/cultural genres that is simultaneously global and local. Dislocalism, that is, traces the rhetorical pressure exerted by the global as a constant movement away from the local that always leads back to some other version of the local once the global threatens to reach the zero point of pure, "liquid" mobility. However, dislocalism now has a concrete social and historical moment as well: America and the American as the simultaneously global and *national*.

But to return now to the question of what I have termed the specific *cultural and social logic* of dislocalism: globalization, considered as metaphor, thought/image, or even as the basis for a kind of phenomenology, is not merely the image of a borderless, total space but of the constant *movement* across borders and all manner of localized barriers. It describes, to return to Justin Rosenberg's phrase, "the process of *becoming* worldwide" (my emphasis), while in the thinking of Zygmunt Bauman it becomes the "liquid," a constant flux.[17] Globalization, in short, while finite in the form of the planetary, also projects the formal image of an infinite *mobility* through and across the space of the planetary.

But the image of pure, infinite, limitless mobility is, of course, an abstraction itself, a mere idea. In order to be visualized at all, to be spatialized, such mobility must be represented in relationship to something fixed.

Thus when a particular, already existing social, cultural, or intellectual form of organization, discipline, genre, and the like, is confronted with the imperative of globalization, when it, in other words, is threatened with the danger of its own *immobilization* as something merely local and hence obsolete, its task, ideologically speaking, is dual: it must globalize, that is, remove or supersede previously sedimented immobilizations or localizing barriers. But, in order not to dissolve altogether into what is, finally, a no less threatening state of total flux and liquidity, it must find—to borrow, in a different context, a term of David Harvey's—a new "spatial fix"[18] or set of localizable coordinates that can appear "global" in relation to the older localism that now threatens it with obsolescence. This is, again, the logic, the rhetorical pattern, that I term dislocalism. But now its variables, its simplest terms, have been specified. That is, as a general strategy for satisfying globalization's rhetorical imperative while also mapping the ideology of globalization itself, dislocalism brings into play both what I will refer to here as a specific metaphor of mobility as well as a corresponding form of "spatial fix."

If examined now as variations on these two (as one might refer to them) phenomenological constants of dislocalism, the book's four objects of critical analysis come into a new, more distinct focus. What we can now map out in each case, in the form of an imagined remobilization of the "genre" in question and its corresponding spatial fixation, is a distinct "imaginary solution" to the contradictions of an ideologically (re)"Americanized" globalization. But let me now illustrate this, and the pattern of variations produced by this interplay of ideological figures, with a concluding survey and schematic analysis of the chapters themselves.

V. MANAGEMENT THEORY

I begin, then, with the first chapter, devoted, on the most general plane, to an analysis of the ramifications of globalization within American management theory during a period ranging from the late 1980s until the mid 2000s. But why include management theory in a study that addresses mainly cultural and literary subjects and that does so, broadly speaking at least, from the disciplinary standpoint of cultural and literary studies? The explanation for this ultimately points to the more direct impact of the increased mobility of capital itself on this particular discipline and the resulting forms of metaphorical remobilization and spatial fix that come into play here. But a more immediate case for taking up management theory is a fact perhaps still unfamiliar to many who work in the humanities and closely related disciplines. Dislocalism in the humanities takes the form of an anxiety that the field itself and its corresponding literary and cultural objects of study have become obsolete in the wake of globalization.[19] Critics and scholars in the humanities often perceive themselves in the position of having to respond to globalization as a corporate-driven phenomenon always already *imposed* on them. There is also registered the implicit belief that the humanities can escape obsolescence only within a corporatized, globalizing university by, so to speak, globalizing itself in advance. But as many cultural and literary critics have turned to questions of business, finance, and corporate culture in order to make sense of globalization,[20] academic management theorists, along with popular management theory gurus such as Tom Peters and Peter Drucker, began, most notably since the 1980s, to turn to culture, literary fiction, and even literary/cultural theory for what were and are ultimately comparable reasons. The real measure of globalization aside, the *idea* of globalization has placed the humanities and what is purportedly its corporate, disciplinary other into an ironic relationship of partly blind interdisciplinarity in which each has, at a certain point, had to turn close attention to the other's field of study in order to secure its own position vis-à-vis what have been perceived as the current realities and threatening implications of globalization. I will have a good deal more to say by way of critical explication about this in chapter 1 itself, but suffice it for now to point out how it is that, via its own dislocalized narratives of obsolescence, knowledge production in the humanities can often unwittingly function to support the very corporate practices that supposedly threaten the humanities with extinction.

Management theory, as one might suspect, joins the rest of the business academy and U.S. corporate culture generally in welcoming the advent of globalization and regarding it as both a justification of the neoliberal policies instituted in and exported from the U.S. and the U.K. in the 1970s and 1980s and an opportunity for further advances toward the global dominance of U.S. capital. But a closer examination of the discipline itself, including both its more strictly academic branch as well as its popular, mass-mediatized wing, best represented by the series of best-selling management "bibles" by the likes of Drucker and Peters reveals a profound, underlying anxiety to match that of the humanities when faced with the globalization "imperative." The latter arises from a sense, not without a definite measure of truth, that globalization's tendency toward the unleashing of capital from all local and national barriers to its mobility has the clear potential to place U.S. corporate managers in a position of increasing *disadvantage,* not only as concerns its more cosmopolitan competitors but also vis-à-vis the *form* of management, a.k.a. "organization" (object of an entire wing within management theory known as organization studies). To state briefly what will be elaborated upon at length below in the first chapter, globalization, insofar as it is equated in the corporate mind with the total flux of capital and the lifting of all restrictions to the transnationalization of its organizational configurations (the new, post-Fordist dominance of finance capital is clearly weighing heavily here), calls for a radical rethinking of corporate management and organization themselves, even going so far as to raise the question of what constitutes the "Americanization" of the capitalist enterprise itself. Where this rethinking leads management theory postglobalization varies in the details, needless to say, but the general direction is clear: management and organizational structure must themselves be able to mimic, to incorporate (literally) in its managers (the future generations of the so-called professional managerial class) the radical remobilization and constant flux of globalized capital. Management must become (again, as we shall see, in the words of lecture-circuit stars like Peters as well as in articles published in management theory academic journals) "post-Newtonian" and even postmodern. Here, then, we have management theory's "metaphor of mobility": a total remobilization of corporate human dynamics in the form of a de-centered, never-in-the-office, horizontally self-displacing managerial subject able to reproduce in living, breathing bodies the total remobilizing of capital in the abstract.

But what is it that makes such managerial agents, once they have—as this variant of dislocalism will have it—internalized as decision-making capacity the pure abstract mobility of globalized capital, *into subjects?*

At least once before—as recently as the heydays of Fordism and the Cold War—American corporate culture would have had a ready answer: corporate "culture" itself, either in the case of the giant enterprise, on the model, say, of Ford, as a kind of nation within the nation, or in the form of "America" as a national corporate subject itself, especially as against powerful competitors such as (in the 1980s) the national corporate subject known as "Japan." But globalization has changed all that and put "America" and Americanization into a question. The latter is now no longer the spontaneous point of departure, but for management theory as one instance of dislocalism, the problematic point of arrival. The answer—and here the sheer complexity in the chain of managerial reasoning will require the full text of chapter 1 to clarify and render plausible—is: *culture itself.* Capital, in reality, never stops moving, erecting barriers as a result of its own development that it must then proceed to demolish and replace with new ones—until its final barrier (itself) is reached—and it breaks down as a whole. Under globalization, at the stage of development corresponding to the period that concerns this study, multiple barriers to this movement certainly remain, but do indeed come close enough to disappearing that capitalism itself must take notice. But so as to internalize both the reality of increasing as well as the myth of total mobility, the new, globalized manager must be able to represent the space defined by this movement, and thus must start out from a point that does *not* move—management's spatial fix. And it is *culture* that, as the field's scholarly and mass-distributed literature as well as the university curricula designed for the training of new managerial cadre bear ample witness, supplies this fix. Culture as such a spatial fix here is globalized and universal but at the same time subjective as well as subject to fixation, both in the form of a tradition or a canon, *as well as,* in the case of the branch of the management academy known as international development, multicultural and ethnic. Nor does the fix stop at culture as such; it often prefers its literary manifestation—here, generally speaking, the more classical, and hence the more "universal," the better. And, to mix it up even more for the humanist who thought corporate reading habits went no further than Ayn Rand and Von Hayek, management theory becomes an avid reader of the theories associated with cultural studies, preferably its postmodern wing, but not excluding Fredric Jameson. For, to the extent that the accelerated, hyper-fungible financialized capital that is synonymous with globalization betokens not only a more frequent recourse to the form of credit that Marx, using the terminology of the English bankers of his own day, termed "fictitious capital," but a trend toward the fictionalization of capital as such—a subject that chapter 1 as well as other sections of *Dislocalism* will also explore—here too management theory senses the crisis this portends. It thus turns to—what else?—fiction itself, as well as the strain of postmodernism that declares everything (including, for Tom Peters, the corporate organization itself) a narrative in any case, for its most ironic spatial fix of all.

VI. (IM)MIGRATION

At this point *Dislocalism* turns to the less direct, more highly mediated ways that globalization and the increased mobility of capital have reshaped the underlying metaphors of mobility and imaginary spatial fixations around which certain cultural narratives of Americanism coalesce. Here, in contrast to management theory, the crucial connection between shifts in the relation of globalized capital as such to shifting forms of national identity formation, above all to Americanization as the latter's "borders" expand and recede, is both less direct and yet also less prone to the blatant mythologizing resorted to by corporate thinking. The ideological and rhetorical strategies of dislocalism thus become, by comparison, more subtle and more difficult to unravel.

It should be noted that the tropes of remobilization and fixation that serve this cultural critique as its basic ideological variables are, in themselves, not historically unique to globalization. The reproduction of an American national identity has long made emphatic use of metaphors of mobility: witness the mythical prominence of the so-called voyages of discovery and settlement, from Columbus on, as well as the traditional figure of the U.S. as a "nation of immigrants." But the historical realities of globalization have, I argue, both increased the resonance of such metaphors and also skewed them and forced their reimagining. As the new dynamic of globalization alters the historical relation of capital and the form of the nation, relativizing the boundaries of the nation itself and positioning global capital as both external *and* internal to the experience of Americanness, the latter's ability to ground itself in a movement of the nation to and from its outside becomes more and more uncertain.

I devote my second chapter to critical analysis of current trends in American immigrant/ethnic literary studies. The latter field is especially vulnerable to the contradictions that arise when, faced with an *a priori* imperative to globalize and the political and ethical opprobrium of intellectual identification of any kind with the Americanism at large in the world today, the broader discipline of American literary/cultural studies undertakes to displace itself from earlier nationalist paradigms—a difficult and paradoxical task indeed for a field with the term "American" already named in it.[21] In effect, a way must be found to displace, or appear to displace a national-American paradigm, that is, to reinvent the metaphor of mobility that is immigration itself, without dissolving any and all semblance of disciplinary object or self-identity—that is, with the insertion of a workable spatial fix. In the case of U.S. immigrant literary studies, this takes the form, for example, of opening up the U.S./American literary canon via a process of critical reading of texts and authors that national-cultural identity once excluded—but in such a way that the readings remain anchored within a horizon of critical interpretation and evaluation that is nevertheless still identifiably and reliably American. Thus I analyze the specific ways that recent U.S. literary scholars of immigrant literature have produced dislocalizing readings of Julia Alvarez's influential novel about Dominican emigration to the U.S., *How the García Girls Lost Their Accents,* readings that effectively categorize and interpret the novel as *already* part of a transnational canon from which most if not all *Dominican* national-historical specificities have been erased—and that thereby remains U.S./American if only by default. Such readings, I argue, make efforts to globalize Alvarez's narrative by privileging the immigrant experience, but this remains immigration *to the U.S.,* and the fact that, for example, globalization and Americanization also shape the lives of Dominicans who never leave the island ceases to be a factor in this version of the transnational. To this extent, the shift within immigrant literary studies to paradigms of the global and the transnational tends to remain on the level of the merely terminological, as opposed to the conceptual.

I also look, from this perspective, at the scholarship that is emerging in the area of Arab-American literature, in particular at how current critical readings of Diana Abu-Jaber's novel *Crescent* structure arguments for the latter's inclusion within the canon of U.S. immigrant/ethnic literary studies. Arab-American literature comes to serve, for some of its critical readers, as one of the remaining pieces of unfinished business for U.S. multiculturalism. This reveals via a different route the dislocalizing project of displacing while simultaneously reinforcing U.S.-national paradigms against the more radical effects of globalization. Yet at the same time, the relatively recent and still somewhat provisional entry of works like *Crescent* into the canon confers on them a kind of outlier status and a more radically globalized sensibility that is especially illuminating. More generally, in this chapter I also critique what I see as decontextualizing moves on the part of immigrant/ethnic literary studies to make globalization into what is primarily a new reading methodology for literary texts rather than to develop a fully social and historical analysis attentive to the ways texts such as Alvarez's and Abu-Jaber's *themselves* reflect on and enter into critical conversation with contemporary global conditions.

In the case of the literary- and cultural-critical interpretations of immigrant fictions, then, dislocalism's "phenomenological constants" display a structure of interaction that diverges considerably from what we have seen in the case of management theory. The metaphor of mobility here is clearly immigration itself, but here reimagined to be what many scholars in the field refer to as migration, that is, as a border-crossing that, in a certain sense, never ends, an instance of seemingly permanent mobility. Unlike immigration, migration, even when it involves physical entry into the U.S., does not end, whether in real or imaginary terms, in assimilation. And yet such a metaphor of mobility is invoked from the standpoint of a critique of Americanist nationalism. That is, at the same time, the transnational is premised on a distinctly Americanized, domesticated version of multiculturalism. It is a multicultural discourse of rights, and the domestic ethnic identity it presupposes that, implicitly, counts as the globalized American here, and that becomes, in the logic of dislocalism, the spatial fix. It should be noted here, however, that not all U.S.-based criticism of racial and gender oppression takes this dislocalized form—that globalized mobility is not always, necessarily subject to the spatial fix.

VII. TRAVEL, TOURISM, AND FOOD

The third chapter of *Dislocalism* examines how contemporary American travel writers such as Robert D. Kaplan (*The Ends of the Earth,* 1996), Mary Morris (*Nothing to Declare,* 1988), and Paul Theroux (*Hotel Honolulu,* 2001) have sought out strategies for redefining an American identity laboring under the global imperative by dislocalizing it along the axis of another, pervasive metaphor of mobility—travel. Globalization for what are here representatives of the sphere of literary writing itself, has, purportedly, already Americanized the world and made the "foreign" itself intangible. Consequently, the meaning of travel itself changes as it becomes a newly privileged means of situating an American national identity—the latter isomorphic in this view with the white middle- and upper-class Americans who generally do the traveling.

Kaplan's account of his journey to the "ends of the earth" in Africa and in Asia can be read as an attempt to produce a globalized update to older travel narratives, such as, for example, those of Paul Bowles. As evoked in his novel *The Sheltering Sky* (1949) or in nonfiction such as *Their Heads are Green and their Arms are Blue* (1963), Bowles's Africa was an exotic and faraway place, one from which the realities of a point of departure and return such as New York seemed, at least on the surface, far removed. In contrast, Kaplan's Africa—and indeed the whole globalized world—is a place traveled to, whether for good or for ill, in search of its *similarities* to the U.S. Thus the main interest in a place like Abidjan, for Kaplan, is its disturbing similarity to poor African-American neighborhoods in Chicago or Washington, DC. Kaplan travels to gain a first hand account of how globalization has affected people on the ground, so to speak. But because of this he produces a narrative that essentially confirms what we already know: that, as opposed, say, to the tiger economies of Asia or to the "BRIC"[22] bloc of rapidly industrializing, formerly "third" or "second world" national economies, most of Africa and poorer parts of Asia itself (Latin America is not on Kaplan's itinerary in this narrative) are not significant participants in the networks of globalization. The sort of dislocalism at work in Kaplan's book proposes the need for travel (and travel writing) in order to see how U.S. foreign policies are working. Yet, at the same time, it produces only information that upholds the credibility of current policy thinking itself, even if it is mildly critical of the latter. Framed as fact-finding mission to survey the dangers of the "coming anarchy"[23] for a *pax Americana*, Kaplan's *The Ends of the Earth* has already seen the world before it sets out. Travel becomes the alibi for globalization, a strange metaphor of mobility in which all movement has already taken place—or is a move in the wrong direction. *Here, in effect, travel has become both metaphor of mobility and spatial fix in one.*

Although taking a far a less overtly pro-imperial stance, something of this same dislocalizing logic pervades Morris's *Nothing to Declare.* Here San Miguel de Allende, virtually a middle-class North American colony in central Mexico, becomes a setting that is something like the obverse of the New York of *The García Girls* (according to certain of its critics, that is.) For Morris it is a setting in which to confront her own domestic travails and, in the process, demonstrate how much better than Mexico the U.S. is for women in abusive relationships with men. Travel, as movement from one place to another that is, at a bare minimum, not the place one has just left, is reduced to its zero degree here. Again we have mobility *as* spatial fix, only here by means of a carefully controlled, timed encounter with poor Mexican women for whom genuine sympathy is expressed, but always with (as Morris openly admits) an exit strategy in place.

In the process of writing a travel narrative about a form of travel that can only begin where the actually existing, globalized world itself "ends," however, an ironic formula is found for giving the *genre* of travel writing itself a new lease on life. Witness Theroux's *Hotel Honolulu*. Distraught and in mourning for a globalized planet that is fast becoming one big tourist spot, Theroux, mainly known for his nonfictional travel writing, turns to *fiction*, here to the novel form to produce a kind of spatial fix for the endangered profession of travel writing itself. In the age of tourism (read: globalization), all that may be left for the professional or intellectual traveler is the perspective gained from having already traveled. But in that case, why draw the line at reporting what one has actually traveled to in order to see? In *Hotel Honolulu* the hero, himself once a heroic travel writer, but who is now stuck fast working in a fictional, second-rate Hawaiian hotel, becomes the ironic, inverted double of Kaplan in *The Ends of the Earth*. Go as far as you like, you're still in Hawaii—that is, in America.

The fourth chapter of *Dislocalism* examines the relationship between food and tourism in popular media narratives appearing in magazines such as *Gourmet* (I analyze Ruth Reichl's *Endless Feasts* [2003], a Modern Library anthology of food-and-travel writing from what were then the last sixty years of the soon to be discontinued magazine's publication [1941–2009]); in the high gloss magazine *Food & Wine* (issues ranging from 2001 to 2007); and on broadcast television in shows such as Anthony Bourdain's Food Network series *A Cook's Tour* (first aired beginning in 2001). Here I demonstrate how such narratives respond to the globalization of cuisine in the U.S., and a resulting if subtle culinary crisis compounded by what has traditionally been seen as the absence of a "true" American cuisine. The crisis is addressed through a recoding of tourism itself as culinary and the seeking out of specifically food-based experiences in places that can be (re)constructed, at least as far as eating is concerned, as "exotic" and "authentic." With the exotic itself in ever-shorter supply, tourism must now be dislocalized and marketed to Americans as the nontouristic. Food becomes a crucial ingredient here, since it is a form of the exotic that can be reproduced anywhere and that is in itself seemingly innocent of the excesses of tourism. Here, as in the case of travel writing, food-based narratives imagine their audience as white and middle or upper class: the implied other of exotic and foreign cuisines, hungry for their appropriation. But in this version of dislocalism it is not food itself but the manner of finding and eating it, whether in real space and time or in purely fantasized modes of consumption, that precipitates out as American.

Here, as will be obvious, the focus as concerns variations of dislocalism has shifted once more: from the corporate sphere, to, broadly speaking, the humanities academy, to that of writing and the literary as such, to, finally, the sphere of mass media and consumption. Of course, this is already an overdrawn schema, far too cut and dry. Management theory falls as much within the academy as does the study and criticism of immigrant and ethnic literature, while questions of ethnicity and multi-culturalism and their narrativization factor into the dislocalizing of management theory no less than in the case of immigration as contextualized within a field of literary criticism anxious to keep pace with the urgency of its own global imperative. The question of gender and ethnicity in America's (Americanized) overseas is also of inevitable importance when posing the question of how to rescue travel as experience, and with it the continued viability of the genre of American travel writing. A constant as well here, if often left implicit, is the form of American identity in relation to which this "multicultural" other is itself constituted *as* other: the white middle- and upper-class subject per se. The latter plays a more explicit role in chapter 3 and does so again in the following chapter. But, having taken this transition as an opportunity to foreground the over-arching, complex pattern of organization and differentiation informing *Dislocalism* as a whole, the question remains: why the focus on tourism *and* food here? How does the cultural logic specific to dislocalism, that of remobilization/ spatial fixation both work itself through *in* and ground the choice *of* object here?

Tourism has, in fact, already made its appearance in chapter 3, in the context of travel and the question of its imaginary remobilization in the face of globalization. Recall that for an inveterate American travel writer such as Paul Theroux, tourism is precisely the nightmare most to be feared, the debased form taken by what had been travel once globalization has completed its conquest of distance and the unknown places on the map. How, from this standpoint, could tourism, as an experience that has purportedly come into its own under globalization and that is already popularly identified as largely American, find itself subject to the fear of obsolescence and the global imperative? What need could it have of dislocalizing itself through the reimagining of itself as a form of mobility with its corresponding spatial fix?

The answer here is too complex for the limits of an introductory chapter and will have to be deferred, in large measure, to chapter 4 itself. But the basic points are these. In the first case, tourism, though lacking the venerable lineage of travel, certainly does have a history that predates globalization. Born, it is safe to say, along with the railroads as a means of mass passenger conveyance, and thrust into adolescence, especially in the U.S., with the automobile and the construction of an interstate highway system, it is only with the introduction of relatively low cost, transoceanic air travel that it becomes literally capable of globalization. By the time of the 1980s and the entry of globalization into mass awareness in the U.S. as virtually a specter of ultimate, end-game modernity, tourism has as much basis to feel the pressure to adapt, hence to dislocalize, as does the corporate or academic spheres, or, for that matter, travel and travel-writing themselves.

What tourism as a mass experience with a steadily more commercial-ized dimension had always offered its consumers—tourism being, as its critics have noted, a mode of consuming "other" cultures as such—was, in a word, *ease of movement* and the chance, above all, to *see*, to have the direct visual experience of something previously inaccessible to most except the more aristocratic and adventuresome traveler. So, for example, by the mid-nineteenth century a resident of the East Coast or the Mid-western U.S. of sufficient means could travel by rail and *see* Niagara Falls. By the middle of the next century, the trip could be made just as easily by car. The introduction of mass air travel, from one standpoint, does nothing to change this except to rationalize even further the ease of movement and to extend the range of exotic visibility, so to speak, to more distant sites: now not only Niagara Falls (by now become quaint and second-class) but Machu Picchu and the Pyramids.

But the increasing globalization of tourist routes and destinations also brings with it the creation of tourism as an industry in the fullest sense. In the form of a package, by the 1980s or so it had become possible in the U.S. and Western Europe for anyone with moderate income to buy a tour, say, to see the museums and architectural sites of Northern Italy or to cruise the Caribbean without ever having to do anything but arrive at an airport and a tour bus on time. Here, then, was a globalized tourism. And here, as well, its metaphor of mobility: ease of movement reduced, thanks to industrial rationalization, virtually to zero, with access to the first-hand, direct visibility of the exotic increased to what seemed the entire globe. Tourism at this point can be considered to be the dialectical flipside itself to another harbinger of globalization: the total immobility of the mass unemployed and social marginality on the "planet of slums."

But along with it comes—as anyone who has experienced such a tour or heard the standard complaints knows—a progressive devaluation of the exotic visual experience, of the actual seeing of the Mona Lisa or the Taj Mahal. Hyper-rationalized ease of movement, combined of course with the massive proliferation of high quality, digitalized images of the exotic sites themselves, circulated via television, websites, social media, and the like, had resulted—in Benjaminian terms—to a shrinkage of the visual "aura" of the touristic site.[24]

Sensory consumption of the exotic site is not, however, limited to seeing. A significant attraction of the packaged tour was and is, as is also common knowledge, the prearranged meals at restaurants serving typical local foods. This, of course, could often turn out to be a bitter disappointment, but the simple fact of its inclusion in the package was an indication of the possibility of sensory compensation, here in the form of taste or the gustatory, for loss of visual aura. And from here it would not be that long a step to an omission of the rationalized movement altogether, and contenting one's self with visual reproductions of the exotic site, together, perhaps with some sprinkling of narrative, and—now at the center of the new package—the culinary experience, whether in the form of verbal and visual descriptions of the latter alone, or, more often, combined with recipes for the reproduction of the exotic tastes. Hardly a substitute in all or even most instances for the visually motivated and centered tour, which doubtless makes tourism into what is still a growth industry in the globalized marketplace—but here we have the formula for another increasingly popular commodity: food-based tourism, whether involving literal travel or its purely mediatized representation in print and/or video formats. And here we have, in the consumption of such forms of exotic experience, whether actual eating takes place or not, what is also the formula for the spatial fix in this particular form of dislocalism.

VIII. TO BE CONTINUED
The Turn to Fiction

Broadly speaking, all four chapters examine, within differing sets of cultural and ideological coordinates, the more general phenomenon in which American literary writers, cultural producers, critics, and management theorists work through the rhetorical/ideological logic of an imaginary global remobilization and a simultaneously local spatial fixation—*dislocalism*—for purposes of securing the U.S. as a global and yet simultaneously nationally and culturally distinctive place. But I also focus throughout the book on another general facet of dislocalism that has particular implications for the humanities and especially for literary/cultural studies—something I refer to here as a "turn to fiction." So, for example, as noted above, in the case of contemporary management theory the study of literary fictions becomes a way of substituting for a sense of national identity that has ceased to reproduce itself reliably on the level of the capitalist enterprise. The professional managerial class, not surprisingly, prefers its fictions to be solidly "timeless" classics on the order of *Beowulf* or Joseph Conrad's *The Secret Sharer,* given the more immediate and palpable threat to management represented by the increasingly volatile, transparently fictionalized quality of finance capital itself. Meanwhile, travel writers, anxious, as I have already observed, that the planet may be turning into one big tourist spot, find themselves impelled to turn their narratives into a paradoxical form of travel fiction as another form of spatial fix. Within immigrant/ethnic literary studies, meanwhile, there can be detected a "turn to fiction" of a different but equally ironic nature. Driven by notions of the obsolescence of the literary itself, critics within this field implicitly or explicitly position the literary texts produced by the experience of immigration as "testimonios," that is, as *post*-fictional documentations of the hardships and abjections of the lives of immigrants as purportedly globalized subjects. Immigrant narratives *themselves* thus also become, for the dislocalizing American critic, something oddly akin to Žižek's "desert of the real." In the end, that is, immigrant literary narratives stand in for reality itself, thus preserving their fictionality *as if* something nonfictional. Dislocalizing food narratives, meanwhile, often take the form of quasi-fictional narratives as well: the articles and stories collected in *Endless Feasts,* for example, are presented to the reader as tantamount to classic American literature, and Reichl's Modern Library collection itself as their would-be literary anthology. In the wake of the globalization of food in the U.S., such narratives compensate by narrating recipes and other accounts of American cuisine within a fictional or quasi-fictional mise-en-scène that itself substitutes for the missing national ingredient.

I should note here that my theory of a "turn to fiction" does not attempt to make any qualitative statements about the political possibilities of the genre of fictional writing *per se* nor of the literary as opposed to other narrative forms. Rather, I show that, however varied in form, dislocalism's "turn to fiction" serves an essentially conservative function. Fiction becomes a mimetic equivalent for dislocalism's contradictory need to situate itself within a global reality that threatens to leave it with no place to stand at all.

CHAPTER 1

Management Fictions

I. GLOBALIZE OR BUST

In his book *Secular Vocations* (1993), Bruce Robbins relates the following anecdote: "In the fall of 1972, when I was starting graduate school, the professor in charge of the first year colloquium asked us all what we would say if a businessman held a gun to our heads and demanded to know why society should pay for us to study literature." This was met by a "painfully prolonged and embarrassed silence. . . . We did not seriously expect to have our brains blown out, but we were, I think, more nervous than usual" (84). This scenario, meant to dramatize what was, already a generation ago, the oncoming crisis of legitimacy of the humanities in the United States assumes, of course, that the legitimacy of business is not itself in question. And what, from the same conventional standpoint, could be less profitable than the work of the literary critic—especially if that work assumes a critical relationship to business and to capitalism generally? The anecdote reaffirms what most of us still tend to take for granted: that the relationship between those who work in the humanities and those in business (and in the academic disciplines associated with business) is an antagonistic one. And it is as evocative today as it must have been in 1972—no doubt even more so, given the increased defensiveness on the part of the humanities as the challenge from corporate interests has come to seem still more threatening and inevitable, virtually total, in the form of globalization.

In the last couple of decades, the term globalization and the kinds of issues associated with it have become familiar territory for literary and cultural critics. My concern here is not to document or question this broad and obvious development, but first to note how it has often seemed—in a subtle replay of the above "gun-to-the-head" scenario—to force the humanist scholar to accept the basic tenets of a corporate-led, and acclaimed, globalization. Take, as one fairly typical example of this, Haun Saussy's edited collection *Comparative Literature in the Age of Globalization* (2006), comprising essays by critics such as Emily Apter, Linda Hutcheon, and Jonathan Culler, and its attempt to take stock of the profession now that paradigms of globalization have become obligatory. Saussy's essay "Exquisite Cadavers from Fresh Nightmares" is rife with questions of threatening budget cuts and the eroding status of literature in its national configurations. David Ferris, writing in the same collection, wonders if the humanities themselves might be a thing of the past (90). Explicitly or implicitly, this impending erasure is attributed to the increasing corporatization of society and the university, spearheaded and championed by business. Writing in a 2001 special issue of *PMLA* on "Globalizing Literary Studies" Giles Gunn confirms this disciplinary common sense, observing how globalization "conjures up in many minds the spectacle of instantaneous electronic financial transfers, the depredations of free-market capitalism, the homogenization of culture, and the expansion of Western—by which is meant American—political hegemony" (19). For Gunn, corporate-driven globalization is a given, even if one remains opposed to it, and it requires literary studies to adapt or face possible extinction. Meanwhile, Grant Farred, himself certainly no celebrant of globalization, concedes that the "susceptibility to corporatization includes . . . not only 'streamlining' or 'upgrading' of academic or bureaucratic functions in the university but the restructuring of academic curricula themselves ("Reconfiguring the Humanities," 42). And the list could go on. With increasing predictions of the end of humanities as we have known them, and the ever-impending threat of obsolescence,[1] the field has felt compelled to theorize and justify its continued relevance—if any—in a global context.

Arguments for how to do this range from denationalizing literary studies to incorporating cultural material from the newly created global peripheries into the curriculum, to articulating more concretely how culture and literature continue to inform us about the intricacies of globalization. But while globalization's internationalizing pull purportedly helps to challenge older, national and regional parochialisms, accepting this new reality appears to require accepting, however grudgingly, the "depredations of free-market capitalism" and similar scripts. The emergent globalized version of literary studies, of course, rarely demonstrates any ideological sympathy for corporate-led globalization, nor, in principle, any reluctance to be critical of corporate practice. But at the same time, one notes a tendency on the part of critics in the humanities to converge in fairly unmistakable ways with the corporate rhetoric of globalization. Take, for example, Paolo Virno's *Multitude: Between Innovation and Negation,* in which the author celebrates the figure of the entrepreneur as an embodiment of innovation and creativity. Although, it is true, Virno is at pains to extract the notion of entrepreneurial innovation from its corporate integument, in the end it is hard to see how his entrepreneur differs in any significant way from the conventional self-image of a corporate CEO. At any rate, the distinction remains a vague one for Virno.

The more significant point, however, is that corporate/business structures themselves are seen as the driving forces of globalization. This widespread acceptance of the corporate narrative of globalization as a *fait accompli* has produced scholarship showing the effects of globalization on literary and cultural texts, and assessing what the larger implications of these effects supposedly are, not only for literary study but, in principle, for all its related disciplines as well. No one, of course, would dispute the importance of questioning these effects, but the questions themselves seem to be prompted by what is, a priori, a perceived need to globalize disciplines, curricula, and so forth, striking an unmistakable note of affinity with a corporate executive's call for the technological upgrade and restructuring of the—in this case, literary-critical—workplace. Unquestioned here is the premise that requires us to imagine and project literary study as something that has to be changed *in direct response* to processes of globalization. Thus prompted by corporate capital, it might seem that literary studies has had in fact no other choice, if it is to preserve a place for itself as a discipline in the new world order, except to become globalized.

Of course, not all responses to globalization from within the humanities are so universally accommodating. A more critically and theoretically oriented cultural studies remains, in fact, one of the few intellectual milieus in which the corporate metanarrative of globalization is explicitly subject to question. Indeed, the critical response to globalization on the part of theorists such as Fredric Jameson, David Harvey, Immanuel Wallerstein, and Saskia Sassen—to mention only a few—has been to link the study of economics, finance, marketing and technology inseparably to the critique of culture. Nor, of course, is this an entirely new trend, reflecting the ways in which Marxist theory has shaped or influenced many of the humanities disciplines, most notably cultural studies itself. The latter field, by extending the tools of literary analysis to objects traditionally considered nonliterary and working via a variety of disciplines, has become, in a sense, the ideal place to house the critique of corporate globalization and of corporate culture. Indeed, the work of cultural studies scholars such as Andrew Ross, Jeremy Brecher and Jim Costello, and Simon During[2] has called for a direct engagement of scholarship with anti-corporate activism, urging an advocacy of corporate globalization's victims that probably could not have been pursued anywhere but in the humanities and other closely related disciplines. Timothy Brennan, writing in *At Home in the World: Cosmopolitanism Now* in 1997, had even called on scholars in the humanities to study and critique the highly influential work of corporate globalization's analysts, mouthpieces, and management gurus, from Robert Reich to Tom Peters and the late Peter Drucker, pointing out that it is this literature that truly shapes decision making at the highest levels in the U.S. Indeed, the critique of global business and of business culture from within the humanities and cultural studies is an emergent field in itself, and includes recent work such as Richard Sennett's *The Culture of the New Capitalism* (2006) Christopher Newfield's *Ivy and Industry: Business and the Making of the American University, 1880–1980* (2003), Luc Boltanski and Eve Chiapello's *The New Spirit of Capitalism* (2006), and Bret Benjamin's *Invested Interests: Capital, Culture, and the World Bank* (2007).

I locate my own work within literary and cultural studies and see it as an extension of this emergent study/critique of corporate globalization from within that discipline. My own analysis in this chapter, however, while it joins the effort to examine business cultures critically, also differs in its scope and focus by subjecting to theoretical scrutiny what has in fact been the turn of business, especially a trend within management as an academic disciplinary formation and a field of practice, to humanistic notions of culture. For while those of us who work in the humanities probably have had—to return to Bruce Robbins's 1972 anecdote—to imagine the businessman's gun held permanently to our heads, the emergent and largely consolidated reality of globalization has changed, in perhaps unexpected ways, the manner in which *both* the humanities and the business disciplines legitimate themselves and—in actual practice—reshape their own objects of study *with respect to each other.*

While others have examined and critiqued corporate capitalism's own "cultural turn," I hope to contribute to that critique by showing specifically how the American academic field of management has found in culture and literature and even in recent literary and cultural (especially postmodernist) theory a strategy for its own adaptation to globalization. This is the kind of adaptive strategy I refer to throughout this book as dislocalism. I have already introduced and briefly characterized this theoretical concept in the foregoing introduction, but to repeat and clarify it at this point: what I term dislocalism is the overdetermining drive to preserve existing theoretical, institutional, and disciplinary boundaries, both within and beyond American literary and cultural studies, in response to the anxiety of the global, to enact certain changes at the sites of knowledge production so as to fend off other, more potentially radical ones. The term itself is intentionally double-edged. Thus, for example, when theorists, authors, critics, and other cultural producers are driven to displace the "local" in order to engage with what they understand as the "global," they engage in a *dis*localism. But, in doing so, I propose, they are simultaneously invested in *remaining* localized—adhering to a dislo-*calism*—so that older institutional practices are not entirely displaced or rendered useless. Thus, as argued in the following chapters of this work, American institutional and literary practices often exemplify a pattern of dislocalism in which American identity must look increasingly to its global others in order to remain, globally, itself: thus American immigrant literary studies, travel writing, and tourism, among others, become sites for the containment of ethnicity and diversity within U.S. borders, helping to construct the United States as a place that is both local and global. The process of defining American identity in relationship to its others is not new in itself but has taken different dimensions in a global context.

But dislocalizing responses to globalization are not restricted to the humanities and cultural studies; in the case before us here, they characterize the changed and changing relation between the humanities and other, seemingly unconnected, or even opposed disciplinary formations. Thus I will focus in this chapter on how the discipline of management, whether in its more theoretically oriented scholarship in journals such as the *Journal of Management Theory,* in its own mass-marketed inspirational literature, or in its course curricula, engages with literary texts on the order of *Antigone, Macbeth,* and *The Secret Sharer* as well as with cultural theorists from Foucault to Baudrillard to James Clifford. This consummately dislocalizing phenomenon is, I will argue, part of management theory's own globalization-inspired narrative of disciplinary obsolescence. My analysis will show, moreover, that this cultural and literary turn accords with the logic of an ideology that in one and the same moment must champion globalization and the breaking down of national boundaries and yet reinscribe a desire for consolidating the American as the only secure place within the new global order. This focus on management and its extradisciplinary, cultural excursions may seem arcane to those of us who practice in the field of literary/cultural studies. But if we are indeed to critique and oppose forces of globalization, we have to understand the functional use of literature and culture for the corporate narrative of globalization and for management theorists in particular.[3]

My choice of objects in what follows has also been shaped by the fact that, unlike what is generally said to be the case in the humanities, the discipline of management sees its central task to be training students—future members of the professional managerial class, or PMC—for nonacademic jobs. Management scholarship, though written for other academics, has a strong applied character, aimed at thinking through administrative work issues. No less than its academic literature, the theories of popular American management gurus such as Tom Peters and Peter Drucker—read both in academic circles as well as by the PMC out in the "real world"— have been influential in the way management as a field thinks about work structures. Analyzing such objects is necessary if one is to understand fully the functional nature of culture and literature for the world of management. I begin by looking at the most immediate implications of globalization as perceived and understood by management theorists and practitioners themselves, and more specifically the question of how these theorists confront the problem of defining what is American in the context of current management practices. I will then turn to an examination of how the question of culture as such becomes central to management discourse, leading finally into the highly specific, dislocalizing function of cultural theory and fiction themselves for global managers.

II. THE GLOBAL VILLAGE AND AMERICAN BUSINESS

As one might have expected, the new, global world order is, at first glance, aggressively championed in management literature. To confirm this one need only page through Tom Peters's various best-selling books.[4] The popular American management guru and famed (co)author of *In Search of Excellence* (1982) markets himself, and is widely acknowledged, as the "father of the postmodern corporation"[5] and has even been likened to Emerson, Thoreau, and Whitman for his writing on American business.[6] (Such incongruous blending of the classical and the postmodern is, as we shall see below in another context, typical of management theory.) In *Re-imagine!: Business Excellence in a Disruptive Age* (2003) for example, Peters proclaims: "The global village is here . . . with a vengeance. . . . The death of distance marks the beginning of (real) competition. The world is catching up. More freedom. Higher Standards of Living. Hooray!" (4). The stock figures of the "global village" and the "death of distance" stand in here for the speed with which money and commodities move unfettered through dissolving national boundaries. Yet this celebration of globalization is accompanied by an ambivalent tone of anxiety and defensiveness: the global village also, says Peters, "puts us [Americans] under the gun. And if we want to continue to stay at or near the top then we must be working on our next act" (ibid.).

This ambivalent relation to the "global village" has become pervasive in management circles. Take, as only one further example here, Wallace Schmidt, Roger Conaway, Susan Easton, and William J. Wardrope, who—without Peters's flamboyance—note in the introduction to their management textbook *Communicating Globally: Intercultural Communication and International Business* (2007) how policies from the 1980s such as the forging of strategic alliances between economic blocs have created "volatile change as globalism has come to dominate international business" (8). The U.S. itself, of course, was at the forefront in instituting these same globalizing policies, and yet it is this "volatile change," as the authors of *Communicating Globally* admit, that has, ironically, threatened an erosion of American business hegemony. The book attributes this anxiety to the changed nature of business in a global context. "An American CEO" cited in the book states: "Before we used to be an American company operating overseas. Now we're trying to become global and there's a big difference in how you think about doing business" (7). The authors see it as necessary for American business to "reassert its leadership role" (8).

Such contradictory responses to globalization can be understood on a number of different levels and provide the occasion to think about two interrelated issues. First, they point to the fact that the globalization-inspired fear of obsolescence pervades management discourse no less than it does the humanities. In works dating from the first years of the "globalization frenzy" in the 1990s[7] Peters, for example, has been relentless in calling on American business managers to keep up with the changing times or face what are likely to be the dire consequences. Post-9/11, in works such as *Re-imagine* and *Talent* (2005), this rhetoric has become increasingly aggressive. For example, in *Re-imagine*, Peters provocatively suggests that it is the "terrorists" who "conceived the ultimate 'virtual organization'—fast, wily, flexible, determined" (4). Underlying this ironic compliment is of course righteous anger over the 9/11 attacks, but it is simultaneously delivered as a reprimand and warning to Americans themselves regarding the dangers not just of future attacks but also of letting the terrorists beat them on the organizational and managerial level. Himself a former Navy Seabee, Peters makes explicit use of military metaphors, exhorting his American audience of businessmen and members of the PMC to take the offensive in rethinking business strategy: "while the American armed forces performed brilliantly in Iraq in 2003 . . . Business Matters! Economics Matters" (1). Perhaps, some years beyond the beginning of the war, such triumphalism would have to be turned down a notch or two, but the perceived dangers of being out-innovated and out-organized remain. American business, too, must fight the "war on terror": the private sector of a "nation of nations" arrayed against "terrorists" who, whether pseudo-identified as Iraq or not, are, clearly enough, another, more sinister name here for globalization. Sounding a similar, but less sensationalist note, Schmidt, Conaway and others in *Communicating Globally*, also call on American business to intervene directly as a player on the global, post-9/11 scene of Realpolitik: "Just as Condoleezza Rice wants to lead the reshaping of America's role in the world through transformational diplomacy," American business should "reassert its leadership role in international business and give direction to this ever increasing globalism" (8).

My analysis will show how the idea that globalization or the "global village" requires a reconsolidation of American business, although given new impetus by 9/11, develops since the 1980s in the context of neoliberalism. The figure of the "global village" convinced many leading management practitioners that if American business remains "just business" it will fall behind and lose the game.

The second thing to consider here is the ironic form of chauvinism underlying the idea that the "global village" places *Americans* "under the gun." While it is obvious, even a cliché, to point out that the potentially negative effects of globalization are felt by people in all parts of the world, whether in the form of increased competition for businesses, or, for the rest of us, through rising food and gas prices, loss of jobs, stagnant salaries, or much worse, this is, at the same time, precisely the point: *everyone*, not just Americans, is affected by globalization. Everyone is "under the gun" and, if one takes the concept of globalization seriously, being American has nothing to do with it. Yet for Peters being "under the gun" becomes a bizarre form of American privilege or exceptionalism. This points to an idea that is perfectly explicit in Peter's writing, if only implied in more sedate, academic management literature, namely that America has not only enjoyed business leadership in the past but possesses the unquestioned and sole legitimate right to that power and advantage for eternity and has a sacred duty not to become complacent about its declining place in the world. Rather than questioning whether national identity categories such as American haven't *themselves* become difficult to shore up, management's response to globalization is a more abstract, and in many ways more extreme form of nationalism, as if the answer to the dangers of the "global village" were to populate it exclusively with Americans. This same "global American" chauvinism is articulated in a somewhat different way by Thomas Friedman, the *New York Times* columnist and neoliberal globalization cheerleader. In his book *The World Is Flat,* Friedman tries to sober up Americans by reminding them that nations such as China and India may well surpass the U.S. in the "race to the top." Here too the "global village" is celebrated only as long as American business is the one sitting atop the globe itself. Otherwise, it becomes a sign of foreboding, a "race to the top" in which all that matters is how the entrance of more and more players such as China and India into global competition introduces a potential of instability for Americans. It is not the emergence of a new world order with porous boundaries, but only the potential loss of American control over that world order that is problematic here. As far as American corporate- and management-thinking is concerned, it doesn't matter what globalization means for political governance in the rest of the world as long as the U.S. remains the global hegemon.

Yet, however obvious and self-serving on its face, such thinking indicates the need to think more precisely about the specific implications of globalization for the discipline of management. For, underlying the anxiety (and corresponding aggressiveness) condensed in the figure of the "global village," whether for ideologues such as Peters and Friedman or for academics like Schmidt, Conaway et al. is the question of what it means, in a global context of porous and complex national boundaries, to speak *at all* of *American* business or management—and of how management theory attempts to grapple with this new dilemma. In fact the increased instability and volatility of life in the "global village" contains an implicit threat to undermine the very field of management itself, insofar as it is fundamentally predicated on the nationalist economic paradigms of the early and mid-twentieth century?

In exploring this question, one should probably begin by observing that both the field of management as well as business generally as an academic discipline has American origins. The University of Pennsylvania's Wharton School, whose existence dates from 1881, is commonly credited with being the first established school of business. The emergence of management itself as a discipline can be traced back to the early twentieth century and the rise of theories of scientific management in private industry. Its origins, that is, roughly coincide with those of Taylorism and Fordism, American capitalist innovations that were indeed to conquer the globe.[8] It wasn't until the 1950s that European universities began in any measurable way to offer their own programs in business and management.[9] If management theory isn't, historically speaking, American, it is indeed hard to imagine what is.

It is also important to understand here that business as a modern academic discipline divided into the various subdisciplines of accounting, finance, marketing, management, and so forth, matured and gained prominence during a period largely dominated by Keynesian economic theory. The latter, with its macroeconomic emphasis on the need for government-led monetarist intervention to prevent recessions and depressions may have ceased to dominate the discipline, but Keynesianism's predication upon the secure existence of distinct, purportedly self-contained national economic spaces is something whose imprint can still be detected, even in the "global village" tirades of someone like Peters.

But it is, of course, the increasing change in the relationship between capital and national boundaries, unmistakable since the beginning of the neoliberal regimes of the 1980s when "globalization" first began to enter the corporate mind-set and lexicon, that shapes the mix of triumphalism and anxiety condensed in figures such as the "global village." The fact that it has been the U.S., along with the IMF, the World Bank, the WTO and other U.S.-dominated international economic institutions, that have led the way in introducing the neoliberal policies that have in turn further destabilized the older national business paradigm only further enhances management's anxious relationship to globalization. To be sure, as the realities of the "global village" have become more and more unnerving, there has also been an increasing tendency in business circles to attribute *all* change, whether for good or ill, to questions of managerial practice on the level of the individual enterprise or administrative structure. Knowing how to cut costs and increase profits by restructuring a company becomes, once global instability becomes the rule rather than the exception, an ironically new form of American macroeconomics. Yet, since the discipline of management has historically focused on strategies for work organizations that are themselves structured by legal, economic, and political conditions within the nation-state, the need to think about strategies within *global* structures introduces both a degree and a kind of complexity and volatility heretofore unseen. All of this is, in a sense, embedded in the essentially dislocalist metaphors of the "global village" and the "death of distance": slogans whose very proclamation contains a not so concealed fear and a longing for the days when America was the village and the distance separating it from its economic rivals seemed fixed for life.

To get at the root of this duality, however, it is necessary to have a fuller understanding of the fundamental, underlying theoretical problem here.[10] This problem concerns the relation between *capital* itself and a global market, the latter conventionally understood as comprised of multiple, competing local economies (or competing *capitals*) housed within nation-states. As suggested by popular slogans such as the "death of distance," management theory has no illusions about the fact that this relation has changed dramatically. But, as a rule, this change, however dramatic, is represented as a purely quantitative one in which capital, understood in management theory (as in most areas of mainstream economics) as simply the inputs to production, whether in the form of raw materials, other commodities, or money, moves across the globe with ever fewer barriers and ever greater velocity. In the case of money itself, whether as a means of circulation or as "investment flows," technologies of electronic transfer make this movement virtually instantaneous. Globalization, in this celebratory conception, becomes the providential and final realization of what Marx once famously referred to in the *Grundrisse* as the "annihilation of space by time."[11]

Capital, however, as Marx has shown in the *Grundrisse* and *Capital*, is not just a thing moving through space at greater or lesser speeds, but a process, an abstract but dynamic form of social relation that has its own, immanent laws of motion which are themselves subject to historical change. In this conception, capital does not simply move more rapidly and freely through space, but has the potential to restructure that space itself, altering, in the process, the fundamental relation between national-economic and global-economic *forms* of space. Globalization, accordingly, would not merely be understood as the quantitative increase in the speed and ease with which capital moves through the space of the global market once national and other protectionist barriers are removed, but rather as the *qualitative* change whereby capital reproduces itself simultaneously and *directly* on a plane that more and more approximates that of the global market as a *single* space. The latter, arguably, is no longer, if it ever was, the merely abstract sum of national economies (as, for example, in Friedman's "flat world" slogan) but, however unequal and hierarchically structured, verges on something that, from the standpoint of capital as whole, supersedes national economic space.

In their representation of the new mobility of capital via the metaphor of a winner-take-all, final round of competition between national capitals whose boundaries have, at the same time, become more porous and less visible, management theorists clearly have more than an inkling of this change. But the phenomenon here is not grasped as one that changes the very relation of national boundaries to capital itself—one in which competition intensifies to the point that its very "law" now dictates the fate, and in some cases even the existence of nations themselves. Much less is this understood as a phenomenon that betokens, at least according to some arguments, a severe and potentially epoch-making *crisis* of capital of truly global proportions. Or to be still more precise: to the extent that the American management theory under analysis here does sense what is truly in the offing, its own subordinate relation to capital and the latter's logic of reproduction leaves it no other ideological way forward but to equate global transformation, whether for good or for ill, with the destiny of *American* capitalist hegemony. The fate of all nations can only be comprehended as the fate of one, the nation that is a "nation of nations."

III. MANAGEMENT'S "CULTURAL TURN"

To the extent, then, that the very categories of management theory themselves presuppose a constitutive, structural relation between the logic of capitalist reproduction as a whole and the existence of distinct, well-defined national-economic spatial spheres, the progressive erosion of such a relation will inevitably produce a kind of theoretical vacuum for management and business generally. For if, as one might put it, globalization has undermined and volatilized the spatial logic of American capital itself, what, to refer back to our earlier speculative question, does or *could* it now mean to manage a business, or individual capitalist enterprise? If America does not name a fixed, structurally integrated space of capitalist reproduction, then what sort of thing does it name? The answer, in a (deceptively simple) word, is *culture*.

Business, in fact, has a fairly long history of addressing cultural issues when they are relevant to the bottom line. Managers have, for example, long made use of cultural or ethnographic profiles on the groups of people in its target markets to sell products/services or in the area of personnel relations.[12] Affirmative action policies as well as fear of lawsuits over discrimination have led firms to institute diversity initiatives and sensitivity training aimed at broadening the cultural perspectives of their employees and giving the appearance, at least, of a culturally diverse workplace. Here culture describes an object that many in management theory circles such as, for example, Fons Trompenaars, have taken to calling "cultural intelligence."[13] I will have more to say below, in my discussion of the subdiscipline of international development management, about the dislocalizing propensities of this idea, but such a traditional, ethnographic notion of culture will not answer to management theory's need for—to borrow David Harvey's useful term—a "spatial fix" able to give the appearance, at least, of closing the dislocalizing breach that globalization has threatened to open up under the very feet of the discipline itself. For that purpose, a much more radical, more theoretically risky notion of culture as, so to speak, subject and not merely predicate of managerial theory and practice becomes increasingly necessary. And, indeed, beginning roughly in the 1980s such notions of culture begin more and more to take hold of the leading figures and movements within management theory.

As I hope to make clear below, this dislocalizing turn toward the concept of culture as subject would ultimately lead management theorists directly to cultural theory itself and even result in the folding of literary fiction into the discursive logic of managerial dislocalism. The burden of my analysis will be to show how such a cultural and literary turn is in itself an effect of how management theorists seek to understand the reproduction of capital on the global plane and their deeply contradictory relation to the latter. For, to reiterate, they must find a way to champion globalization's uneven flux and dissolution of national boundaries while at the same time continuing to theorize about how to reproduce *American* know-how and business sense across the world. What I posit here, to formulate this same idea in terms more familiar to theory in the humanities and cultural studies, is that culture, literary fiction, and cultural theory—the latter, above all, in its postmodern variant—come to provide business theorists with a way to renarrate the nation in a new, global context. I will analyze this variant of dislocalism within two distinct areas of the field of management: organization studies and international aspects of the field as in international management, development management, or, as it is also sometimes referred to, international development. I will analyze both at some length, but for now I offer a thumbnail sketch of each area, stating my specific purpose for examining them.

Organization studies, or OS, arose in the 1980s as the notion of culture was gaining more currency among business theorists due to the perceived threat of competition from Japanese business. Michael Rowlinson and Stephen Procter in "Organizational Culture and Business History," explain that "Japan's economic success was believed to owe something to the cultural characteristics of its corporations. In response, several American writers perceived a need to celebrate the cultural virtues of successful American corporations" (370). Along with the idea of a national-cultural business organization, then, came a different notion of culture itself, one that was no longer limited to the "cultural intelligence" paradigm with its focus on better management of employee relations and target markets.

Culture was now also to provide managers with more effective ways of narrating American organizations themselves. The category of culture, that is, underwent a needed expansion so as to be able to link it directly to the national.

However, as, since the 1980s, global economic interlinking has increased, the ideas of corporate culture and identity have themselves become increasingly *delinked* from the national. Or to put it another way: analyzing the *national* specificity of organizations must now have factored into it the added complexity of the new, vastly increased mobility of capital. Along with this, there is a growing sense that *all* organizations must be run like for-profit corporate institutions, and the very distinction between public and private institutions is blurring. Here OS itself comes to overlap with public administration, the subfield that has traditionally theorized governmental and public sector organizations. That is, in the wake of an accelerating tendency toward the dissolution of both national and institutional boundaries as well, OS has implicitly come to think of the organization itself as something transcending the national and the regional. The organization becomes what is in effect a universal, leaving OS with the task of theorizing the idea of organization *as a culture in itself*. (But while presented in denationalized terms, OS as practiced nevertheless tends to theorize about management of people—their behaviors and social interactions in relationship to existing and emergent work structures. These concerns have also become more emphasized in the field of management as a whole.)[14] From here it is a relatively short step for management to turn to theories of postmodernism, given the latter's emphasis on the ubiquity and sheer complexity of culture—on culture as that which, as Jameson once put it, appears to "coat" everything else.

Nevertheless, this very embrace of cultural complexity and polymorphism as the key to understanding the universal corporate organization masks a nervousness and anxiety lest, in the end, OS should find itself adrift in a global, transnational no man's land with nothing left any longer to organize or manage. It is this anxiety, I will argue, that then prompts OS's academic and popular turn to literary fiction as a way of hedging its bets, of staging its restorationist desire for a simpler, more stable version of culture, and a reconsolidation of the nation on the level of the new, global cultural "rhizome" itself.[15] That is, I argue that while OS purports to theorize the universal corporate organization, it is all the while unwittingly narrating and reconsolidating Americanism. This point becomes clearer if we juxtapose the field of organization studies with those areas of the field that explicitly deal with questions relating to managing globally. As I read it, OS is part of the trend of the entire field of management focusing more on international aspects of management concerned with managing multi/transnational corporations. The institutionalization of organization studies has kept in step with the rise of multi- and transnational corporations that began to be theorized in the area of "International Management." As a result we have seen an emphasis on organizational culture that at the same time attempts to deal with issues of management in different parts of the world. Moreover in an increasingly globalized world, there have been correspondingly increasing arguments for interdisciplinary work in international management so that issues of managerial expertise can be related to questions of policy and governance—an area that deals with international development issues.[16] I will focus some of my analysis on the field of international development management, or IDM, by relating it to questions of management and managerial expertise in those areas of the world considered in need of development.

IDM addresses issues of concern to managers in a highly global network of institutions such as USAID and the World Bank, managers responsible for instituting U.S.-led neoliberal policies and for the global reproduction of American business interests and know-how. It also deals with management strategies for international agencies lending money to developing nations for specific projects and also with governance policies. As the international branch of public administration (encompassing governmental and nongovernmental organizations alike) IDM emerged after WWII as the principal academic discipline charged with the design and implementation of modernization policies for the developing world—the very developmentalist models that would be critiqued in places like Latin America by so-called dependency theory. OS, it should be noted, has maintained a distance from IDM, viewing the latter as more in the nature of a specialized subfield, whose concern for "nation-building" OS proper considers to be outside of its purview. It will thus come as no surprise that, in questions of culture, IDM often appears to fall back on what, from the OS perspective, are more traditional theories of "cultural intelligence." Those charged with administering foreign loans must, after all, cultivate an understanding of the culture of their prospective debtors and client states. So, for IDM, the notion that American culture is essentially different from, say, Sudanese, Chinese, or Mexican culture remains very much in force.

However, in an increasingly globalized context, even IDM's more conventional, nation-centered notion of culture has suffered complications, and the national qualifiers of culture have had to be supplemented here theoretically by other kinds of cultural formations such as those of race/ ethnicity and religion. It is thus now not uncommon to find in the management texts used to train future international development managers, discussions, say, of Islamic, Native American, or Chicano cultures. IDM, then, narrates America via concepts of race and ethnicity that in turn betray its own version of the desire for a simpler, more sustainable version of culture—given the specter of a total, global flux that would erase cultural boundaries of all kinds, be they national or not. If, for OS, the idea of organization as itself a culture supplements the lost unity of the national business entity, for IDM it is race and ethnicity that must be summoned to help restore the national-cultural boundaries underpinning the field itself.

It is important to note here as well that IDM is generally aware of radical critiques that charge it, along with the powerful institutions it serves, with implementing and defending neocolonial policies around the world. Such awareness has, in fact, led IDM to incorporate these critiques into its own discourse, so that it is not uncommon to find discussions of postcolonial theory cropping up in IDM circles. I argue that, in fact, by incorporating such theories as would-be self-critiques, IDM in effect attempts to Americanize itself, that is, to distance itself from a European-style colonialism. Here too, ironically, the vision of an American-originated, benevolent hand held out to the other, "developing" nations of the world must frame itself in a neutral, universal language of culture—a language that IDM, too, will find in notions of postmodernism and fiction. These notions remain unacknowledged but are nevertheless subtly operant.

I should also point out that, in addition to their ideological alliance with the concept of Americanism, both OS and IDM largely remain institutionally American in the sense that the publishing venues in the fields and those who write in them are mostly affiliated with American academic institutions. European academics, especially from the U.K., have some scholarly representation in this area; but there is very little representation from other parts of the world. I will first analyze OS at length and in greater detail by examining recent scholarship by management theorists and the curricula of management courses themselves. In my subsequent analysis of IDM, I will, in addition to scholarship and curricula, also examine several case studies appearing in management textbooks. And I will also fill in more historical and descriptive detail as needed.

IV. ORGANIZATION STUDIES, THE SHIFTING NOTIONS OF CULTURE, AND THE DENATIONALIZED ORGANIZATION

The dislocal reshaping of OS, with its increasing emphasis on the active role of culture, is inextricably connected to what the field now imagines as its essential object, namely, the *global* enterprise and the latter's changed relationship to the nation-state, as well as the role of managers in leading such new organizations. Analysis of this particular field-imaginary will also allow us a more detailed glimpse into management theory's understanding and simultaneous mystification of the globalization of capital.

If, before the 1980s, the notion of culture was not explicitly connected to the notion of a national business organization, this reflected a historical context in which the lines between nation-states seemed more defined and fixed. Production and consumption were presumed to take place largely within national economic space, while nation-states themselves appeared, to some extent objectively, to exert greater control over economic and financial decisions. It is also important to remember that the post–World War II decades had seen the rise of many anti-colonial movements for national independence and sovereignty and for economic control over resources within the newly created nations—something that further helped to concretize the notion of firmly entrenched national boundaries. But during the 1980s the idea of a shrinking, spatio-temporally "compressed" world was already starting to take greater hold on management theory, and the corresponding need to establish a direct relationship between culture as such and the national business organization anticipated the delinking, qua capital, of nation and business organization that was to take hold of the field-imaginary (or unconscious) in the not too distant, global future. Take, for example, the case of the "father of modern management," the late Peter F. Drucker. In "The New Society of Organizations," Drucker pronounces that—in a "globalized knowledge economy"—"every organization has to build the management of change into its very structure." (144).[17] How to produce this structural change? For Drucker, significantly, it is the notion of the culture of the organization itself, disconnected from the culture of the locality surrounding it, that holds the key. He acknowledges that "an organization's members live in a particular place," and that there exists a "need to feel at home there" (ibid.). Yet, Drucker claims, "the organization cannot submerge itself in the community nor subordinate itself to the community's ends. Its culture has to transcend community" (ibid.). This emphasis on organizational culture appears in a variety of Drucker's writings.

The question of the "transcendence" of organizational culture vis-à-vis the culture of the "community" has itself become a regular curricular topic in university courses. Consider, for example, "Organizational Culture and Culture Change," a course that appears in the 2008 catalogue at the Dartmouth Business School. According to its catalogue description, the course seeks to "introduce organizational culture concepts and give [students] some first hand experience in understanding the cultural values of an organization." It goes on to state that "after arming [students] with tools and frameworks that can be used to identify and evaluate the cultural values of an organization," the course "will also equip [them] with some tools and techniques about changing the corporate culture to increase satisfaction and performance. At a personal level, these insights in organizational culture will help [students] find [their] fit for [a] future job and connect with [their] company's culture" (*The Tuck MBA: Organizational Culture and Culture Change*).

There are several issues to be explicated here, beginning with the question of the nature of organizations themselves. Note that in both Drucker's more abstract, almost philosophical formulations as well as in the boilerplate of the course description the culture of organization is also different from the culture of the people who make up the organization. Managers and members of the PMC are expected to cultivate a sense of organizational culture that is not shaped by the culture or identity of employees that the latter may have developed through other affiliations such as family, religion, ethnicity, or nationality. In this configuration, organizational culture is supposed to define the people affiliated with it and is itself free of any national, regional, or local referent such as American, Chinese, German, Midwestern, Eastern, Southern, and so forth. Note as well that there is no need of any reference here to other, legal distinctions as to the size and nature of the organizations, that is, whether they are small or large businesses, for profit, nonprofit, governmental, S corporation, C corporation, business trust, sole proprietorship, and so forth. At one level, of course, theorizing the organization as a whole, that is, as a form, is bound to introduce some level of generality. However, an increasingly global context has tended to theorize away not only the borders between nation-states but also the practical if not legal borders between different kinds of organizations as well. This is in keeping, as mentioned already, with the widespread belief that all institutions must be run efficiently in the manner of for-profit privatized firms. The overlap between the fields of OS and public administration (the latter charged with theorizing governmental organizations and now also NGOs) then, is itself one further manifestation of how pervasive the rhetoric of dissolving boundaries of all kinds has become. Scholarship on notions of culture and literature from both disciplines continues to be published in the same journals—for example, the *Journal of Management Inquiry* and *Organization*—making OS even more the disciplinary default setting for management as a whole. Another reason behind the supposed need for organizations to define their own, "transcendent" cultures is the speed with which companies change affiliations, ownership, or locations—whatever that now means—in the course of having their stock bought and sold on the global market. The idea is that culture can remain the constant among the many, multiplying variables. But this, again, is precisely where the dislocalism of the field comes into purview.

For Drucker's notion of the culture of the organization as transcending that of the community, while clearly a symptom of increasing globalization, also signals a definite limit intrinsic in OS and management theory's understanding of the globalization of capital. According to OS, the increasing universalization of the organization—imagined as a structure with ever broadening operational ties spilling across national borders—is the direct result of increasing globalization. But, although OS explicitly refers to "transnational" and "multinational" corporations, terms Drucker himself has helped to define and popularize, such terms are implicitly inadequate to the idea of the universal, culturally autonomous, or "transcendent" organization. What Drucker and OS fail to articulate here is how the new, global firm has become not merely a transnational/multinational but what I want to call a *denationalized* structure. Regardless of whether organizations become international in their operations, or whether they move from one national or even regional location to another, their very relationship to the nation, and to the regional and local generally, has changed in the wake of globalization. It is, at any rate, safe to say that the idea of a *trans*national or *multi*national corporation/organization captures only one aspect of the nature of organization in a fully global context. In effect, despite having assumed the task of rationalizing emergent work structures, and even as it proclaims the delinking of organizational culture from the community, OS is still not quite able to put its finger on the realities of organizations themselves—structures whose connections to their localities are changing due to fundamental and unperceived changes in social relations themselves.

And yet, even as OS has, implicitly, reached the threshold of theorizing the universal organization as denationalized, as fully detached from the national, its own ideological affinity nevertheless lies with corporations operating largely out of the global North and West, and primarily within the U.S. (I will analyze this at length in the section on IDM.) Consider, for example, that when Drucker advocates a delinking of organizational culture from that of its surrounding community, he links the importance and necessity of this detachment to what he terms a "globalized knowledge economy." While the "knowledge economy" is an allusion to globalization here, it is, even more specifically, a commonly employed descriptor for the rise of a postindustrial service sector in the global North/West, primarily in the United States. Though of course goods are still manufactured in the U.S., even as more and more industrial production is farmed out to the global peripheries, the term "knowledge economy" in Drucker's conception does not describe the world at large. What it describes, in a quintessentially dislocal move, is a "denationalized" United States. On this level it becomes more apparent how the emptying out of the national referent from culture has as much to do with OS's own narrative of obsolescence as it does with the celebration of a transnational era.

There are, in fact, myriad sources for such dislocalizing contradictions, but underlying them all is the fact that both the institutional and the ideological apparatus for theorizing the global, transnational, or, more accurately, the denationalized firm exists largely if not exclusively in the United States. In this context, the denationalized "American" speaks to a specific form of globalization anxiety. Celebrations of globalization, summoning up the standard topos of the *transnational* organization with its increasing international links, mask what is at the same time, and more primordially, the fear of the *denationalized* organization. Implicit in the rhetoric of the "global village" with its correspondingly *global* firm and organizational culture is not only the fear of going out of business but an underlying apprehension over the potential to rationalize away the function of management academics and the PMC themselves, leaving them with no clear locus from or in which to manage, whether in theory or in practice.

And this same tacit fear is, arguably, reflected in post-1980s curricular changes that management theory and OS have undergone in the American university as students are increasingly being trained to employ culture as a tool of for business creativity and innovation. Behind the innocuous-sounding emphasis on the ability to connect to and transform an organization's culture as key to the career success of the future PMC in the above-cited Dartmouth course description, for example, there is a palpable sense that culture may soon be all there is standing between management and the void. Although the course does not state it as such, a manager's skill at shaping and sustaining organizational culture will likely appear to be most critical in times of layoffs and restructuring. The potential need for an (perhaps unsuccessful) attempt at arousing an organization's cultural *esprit de corps* so as to make periods of crisis, increased extraction of labor power, and threatened job cuts more palatable does not bode well for the job of the manager either. The Dartmouth course also provides a suitable supplement to the aggressive but clearly defensive call to restore American business leadership sounded by Schmidt and Conaway's and Peters's specter of "Americans under the gun."

There is, moreover, the irony here that in learning to utilize culture as a tool, the students are expected to develop cultural blueprints for what they consider to be efficient universal organizations exclusively from within *American* universities. The cultural universality of the latter is taken for granted. Once developed, these blueprints can then be exported globally. (This latter point will be made clearer in the section on international development management.) For this reason, the field of organization studies and management as a whole positions itself to theorize innovative up-to-date strategies using cultural theory and literary fiction as seemingly applicable to any global firm. Even as courses such as "Organizational Culture and Culture Change" adopt a consciously neutral tone, the dislocalizing contradictions implied in such an endeavor become all too clear. I will first address this dislocalism in the field's adoption of cultural theory, largely postmodernism, and then move on to examine the same trend in management theory and OS's turn toward literary fiction—a trend that solidified in the 1990s.

A Manager's Guide to Postmodern Cultural Theory?

It should not come as any great surprise that, as its preoccupation with culture grows, management theory would eventually gravitate toward the humanities and cultural studies to seek out scholarship on the concept. In the same vein, it is also understandable how the notion of a denationalized knowledge-based firm would eventually discover a certain affinity for theories of the postmodern. As Tom Peters says in *Liberation Management*, "let's hold applause for chaos theory" [the emphasis here being on "theory"]. Instead of the frantic pursuit of total comprehension (via central-control schemes) let's revel in our very lack of comprehension!" (491). In some sense postmodernism, with its emphasis on the nontotalizing virtues of chaos and the inevitable nonclosure of theoretical comprehension serves an immediately descriptive purpose simply by furnishing a preexisting language for representing the often seemingly incomprehensible appearance of global capital's financial flows and fluxes. Postmodernism also seems as good a way as any in which to frame the issues brought into play by not only the speed with which organizations change locations and affiliations but also the reconfigurations of the spatio-temporal axes affecting notions of office space and work time, as managers telecommute and transact with each other across multiple time zones.

However, many management theorists have also sought to make a case for postmodernism as a direct tool for problem solving and a source of innovation. For example, in the essay "Decoding Postmodernism for Busy Public Managers," appearing in the Spring 2007 issue of *The Public Manager*, Kenneth Nichols writes, "postmodernism encourages organization theory, and public administration . . . to rethink fundamental assumptions and concepts, mind the larger perspective and the longer view—much like what good public managers do" (63). Similarly in "Strategy as Simulacra," published in the *Journal of Management Studies*, Gina Grandy and Albert J. Mills, following Baudrillard, explain that postmodernism makes it possible to think about "strategic management as a model of simulation" and to examine the "practice of strategy as a discourse attempting to understand the 'truth effects' of the those discursive practices" (1153). And Jay D. White in "Knowledge Development: Views from Postpositivism, Poststructuralism, and Postmodernism," references the works of theorists such as Jameson, Derrida, Lacan, and Lyotard, among others, for their usefulness in explaining "local interconnected problems" in public administration (171). "The narratives that guide public administration," White openly affirms, should be "considered in light of postmodernism" (173). Invoking the postmodern disbelief in grand narratives, he further claims that "problem-solving in the postmodern era will proceed incrementally as small problems are addressed one at a time using local knowledge" (174). It is, again, fairly obvious how postmodernism—especially when the grand narratives of global capital take on increasingly overwhelming proportions—could come to serve as a conceptual back-stop for a preexisting inclination to focus on the local knowledges and micro-practices of OS and public administration, and also how it lends a theoretical gloss to the post-Fordist flexibility of labor that David Harvey analyzes in *The Condition of Postmodernity*. But what *are* these organizational and administrative problems that postmodernism can purportedly help solve?

The Labor-Intensifying Virtues of Egalitarian Postmodernism

As the internal contradictions of capital deepen along with its increasing mobility and volatility, the PMC, as I have argued, finds itself in need of new ways to produce cultural identification with the firm. To this extent, a postmodern-inflected organization theory steps in to assist the PMC to better manage employees and build a culture of employee participation in the newly globalized context by legitimating the adoption of a more egalitarian managerial pose. Such a turn to postmodernism represents itself, in part, as a reaction to the traditional approach to organization theory, which typically emphasizes rationality, formality, rule-reliance, and hierarchy. According to Nichols, "postmodernism refers to a skeptical approach to orthodox theories of organization, management, and culture, with an emphasis on adapting to circumstances" (60). Such "adaptation" will require openness to difference and the multiplicity of management "narratives." Writing in "The Role of the Researcher," Mary Jo Hatch cites Gérard Genette along with Derrida, Geertz, and Foucault to argue that "different ways of knowing are constructed within and through different narrative perspectives" (370) and that "the analysis of the narrating practices of organizational researchers may have direct benefit for managers" (371). "The acceptance of varied writing practices with respect to narrative positions," reasons Hatch, "should contribute to greater pluralism of perspectives" in management (374), a pluralism that could help "organizations transition from the authoritarian relationships typical of hierarchical structures to the influence-based, largely egalitarian relationships" (371). Hatch's notion of pluralism in fact fits perfectly well within the contours of a corporate ideology, which, ever since the adoption of affirmative action policies has moved to, in effect, redefine discriminatory policies as "pluralistic" through retooled corporate and managerial rhetorics and mission statements. As the looming shadow of globalization has driven management theorists in the direction of postmodernism, the question of pluralism has become all the more emphatic as corporations realize that to compete in a global market they need to employ in a systematic way the expertise of diverse sets of people from across the world. Even so, however, pluralism, in addition to being an ideology to be cultivated in keeping with the postmodern leanings of various corporations, has also emerged as a problem. So, for instance, in "Managing Multicultural Teams," a 2006 article by Jeanne Brett, Kristin Behfar, and Mary C. Kern, published in the *Harvard Business Review*, the authors acknowledge that, while "multiculturalism teams" can offer many advantages, a number of problems nevertheless arise due to such things as miscommunication based on differences in accents, in work values, and so forth. Although the authors propose dealing with such issues by implementing better communicative systems, the subtext here is clearly enough the fact that pluralism has become as much a part of the problem as it is part of the solution.

That is, in addition to being an ideological guide for purportedly less hierarchical employee relations, postmodernism also, in an even more overtly and ironically dislocalizing move, offers a chance for management to adapt to new, globalized conditions while at the same time reconsolidating its own disciplinary position. For White, here representing the view from public administration, postmodern theories can help identify and solve problems such as those resulting from "job dissatisfaction, or low organizational commitment, or job stress, or work overload, or occupational burnout"—and in so doing "preserve a greater sense of public administration as a whole" (175). It is as though the postmodern advocacy of the horizontal and nonclosure offered the PMC a way, not just to put a more positive spin on a crisis of management and administration, but to translate that crisis into an image of management itself.

But, however genuine the egalitarian desire may be here in the abstract, there is nothing in either White's or Hatch's analysis to suggest that such egalitarianism would really be the outcome—even if it were possible— of a postmodern managerial style. The emphasis here seems purely to be on getting conservative, top-down managers to understand how an egalitarian pose might help them motivate their employees into becoming more productive workers—and perhaps on getting rewarded for better managerial performance in the process. Whatever its merits may or may not be *per se,* postmodernism, no less than the idea of culture, functions within management discourse in a quintessentially dislocalist mode: apart from standing in for a new theory to match the sense that global capital has become a bewilderingly complex question of accelerating flows and fluxes without any apparent stable ground, it gives closure to management's narrative of obsolescence by recasting the centrifugal forces of globalization that threaten to undo it as if these were already contained within the field itself.

Such dislocalism becomes especially clear in White's appropriation of postmodernism. White begins by claiming that postmodernism can help solve administrative problems by licensing managers to reframe such problems as stories—stories that thereby become open to reinterpretations leading to "creative solutions." But in further thinking through this idea an odd sort of switch comes into play, and White appears to end up arguing *against* the application of postmodernism for such a purpose. This becomes apparent in his discussion of Jameson's well-known analysis of postmodernism:

> Jameson argues that Westerners have lost their ability to deal with the present or the future. He calls this "pastiche," meaning the imitation of dead styles. One example he uses is the Western fascination with nostalgia film, suggesting that only the past is meaningful . . . His second argument starts with Lacan's definition of schizophrenia as the inability to engage fully in speech and language . . . One corrective for the problems of pastiche and schizophrenia is the willingness to engage in telling stories about the past, the present, the future. (171)

Although Jameson's general characterization of the postmodern is vaguely recognizable here, note that White does not distinguish Jameson's profoundly critical metacommentary on postmodernism from those postmodern theories that are more affirming of "fragmentation" and the "dissolution of metanarratives" as interpretive strategies. Jameson, as we may recall from *Postmodernism, or the Cultural Logic of Late Capitalism,* does not claim that pastiche is merely an imitation of "dead styles," nor that pastiche in its postmodern form could be overcome by storytelling, the latter conceived here by White as a sort of executive tool capable of solving muddled administrative problems. What drops out of the picture entirely here is the fundamental difference between the Jamesonian theory of the postmodern as an attempt to read the contemporary narrative of capital itself and what White and other postmodern management theorists are doing, namely, reading the organizational forms of capital themselves as just narratives. Why, then, if the content of the theory is either glossed over or itself converted into a pastiche, invoke the authority of Jameson at all—or that of the other cultural theorists of postmodernity making regular appearances in management theory? Part of the answer here is simply that it authorizes management theorists such as White to introduce the concepts of culture and narrative into a management discourse in which such notions are otherwise unavailable. White invests in the narrative of "dead styles" because this reading of pastiche allows him to imply that those who continue to use older or past management practices to solve present and perhaps future problems employ dead *management* styles. The concept of pastiche is employed so as to code certain practices and people as obsolete in favor of those considered up-to-date. According to White, storytelling can be a corrective to these outmoded management methodologies. His claim is that scholarship in management theory and public administration "most closely approximates the conventional meaning of a story" because it "include[s] case studies, descriptions of administrative and political events, logical arguments, and interpretations" (172). While case studies and "administrative events" can indeed be treated as stories, postmodern theorists would probably not even agree on what the conventional meaning of a story might be, much less on how to apply it to solve administrative problems.

White's appropriation of the cultural theorists of postmodernism is thus deeply paradoxical. On the one hand, he sees himself as their proponent, reading them in a purely instrumental spirit as providing ways to identify problems. He advocates casting aside the possibility of "a grand narrative for public administration as a whole" so as to study only "the development of interconnected, local problems of society" (175). Although lacking entirely the philosophical overtones of, say, a Lyotard, the distrust of totality typical of much postmodern theory (Jameson obviously excepted) here seems to have found a secure home in the world of organizational administration. But, in that very moment, White equates postmodernism with pastiche, or as he says, with "dead styles," suggesting that postmodernism is a pathology that is to be overcome by storytelling. He asks: "What should be the role of public administration, if any, in dealing with the problems of postmodernism such as the pastiche and schizophrenia that Jameson fears? If society is really as fragmented as Lyotard claims, what role, if any, does public administration have in bringing it together?" (173). That is, the fact that the "grand narratives" have become eroded within the organizational wing of business (as well as in the world at large) is itself seen as purely a problem of organization. Evidently the underlying anxiety in business circles—that the complexities of globalization have now exceeded the organizational capacities of conventional business and management thinking—is to be dispelled by a corresponding panacea, according to which all one has to do is insert, somehow, this new level of complexity itself into the offices, production lines, and boardrooms in order for the grand narrative of global capital to piece itself back together again.

But the contradictions in White's appropriation of postmodernism reach their full expression only in management theory's instrumentalization of literary fiction—one in which fiction becomes not only a central form of knowledge for organization studies but also a model for organizations themselves.

V. THE TURN TO LITERATURE AND FICTION

It would perhaps have come as a surprise to the imagined, gun-wielding businessman in Bruce Robbins's 1972 graduate school anecdote—or to the professor who used it to humble his literature students—to learn that in the late 1980s Harvard Business School introduced and has regularly offered a course entitled "The Moral Leader" in which students have been required to read, *inter alia,* Shakespeare's *Macbeth,* Conrad's *The Secret Sharer,* Fitzgerald's *The Last Tycoon,* and Ishiguro's *Remains of the Day,* along with selections from the philosophy of Aristotle, Confucius, and Machiavelli. Such readings, according to the course catalogue description in 2003, will help future corporate leaders and managers think through "issues of personal character and sound practical judgment" (Elective Curriculum MBA Courses, Harvard Business School).[18] A light meal of "cultural capital" in what is otherwise a no-nonsense curriculum aimed at schooling America's future business leaders in the practical, hard-nosed realities of competing in the global marketplace? One might think so, but in fact a survey of business and management programs in American universities since the 1990s suggests otherwise. Along with the increase in combined BA/MBA programs that encourage business students to engage in a serious study of the humanities, courses like "The Moral Leader," in which works of literary fiction take center stage, have come to occupy a more stable place in management curricula.[19] What, to any advanced contemporary student of the humanities, must seem the superannuated, Arnoldian or Leavisian overtones of such catalogue descriptions are obvious and ironic enough. But the increasingly literary turn of the management academy indicates a widespread conviction among business educators not just that the great works of literature will make you "a better person"—or make you feel like one when you are faced with the "moral" dilemmas of having to "restructure" a company or wipe out your competition—but that they will make you a better *business*-space.

Fiction, however, offers management much more than simply a way to measure what is immeasurable, say, in a productivity or feasibility report. Even more than learning from the "leadership roles" depicted in *Macbeth* or the *Secret Sharer,* such fictions, in some sense the purest possible instances of storytelling (and to this extent in keeping with management's reading of postmodern theory), become a tool for problem solving. For example, "Literature, Ethics and Authority," a course offered at MIT's Sloan School in which students are assigned readings such as Melville's

Billy Budd, Sophocles' *Antigone,* and Timothy Mo's *The Monkey King,* explicitly states in its 2003 catalogue description that "unwittingly, we use stories and story-telling as managerial tools: properly applied, they help us motivate a workforce, define a company mission, *focus our thinking in moments of crisis*" (my emphasis; MIT OpenCourseWare). The point of the course, then, is to make this unwittingly literary approach to management conscious and methodical. Stories and the practice of storytelling here become a way of dealing with employee-related problems by furnishing direct models of organizational process and behavior, helping to shape and guide a culture of innovation and change in a globalized context. In effect, the concept of fiction has become an integral part of that cultural development.

But OS's penchant for fiction goes further still. Alongside helping to guide managers in their organizational decision-making by providing ethical templates and by furnishing simple and compelling behavioral models capable of reflecting complex situations, fiction itself becomes a blueprint for organization. Thus the ever trend-setting Tom Peters, writing in *Liberation Management* asks "if fiction and poetry (drama, opera, etc.) capture life better . . . then why not think of fiction as a model for organization?" (375). But he goes even further here than advocating the use of literary fiction to infuse organization with newness and creative thinking, openly declaring that "organizations *are* fiction—especially the knowledge based, professional service firms that are tomorrow's best models" (ibid.). Why pose fiction as model for organizations? According to *Liberation Management:*

> If you're lucky, your organization—that is "organization"—doesn't exist. You can't find it. People aren't in their offices. They're not doing what they're supposed to be doing—not passing paper to and from . . . Where are they damn it? If you can answer that question you are Newtonian and in trouble. In the old days we wanted an answer to that question . . . "He's in the office . . ." But now ambiguity defines the market. So doesn't it follow, as day follows night, that ambiguity must be . . . the organization? Um, how do you do a "chart-and-boxes" depiction of ambiguity? (379)

At this point, not only does Robbins's anecdote about the Benthamite businessman holding a gun to the head of the literary scholar begin to lose its terrors, but, to hear Peters tell it, it becomes curiously reversed. But organization *itself* as fiction? Apart from Peters's customary hyperbole, there are, of course, certain obvious caveats here. As is generally the case with Peters's brand of management discourse, it is the so-called knowledge-based firm, tacitly assumed to belong in the global North and particularly in the U.S., that is claimed to have crossed over into the "fictional" realm. And in this context it perhaps makes some sense to observe that the more employees telecommute and the less time they spend physically located in any single, nonvirtual office space, the more does their organizational presence appear to be a "fiction."

Yet Peters is not the exception here, for, as with the case of postmodernism, the more scholarly and academic wing of management theory has for some time now been making much the same kinds of argument.[20] Moreover, according to Peters and the standard corporate view of globalization, it is the "knowledge-based firms" that, along with the financial sector itself, ultimately organize not only knowledge and finance but also all of production worldwide. Odd as it may at first seem, the theory of organization *as* fiction is meant and is to be taken quite literally here. Analogy gives way to homology. For Peters, the essential attribute of fiction—and its great virtue as a model over the "Newtonian" school of OS—is its "ambiguity," the fact that flux and indeterminacy are perfectly at home in the fictional realm. Organizations must be ambiguous and in flux, hence must be "fictional," so as to match, to internalize directly within their own structure, what is universally understood as the flux and ambiguity of the market itself.

It is hard to avoid the speculative conclusion here that, however unwittingly, unsystematically, and, so to speak, facing backwards, management theory and OS have been driven to formulate or at least to imagine something like the Marxian category of—as it now tends to be termed— "fictional capital." In the third volume of *Capital*, Marx refers to the system of credit in general as "fictitious capital."[21] So, for example, the buying and selling of shares on the stock market neither creates new value nor injects increased capital into the firm whose shares are being traded. "Fictitious capital" is different from the money originally supplied for use in production. It is an additional amount of money that simply allows for the *circulation* of income or profit. In fact, this circulation represents claims to future, still unrealized surplus value, making it appear that the amount of capital has increased. Thus the increase in the price of shares, to take the most obvious example of fictitious capital, creates the illusion—the stuff of everyday economic life on Wall Street—that the stock market itself is creating value. Essentially, fictitious capital refers to a form of financialization—the listing of a given amount of prospective money capital on the books—that makes a claim on the future generation of real, nonfictional profits or surplus value.[22]

None of this poses any real threat to the reproduction of capital as a whole as long as such claims themselves are eventually made good and fictional is converted into real capital. But what happens if—or when—a point is reached beyond which this realization (in more than one sense here) ceases to be possible, and, to avoid defaulting on the claims already lodged against fictional capital, still *more* fictional capital must be injected into circulation in the hopes of putting off the inevitable day of reckoning? Here one encounters what has become a major question in discussions of contemporary political economy, one to which I cannot do real justice here. The most recent U.S. financial crisis, set off in 2007–8 by massive defaults on subprime home mortgages and the resulting deflation of what had been Wall Street's latest, real estate–based speculative bubble is only the latest indication that such a point—what we might term hyper-fictionalization—may have been reached.

But one does not have to be knowledgeable on this point of Marxian critical political economy to have more than an inkling that, as increasing masses of fictional capital remain unrealized, as more and more "good" money is thrown after "bad," a "tipping point" will be reached beyond which capital itself must come to function more as a "fiction," a financial *fictio juris,* than as anything with a *real* basis in production. If, however, for ideological reasons, "theory" is prevented from entertaining the thought that such hyper-fictionalization calls into question the continued viability of global capitalism itself, then, as bizarre as this undoubtedly may appear, it is hard to see what alternative remains but to complete the ideological inversion itself and conclude that the whole business is a fiction anyway, and the sooner one realizes this, and sets about the task of selecting the fictions best suited to getting the job done, the better.

Affirming the business organization *as* fiction is, after all, one way of dislocalizing the more deep-seated, largely unconscious anxiety, observed repeatedly above, that globalization and the volatilization of capital have pulled the rug from under the organization as such, have made capital borderless and, in a sense, unorganizable. At least "fictions" have boundaries.

To put this ideological escapade into perspective one must be reminded of just how *un*manageable and bewildering the current global scene with its huge proliferation and decentralization of financial markets and instruments must seem to anyone charged with the task of managing a firm who is somehow to register all this and act accordingly. As David Harvey remarked in *The Condition of Postmodernity,* the global financial system has become "so complicated that it surpasses most people's understanding. The boundaries between distinctive functions like banking, brokerage, financial services, housing finance, consumer credit, and the like have become increasingly porous at the same time that new markets in commodity, stock, currency, or debt futures have sprung up, discounting time future into time present in baffling ways" (161).

Indeed, the giddiness of life in the moment of hyper-fictionalization appears, if anything, to magnify a sense of empowerment in the case of the management and marketing disciplines responsible for coming up with cultural or fictional strategies for gaining market share or managing cultural diversity. If the valorization of capital itself depends on a future return to general profitability that may turn out to be fictional, that is, if it all comes to depend on what buyers and sellers imagine will happen, why waste efforts on "Newtonian" organizational structures? Consider, as one indication of this, the article "Truth or Consequences," collaboratively written by Hans Hansen, Daved Barry, David M. Boje, and Mary Jo Hatch. The authors affirm that "not only is there truth in fiction, there is truth through fiction," further observing "fiction's special capacity to furnish us with knowledge about the 'actual' world that the 'actual' world cannot provide" (113)[23]. This is a plausible, not to say conventional view insofar as works of literary fiction themselves are concerned. But when, as here, it is adduced as an organizational or managerial principle in the face of globalization, it suggests that the "actual" world has become too volatile and unknowable to be "managed" *except* through its fictionalization. The authors of "Truth or Consequences" also cite Barbara Czarniawska's *Narrating the Organization,* another management theory text that draws upon fiction and culture, stating that "stories capture organizational life in a way that no compilation of facts ever can; this is because they are carriers of life itself, not just reports on it" (ibid).[24]

Like Peters, who in *Liberation Management* muses that the "conundrums" of running an organization have "more in common with convolution within convolution in Norman Mailer's *Harlot's Ghost* than with [management theory's] latest pronouncements," the authors of "Truth or Consequences" again indicate how literary fictions not only are claimed to assist in producing novel and creative thinking but have come to *stand in* for the complex relations of fictional capital themselves (379). It would seem that the current realities of finance capital—especially its increasing flight forward into the realm of essentially fictional future realization and profits—have become so complicated that attempts to understand them slide out of the *business* narrative entirely, leaving behind *only* the *cultural* as that which encompasses the fictional in both senses, literary and financial.

Management Narrates the Nation

But the dislocalism evident in management's penchant for fiction and high postmodern theory has still another surprise in store here: for it will perhaps already have been noted above that OS's affinity for postmodern theory is not matched, as one might have expected, by a taste for more of the contemporary or postmodern fiction. Certainly Peters's bold, "liberated" willingness to question whether organizations really do exist and his fascination for postmodern ideologemes such as chaos, conundrum, convolution, ambiguity, and the like, also ought to lead him and the conceptual mindset of management theory he represents toward a corresponding interest in primarily postmodernist fiction on the order, say, the work of Kathy Acker, or at least of Don DeLillo. But for Peters, Norman Mailer's work seems to be as close as it gets. This could be said to be true of management theory generally. Jay White's simultaneous argument both for and against postmodernist theories is again symptomatic of this contradiction. What attracts White and other OS and public administration theorists to postmodernism is its emphasis on the fluidity and free-floating properties of culture—analogs for and even, so to speak, possible homeopathic cures for the hyper-complex and boundaryless world of the global market and fictional capital. But in OS this attraction goes hand in hand with a no less persistent longing for a simpler, homogeneous culture, before postmodern pastiche, and able to restore the loss of both national and disciplinary boundaries.

That is, management theorists effectively dislocalize postmodernism itself, making it the cultural-theoretical accompaniment to authors and titles that for the most part are not an easy fit with postmodernist paradigms. Typical reading lists in management theory courses follow the canonical pattern evident in the Harvard and MIT business courses already cited above: an ancient or medieval classic, along with something by Shakespeare; a nineteenth century standard by writers such as Conrad or Melville; and one or two lesser known contemporary works that stay well within the mainstream. Some lists include one or two works by non–Euro-American authors such as Chinua Achebe, Wole Soyinka, or Toni Morrison. But these works are also generally part of the canon of literary readings in the United States. I see the inclusion of such texts as part of the process of utilizing multiculturalism in the corporate and management sector analyzed later in this chapter. The course description for "Management through Literature" at Maryville College in Tennessee in 2002 explains the value for the future PMC of what it terms "great" literature as follows: "Great literature affords us the opportunity to learn from others who have wrestled with . . . perennial questions about our nature, our experience, and our existence" (*Management through Literature, Maryville College*). Even as literary fictions offer management theory a way to infuse the field with newness, that is, literature also provides it a secure anchor in what is "perennial." After all, "perennial questions," even if they must be wrestled with, can still appear to have answers in a world mystified by the global and increasingly fictional nature of finance and capital itself. Narratives and storytelling may, as we have seen, provide management theory with risk-free ways to promote diversity and egalitarianism in the workplace, but classical fiction is nevertheless clearly preferable thanks to its perceived emphasis on purportedly universal motivations and behavior, categories that, in a time of increasingly diverse markets, appear to be in ever scarcer supply. "Great" works that have "passed the test of time," seem in a better position to provide answers for an incomprehensible present in apparently constant flux. In a sense, the postmodern and the premodern converge on each other in management theory's literary aesthetic. Indeed, in a maneuver that demonstrates just how abstract and tenuous the game has become, management theory eventually finds that it must turn to classical literature and philosophy for the "knowledge" needed to run the "knowledge-based" firms. Here again we are lead back to the literal double meaning of "fictional capital," since, with industrial production being farmed out to the peripheries, such a fictional principle helps to cement the illusion that firms do not sell products at all but only "knowledge." It is as if the potential crisis of fictional capital—given the distinct likelihood that the future valorization of this capital through real production and profits will not come about—could be warded off by reverting to a dimension in which "knowledge" and indeed all values are the stuff of fiction. Such a readiness to mine literature and culture for purposes of supplying the product itself to "knowledge-based firms"—always tacitly assumed to be of U.S. and European provenance—is symptomatic of the way the discipline of management, no less than literary and cultural studies, is plagued with anxiety over globalization and what it takes to be the implicit threat of its own obsolescence and potential disappearance. At the very least, the turn to these particular works of fiction in management theory masks a nervousness about capitalism to which management theory may be understandably unwilling to admit.

Finally, and not least importantly here, there is the fact that canonical fiction not only provides to the world of business and management the welcome sense of being able to slow down time in the spatio-temporally compressed universe of globalization. It also offers an indirect, imaginary way of reproducing national boundaries themselves, given that fiction—in this *unlike* globalized capital—appears to have a spontaneously national character. Although, management courses generally do not stress the organization of their literary reading lists along national lines per se, the fact remains that it is difficult, not to say impossible to discuss these works of literary fiction (especially those on management reading lists) without references to settings, time of publication, a minimum of historical context, and indeed a definite geographical location—all of which betoken the presence of a nation-state, whether real or projected back into the past. Even if a novel, say, is set in different parts of the world it generally narrates the lives of characters as they move from one place to another—safe, as it were, from the abstract vertigo of globalization. A survey of such courses reveals, not surprisingly, what is, with few exceptions, a decided penchant for North American and British authors and texts. Schools of business and management on the whole regard English as the language—and the Anglo-North-American global sphere of influence as the space—in which to "wrestle with the perennial questions." And this is clearly no coincidence, given the implicit and near universal desire of management theory to be a discipline for preserving, or restoring, American business hegemony.[25]

To this degree, management's turn to literary fiction, as a function of its more general cultural turn, can be read as an indirect method for "narrating the nation"—given that the nonliterary, nonfictional nation itself no longer has a place in management's own globalization-inspired narrative of obsolescence. OS's fascination for the idea of the virtual, postmodern organization, with its professed respect for the varied cultural perspectives or narratives of its personnel and its anti-hierarchical pose, exists, here as well, in a simultaneously overlapping and contradictory relationship to an aggressive rhetoric of Americanism and a fixation on the nation-state in general. In consummate dislocalist fashion, OS celebrates the global village in the very moment it is nervously attempting to reconsolidate national boundaries and Americanness. The postmodern move to appropriate a traditional, mainly Anglo-American literary and philosophical canon that is itself at odds with postmodernist paradigms speaks to that nervousness, since affirming the relativizing and anti-universalist principles of postmodernist fiction might be tantamount to an admission that those who have been responsible for understanding (so as to exploit) the workings of capital may not be competent to do so any longer. Even this ambiguous nostalgia for the history of Western thought and great literature seems somehow coerced, a displaced form of globalization anxiety. What is "new" to the disciplines of business and management is in fact valued for its being "timeless"—an antidote to both the dangerous fictionality of the present material conditions and the lurking material dangers of the new. Given such an uncertain, potentially chaotic horizon, turning to old standards such as *Beowulf* and *Billy Budd* provides management theory with a way to hold onto something that, for it, seems to be both established and creative, new and yet old: a venerable, if fictional nation to fill in the strange vacuum of the denationalized business organization itself.

VI. FROM POSTMODERNISM TO MODERNIZATION
International Development Management (IDM)

The shift from an interest in culture as a predicate of organizations to the theory of organization itself *as* culture that has characterized OS and produced its preoccupation with literary fiction and postmodern theory appears on the surface not to have influenced the other major area in management, international development management (IDM). As already noted, the field of IDM addresses issues of concern to managers who are part of the global network of institutions responsible for instituting U.S.-led neoliberal policies as well as disseminating American business know-how abroad. This field, sometimes referred to simply as development management, has traditionally been considered the international branch of public administration. It is generally distinguished institutionally from organization studies (even perhaps from international management insofar as it arose to theorize managerial issues in a global context). Given its involvement with the so-called developing world, it includes the work of "nation-building." Although of late, the emphasis on the rhetoric of "nation-building" per se has been downplayed while still looking at politics and policy analyzing conceptual and technical issues of pertinence to officials in charge of modernization projects across the world. In addition, as mentioned above, ideas that international management could benefit from a closer relationship with development management so that managerial questions can be considered in relationship to questions of governmental policy are also being explored. My analysis of the material under the label of IDM then is cognizant of the divergence and convergence of these areas of management.

Derick W. and Jennifer M. Brinkerhoff, academics who also consult for development banks and other agencies, write in their 2007 essay "International Development Management: Definitions, Debates, and

Dilemmas,"[26] that "the field addresses organizational and managerial problems in the developing countries of Africa, Asia, and Latin America, and in the transitional economies of Eastern Europe and the former Soviet Union" (823). But IDM has also recently begun to consider that "the same types of problems that confront the developing/transitional world can be found in pockets of poverty, marginalization, and inequality in industrialized countries as well" and that, therefore, IDM can also be applied to "poverty alleviation and community organizing in the industrialized world" (ibid.). I will subsequently analyze the way in which this latter "first world" encroachment of IDM is lending implicit managerial support to the policing of ethnic and racial minorities in the United States. But for the most part development management is connected to projects in developing nations that are "sponsored by international money donor agencies" (ibid.)—all of which have their own priorities and corresponding agendas. IDM professionals are often dispatched from a donor agency to an onsite assignment (in the global periphery) for a "pre-determined task or a sponsored development project" (829). While this paradigm of lender and debtor nation may be consistent with a more generalized East/West, North/South model of center and periphery, the centrality of American hegemony in terms of both financial power and the ability to dictate management practices cannot be denied here. Some of the most prominent donor agencies served by IDM include the World Bank, the IMF, and USAID, whose legions of consultants and officials in developing nations are in many ways today's version of erstwhile colonial administrators, still working to help these nations "find their place" in imperial modernity. As a result of its neocolonial reputation, IDM has, not surprisingly, been the object of widespread criticisms, including many organized protests at public meetings and events. But, perhaps even more significantly, the response from IDM has been to try to accommodate such criticisms within its own theoretical discourse, to distance itself from charges of imperialism by adopting some of the language of postcolonial theory[27] (more on this below as well). As it tries to reposition American-sponsored neoliberal policies and its vision of modernizing corporate practices in what is purportedly a departure from older colonial and neocolonial models, a more traditional, ethnographic idea of culture and a corresponding notion of "cultural intelligence" come into play as important tools in this endeavor.

"Globalization, Culture, and Management: Managing Across Cultures," a course that has been offered periodically in the last eight years at the Harvard Business School, is a good example of how the older, cultural intelligence paradigm still retains its importance for managerial work in a global arena. As the course description (2003) puts it: "the liberalization of markets around the world has created new opportunities and challenges for managers everywhere. Increasingly, they must develop effective working relationships with people of diverse cultural backgrounds" (*Elective Curriculum MBA Courses, Harvard University*). Managers, the blurb continues, "must decide whether principles, practices, and strategies that make sense in one cultural context are equally suitable for another. As they build organizations that span the globe, they must take into account a complex set of cultural variables that shape the attitudes and expectations of their varied constituencies."

Here we clearly have an ethnographic notion of culture being used to theorize employee relations and target markets. But note that its deployment has in fact already moved beyond a local, more conventionally ethnographic to a global, transnational context. For example, "Globalization, Culture, and Management" declares its intention to study "Latin American, Hindu-Buddhist, Japanese, Chinese, Russian, Islamic, and African cultures," making this diverse set the lens through which to "take a global perspective." The course promises to examine the "difficult choices for managers whose activities span many cultures" and, eventually, even to "explore the possibility of a transcultural model of corporate excellence." The image of globally mobile executives interacting with multiple cultures and standing in need of training in the latter's complexities has, of course, long been a familiar one. But note that, as would not have been the case, say, a generation ago, the notion of "culture" itself no longer lends itself here to ready differentiation along national lines. The juxtaposition of Hindu-Buddhist and Islamic cultures alongside Russian and African is already a clear indication of this. While the notion of the "transcultural" can help understand the complexity of group dynamics, it presence represents an implicit admission of how difficult is has become to organize this complexity along traditionally national lines. As a result of hyper-mobility and time/space compression, culture in the conventional national or ethnic sense has become too "messy" to articulate the movement of peoples and capital across the globe. All the various "cultures" listed in the Harvard course description, for example, are to be found both within and outside the borders of the U.S. It is not so much that this complexity of culture is new per se, but the unprecedented scale of cultural complexity presents particular challenges for the purposes of "managing" capital and its reproduction. Thus, for example, Michael Veseth, who writes on marketing and management, points out in *Selling Globalization* that "international marketing textbooks are filled with studies of global strategies defeated by language, culture, or local practice" (53). It is just such cases of "international failure" that have led management theorists to the conclusion that previously held notions of culture and cultural intelligence have to be carefully rethought if management as a field is to avoid becoming globally obsolete. And yet, as the analysis to follow will attempt to show, this very recognition takes a dislocalized form, articulating, at the same time, an anxious desire for a return to a simpler, prelapsarian state of culture that could allow for a clear differentiation among the nations over which to reassert IDM's *sine qua non* here: American business hegemony. Much like OS, although in different contexts and via a different route, IDM theorists, nervous about the effects of the mobility of capital and time/space compression, betray a semi- or unconscious wish to restore and fix the distance between nations even as they champion the speed with which global capital travels through a borderless space.

Indeed, although on the whole culture remains, for IDM, an object to be "managed" via an enhanced "cultural intelligence"—while for OS culture has, so to speak, moved into the subject position itself—the very form of this relative difference within management theory speaks to the fact of globalization and its dislocalizing effects on the business disciplines. For in the case of the "developing" nations that are the focus of IDM, whose aim it is to place these countries firmly on the path of a metropolitan-guided capitalist modernization, the nation itself seemingly remains a coherent, unified cultural entity. Globalization as a socio-historical process is uneven: the same globalized capital that reproduces itself directly on the plane of the individual denationalized capitalist enterprise, thereby pulling the rug out from under the national identity of these organizations themselves, simultaneously requires for its reproduction the "modernization" of the "developing" economies—that is, their firm incorporation into the global capitalist order. IDM trains and assists those members of the PMC who oversee the investment of capital via "donor agencies" such as the World Bank in the expectation that it will yield ample returns for corporate and financial elites in the U.S. and elsewhere—but mainly in the U.S. In effect, the same dynamic within global capital that threatens to denationalize the major capitalist enter-.prise renationalizes the socio-economic formations of the "developing" world from the standpoint of these global enterprises themselves. For this reason the "developing" nation retains what looks like its traditional role for capitalist reproduction—whence what also appears as a greater stability and fixity of the cultural. To this degree, ironically, globalization positions the peripheral nation in a more direct, immediate relation to the firm itself, thus—with the assistance of IDM—making it easier, in one sense at least, for an American-based PMC to draw the national-cultural lines between the U.S. and, say, Mexico.

This relative difference becomes clearer in relation to what is, for IDM as well as OS, a distinct move in the direction of the postmodern. In their focus on modernization, IDM professionals, unlike their OS counterparts, do not sense any compulsion to argue for postmodern theories per se. In the context of management theory, just as in the humanities, postmodernism, for all its claim to de-centeredness, is a tacitly metropolitan prerogative, a kind of code for reinventing and updating the field that also functions as a qualifier for a denationalized U.S., helping to position the global North as ahead in time of the developing global South.[28]

However, even if the theories themselves are not directly invoked, the very language employed by IDM in this context, echoing OS's emphasis on the multiplicity of perspectives and an "egalitarian" destabilizing of traditional hierarchies, indicates the influence of postmodernism here as well. And here dislocalism is again at work, for postmodernism effectively steps in to help IDM rethink, from the corporate standpoint, the task of peripheral *modernization* itself in an age when global, neoliberal capitalism, with its far greater and more locally mediated penetration of the economies of the global South, requires a deepened appreciation of the cultural pluralism and complexity of the markets it is driven to exploit. What is new and different—postmodern—about contemporary IDM is the explicit acknowledgment that in order for the PMC charged with managing development internationally as well as in less-developed pockets of the global North/West, it must learn to drop the notion of a single, standardized culture of modernity even as its pursues the economic and technical objectives of modernization.

This tacitly postmodern standpoint is reflected as well in the way that, as already noted above, IDM parries the charges often leveled against it, and its donor agency sponsors, of complicity with neocolonialism. But rather than strike back at its critics—say by employing the old, Cold War tactic of dismissing them as left-wing radicals—IDM simply deploys the more neutral postmodern language of egalitarian de-centeredness and diversity of perspective, thereby appearing to distance itself from a self-evidently centered and hierarchical policy of neocolonial exploitation.

IDM has, in fact, managed to build what appears to be its *own* critique of imperialism into its theoretical metalanguage. The Brinkerhoffs, for example, openly concede that "development management is a means to enhancing the effectiveness and efficiency of projects and programs determined and designed by outside actors," acknowledging the view, albeit characterizing it as "radical," that IDM retains a "connection to the imperialist agendas of colonialism, and that today's development management is the instrument of donor-imposed priorities just as colonial administration enabled Western imperialists to rule their acquired territories for their own purposes" (827). They admit the potential for conflict within IDM between the latter, when viewed as an "instrument of external institutional agendas" and "the agendas of groups within developing/transitional countries" (838). "This," they go on to say, "is often a contest among unequal actors, with predominant power residing with the international donors in the case of negotiations between international funders and national governments" while, moreover, "internal to the recipient country, power tends to be concentrated in political and economic elites, whose agendas overrule those of the poor and marginalized" (838).

This may sound like the script for a left critique of corporate structures, albeit just distanced and descriptive enough to place IDM somehow in the rhetorical middle space between the "outside" and the "internal." But it is precisely alongside and *through* such a slightly displaced—more precisely, a dislocalized—critique of imperialism that IDM opens up a rhetorical space for resituating a "postmodern" American, and, so to speak, "nonimperialist" imperialism, seemingly as far removed from European colonialism as are the local, internal recipients in potential conflict with the outside actors of the donor agencies—and leaving an American PMC to play the role of innocent, potentially helpful actor.[29] The crucial rhetorical instrument here is the seemingly neutral language of management theory itself. The Brinkerhoffs and other management theorists may in fact be genuinely sympathetic to the plight of nations being restructured according to the neoliberal agenda. However, the problem as they—"managerially"—see it is not that developing nations are being exploited to further the interests of the donor agencies—how can a donor be an exploiter or expropriator?—but that these same agencies have tended to work according to agendas that make it "difficult (although not impossible) to accommodate local political realities, or to take a process approach" (830). And this in turn leads to an even more serious problem when local priorities contradict those of a "foreign assistance funder" but the recipient country governments give in simply in order to receive the funds, leading to a "superficial commitment to reform and pro forma meeting of targets" (830). The problem here is not the existence of an unequal relationship itself but rather the *perception* of unequal frameworks, a failure to incorporate "local realities" or take a "process" approach to following through on donor priorities. Note here as well that this is precisely the rhetorical moment at which management theory must check its own instinctive celebration of globalization's dissolution of national borders and revert to the dislocal drive for a more coherent notion of the nation-state, one that can accept donor agency priorities and reforms on behalf of its citizenry without potential conflicts.

Still further evidence of IDM's dislocalized, modernizing postmodernism can be detected in the name of the discipline itself. As the Brinkerhoffs tell us, the field of international or development management (IDM) previously went under the rubric of "Development Administration," a "sub-field of the field of public administration [but] in the developing world" (824). The replacement of term "administration" by "management," they further explain, reflects the change in emphasis from the "tasks and tools of routine administration in bureaucracies" to emphasis on "nimble organizations, flexible strategies, and proactive managerial styles" (824). "Flowing from [a more] polycentric concept, where numerous actors are actively engaged in the tasks of improving people's lives and generating socio-economic benefits, development management is not restricted to the public sector" (824).

Several things need unpacking here. The first is simply to note how, in what has become one of the most familiar and insidious rhetorical sleights of neoliberalism, the language of the "nimble" and the "flexible," here qua "organizations" and "strategies," turns what is for the majority of the global population the social catastrophe accompanying the qualitatively increased mobility of global capital into a managerial virtue. The second is to note how, by replacing the term "administration" with "management" IDM already distances itself semantically from charges of neocolonialism: one speaks customarily of colonial "administrators" or bureaucrats, but not necessarily of colonial "managers." Finally, the switch from "administration" to "management" here—or rather, the collapse of the public/private sector distinction implied in the difference—paints as a purely technical, managerial advance in the direction of "flexibility" and "process" what is, for those targeted by the donor agencies, the effective removal of all local state barriers to globalization and the penetration of capital. In relation to the management of development, such barriers come to seem little more than outdated, parochial practices.

But of course management does have available to it, when needed, a political synonym, and one that is perhaps more at home in a postmodernist, globalized cultural register than ever: "democracy." According to the Brinkerhoffs, development management "is crucial in helping governments build the capacity to respond to citizen expectations and to put in place the institutional structures that allow democracy to function effectively" (839). The note of similarity here between George W. Bush's post-9/11 call for the U.S. to lead a world crusade for "democracy" is striking, but it is culture rather than guns that has become the weapon of choice here. The Brinkerhoffs exhort IDM to explore "various institutional options for democratization that fit with particular country circumstances, and of recognizing that the U.S. model is but one path among many" (836). The figure of the "one path among many" seems to be adapted right from a manager's guide to postmodernism. Thus traditional village governance structures in Africa, for example, despite what are perceived as their political limitations qua models of consensual or representative organization, are conceded to be as worthy of being considered as "democratic" as the U.S. model. Still, whether U.S. style or not, "democracy" is to be encouraged, or, when necessary, ushered in under the strict guidance of American-dominated donor agencies armed with managerial know-how. Here, as noted above, the postmodern inflection is precisely what allows IDM both to appear to critique an older style of European colonialism and to position itself, and its U.S. sponsors, as *modernizers,* as coming to the aid of developing nations that aspire to catch up in time. The emphasis on "flexible" and "participatory" structures becomes a managerial rhetoric for modernizing in a postmodern way. The Brinkerhoffs advise managers to place emphasis on "multi-sectoral solutions" as "no single discipline or perspective has a corner on 'the truth'; the best solutions emerge when the insights of many viewpoints and sources of expertise are brought to bear" (840). Just as, for OS, management must become conscious of the existence of its own, as well as that of other "master-narratives," IDM officials need to be aware of what their values are and then make those values explicit in order that the process of democratization can become more egalitarian. But note here how postmodernism, à la IDM, not only culturalizes and pluralizes what would otherwise be a too transparently U.S.-identified "democracy." It also becomes a way for the management theorist to narrate the nation even while championing globalization and the sweeping away of national borders. The very language of postmodernity, here functioning as a code in which to represent the flux of global, increasing fictionalized capital, also becomes a way to appear to undo the time-space compression that has produced the "global village." The ideal manager emerges here as someone who plays up the rhetoric of globalization, participation, and democracy for all, but precisely in order to put in place the institutional structures that will make it possible for the U.S. to remain a "nation of nations."

Narrating American Business in the World

The question of practice remains, however: how are these theories actually supposed to work "on the ground"? Recall that for management theorists and academics, theory is required to produce—or appear to produce—workplace and organizational results. One of the principal, pedagogical methods the field at large employs in order to attempt to mediate theory and practice is that of working through case studies that are intended to simulate real-life scenarios. The case studies themselves are either purely fictional or quasi-fictionalized narratives based on actual events that present a set of problems for students to assess and analyze from different points of view, in the manner of an exercise. I want now to turn to a close analysis of several of such case studies, taken from editors Linda Catlin and Thomas White's 2001 textbook, *International Business: Cultural Sourcebook and Case Studies.* I have chosen to analyze this text because it is typical of numerous textbooks in the area of international business used in university classrooms since the 1990s that attempt to teach students issues in "cross-cultural management." In particular, I want to explore two theses here: 1) how management's own form of the dislocalized drive to return to or preserve a simpler, localizable culture amidst the flux and vertigo of globalization also produces a gravitation toward a certain kind of fiction; and 2) how the undermining of the national point of view and the transnationalizing of cultures has led management to focus increasingly on race and ethnicity themselves, both outside and within the U.S.

In both cases, significantly, culture remains a crucial, guiding term. Like OS, IDM operates on the assumption that the political, economic, and legal changes required to ensure the successful management of capital investment cannot take place without cultural change. Because, in the case of IDM or international management, culture itself is potentially an exotic and complex entity, the PMC it is charged with training must, as we have seen, develop a minimum quota of cultural intelligence. But if the international management textbooks of the 1980s tended to employ case studies largely focused on distinct national cultures, then since the 1990s textbooks have steadily complicated this pattern. *International Business,* for example, includes case studies relating to cultural patterns in Germany, Australia, Japan, and Mexico, but also exercises involving the more ambiguously "national case" of Puerto Rico and those of the explicitly U.S. regional cultures of Native Americans and of the American Southwest. Without at any point questioning its own implicitly Americanist point of view *International Business* concedes the need of management and the PMC to manage and develop the cultural otherness not only of overseas markets but of the U.S.'s own ethnic minorities—in relation to whom the aspiring manager is, of course, consistently if also implicitly coded as white. To the degree that acknowledging cultural complexity *within* national boundaries makes that a more difficult task conceptually, the categories of race and ethnicity step in here as dislocalizing agents, able both to displace and to reconsolidate national boundaries. But it is also, as we shall see, the fictional, if nonliterary quality of these case studies that provides invaluable assistance here in dislocalizing—and re-Americanizing—the global, and helping to protect the field of management itself against increasing suspicions of its own obsolescence.

So as to further narrow down my narrative object here, I have chosen to analyze case studies in *International Business* that deal explicitly with cultural issues of time and space. Here the underlying link (within the dislocalized imaginary) between culture, nation, ethnicity, and the abstract fungibility of globalized capital becomes especially vivid. Framing the case studies are short write-ups and articles asking students to consider the ways in which cultural values affect people's perception of time and space, as, for example, in statements such as: "Time is money. Don't stand so close. You're breathing down my neck." Such clichés, according to Caitlin and White, in fact describe "ideas held by many Americans about the value of time and appropriate amount of physical space between individuals," and they advise students to consider that "all cultures have specific values related to time and space. When your cultural values relating to time or space conflict with another culture's values misunderstandings or even animosity can occur" (26).

An article entitled "Relearning How to Tell Time" is introduced to help coach students into greater flexibility in relation to the "time" of other cultures, focusing, as one example of such flexibility, on the many thousands of Mexicans who live in Tijuana and commute daily to jobs on the California side of the U.S.–Mexico border. It includes an anecdote about a Mexican psychologist, Vicente López, who spent five years making the Tijuana-to-San Diego commute and is indirectly quoted as saying "that each time he crossed the border, it felt like a button was pushed inside him. When entering the U.S., he felt his whole being switch to rapid clock-time mode: he would walk faster, drive faster, talk faster, meet deadlines. When returning home, his body would relax and slow down the moment he saw the Mexican customs agents" (93). According to Catlin and White, the case of Vicente López shows that people can master unfamiliar time patterns.

But note how telling this anecdote of postmodern existence is of the ways in which people's bodies must be adjusted to the needs of capital. Under the cover of a cultural relativization of time, here the mobility of capital comes to be narrated and represented as if it were simply a question of the mobility of people. Spatio-temporality here is deployed in such a way as to maintain the conceptual and narrative boundaries between Mexico and the U.S. even as global capital itself is presumed to be free to ignore them. And the U.S.–Mexico border setting is surely no coincidence, Mexican workers standing in here as stereotypical embodiments of the flexible and the temporary, as a population easier to dominate and police than others. For those looking to move their businesses across the border to Mexico, *International Business* even has a section that contains a list of guidelines on Mexican labor, observing that Mexicans are flexible, respectful of authority, and always poised to show camaraderie to their peers. But, the book adds, "most employees desire that authority over them be wielded in a kind and sensitive manner" (88).

To be sure, "Relearning How to Tell Time" is also intended as advice to managers on how to adjust themselves to other time-cultures, for, as the textbook states, "most intercultural travelers would prefer to avoid the five years of onsite mistakes that López endured before achieving multi-temporal proficiency" (94). *Inter alia*, managers in need of "multi-temporal proficiency" are advised to learn a culture's customs for making and keeping appointments as well as the line between work time and social time. Mastering the language of time will, of course, require time and practice, and so the student manager is also exhorted to follow management theory's version of postmodernism by becoming more aware of his or her own cultural values as well as humble and open to criticism in relation to the spatio-temporal values of others. But managerial postmodernism goes only so far here. Contrasting the "multi-temporally proficient" border-crossing Mexicans to those who live and work in Mexico proper, *International Business* states that the latter "may permit themselves to be guided by their own inner clock rather than the clock on the wall. Consequently many U.S. firms provide buses to pick up workers at various locations so at to avoid uncertain arrival times as well as complications due to traffic problems" (90). Again, although there is a formal recognition of the nonhierarchical and diverse here, there is also, when work is involved, really only one clock on the wall, and cultures in the developing world that lag behind will, however worthy of cultural respect, have to learn to tell its time. Consider that the same book that advises American managers to respect—so as to correct for—the internal clock of Mexicans advises them never to adopt the persona of the "relaxed

American" and be late for an appointment in Germany. In some places even Americans can be "Mexicans."

Such scenarios are thus, in a sense, perfect examples of dislocalism itself. Ethnocentric views of culture are displaced in favor of diverse cultural points of view, but this in turn becomes a technique for managing diversity itself, and ultimately for fixing cultures and people in a newly framed spatio-temporality in which the PMC is permitted the time and space to learn and practice "multi-temporal proficiency" the more effectively to speed up the work of their cultural "equals" and limit their mobility in relation to capital. This slowing down in order to reaccelerate, de-centering in order to cement more securely in place becomes even more evident in the consciously fictional—and themselves effectively fictionalizing—management scenarios to which I now turn.

FICTIONALIZED CASE STUDIES

United States/Mexico: "Fish Farming Enterprise in Mexico"

"Fish Farming Enterprise in Mexico," one of the fictionalized case studies/exercises included in *International Business,* tells the story of the Amica Corporation, a construction company in Albuquerque, New Mexico owned and operated by a chemical engineer, Arthur Jackson. Jackson wants to sell this business and start a catfish farm in a small town in Mexico. Students are asked to imagine themselves as consultants to Jackson, providing analysis that would "complement the Mexican perspective" (24). They are also to imagine that they have conducted an interview with the Mexican Consul-General in Denver, "discussing the subtle cultural differences between Mexicans and Americans and how a knowledge of these differences is important to business success in Mexico" (24). The students are instructed to advise Jackson primarily on cultural matters, including language, religion, social class structure, gender roles, values related to work, and time. But the fictional exercise also provides the students with additional cues for aligning their own point of view with Jackson's. They are told, for example, that Jackson and his family used to own a fish farm in Louisiana; thus he is framed not just as an entrepreneur but also as someone who is carrying on an American family tradition. Jackson is also, according to the fictional case study, aware that "U.S.–Mexican relations have been characterized by war, and misunderstandings," as well as by numerous and important cultural differences (23). He is presented as a sympathetic character, who, although his "primary goal is to make a profit," nevertheless has the goal of supplying "inexpensive, high quality protein" to customers in both Mexico and the U.S. while bringing new jobs to poor and unemployed Mexicans (23–24).

Here, however, the foregrounding of cultural differences becomes a way of displacing—and, in the process, mystifying—the various economic, profit-driven factors that form the real "story" in this case study. Among the reasons Jackson wants to operate his fish farm in Mexico are the availability of a cheaper source for labor, land, and water and a warmer climate in which the catfish will mature faster (23). Also factors here are the relaxation of laws restricting foreign company ownership in Mexico and reports that "Mexico is interested in importing agricultural products from the U.S." (ibid). In effect, Mexico here could be anywhere that offered Jackson's new venture the same legal, geographical, climatic, and cost advantages. The fact that the case study narrative centers on notions of cultural awareness and sensitivity becomes, in the end, a kind of tautology, a way of re-producing the idea that there are fixed differences between Mexicans and Americans. This cultural difference in turn obfuscates the fact that, in the current global order, national borders do not neatly divide off the center from the periphery and that the movement of production facilities, whether across national boundaries or within them, invariably works to concentrate resources in the hands of a select few. Since Mexico already functions as a naturalized, self-evident periphery in the U.S. business imaginary here, Mexico's purported interest in importing U.S. agricultural products need never be subject to question. Neither does the case study indicate why or how it happens that the laws restricting foreign firms have been relaxed. This too falls outside the culture-driven "plot"—so to speak—of "Fish Farming." The practical, historical realities of globalization already foreground the story so completely that, *within* its diegesis as such, the "global" can become simply a question of *managing* cultural complexity and difference. The deeper, nontautological narrative function of culture here, however, is not to remind prospective managers of the need to learn about the life-ways of others but to naturalize and thereby to deflect any possible critique of the center/periphery relation itself. It confirms preexisting notions about Mexicans as cheap laborers, and Mexico itself as a dehistoricized cultural and natural resource. Like the warm weather that will make the catfish grow faster and the physical location of the land and water themselves, cheap labor is transformed into something inherent, culturally if not naturally, to Mexico. Culture is what has already drawn the national boundary between Mexico and (North) America such that capital lies to the north and labor to the south of it. The fact that Jackson is presented as a would-be "postmodern manager" who would be sensitive to the unfamiliar culture of his Mexican employees deflects from the fact that the cultural awareness, say, of the supposed fact that Mexicans sense time as slower than do Americans is an advantage if one's goal is the speeding up production.

Puerto Rico/United States: "Script for Juan Perillo and Jean Moore"

Written as a series of dialogues, "Script for Juan Perillo and Jean Moore" again asks students to consider their own "culturally determined values of time and space" in order to gain a better understanding of such values in the case of others. Jean Moore is the American manager who works at the Dayton, Ohio-based plant of the same firm that operates a subsidiary in Puerto Rico, the latter managed by Juan Perillo. The Puerto Rican plant is given the responsibility of manufacturing newly designed computers ordered by the U.S. Department of Defense. This fictionalized scenario takes Jean's point of view, assumed here to correspond to that of the students. On her visit to Puerto Rico, Juan greets her, and they exchange pleasantries. He tells her that his daughter has broken her arm while playing rough with other children. Juan further starts to say "just last week, my son . . ." (28), but before he can finish Jean says that she's sorry to hear about his daughter and immediately asks Juan if his plant can deliver the computers by June 1 (ibid.). He is hesitant, but Jean insists: "you have a lot of new employees and you have all of the new manufacturing and assembling equipment that we have in Dayton. So you're as ready to make the new product as we are" (ibid). Juan agrees and says he sees no reason why they shouldn't be able to fill the order on time. On May 1 they have a further interaction via the telephone in which Jean asks if the order is ready. Juan then tells her that he has had to take time off to see that his daughter gets medical treatment and that a few of the other Puerto Rico-based employees have had to work reduced hours as well. He is not sure if the order can be filled on time. The exchange between them ends here.

Perhaps inadvertently, this scenario illustrates the problems that can arise in the spatial rationalization of production. Moving production to sites with lower costs often entails other, unforeseen expenses that threaten to eliminate any savings, as exemplified here by potentially greater diffi-

culties in guaranteeing on time delivery of orders. The fact that the presumably lower-cost location here is Puerto Rico—formally a part of the
United States but at the same time culturally Latin, not North American
and hence "foreign"—draws our attention to the relative meaningless of
national borders in the movement of capital. But this fictionalized case
study narrates the problem strictly in terms of ethnic identity, making it
a point to draw a clear line of demarcation between Puerto Rico and the
U.S. And although race is not explicitly mentioned, the scenario is narrated in such a way as to imply that Puerto Ricans are racial others. (I
will analyze this ethnic/racial dimension below in relationship to a case
study on Native Americans.) Here, too, *fictional* devices such as point of
view and dramatization become key elements in conveying the central,
problematic importance of cultural misunderstanding. Jean Moore, for
example, is referred to as the "American Manager" while Juan, legally
just as American as Jean, is not. Although, to be sure, this accords with
the fact that most Puerto Ricans do not consider themselves "Americans," nevertheless this casual distinction is one of several ways that the
narrative posits the continental U.S. as the cultural norm against which
Puerto Rico is defined, and to which it must catch up and become tempo-
rally commensurate if it is do business with—or *as*—the U.S.

Consider again the manner in which Juan explains the possible delay
in meeting the production schedule. A few employees had to attend to
"serious illnesses in their families" and that his own daughter's medical
treatment for her broken arm took more time than expected (29). To this
Jean responds by asking what that has to do with the computers being
delivered on time (ibid.). The tension in this scenario is thus built around
potential misunderstandings having to do with different and potentially
conflicting ways of assigning value to time. The exercise prompts students to become aware of the need for cultural flexibility on the part of
the managers and gives them clues as to where they can look for Jean
Moore's cultural insensitivity. Juan says: "My daughter Marianna broke
her arm. She was out playing with some other children when it happened. They are rough and it's amazing they don't have more injuries.
Why just last week my son. . . ." The ellipses here represent Juan's unfinished sentence as Jean breaks in: "I'm very sorry to hear about Marianna and I'm sure everything will go well with the surgery. Now shall we
start work on the production schedule?" Jean's comment functions as an
alienating rupture in their conversation rather as a moment of connection
between them. The textbook editors explicitly instruct students to take
away from this case study an awareness that the U.S. works on "monochronic" time—in the office, work takes precedence over personal con-

cerns—while those outside the United States may often function within a "polychronic" time in which social concerns are part of the work culture itself. But at the same time that the students are asked to become aware of their own cultural norms regarding time, the fictional exercise tacitly assumes that these norms are "monochronic," thus forcibly and from the outset aligning their own implied viewpoint with Jean's. Successful management requires cultural intelligence, but making a profit requires strict adherence to the monochronic clock. Indeed, the case hints at the fact that better cultural understanding on Jean's part is, in the end, not going to solve the strictly profit-related problems resulting from different time cultures.

Indeed, the important unasked question here is: how *could* cultural flexibility on the part of American managers, touted as a virtue, work as a strategy of adaptation to space/time compression? The spatial rationalization of production requires changes in social structures that in turn require time and expense. So in some sense, the spatial fix of outsourcing production overseas does, in fact, become especially meaningful in the case of Puerto Rico—highlighting the reality that it may not matter much in the end whether companies relocate overseas or move across town: the effects of the corresponding consolidation and concentration of capital will be experienced everywhere, however unevenly, in terms of job loss, unmet production deadlines, and the need for employee retraining. In fact the ending of this particular narrative illustrates this well, as Juan says to Jean: "you have many of the same problems in the Dayton plant, don't you?" This is the last line in the scenario.

We don't get to hear Jean's answer, but, at one level, there is a clear acknowledgment here that certain cities, given the current form taken by the mobility of capital, are connected to each other directly within a spatiality that is not nationally divisible, even if, as the case study itself indicates in dramatic terms, such sites retain their differences. Dayton is generally known to be an economically depressed city, suffering from a steady drain of manufacturing jobs. The outsourcing of such manufacturing to places like Puerto Rico, of course, obeys the abstract capitalist dictate of rationalizing production and reducing costs. But such rationalization itself also connects one place to another here by helping to better police potentially restive workers in Dayton. At one point Jean mentions to Juan that if Puerto Rico can deliver the computers on time "then they will be doing as well as the Dayton plant" (28–29). Add to this the fact that outsourcing or relocating production can often end up costing more than it saves, and we get an especially keen, if unintended insight into the very real potential significance, for capital, of policing and speeding up workers via cultural management techniques. But fictionalization here again steps into this case study to coax students into assuming that the Dayton plant does *not* have these problems, redrawing the boundaries erased by capital. The cultural solution sought here then must take place within the framework of what is, for the students, the process of understanding a "foreign" culture. Here again, borrowing from management theory's version of postmodernism becomes a roundabout, but more adaptive way of reaffirming the fundamental supremacy of "monochronic" production time. Culture emerges as a significant category here precisely because the fictional narrative purposefully shapes it as such. By advising students to slow down and become more aware of diverse cultural values, a more egalitarian, process-oriented, and participatory management paradigm, inspired by postmodernism, is reinstrumentalized in the service of pushing Puerto Rican workers to adjust to the time standards of the U.S.—even though they, unlike the border-crossing Mexicans, are not moving anywhere themselves. They too must be molded into flexible workers and keep up with the one time that, finally, measures all the others.

Peripheries in the United States: "Southwest Manufacturing Company"

The convergence of race and problems relating to time and space emerge even more sharply in the fictional case study that follows, entitled "Southwestern Manufacturing Company" (51). The latter is narrated from the point of view Judith Vincent, the co-owner, along with her husband Ken, of the Southwestern Manufacturing Company in Lobos City, New Mexico. The company manufactures and sells Native American artifacts such as drums and lampshades. The story begins as Judith completes a drive from Lobos City to Dallas to attend a trade show. After checking into the hotel, she calls home and finds out that there has been a fire at the factory. She decides to drive back immediately. The rest of the narrative is made up of her internal monologue, as she thinks about the trials and tribulations she and her husband have suffered over the past three years in trying to build a business that was just beginning to be successful. The problems are mainly related to their workers. We learn that their "fifteen employees represent the three ethnic groups who make up the population of northern New Mexico: Pueblo Indians, Hispanics, and Anglos" (52). Judith wonders to herself whether in fact it would be worth rebuilding the business at all, given the way in which numerous and severe problems of cultural misunderstandings (primarily between the Native American and the other ethnic groups in the factory) have slowed the successful development of the business. The scenario ends as she arrives home, but without having reached a decision about whether to rebuild.

That decision is left to the student readers of the case study, who are asked to imagine themselves in the role of cultural advisors to the Vincents. "How," the textbook editors ask, framing the problem, as in the above examples, as a potential deficit of "cultural intelligence" on the part of management, "would you suggest [Judith and Ken] educate themselves regarding their employees?" (56). As an aid to the students, the textbook points them to supplementary sections containing digestible informational capsules about Native American cultural practices and stressing the importance of becoming familiar with Native American governance and business structures as well. Becoming better educated about such matters in "regions of relatively large proportions of American Indians," argue Catlin and White, can "help improve economic development activities" for Native Americans themselves and work as a "as a postcolonial bridge" between American Indians and other communities to create greater awareness (104). The textbook refers students to "recent work by postcolonial scholars that exposes biases and assumptions of Western scholarship" (Guerrero, Jaimes, Mohanty) and that can help management scholars to "question dominant culture assumptions of pedagogy and research in which historical legacies are omitted" thereby helping to undo the "white man's version of warfare and conquest and its racioethnic stereotypes" (104).[30] Positioning itself as a potential benefactor to Native American businesses, IDM explicitly sees itself as coming to the aid of poverty-stricken Native Americans. As a subset, in this context, of postmodern theory, postcolonial theory is directly invoked as a means of helping managers and owners strike a more benevolent and egalitarian pose—but betraying, at the same time, a definite set of rather less than egalitarian attitudes about race and ethnicity. Just as the latest cultural theories have come to the aid of development theory's task of exporting neoliberal policies abroad, here postcolonialism will, it is hoped, help to pry open native American governance and business structures. Advocating what is called "developmental economics" in relationship to Native Americans, Catlin and White here embark on what is in fact an explicit attempt at "narrating the nation" in terms of race.

The structuring of the fictional narrative itself, however—as in the case of "Script for Jean Moore and Juan Perillo"—implicitly foregrounds Judith's point of view, thus, in the end, aligning the students' "postcolonial" point of view with that of the white owner/manager. The difficulties in running the business that Judith recalls on her drive back to New Mexico are narrated in such a way as to single out the Native American employees and blame them for the tensions with the other, mainly Hispanic workers. We learn that the Pueblo men, Carlos and Juan, make the drums, while the Pueblo women, all relatives of Carlos and Juan, make lampshades, together with one Hispanic woman. Another woman, an Anglo, makes drums, but she works from home. The Anglo male employees work in a separate room doing shipping and billing. In fact, all the employees in the case study are consistently referred to in terms of their racial and ethnic identities, but the Pueblos are made out to be the most problematic group because, according to Judith, they do not seem to understand what makes a successful business. Judith runs down a kind of checklist of Pueblo maladjustment. For example, one day all of the Pueblo men fail to show up for work because instead they go out to "irrigate their fields" (54). By contrast, and in an ironic twist, they are irritated by the decision to close the factory for the long Thanksgiving weekend and have no inclination to take the day off for the Fourth of July—an attitude that does not prevent one of the Pueblo workers taking an entire month off for a series of important Native American ceremonies. Judith also recalls the tense work atmosphere that had resulted when minor squabbles erupted between the Pueblos and the Hispanic women. One of the latter, Rosa, for example, had complained that the Pueblos were saying "something bad about [her]" but didn't know exactly what because they were speaking Tewa (55). These recollections are framed by the question that concludes Judith's internal monologue, namely, whether to rebuild or not—a question that appears to hinge on whether it will be possible to resolve the problems caused by the Pueblo employees.

This narrative points to issues of time as well. In effect, Judith and Ken become frustrated with what they see as the Pueblo's disregard for the factory clock. But the temporal structure of the case study is itself a case in point here. The incidents at the factory have taken place at irregular intervals and over a long period of time. But Judith recalls and narrates all of the problematic incidents with the Pueblo workers sequentially, weighing each in connection with all the others on a scale of severity. Indeed, the story reads almost like a national allegory, restructured along an axis of "empty, homogeneous time," with the Vincents depicted as concerned owners and benefactors, frustrated with the apparent national disunity that threatens due to the discord arising between native populations and more recent immigrants.

Once again, as in the above case studies, problems relating to spatio-temporal compression and mobility of capital are articulated exclusively as cultural, even, here, as openly racial/ethnic in nature, and then refor-mulated as forms of knowledge useful in the management—that is, in effect, the policing—of ethnic and racial groups. The fracturing of ethnic groups in the workplace, in direct relation to the needs of valorizing cap-ital, while acknowledged by management theory as a problem that cannot be resolved by purely administrative, top-down measures, is so acknowl-edged only by being recast as a cultural problem. Pueblos, like Puerto Ricans, have evidently not learned the lessons of postmodernity that the Tijuana, border-crossing Mexicans of "Relearning to Tell Time" have. They have not learned to install or when to push the automatic button that would make them speed up at the factory. As the "postmodern" owners, Judith and Ken's attempts to bring people together, described as benevolent "team building," are foiled because of the ethnic/racial ten-sions among employees, and especially because of Pueblo intransigence. Ken's requests for universal participation from the employees so as to come up with ways of cooperating are, according to the case study, met with silence and resistance. So, disappointedly, Ken decides to "appoint a leader for each group, rather than allowing leaders to emerge as he had hoped would happen when the employees got together for their discus-sions" (55). Such details are obviously intended to represent the Vincents as enlightened managers, concerned for their employees, and to facilitate the identification with them on the part of the student readers of the case study, even as they comply with the exercise and propose strategies for improvement. But, if anything, "Southwest Manufacturing Company" sounds, at this point, like the story of a frustrated but benevolent colonial administrator, unable to quell intertribal warfare among his local wards. Enter, then, postcolonial theory, which, like postmodern theory generally for management discourse, will, it is hoped, help suture the organization like it would the nation.

But, with the latter already assumed to belong to its white owners/benefactors, what this "postcolonial" narrative in fact signifies is that a nationalized global capital must be ready to pry open the seemingly irrational enclosures and special protections inscribed in earlier policies regarding Native Americans. Thus, for example, in the supplementary material included along with the case study narrative, Catlin and White advance the view that paying greater attention to Native American busi-ness structures and culture, along with admitting more Native Americans into university business programs, would help them adjust and become more productive. This is conveyed in the story through Judith's frustra-tion at the fact the Pueblo workers have refused their bosses' offers to help them make more money for themselves by making rattles (after regular work hours) on a piecework basis, an offer which they refuse. This behavior is contrasted with that of the only Anglo woman drum-maker, who, according to the case study, earns more than the other employees by working at home, exclusively on a piecework basis. Her productivity levels are reported to be higher than those of the men who work during regular hours inside the factory. The fire, raising the question of whether it is worthwhile to reopen the factory at all, well illustrates the fact that by choosing stability over the "flexibility" of piecework and perhaps higher earnings, the work and time culture of the Pueblos translates into greater *instability* for the owners. In fact, Judith and Ken now see themselves forced to pay their Pueblo and Hispanic employees for making the drums that burned in the factory fire, and even perhaps forced to compensate their workers for the time the factory is out of production. Finally, it is related in Judith's narrative that the Pueblo workers had, in fact, refused to accompany her to the trade show, evidently not swayed by the "excitement of crowds" and the "intensity of the big city" (56). They have refused, in essence, not only to internalize the factory clock but to enter into the life world of business culture itself. The postmodern advice the students are expected to devise for Judith and Ken—for example, seeking a better understanding of the cultural and family practices of tribalism and communalism—must not only help rationalize the work practices of Native Americans but help the owners to incorporate the latter into the time of capitalist modernity itself.

Carefully read and analyzed, such case studies, emblematic microcosms of management theory's dislocalized deployment of culture, literature, fiction, and postmodern cultural theory, can be made to disclose the ideological workings of the field itself. Analysis of the *functional* quality of concepts, categories, and theories originating from within the humanities for the purposes of the seemingly antithetical and hostile discipline of management shows what is in fact their dual and seemingly contradictory nature. This functional quality is both an answer to a perceived need on the part of management—to reinvigorate and adapt itself as proof against the implicit threat of obsolescence represented by globalization—and yet at the same time a strategy for nonadaptation, for keeping the boundaries of the field itself fixed within their familiar coordinates. But alongside such a critique of the field of management, I have also attempted to reveal, however indirectly up to now, some of the blind spots in cultural theory itself—blind spots in its own assumptions and perceptions of business and its affiliated academic disciplines. Oppositional practices and currents within cultural studies cannot, in my view, successfully form and advance without understanding the ways in which business theory understands itself, and how, in accordance with this self-understanding, it neither ignores nor dismisses but in fact seeks to appropriate cultural theory. Although definite radical developments in cultural studies have been able to formulate a genuinely critical approach to the corporate world and to management theory, it seems safe to say that a good deal of what passes for radical critique in the humanities and the cultural disciplines, transfixed by the discursive idols of globalization, still imagines the proverbial businessman's gun held to its head and thus fails to grasp how, for example, theories of postmodernism lend themselves with relative ease to the theoretical needs of corporate capital. But this then, obviously, raises the question of dislocalist practices in the humanities itself. As such, this is a subject far too extensive to fit within the pages of this book, but I want to begin to explore it in what follows through the critical analysis of dislocalism at select set of sites within humanistic and cultural theory and practice. One of these is the field of immigrant literary studies, and it is to this topic that I turn in the next chapter.

CHAPTER 2

(Im)migration and the
New Nationalist Literatures

I. NATIONALIST PARADIGMS

Dislocalism in literary studies is a strategy that critics employ to produce a larger transnational context for various categories such as American literature or British literature—categories whose partial displacement is advocated only so as to solidify the nationalist category per se. In this chapter I will analyze dislocalism in American immigrant/ethnic literary studies. I have chosen to focus on this field because each of its defining terms has come under pressure and serves to emphasize the difficulty of engaging with theories of globalization from within the field itself. The term American presents particular problems partly because globalization can often be perceived to be synonymous with Americanization—a problem of which the post-9/11 wars in Afghanistan and Iraq have provided a vivid manifestation. In such a context it has become more urgent than ever for American literature and American studies to disassociate itself from nationalist paradigms of critique. The term immigration too has come under pressure because the mobility of people through and to the U.S. is too varied and occurs in too great a variety of directions to be contained any longer by the idea of a definitive passage from one nation into another. A result of this has also been to bring into question U.S.-localized ethnic identity categories such as Latino/a, Asian-American, African-American, and the like. This more complex form of mobility also affects the notion of a multicultural politics based on categories of race, ethnicity, and gender, disrupting American nationalist narratives in a domestic context. And the term literature itself can present problems insofar as it is equated with fictional and imaginative genres of writing whose ability to convey the urgency of global realities is often placed in doubt.

My goal here is to analyze how the field of immigrant literary studies, under institutional as well as internal pressure, attempts to displace all of the above concepts, whether of Americanness, immigration, ethnic identity, or the literary-as-fiction, but only so as, in the end, to reconsolidate them and keep the field as a whole from suffering a total displacement. So, for instance, while the figure of the immigrant has long helped the U.S. to produce a national imaginary, that figure must now be dislocalized in order to serve the same purpose in globalization's new era. To demonstrate this I concentrate in what follows on scholarship generated on two specific works of fiction that are frequently categorized as immigrant/ethnic texts: Julia Alvarez's *How the García Girls Lost Their Accents* and Diana Abu-Jaber's *Crescent*. The former work has now become canonical within American ethnic literary studies, and the latter is steadily acquiring a similar status, especially as the field looks to expand into the area of Arab-American writing.

I will focus in what follows on how dislocalist practices in immigrant/ethnic literary studies show the contradiction of the contemporary moment, a moment in which globalizing the field becomes imperative but in which it must be saved from the complete displacement threatened by globalization by consolidating its concepts of analysis. I argue that the curricular locus of texts such as Alvarez's *The García Girls* and Abu-Jaber's *Crescent* as immigrant/ethnic fiction helps critics to reproduce a dislocalized nationalist imaginary within domestic paradigms of race and gender. I have chosen to focus on the scholarship centering on these women writers for several reasons. It is representative of the ways in which the field has produced a canon of immigrant/ethnic literatures with a heavy concentration of women writers—partially because women writers and their female protagonists allow for conversations about issues relating to construction of race and feminism to occur simultaneously. It is also common to see the appropriation of these aspects of the texts in readings that work, consciously or not, to consolidate American paradigms of immigrant/ethnic literature. And yet at the same time the novels themselves function as portraits of certain aspects of the contemporary conditions of (im)migration, for example, by following the transnational trajectories of low-waged and temporary labor or the flight into exile due in no small part to conditions created by the U.S. itself. That is, the texts allow us to see how they are themselves in conversation with the recent history of globalization and serve to complicate issues of localized American immigrant identities. But let me begin with the question of "America" in American literature.

American Literature

How should critics respond to the imperative to globalize the field of American literature? Wai Chee Dimock and Lawrence Buell's edited volume *Shades of the Planet: American Literature as World Literature* is one example of how this is being attempted. It begins by taking up a by now familiar question: what is American literature in a global context? The editors suggest delinking the word American from its denotation of national and geographical boundaries. Such delinking has become particularly urgent in a context of increasing U.S. military and economic aggression. As Shelley Fisher Fishkin states in her 2004 American Studies Presidential address: "The goal of American studies scholarship is not exporting and championing an arrogant, pro-American nationalism but understanding the multiple meanings of America and American culture in all their complexity" (20). This understanding, she says, "requires looking beyond the nation's borders, and understanding how the nation is seen from vantage points beyond its borders" (20). But this is a difficult task indeed for a field with the name American in it.[1] A number of Americanist projects have attempted to displace and de-center the field in specific and highly conscious ways, and in the process they helped to reinvigorate it.[2] However, such a body of work also shows the particular difficulties in de-centering the field. *Shades of the Planet* points to such issues. In their introduction, Dimock and Buell suggest treating American literature as a subset of, and a "taxonomically useful entity" within, the field of global literature (4). This invocation of the planetary allows them to "modularize the world into smaller entities able to stand provisionally and do analytical work, but not self-contained, not sovereign" (4). That is, the entity of American literature is not displaced entirely but is repositioned within the space of the "planet"—although Dimock and Buell are careful to argue that this "should not lure us into thinking that this entity is natural" (4).

Each of the essays contained in the volume proposes its own particular way of de-centering American Literature, ranging from the inclusion of literatures written in languages other than English to reimagining the spatial coordinates of America as existing beyond national boundaries. But I want to take a brief look at Jonathan Arac's essay "Global and Babel:

Language and Planet," since it serves as an especially good example of the difficulties encountered by scholars of American literature as they attempt to deal with issues of globalization.[3] The essay proposes a dyad: the "global," defined as "a movement of expansion that one imagines may homogenize the world," and "Babel," defined as a "movement of influx that diversifies our land, as in multiculturalism" (24). A major part of the essay deals with the reading of literary texts in a manner that delinks them from nationalist paradigms. Some of the authors whose work exemplifies the "global Babel" here are Emerson, Thoreau, Whitman, Henry Roth, and Ralph Ellison. Consider Arac's reading of Thoreau's *Walden,* from which he quotes as follows: "observe the forms which thawing sand and clay assume in flowing down the sides of a steep cut on the railroad" (25–26). Here Thoreau, says Arac, "feels as if he is in the 'laboratory of the Artist who made the world,' and is 'nearer to the vitals of the global,'" the global as that which "'continually transcends and translates itself and becomes winged in its orbit'" (Arac's citations from *Walden,* 26). Arac interprets this for us, stating that "Thoreau's globalism at home provides the most morally reassuring babble" (26), and finds in Thoreau a guide for American literary critics to think globally. But here the focus is largely on the language and terminology of globalization and not on the socio-historical conditions that might help us better understand the global context of Thoreau's work. Arac reads Ellison's *Invisible Man* in a similar way, citing the famous passage in which the narrator, looking at yams for sale on the streets of Harlem, proclaims: "I Yam what I am." Arac's essay presents this as an example of heteroglossia—that is, of "Babel"—as it "sets against each other radically different social registers of language," observing further that the "root and its name aren't simply southern [that, is, American,] but also African" (27). Such connections can indeed lead to a broader interpretation of the text. And Arac is careful to note what he calls the imperialist *thinking* of the authors in question. For example, while invoking the global dimension of Whitman, he also draws upon Edward Said, whose work, he says, "enables us to think openly, rather than defensively, about the imperialism that inescapably grids the planetary reach of Whitman's democratic idealism" (27). Arac cites Whitman's poem *A Broadway Pageant* as an example of this: "'Comrade Americanos!, to us then at last the Orient comes . . . Lithe and Silent the Hindoo appears, the Asiatic continent itself appears the past, the dead'" (27). The problematic aspect of this language, from the standpoint of "Global and Babel" is the imperialism of Whitman's vision. However, globalization here remains primarily an issue of language, a linguistic globalism, as practiced by authors who already have a secure place in the American literary canon. In arguing for this kind of globalism, Arac thus allows the history of the U.S. imperialist economic and military policies to slide out of consideration

No doubt the works of Thoreau, Melville, Emerson, and Whitman remain essential ones for students of globalization today. But it is notable here that despite the inclusion of Ralph Ellison, whose notion of America is often positioned against that of Thoreau or Whitman, the centrality of a traditional canon is left intact. In the very attempt to de-center American literature—here via interpretations that discover a *language* of the global within the national—there is a simultaneous move to shore up the canon to which such de-centered works belong. In this respect "Global and Babel" has much in common with other moves in literary and cultural studies to globalize the field while leaving the older curricular paradigms to continue essentially unaffected and unthreatened.[4] I argue that this is a *rhetorical strategy* that critics employ to produce a larger transnational context for categories such as American literature–categories whose partial displacement is advocated only so as to resolidify the *nationalist* basis of the category per se. I would also insist on distinguishing between this rhetorical strategy and the historical processes of globalization themselves, processes that cannot be reduced to the former.

In Arac's case this rhetorical strategy is to de-center nationalist paradigms and American literature itself by linking the established writer's work on the level of language and style directly to the "global," doing so in ways that leave the centrality of the already established writers in the canon (Thoreau, Melville, etc.) intact. Other critics—notably but not exclusively those working in the field of immigrant/ethnic literary studies—have attempted, in what may appear to be a diametrically opposed move here, to de-center American literature by *displacing canonical works themselves,* thereby making room for other, less sanctioned writers within American literature. But how different, in the end, are these two approaches to globalizing the field? I will examine how, in fact, the concepts of immigration and immigrant literatures—in ways subtly *analogous* to the rhetorical strategy described above—also assist American literary studies in reconstructing a nationalist paradigm even while attempting to globalize or update disciplinary practices.

But in order to do so it becomes important to look first at the concepts of immigration and ethnic identity themselves in relationship to globalization. These concepts have played a central role in the de-centering of American literature, not only through furnishing a standpoint from which to produce destabilizing readings of canonical literature (as in the above case of Arac's essay), but also by grounding the field of American immigrant/ethnic studies per se. Yet the very field that has helped to raise the questions of race/ethnic/gender identity as multiple sites of oppositionality and that has become a vehicle of interrogation indispensable to the broader discipline is now itself in need of displacement if it is to avoid becoming obsolete in a global context.

II. IMMIGRATION AS A DISLOCALIZING CONCEPT

The rhetoric of America as open to immigration and subsequent happy settlement has long inhabited the American imagination and has come to take on the status of a cliché. William H. A. Williams suggests in "Immigration as a Pattern in American Culture" that immigration has become such an integral part of the definition of the U.S. that it comes to define America in ways that affects nonimmigrants as well. As he says, the "impact of immigration is the quintessential American experience, establishing a pattern that is replicated in almost every aspect of American life" (19). "Whatever it is that sets us moving," he continues, "many of us, like immigrants, experience at some level the sense of loss of the old and the familiar, and varying kinds of "culture shock" still await even those of us who have been born here, as we move from one part of America to another" (22). Williams elasticizes the concept of immigration to describe the everyday experiences of people within the U.S. But despite Williams's claims that most Americans experience dislocations similar to those experienced by immigrants, and that immigration is a central aspect of being an American, the term immigrant and the condition of immigration are also exclusive to those on the outside or on the fringes of what can be called the dominant American experience. This notion of immigration as essential to American identity is inseparable from the idea that the immigrant is always an outsider, and is implicit in the very production of the U.S. as both a local and a global place.

That is, along with its centrality, there has been and remains something fundamentally marginal about the figure of the immigrant.[5] It becomes evident that in discussions on various issues regarding immigration—questions of economic benefit, for instance, or of the nature of assimilation—attempts are being made, via this figure of marginality, to delineate American identity itself. This delineation has been especially crucial since the rhetoric associated with questions of American identity has been preoccupied with preservation of "old" ways that seem threatened with each major wave of immigration. The worry over American identity is reflected in concerns about whether various groups will be able to shed their "old world" identities and assimilate into existing structures within the United States. Thus, for example, writers in the eighteenth and nineteenth centuries, including Benjamin Franklin and Ralph Waldo Emerson, consciously took on the task of defining the American as the self-reliant and self-sufficient. But these writings simultaneously drew upon the notion of the "foreign" to define Americanness and thus positioned the United States as a unique nation—an idea employed even today in chronicling the accomplishments of immigrants. Ronald Takaki has shown that the policy of bringing immigrants to the U.S. to produce a glut of labor and thus keep wages low has from the first been an indispensable part of nation building. More importantly, the image of immigrants coming to the U.S. with nothing and working from the ground up in order to make a living has remained a powerful one for the way that it suggests the rebirth of the immigrant upon reaching the U.S. and the repositioning of the "foreignness" of the immigrants within the domestic borders. This repositioning then provides the immigrants with their particular identities in relationship to the United States. In turn, each major wave of immigration has renewed conversations about the nature of American society and about who counts as an American and in what capacity. The 1968 immigration act served as one such an occasion by legally prohibiting discrimination based on race, gender, or place of birth and rescinding the remaining bans on immigration from parts of Asia. As Michael Lind has pointed out in *The Next American Nation,* "Mexicans and Cubans join Hispanic America; Chinese, Indians, and Filipinos join Asian and Pacific Islander America, and so on" (98). Moreover, each race, in addition to preserving its cultural unity and distinctness, is expected to "act as a monolithic political bloc" (ibid). In effect, immigrants become localized ethnics in the United States.

Theories of globalization, meanwhile, have responded to such stable and localized ethnic identities, positioned as either insider or outsider, by calling this move itself into question. In fact the very idea of immigration as movement from one nation and "into" another has itself come under critical scrutiny. For example, in "Change and Convergence?" Thomas Heller considers whether immigration can still serve as a defining idea for the United States, given that immigration has now become an integral part of the definition of the European Union as well. This is only one example of the many ways in which new forms of (im)mobility across the globe exert pressure on the United States to reassess its foundational concept(s) of immigration. Furthermore, in "Patriotism and its Futures," Arjun Appadurai suggests that the U.S. is not so much a nation of nations or of immigrants but "one node in a postnational network of diasporas"

(423). The United States, writes Appadurai, is "no longer a closed space for the melting pot to work its magic, but yet another diasporic switching point, to which people come to seek their fortunes but are no longer content to leave their homelands behind" (424). He goes on to say that "no existing concept of American-ness can contain this large variety of transnations" (ibid). In this context the "hyphenated American might have to be twice hyphenated" such as "Asian-American-Japanese, or Native-American-Seneca" as "diasporic identities retain their mobility and grow more protean. Or perhaps the sides of the hyphen will have to be reversed, and we can become a "federation of diasporas" (ibid).

These sorts of observations speak to the real complexity of the movement of peoples across the globe. Yet while the adequacy of immigration itself as a term for describing this movement comes increasingly under question, the rhetoric of immigration is clearly alive and well and has become much more inflammatory, especially, since 9/11, as not only the U.S. but other nations have rushed to militarize their borders as part of the strategy of the "war on terror." While people move across the world in unprecedented numbers, this movement itself reflects growing social inequality. For the global upper class mobility means holiday or business travel without the need to change national affiliation. (This phenomenon will be addressed in detail in the following two chapters.) Meanwhile for the vast majority of mobilized humanity for whom mobility is, in effect, forced and the means to a necessary end, immigration papers come to signify a means of obtaining a much-needed stability even if that stability itself becomes more illusory than ever. At the turn of the twenty-first century, the immigration debate has raged, instigated by controversies surrounding the construction of the U.S.-Mexico border wall, rallies against tougher immigration bills, and by a general atmosphere of heightened suspicion of the foreign other. For example, recent conversations about immigrations often conjure up images of people arriving to the U.S. without documentation. The term "illegality" becomes the central focus in these arguments.[6]

No doubt the ratcheting up of the political rhetoric is itself another symptom of a complexity that makes it increasingly hard to define the concept of immigrant in a globalized reality. This same complexity can be read in the proliferation of alternative terminologies: see here, *inter alia*, James Clifford's conscious introduction of terms such as "pilgrimage" and "tourism" to make distinctions that "immigration" alone cannot make. While Appadurai may have been a bit too quick in claiming that "immigration" has been supplanted by "migration," his terminological innovations suggest just how complex the positioning of (im)migrants as outside of the American dominant experience has become. Appadurai's "federation of diasporas," implicitly skeptical of the idea of a définitive passage to the U.S., speaks, rather, to Saskia Sassen's contention that the forces of globalization do not produce movement toward other nations so much as toward cities. In *The Mobility of Labor and Capital,* for example, Sassen theorizes that people moving both from within various parts of the U.S. as well as from other nations to, say, New York are part of the same complex global system that produces migration toward cities, regardless, to a certain degree, of their national location. The forced movement of people from countryside to urban areas and the production of mega-slums across the world are well documented in Mike Davis's *Planet of Slums.* The very distinction between inter- and intranational forms of movement becomes less clear.

Whether "immigration" retains anything of its former, "simpler" meaning, what is certain is that this underlying complexity has significant implications for immigrant/ethnic literatures as objects of scholarship. Thus, for example, while a significant number of earlier narratives portrayed immigrants as negotiating their ethnicity and their status within the bounded space of the U.S., more contemporary narratives represent immigrants to the U.S. as conducting the same negotiation in a world much more interconnected.[7] There can, in any case, be little doubt of the decisive importance to the field of the literature of (im)migration of the contemporary conditions in which people move across the globe: 1) that immigrants themselves live a life that is often divided between their homelands and the U.S; 2) that in some sense people need not *physically* immigrate in order to experience the conditions of immigration, because they are in contact with those who have immigrated and are living in a world where movement has become so much a part of normal life that those unable to move are nevertheless formed by this experience; and 3) that the nations sending the largest numbers of immigrants into the U.S. are themselves, as nations, conditioned by, if not the products of, the history of American influence on and intervention in these locales. If nothing else, these realities bring to light the problem with conceptualizing immigration as a neat movement from another nation into the U.S. and in turn, the assimilation of immigrants into localized ethnic identity groups.

III. THE QUESTION OF IDENTITY

As part of the wider culture wars for canon expansion that ensued in the wake of the Civil Rights era, ethnic studies programs made their case for inclusion of texts and authors based on previous exclusion and marginalization. But in taking up the figure of the excluded, literary studies not only seek to criticize the marginalizing of certain groups of people, but also appropriate that very same figure and transform it into something positive, something manifesting a desire to *remain* outside the dominant. This particular critical move has also come to be associated with approaches to contemporary American ethnic and immigrant literatures and has provided a way to critique dominant cultural practices as well as to challenge more traditional, parochial approaches. Such arguments and approaches clearly drew upon the rhetoric not only of the U.S. Civil Rights movement but also of national and social liberation movements around the world. While many including Michael Denning have been, no doubt, right to point out the fallacy of characterizing the liberation movements of the 1960s as restricted to identity politics, identity as such comes to be a crucial term in what was to count as politics within both the broader public sphere as well as the university and the field of literary/cultural studies. The topics and arguments loosely organized under the category of identity politics have, to be sure, resulted in a significant body of scholarship and criticism that has both examined discrimination based on identity categories and done much to challenge such discrimination. However, identity politics has for some time now become the subject of considerable critique. In "The Politics of Recognition," for example, Sonia Kruks proposes the gist of identity politics to be: "what is demanded is respect for oneself as fundamentally different" (123). "Questions about 'What is to be done,'" she continues, "are frequently displaced on the Left today by questions about who 'we' are" (122). Kruks goes on to suggest that "what makes identity politics a significant departure from earlier forms of the politics of recognition is its demand for recognition on the basis of the very grounds on which it has previously been denied: it is qua woman, qua black, qua lesbian or gay—and not qua incarnation of universal human qualities—that recognition is demanded and moral superiority sometimes asserted" (123). In this way, what was previously the basis for marginalization becomes the source of self-identification.

But if, when working with ethnic identity categories, identity politics typically positions the latter as necessarily outside of and in critical opposition to dominant cultural groups, analysis of identity need not remain within this framework. A wide range of scholars, among them Anthony Appiah, Linda Alcoff, and E. San Juan, Jr., have weighed in on the essentializing and liberal tendencies of identity politics and multiculturalism. Still others have noted a significant shift in what counts as politics both in and out of the university. As Michael Denning explains in *Culture in the Age of Three Worlds,* the movements of the 1960s targeted the "welfare, warfare and interventionist state demanding the right of women to divorce, sexual freedom, the civil rights of racial minorities" (43). However, a new era of politics since the 1990s targeting IMF, World Bank, and WTO represents a shift away from the nationalist liberation movements (35).[8] Multiculturalism presupposes a politics of representation and recognition *within a national frame*—a politics that overlooks and even obscures the supranational power relations represented by international organizations such as the World Bank and the WTO. Furthermore, as analytical frameworks that consider identity in its socio-historical context are able to show, race, ethnicity, and gender identity paradigms are themselves part of the structural makeup of a historically specific form of society.[9] Critics such as Jon Cruz, Paul Smith, Avery Gordon, Wahneema Lubiano, and Lisa Lowe have provided models for a scholarship that analyzes the production and appropriation of identity categories by and within relations of capital. Lowe's argument in *Immigrant Acts* is that the production of multiculturalism with a fetishized focus on identity as a positive force "'forgets' history, and in this forgetting, exacerbates a contradiction between the concentration of capital within a dominant class group, and the unattended conditions of a working class increasingly made up of heterogeneous immigrant, racial and ethnic groups."[10] In addition, as Jodi Melamed has written: "Race continues to permeate capitalism's economic and social processes, organizing the hyper-extraction of surplus value from racialized bodies and naturalizing a system of capital accumulation that grossly favors the global North over the global South. Yet multiculturalism portrays neoliberal policy as the key to a postracist world of freedom and opportunity" (1). In support of the latter claim, Melamed refers to the fact that, since the 1990s, "multiculturalism has become a policy rubric for business, government and education." For instance, reading the 2002 Bush administration *National Security Strategy,* she notes its reference to the "opening" of "world markets" as a "multicultural imperative . . . opening societies to the diversity of the world" (16). In another example, Melamed reminds us that Bush has consistently used the language of multiculturalism to justify the indefinite incarceration of Arab and Muslim prisoners at Guantanamo. His much-publicized policy of supplying prisoners with Korans and time to pray is supposed to work as a marker of racial sensitivity. This new racism uses the language of multiculturalism so as to give the appearance of having overthrown older racial binaries such as Arab vs. white/American/European and thus works to obscure the fact of their continuation (16). That is, questions of racial identity become, if anything, even *more* salient in the global context as outlined by Melamed. Clearly, an analysis of identity that examines the uneven cooptation of groups of people in a globally structured economy must be distinguished from identity as a politics of recognition and representation.

The questioning of U.S. multicultural identity as a critical and oppositional term then simultaneously tends to shift the target of critique from the nation-state to the international agencies of capitalist globalization—however closely aligned these are with the United States. And even though there is disagreement in critical circles about whether the nation-state is meeting its demise,[11] there is a pervasive sense that politics and scholarship based on what are by some accounts the parochial domestic paradigms of multiculturalism and identity as a politics of recognition are inadequate or even out of date. A new theoretical emphasis on the critique of political economy—especially concerns regarding labor and commodification—seems in some estimations to threaten the very paradigms of ethnic/immigrant studies, not to mention the field of literary studies, as so aptly invoked in Bruce Robbins's anecdote of the businessman with the gun. How, then, in the face of this historical and theoretical change, is a field such as immigrant/ethnic literature, given its reliance on paradigms of ethnic identity and marginality, able to reproduce its own identity *qua* field when the very categories on which it is founded are, apparently, rapidly shifting?

In keeping with the general trend toward dislocalism, the answer here, I will argue, is that the very pressure to move beyond previously accepted paradigms within immigrant/ethnic literary studies, results in a countervailing pressure within the field to find *new* ways to consolidate the older paradigms. And since immigration signifies moving from one nation into another—meaning that, these paradigms are themselves predicated on the nation—we encounter in this process a *new* way of consolidating the nation and nationalist paradigms as well. Again, I want to emphasize that not all attempts to rearticulate the relevance of literary studies in a global context can be reduced to dislocalism. In the contemporary, globalized context, critics turn to immigrant/ethnic literatures as cultural texts able to mediate current discussions on globalization because such literature has historically produced an imaginary of dislocation and allowed a connection between the U.S. and the rest of the world. Yet to a large extent this broadening of literary scholarship continues, under new conditions, the work that has always defined the field of what has been considered American marginal literatures. The figure of the marginal—here in the guise of the immigrant—is itself dislocalized. For the latter figure is taken up in literary studies not simply out of an ethical opposition to the marginalizing of certain groups of people, but also so as to valorize this figure itself—to valorize it not only for being outside the dominant but also for the less obvious way in which it leaves what is *inside* the dominant intact. The figure of the immigrant comes to occupy the position of an "outsider" that helps make the "inside" seem more secure. Critics find ways to reposition the figure of the immigrant within their own project of universality, in such a way that this project remains, fundamentally, a nationalist one.

But before I proceed to analyze this instance of dislocalism in detail, there is still at least one other formal, categorical factor to be considered here. For the project of rescuing nationalist paradigms in literary studies of whatever sort cannot be adequately grasped without a consideration of questions relating to form and genre, specifically of how literary forms conventionally thought of as fictional or imaginary position themselves critically in a global context. At one level, it is important to consider the question of fiction if for no other reason because fictional works tend to be generally labeled as such in relation to their national points of origin, hence to nationalist paradigms. Immigrant literary *fiction*, then, will afford us an especially apt point of view from which to consider the global politics of national borders.

IV. THE LITERARY, THE FICTIONAL, AND THE REAL

As Bruce Robbins's anecdote about the businessman and the gun to the head (see chapter 1) reminds us, narratives of the impending obsolescence of literature and of literary studies have been circulating within the humanities for at least a generation now. One could argue that such narratives were effectively institutionalized when the field began the process of "culturalizing" itself in response to the advent of cultural studies. And, despite the fact that it has now become difficult if not impossible to separate the cultural from the literary, these same narratives of obsolescence now reappear, albeit for different reasons, as the field attempts to negotiate the implicit demand that it globalize.

The resulting dislocalism takes various forms. One of the more parochial is the search for ways to redescribe literature and the literary-critical *status quo ante* as global while leaving everything else more or less intact. Such parochial dislocalism has a particularly good representative in the literary scholar Marjorie Perloff, who has made a case for a return to aesthetics, single-author studies, and the "merely literary." In her 2006 MLA Presidential Address, for example, she brushes off the call to globalize but also attributes to certain prominent literary figures the condition, as one might put it, of being "always already" global. She cites the work of Samuel Beckett and the fact that it is read and celebrated the world over as proof, if one were needed, that Beckett is "global." [12]

But the same perceived opposition between the literary and the global that elicits a parochial reaction from Perloff is evoked in a variety of different, less defensive registers as well. For example, Masao Miyoshi in his essay "Turn to the Planet" notes how, along with changes in the notion of the literary itself, the interest and investment of the literary-critical discipline in literature has fundamentally altered. "Gone" he says, "is the argument concerning the relationships among nation-states and national literatures"—noting the decline of the idea of nation-state in intellectual discourse as a whole (287). Moreover, he argues, along with the declining importance accorded to the idea of national literatures, the "grammatical/formal analysis of literary products seems to interest very few scholars . . ." (ibid.). However, the connection that Miyoshi traces between the decline of the "literariness" of literary studies and the latter's growing interest in questions of the global does not prompt any effort to rescue the former by resemanticizing the latter, as it does in the case of Perloff. Instead he quite aptly argues for a renewed inquiry, under the sign of the "planet" rather than the nation-state, into the connection of literary objects to their social, cultural, and economic conditions. Other scholars in literary studies—Frederic Jameson, Pascale Casanova, Franco Moretti, Lisa Lowe, and Frederick Buell, to mention only a few—have also taken the rise of the global as an invitation to rethink the limits and the dimensions of the literary.

But note here as well how, in almost all current metanarratives of the erosion of literary studies, whether of parochial or nonparochial bent, the rise of globalization is posited as occurring in *inverse* relation to the viability of the literariness in literary studies. The global and the literary appear to compete as claimants to intellectual and scholarly attention, nearly always to the advantage of the former as seemingly more attuned to contemporary secular realities. The globalizing of literary studies has in fact, emphasized a form of interdisciplinarity in which the most imme-diate and urgent questions of global existence—political oppression, declining living conditions, and the proliferation of new regimes of vio-lence—impinge directly on the study of the literary or cultural object. Even in cultural studies this can be confirmed in a tendency to cede what had been the privileged position accorded to anthropological theories of culture in preference for theories and theorists directly concerned with questions of political economy, labor, urbanization, and finance. As the discipline has sought to address more global issues, the theories of critics such as Clifford Geertz, James Clifford, and Renato Rosaldo seem, in relative terms at least, to be of less concern than do those of, say, Harvey, Arrighi, Sassen, and Robert Brenner.[13]

My interest here, however, is less the question of the literary *per se* than it is the way in which the opposition between the global and the literary also tacitly takes the form of an opposition between the fictional or the imaginative, seen as falling within the purview of the literary studies, and the *real*, perceived as the spontaneous correlate of the global. Within the terms of this binary, the literary is threatened with obsolescence in the face of globalization not only because of its genealogical tie to the nation but because the global has somehow become synonymous with a form of reality so urgent and exigent that even the fictive and the imaginary suddenly appear to have become luxuries, of concern only to the intellectually effete.[14]

This specific form of binary opposition between the global, read as reality, and the literary, read as the fictional, has the potential of generating a no less specific form of dislocalism—and it is the latter that I will attempt to map and critique in what follows. I stress here that I am not the least bit interested in rescuing the literary by proving its continued viability in a global context, as Perloff attempts to do. Nor do I want to join Miyoshi and others in the project of reconnecting the literary or the fictional to the newly globalized questions of the social, the historical, and the cultural, although I readily align myself with such a project. Rather, in what follows, I want to show how transposing the fictional vs. the real onto the literary vs. the global opposition can all too readily become another (dislocalizing) way of *evading* the real, objective, historical processes of globalization.

I will analyze this latent tendency within literary studies by focusing on scholarship in the area of immigrant literature. But before turning to that, I want first to consider further what this specific form of dislocalism entails as a broader phenomenon. More specifically, I want to argue that the fictional vs. real binary opposition works dislocally so as to extricate itself from a full engagement with global, historical reality by putting a simulacrum in place of the latter—a simulacrum that comes to function as what, in Lacanian psychoanalytical theory, is designated as the "real." This latter notion has of course been the subject of an enormous amount of analysis and dispute on the part of Lacanian theorists, but I want in what follows to develop my analysis of the question of the real in immigrant/ethnic literary studies through an extrapolation from Slavoj Žižek's widely read *Welcome to the Desert of the Real*, written initially as a theoretical reflection on the social and psychic landscape that emerged in the wake of the 9/11 attacks.

Žižek begins this work by observing that those who live in the global North/West typically find themselves in the grip of the paranoid fantasy that they inhabit a fake world. The role of the media is crucial to the perpetuation of this fantasy. Žižek illustrates this at one point by reference to the popular 1998 film *The Truman Show,* in which the main character discovers that he has unwittingly been living his entire life as the hero of a long-running reality TV show. According to Žižek, the deeper point of the film is that life in the postmodern metropolis, in its very "hyperreality," is in its way simultaneously *"unreal,* substanceless, deprived of material inertia" (13). The real, he notes, even becomes the "ultimate 'effect' sought after from digitalized special effects" themselves (12). But, he argues, it is not only Hollywood that produces the semblance of such a "weightless" real life. In "late capitalist consumerist society 'real social life' itself somehow acquires the features of a staged fake, with our neighbors behaving in 'real' life as stage actors and extras" (12–13). Žižek further speculates that the feeling of living in a more and more artificially constructed universe gives rise to "an irresistible urge to 'return to the Real,' to regain firm ground in some 'real reality'" (19). Thus "the real which returns," he argues, "has the status of an(other) semblance: precisely because it is real it has a traumatic character and we are unable to integrate it into our everyday lives and [thus] experience it as a nightmare" (ibid). "What do well-to-do Americans immobilized in their well-being dream about?" he asks, rhetorically. The answer follows: "About a global catastrophe that would shatter their lives" (17). Žižek grounds his explanation of how such a nightmare could become part of the American psyche in a fairly strict version of Lacanian psychoanalytic theory, but I am much more interested here in how, according to *Welcome to the Desert of the Real,* the desire/passion for the real "culminates in its apparent opposite, in a theatrical spectacle" and more significantly in how this spectacle works to uphold middle- and upper-class American ideological presuppositions (9), that is, in how the fiction vs. reality binary, as Žižek rethinks it here via the dialectic of semblance and the real, has come to underlie popularized notions of American nationalism and the ideology of Americanism itself.

But to see how this ideological mechanism works, we must delve a bit further into Žižek's theoretical analysis. The most prominent example of the real as "today's fundamental terror" would of course appear to be "terror" and "terrorism" themselves, experienced by most people as televised spectacle—with the 9/11 images as the archetypal instance. Terror-as-spectacle, according to this notion, is designed to "awaken us, Western citizens, from our numbness, from immersion in our everyday ideological universe" (9). But Žižek suggests that we should invert our standard way of thinking, in which the destruction of the World Trade Center towers is read as an "intrusion of the Real that shattered our illusory sphere" (16). "It is not that reality entered our image," he argues, but rather that "the image entered and shattered our reality" (ibid). Before 9/11 we lived in a particular form of *our* reality, "perceiving third world horrors as something . . . not [a] part" of it (ibid.). After 9/11 these "third world horrors" do enter first world, metropolitan reality, but precisely *as* simulacrum, as a new form of *semblance* that obeys the logic of the Lacanian real. The desire or "passion" for the *real* as opposed to semblance is thus, according to Žižek, precisely what helps us to *maintain*, in the face of new threats to close it, the distance between the first and the third world. Thus he points out that, in clear contrast to first world reporting on third world catastrophes, where the whole point is to produce a "scoop of gruesome detail"—say, "Somalis dying of hunger," or "raped Bosnian women"—reporting on the 9/11 attacks showed "little of the actual carnage . . . no dismembered bodies, no blood" (13). This spectacular real then helps to "separate Us from Them" shoring up the sense that "the real horror happens *there* not *here*" (ibid). Žižek even draws the connection between fictional digitalized images and 9/11. He recalls here the 1999 film *The Matrix*, in which the hero Neo awakens from the slumber of simulated reality into a "real reality"—a "desolate landscape littered with burnt out ruins—what remains of Chicago after a global war"—and receives the ironic greeting—"welcome to the desert of the real"—from the resistance leader Morpheus, from which Žižek takes the title of his book (15). Žižek's point here is that Americans experienced the 9/11 disaster as a spectacle reminiscent of the "most breathtaking scenes in big catastrophe [movie] productions," not out of some robotic incapacity to see reality at all, but rather according to the logic of a defense mechanism, a digital sanitizing of the space of the U.S. designed to keep it from becoming the "desert of the real" (15). It is also important to recall here, as Žižek also reminds us, that, post-9/11, Hollywood postponed release of previously produced films that contained images similar to the ones we saw on the television screens when the planes hit the towers. Perceiving the real scenes of 9/11 not as fiction per se but as irresistibly paralleled by, even *preceded* by their fictional equivalents here, according to Žižek, works to uphold the ideology of American exceptionalism, and, under the new mapping of semblance and reality the 9/11 events ushered in, to relegate once more the real suffering (that must *not* be represented or experienced) to a "desert of the real" locatable somewhere in the global South.

In this ideological climate, then, immigrants, generally depicted in the U.S. media as interlopers from the global South who, if not potential terrorists, have at the very least come to take away American jobs, must also be resituated within the "desert of the real" in the American collective imaginary. Consider here, as one such example of how the media constructs immigrants as the real, Lou Dobbs's "Broken Borders" commentaries on his (now canceled) CNN show "Lou Dobbs Tonight"— especially during the surge of anti-immigrant demagogy that followed the public controversies over the (failed) "Border Protection, Anti-Terrorism, and Illegal Immigration Control Act" (also known as the Sensenbrenner Bill) of 2005. Speaking on a segment on the U.S./Mexico border fence aired in January 2007, for example, Dobbs, who has continually given voice to the most aggressive right-wing nationalist and populist sentiment in the U.S., openly refers to immigrants as "those that would cross the border with an intent to harm us" and praises the fence as a "principal mainstay against illegal immigration and unlawful entry into this country whether by terrorists or illegal immigrants."[15] The elision, achieved via regular juxtaposition, between "terrorists" and "illegal immigrants" already gives some idea of the pathological need to redraw the symbolic U.S. border so as to keep immigrants, no matter which side of it they are actually on, quarantined in the "desert of the real." But to get an even more vivid sense of this, consider the media controversy that erupted in May of 2007, after the CBS show "Sixty Minutes" aired an interview segment with Dobbs in which the interviewer, Leslie Stahl, brought to his attention that in 2005 a correspondent on his show reported that there had been a sudden increase in leprosy (purportedly 7,000 new cases in the three years leading up to 2005) and attributed this partly to "illegal immigration." Stahl challenged these statistics, and similar charges were soon to come from various other sources. Dobbs went back to his show and insisted the original reports were accurate. He reiterated that the upsurge in leprosy was at least partly due to "unscreened illegal immigrants coming into this country." This claim was subsequently proven in decisive terms to be false.[16] However, Dobbs continued his backlash against those who had challenged him, indicating the degree to which the mass, psychopathological dimensions of the leprosy narrative had made the facts of the case irrelevant to Dobbs's large, hardcore audience. Note how, in this narrative, the spurious linkage between leprosy and immigration goes beyond the idea that immigrants "harm us" because they take away jobs or are potential terrorists and maps the real onto their very bodies, seen as *ipso facto* infectious. No matter who they are or what they do, or whether they are "legal" or "illegal," immigrants are already projected as those who would carry the ills of the desert of the real into the United States. Even liberal challengers of Dobbs such as Stahl, who essentially sought to reassure the "Sixty Minutes" audience that, in fact, diseases such as leprosy are not crossing the border into the U.S. and remain safely quarantined *outside,* reveal how invested they are in this notion as well. Either way, infection and pandemic inhabit the desert of the real. No one expresses much concern over the possibility of increased cases of leprosy, say, in Mexico or diseases like dengue fever in India or Bolivia. In these renditions, immigrants have already *become* the real, having no connection to history and leaving the U.S. free to go on imagining itself, digitally if need be, as a symbolically sanitized space.

Virtually without exception, current work in immigrant/ethnic literary studies expresses a much-needed diametrical opposition to the idea of immigrants as job stealers, terrorists, or disease carriers. The field consistently strives to represent immigrant/ethnic groups as complex, humanized subjects and serves as one of the relatively few established counterweights to the reductionist and pathologizing metanarratives surrounding immigration, whether on the right or in mainstream liberal circles. One of the major contributions of the field has been to challenge as parochial all American nationalist metanarratives that exclude immigrants and (most) ethnics *per definitionem.* Immigrant/ethnic literary studies, I argue, enacts a dislocalized strategy for a more inclusive remapping of the frontiers between immigrant and citizen—but largely *within* a domestic-national space/paradigm. This it does via its own version of a binary of semblance—the fictional vs. the real (the global) in which the fictional functions simultaneously as a genre and as something opposite to fact, and the real situated as closer to the global and nonfictional reality.[17] By evoking a notion of fiction as, at one and the same time, both literary genre and something opposite to factual truth, immigrant/ethnic literary criticism also constructs a particular version of the real as global.

Let me begin by noting that even though fiction as genre does not entail the factual in the same way as do, say, nonfictional genres such as documentary, the *non-fictional*—and with it, potentially, the specter of the real—has become a key part of the way that immigrant/ethnic *fiction* is circulated and promoted in publishing and reading circles. Fictional works labeled as immigrant or ethnic are, for example, often marketed on the basis of how well they introduce the reader to a "different" culture not their own, one the reader is invited to experience, as *factually real,* through the fiction itself.[18] Of course, any fictional narrative is liable to be read for its "local color" or as a kind of supplement to nonfictional accounts, but this effectively becomes the rule in the case of immigrant and ethnic fictional narratives, one that stipulates that they be read as uncomplicated reflections of geographic settings outside or cultural practices of immigrant groups within the United States. The field of immigrant/ethnic studies has routinely made critical arguments against reading immigrant/ethnic fiction as a window onto culture. However, by virtue of what has become the field's structural positioning over and against the study of literature considered mainstream, it has come to see its own task as infusing the traditional literary canon with a dose of reality, jolting it out of its insularity. Thus, even while challenging the systematic exclusion of immigrant/ethnic texts from traditional canons, immigrant/ethnic literary studies bases this on a paradoxical capacity of immigrant fictions for conveying a more "real" reality.

Reading immigrant/ethnic literary narratives as vehicles for the "real" situates them within a peculiar generic space, the best term for which is probably "testimonio." "Testimonio," Spanish for testimony, was first used in Latin American literary circles in the late 1960s and early 1970s to describe nonfictional narratives that told the often-unknown stories of socially marginalized, oppressed individuals and groups. The Cuban anthropologist Miguel Barnet's *Autobiography of a Runaway Slave,* an edited and reconstructed version of interviews the author conducted with the former slave Esteban Montejo in the 1960s, was probably the first narrative to be classified in this way. The term was then used in the 1970s by Mexican author Elena Poniatowska to characterize what she called "testimonial novels," among them her *Hasta no verte, Jesús mío* (1969). The latter mixed fictional and nonfictional content in new ways. "Testimonio" first enters North American critical discourse in the early 1980s, propelled by the notoriety of Rigoberta Menchú's autiobiographical narrative *I, Rigoberta Menchú* (written with the anthropologist Elizabeth Burgos). Critics such as John Beverley, George Yúdice, Doris Sommer, and Barbara Harlow were among the leading critics arguing for testimonio's significance for literary and cultural theory as a whole. One of the principal aspects of the ensuing intellectual conversation over testimonio has been to position it as a generic marker for *both* fictional and nonfictional narratives and emphasize its apparent ability to elide this difference. By enabling this slippage between the fictional and the nonfictional, testimonio becomes a way for fields such as immigrant literary studies to introduce the notion of the global-as-the-real into the genre of fiction itself. Testimonio, in this context, becomes the perfect dislocalizing device: displacing the fictional with an infusion of the real, but only in order to consolidate the fictional itself as a vehicle for directly conveying the real.

This is especially evident in the work of the U.S. critical theorist most associated with work on testimonio, John Beverley. Focusing almost exclusively on *I, Rigoberta Menchu*, Beverley initially characterizes the testimonio as an eyewitness account, taking its name and many of its formal properties as a genre from the conventions of legal testimony. But he also defines testimonio as a new kind of narrative that, because of the extreme, often traumatic circumstances that produce it as well as its "non-traditional author-function" raises the question of whether literary fiction itself, at least as a mode of portraying such circumstances, has become obsolete. Testimonio becomes, for Beverley's work and for other theoretical writings on the concept authored for the most part by critics in the U.S., a kind of catalyst for destabilizing traditional notions of literature and inserting a new kind of "reality-claim" into the discourse and protocols of work that had conceived fiction primarily as a genre of imaginative writing.

But Beverley's theory of testimonio as a form of, so to speak, "post-literature," offering direct, unmediated access to the real came under severe pressure after the veracity of key sections of Rigoberta Menchú's testimonio was challenged by the U.S. anthropologist David Stoll. However accurate or not Stoll's charges may have been, their effect was to force Beverley (and other champions of testimonio and Menchú such as Arturo Arias) to mount a defense of his earlier theoretical moves and to emphasize the more fictional aspects of the genre such as point of view, intentional gaps in narrative continuity, and, in the general, the mediated, constructed property of all forms of textuality. If only so as to immunize it from the effects of Stoll's exposé, the claim that testimonio was a genre conveying the immediate truth of the oppressed/subaltern was revised, at least to the degree that fiction-like devices were now seen as no less important to this end.[19] Yet even here there persists the seemingly *a priori* imperative for preserving a qualitative distinction between fictional texts and the unique capacity of testimonio for delivering a dose of the real. In the second chapter ("Second Thoughts on Testimonio") of a 2004 book-length compilation and updating of his key essays on the genre, *Testimonio: The Politics of Truth*, Beverley writes that "testimonios in a sense are made for people like us in that they allow us to participate as academics and yuppies, without leaving our studies and our classrooms, in the concreteness and relativity of actual social struggles" (47). In a quintessentially dislocalist move Beverley both invokes a real/imaginary duality between actual struggle and academia, and then also dispenses with it by saying that university classrooms are also places of struggle. He argues that, via testimonios, students, indeed all readers "can be interpellated in a relation of solidarity with liberation movements and human rights struggles" both in the United States and abroad (ibid.). Testimonios can accomplish this because they are texts "whose discourses are still warm from the struggle," and yet the testimonios are "still *just* texts" and "not actual warm or in the case of the victims of death squads, not so warm bodies" (ibid).

The "warmth" of the testimonio is thus effectively admitted here by Beverley to emanate from the desert of the real. Beverley himself acknowledges that "what we encounter in testimonial is not the Real as such, in Jacques Lacan's sense of 'that which resists symbolization absolutely'" but an effect of the real "created by the peculiar mechanisms and conventions of the text, which includes a simulacrum of direct address" (2). Yet it is hard to avoid the conclusion here that testimonios are "just texts"— simulacra of the real—when their truth-claims are challenged, and yet quickly revert to their privileged role as direct embodiments of the real as soon as they become emissaries of the third world in first world universities. In this roundabout, seemingly self-ironizing way, Beverley's arguments would seem to be as invested in keeping a safe distance between the U.S. and the desert of the real as is any current within mainstream Americanism. Promoting a big picture of ethical solidarity with liberation struggles while deemphasizing any issues having to do with the verifiability of the facts in testimonial narratives, he is able both to disavow traditional, aesthetic notions of the literary as the province of (in a phrase he adopts from Jameson) an "overripe subjectivity" and yet at the same time to invoke quasi-literary "conventions of the text" in order to rescue the testimonio genre from charges of falsification. Whether directly referenced in specific works or not, Beverley's arguments have had a significant impact on critical scholarship on many levels, where testimonio—now routinely used to describe a variety of forms of writing such as novels, memoirs, and personal essays—has come to be broadly understood as a genre able to convey experiences of social and ethical urgency in ways that traditional literary forms cannot. And Beverley has recently argued that reading and debating testimonio remains relevant in the global context of a "world dominated by U.S. military and geopolitical hegemony" (x, Preface, *Testimonio*). In other words, according to Beverley, the testimonio has the ability to deliver us the "real" not just of a *third* but of a *globalized* world.

Unsurprisingly, testimonio, as both genre and theoretical topos, has also entered the lexicon of scholarship on immigrant/ethnic literature, where it is used to uncomplicate, so to speak, references to the fictional-ized experiences of oppression and trauma depicted in immigrant texts as, fiction notwithstanding, instances of a more "real" reality. Here, as in Beverley's defense of Menchú's testimonio as though endowed with an almost metaphysical truth in relation to its author's experiences (outside the U.S.) and yet as "just a text" in relation to readers who do not share in these experiences (as would be the case for most readers inside the U.S.), the invocation of testimonio facilitates the transfer of the preim-migration experiences of immigrants to the U.S. into a version of the real. But to see more concretely how that is so I will now turn to a critique of some of the testimonio-oriented scholarship two such immigrant texts have generated, and will offer some analysis of the texts themselves.

V. GLOBALIZING AMERICANISM
Julia Alvarez's *How the García Girls Lost Their Accents*

Alvarez's novel tells the story of the flight of the García family—father Carlos, wife Laura, and their four daughters, Yolanda, Sandi, Sophia, and Carla—from the Dominican Republic to the United States. In Santo Domingo the Garcías had been a wealthy and prominent family employing maids and servants. Carlos's father has a post in the United Nations. But this is not enough to protect them when Carlos is implicated in a failed CIA plot to kill the dictator Trujillo, and they must flee or face certain and violent retribution. The narrative itself begins in the 1980s, chronicling the life of the family as the García girls grow up in New York City, making frequent visits to the Dominican Republic, the actual circumstances leading to the family's emigration from Santo Domingo not being related until the end of the novel, in a flashback to the 1950s. It is important to note at the outset, however, that life in Santo Domingo in the 1950s, as portrayed in the novel, already betrays the fact of wide-spread Americanizing influences on the island, and that even after their emigration to New York—and the death of Trujillo in 1961—the family returns frequently to the Dominican Republic.

The *García Girls* is a widely taught text in courses on American ethnic and immigrant as well as women's literature and has become an almost permanent fixture in these categories. Critical scholarship on the work has highlighted issues of cultural conflict and Latina identity in the U.S.[20] But the novel has also begun to make regular appearances in conversations about globalization—an indication of a certain pressure for a shift in the framing of such texts as simply U.S. ethnic. However, such a shift is by no means tantamount to an unambiguous desire on the part of literary studies to replace the U.S. nationalist framework with a more global one—or at least not in the case of *The García Girls*. One of the reasons *The García Girls* has been so readily accepted into the canon of American literary studies surely has to do with the assimilation narrative it contains. This, together with the need perhaps to keep up with the demand from both publishers and readers for coming-to-the-U.S. (and finding liberation) narratives has also disposed scholarship to emphasize identity-based readings. And, to be sure, one could read certain aspects of the novel as reproducing dominant, assimilationist ideologies. My critique of how the novel is read by current American scholarship is thus mindful of the complex locations of both the text and its critics. I will first trace dislocalist tendencies in the critical writings about the novel and then indicate aspects of the novel that simultaneously resist such tendencies.

My analysis will focus primarily on three critical readings of *The García Girls*: Lucía M. Suárez's "Julia Alvarez and the Anxiety of Latina Representation," Pauline Newton's "Portable Homelands in Julia Alvarez's *How the García Girls Lost Their Accents*, *¡Yo!*, and *Something to Declare*," and Maribel Ortiz-Márquez's "From Third World Politics to First World Practices." These essays are broadly representative of work on Alvarez that has attempted to reframe her work in keeping with the overall drive to globalize American ethnic and immigrant literary studies.[21]

Even more to the point, all of the essays position the fictional text as a testimonio, explicitly so in the case of Newton and Suárez even if on a more implicit level in Ortiz-Márquez. Consider for example the claim made by Newton. She draws upon Beverley to say that, read as testimonios, Alvarez's works and her fictional characters put on the agenda problems of "poverty and oppression" that are normally not visible in the dominant forms of representation for "Dominican and US American readers and citizens" (52). It is, Newton notes, repercussions from the indelibly real traumas of the Trujillo dictatorship that have resulted in the emigration both of Alvarez herself and of her characters and that trigger the formation of the "multicultural states" explored in *The García Girls*, in her novel *¡Yo!* and in Alvarez's memoir, *Something to Declare*. (51). Alvarez's fictions, that is, are claimed to function as testimony not only to the brutality of Trujillo but also to the problems that arise in the formation of her characters in their relationship to racism and cultural difference in the United States. This point is underscored by Suárez, who writes that the novel can be studied as a testimony to the complexity of memory. In her words it "foregrounds the deep psychological problems that manifest themselves through memory, or lack of it, for those who are both challenged by bicultural and bilingual experiences and haunted by a silenced, and escaped, past of state repression" (117).

Reading the novel as testimonio allows a number of moves to take place simultaneously. First, it destabilizes certain accepted categories of analysis stemming from nationalist paradigms—categories such as immigration and ethnic identity themselves, both of which appear to be the result of simply moving from one nation to another and adapting to a new living situation. The movement from the Dominican Republic to the U.S. becomes, in the interpretive space of testimonio, more complex than simple ex- or repatriation. Moreover, both essays reason that reading *The García Girls* as testimony has become a necessity in a world where stories of real brutality, subsequent escape from it, and the resulting pain of readjustment transcend questions of fictional versus nonfictional portrayal. Although less directly, this overriding emphasis on the urgent flight from terror and the almost therapeutic need to tell its story is also present in Newton's reading of the novel. Indeed, to varying degrees all three essays make some attempt to link the emigration of the García family directly to American intervention in the Antilles and to the historical particularities of the Trujillo dictatorship. The implied thinking here is that the forms of mobility resulting from a global politics cannot be entirely contained by the notion of immigration. The new urgency of flight transcends national boundaries—a reality that is then to be conveyed, analogously, by positioning Alvarez's novel beyond the formal boundaries the novel itself—as testimonio.

But what is really at stake in positioning these works as testimonios? Consider, again, Newton's claim: that the works of Alvarez "put on the agenda oppression that is not normally visible in the dominant forms of representation" (51). Although Newton is referring to Alvarez's personal essays here as well as to her fictions, such a statement begs the question of why a fictional form—such as the novel—should be unable to put such oppression "on the agenda." What exactly then is the advantage of reading *The García Girls* as a testimonio? Recall Beverley's suggestion that testimonios are still "warm" from struggles in the real world. The notion here is that testimonio is formally necessary in order to convey an urgent reality beyond the limits of fictional representation or indeed of any form of *mediated* textuality. Nevertheless, as I have noted above in reference to testimonio theory in the wake of the Rigoberta Menchú controversy, testimonio is promptly rescued from charges of factual inaccuracy by invoking the fictional and what is generally the cultural and textual mediacy of truth-claims, thus allowing the critics to, in effect, dislocalize the fictional, to position themselves as if beyond its mediacy, but still able to fall back on it when necessary. This is possible precisely because the notion of testimonio is itself *already* positioned in such a way as to blur the boundaries between fiction and nonfiction. Newton, for example, argues outright that we need to get beyond asking whether Alvarez's narrative is autobiography or fiction. Suárez explains, in turn, that, after reading Alvarez's autobiographical essays, she "cannot help but make the connection between [the] reminiscence of her past and her fiction." The "essays," she states, "have led me down [a] slippery path" in which the distinction between memoir and novel itself disappears. (143). And Ortiz-Márquez claims that the blurring of boundaries between fiction and autobiography is crucial to understanding the "social reality" that "lies at the margins of the text—namely the escape from Trujillo dictatorship" (236).

At one level, it makes a certain sense to read testimonios as these critics do. Nonfiction and fiction alike are, as forms, necessarily mediated. And there can be no question that fiction as form has the capacity to explore and explain factual and historical truth about oppression, poverty, and so on, and that the nonfictional is just as "constructed" as the fictional. Lisa Lowe has, for one, pointed out in "Work, Immigration, Gender," that reading testimonios should not become a pretext for ceasing to attend to formally "aesthetic" genres such as the novel, or for ignoring the question of why testimonios emerge at particular political and historical moments. However, most of the conversations centering on testimonio have, as in the instance discussed here, been able only to gesture toward the kind of broad and contextualized reading advocated by Lowe. If anything, reading fiction as testimonio in cases such as the above has led, as I will show in what follows, to a particular kind of traditional disciplinary consolidation. At the same time it is important to note how these reading strategies have emerged within a larger global, political context in which literary critics are chastised for occupying themselves with the "imagined" world of fictional texts purportedly far removed from the realities of globalization. In this atmosphere, the dislocalizing possibilities of testimonio are readily mobilized to blur the boundaries between fiction and nonfiction and, in a moment of globality that champions the "real," to increase the reality quotient of the latter.

However, such attempts to blur the boundaries between different forms of writing also lead toward a blurring of another kind of boundary: that between fiction and fact. While we certainly get a certain quantum of historical information in these readings of *The García Girls,* this does not translate into helping us better understand either Alvarez's fictional texts or her memoirs in relation to the specific historical circumstances and conditions reflected in the novel itself. The scholarship here advocates what is, rather, a deliberate ambiguity in relationship to history, reducing historical information to the real where the reading of the novel remains disconnected from history itself. Both Suárez and Newton, for example, argue that testimonios (fictional and nonfictional) give voice to the silences and the unknown aspects of the Trujillo regime. As Suárez puts it: "I would argue that Alvarez not only renders justice to the visible and obvious universe, but that she also makes way for an array of invisible elements in a less clearly definable globalized world, where memory is tainted by amnesia, fear, pain, and trauma" (120). However, nowhere is there an attempt to theorize the historical specificities in relationship to trauma. Nor do we learn here about the historical specificities that produce amnesia or that give content to trauma. Terms such as amnesia, trauma, and invisibility remain abstract and unconnected to the history invoked elsewhere in the criticism itself. The American occupation of the Dominican Republic and the murderous brutality it produced and left behind after placing Trujillo in power, invoked here, seems to obfuscate memory and history rather than sharpen it.[22] Such history comes to function, in effect, as the real, and part of the reason is that the trauma and terror experienced under Trujillo is assumed here to have been left behind when the immigrant crosses into the United States. This crossing, I would argue, is already implied here when the past becomes a memory that is "tainted by amnesia." Remembering, according to Newton and others, is given shape only in stories that blur the formal and generic boundaries between fiction and nonfiction, that is, in testimonio. According to all of the essays being discussed here—and this is anything but atypical of current scholarship in ethnic and immigrant literary studies—telling such stories is important not because the memories they contain are produced by the realities of history but because of the larger work they do in service of fighting racism and sexism in the United States. There can be no gainsaying such work; of course, I would add here that the additional benefit of emphasizing memory and trauma and their testimonial medium as if somehow *prior* to their historical truth is to contain terror and trauma *within* the space of the real—the Dominican Republic in this case. The focus on amnesia furthers this process of containment. These are, in effect, the only aspects of history to be invoked, because it has already been assumed, however unconsciously, that once immigration into the U.S. has taken place, personal trauma and terror can safely be worked through in therapeutic, "testimonio" fashion. Terror is relegated to the past as a result of a spatial displacement along an axis of decontextualized culture and identity, rather than through historical transformation.

But there is still another dimension to the process of reducing the details of the preimmigration past to the real. Throughout the criticism under analysis here, both the Trujillo dictatorship and the history of U.S. intervention in the Dominican Republic and the larger Caribbean are coded as exceptional rather than continuous with a "normal," postimmigration life in America. In place of the larger, global historical context, chronology—for example, particular dates such as the 1965 U.S. invasion of the Dominican Republic—becomes the focal point when referring to preimmigration reality in *The García Girls*. Suárez for instance is careful to cite 1965 and the wave of emigration from the Dominican Republic that followed during the postinvasion period (123). These are crucial realities, of course, but with focus on them as "events," they are rendered as exceptional and outside the global, imperial context that generated them. Constant references by critics such as Suárez, Newton, and Ortiz-Márquez to the Trujillo dictatorship as a "regime of terror," while true enough, nevertheless tend to fetishize it as event, and thus to further reinforce its banishment to the desert of the real and its effective removal from history.[23] The terror indubitably unleashed by such events, to the extent that it is rendered as exceptional, is reduced to little more than the motive for flight, something to leave behind—after which a return to normalcy is declared, or assumed, even if attained in an uneven manner.

In this way, moreover, the representational space of the U.S. is also kept free from the exceptional terrors of the real. Dominican immigrants, like others, must of course face the realities of racism and sexism in the U.S., as critics such as Ortiz-Márquez, Newton, and Suárez are right to emphasize. But the accompanying implication here is that immigrants are nevertheless free to reinvent themselves as Americans, even when struggling with the pain of adaptation. Terror *within* U.S. borders is seen as something dream-like, nightmarish, amnesiac—purely psychological and thus removed from the material. In this context, then, the "testimonial" blurring of the boundaries between fiction and nonfiction works not only to displace ideas of aesthetic mediation but to seal off the space of the U.S. itself as one in which writing—all writing—can be inventive, creative, and playful. Indeed, the possibility of testimonio itself as a form of writing that transcends boundaries would appear to presuppose a freedom to pursue personal recovery and reinvention that only the space within the boundaries of the U.S., where the terrors of the real are safely psychologized and dehistoricized, can provide. The question of identity itself becomes separated off from geopolitics, economics, and culture. To be sure, both Alvarez and her characters are portrayed by their critics here as global and transcultural subjects, but precisely *because* such characteristics are acquired through immigration to the United States. The question "who am I?" becomes possible primarily for those whose immigrant status is assured and who are learning to adapt and become Americans, however incompletely and against the odds—but seemingly not in the case of those for whom immigration itself has yet to take place . . . or never will. So, for example, Newton's reference to "portable homelands" assumes a space—as preexisting "homeland"—in which cultural identity is individually "portable," a matter of personal choice (51). The echoes of the "melting-pot" and quasi-official multiculturalism are distinctly audible here, in what has effectively become a gesture of rethinking, via immigration narrative and testimonio, a literary canon already assumed to be *American*. The identity of immigrant subjects comes into sharp focus not so much because these particular subjects have spent a part of their lives outside the U.S., but because such identity has become a unique staging site for that synthesis of the local and the global now required to reproduce the dominant imaginary of the U.S. itself as an "identity."

(Im)migration and Gender

At no point does any of the scholarship I am examining here, it must be emphasized, espouse much less attribute an overtly assimilationist stance to Alvarez's novel itself. If the García girls lose their accents, the new identity they acquire as a result is never explicitly claimed in these readings to be—much less celebrated—as "American." In keeping with the dislocalist strategy of displacing fiction onto the real through the invocation of the genre (or nongenre) of testimonio, the national question raised in this is displaced here as well—onto questions of gender. Consider for example how Ortiz-Márquez's essay lays out this dislocalist strategy. "Belonging" she writes, "is the privileged feeling" in Alvarez's narrative. "Belonging expresses the need to be somewhere where the boundaries of 'here' and 'there,' can be easily defined, where the sense of estrangement can be easily defined" (233). Ortiz-Márquez cautions against any easy acceptance of a "defined" identity as such, preferring instead to cast the "negotiation" of belongingness in *The García Girls* in terms of gendered identities, concentrating on how the novel's female protagonists struggle to find their place in the U.S. through their bodies. But if such gendered identities turn out to be vexed—requiring "negotiation"—this, then, is so precisely because of issues of assimilation to and from within the United States.

Thus, Ortiz-Márquez goes on to observe, "differences between male and female reproductive organs . . . translate . . . into differences in the way boys and girls are to behave once they enter puberty. The meaning of those differences is tied, in the novel, to Yolanda's understanding of language and language acquisition in the United States" (233). Note what is, in fact, the double displacement here: the Americanizing assimilation of immigrants becomes a question of language acquisition ("losing accents"), but this question in turn is claimed as, a priori, something "related to the configuration of sexual and gender identities" (233)—that is, *girls* "losing their accents." Gender questions would appear then to act as a screen for a more assimilationist reading of the novel.

The boundaries between the Old and New World are themselves, in fact, "negotiated" through notions of gender. This becomes clear if we consider how Ortiz-Márquez reads the novel's inaugural scene. The first chapter of the novel, the first of a series that covers (in reverse order) the time period stretching from 1989 back to 1972, opens with Yolanda returning to the island on one of her regular trips from the United States. Here is the description of Yolanda's arrival, narrated from her own vantage point:

> The old aunts lounge in the white wicker armchairs, flipping open their fans, snapping them shut . . . [T]he aunts seem little changed since five years ago when Yolanda was last on the Island. Sitting amongst the aunts in less comfortable dining chairs, the cousins are flashes of color in turquoise jumpsuits and tight jersey dresses . . . Before anyone has turned to greet her in the entryway, Yolanda sees herself as they will, shabby in a black cotton skirt and jersey top, sandals on her feet, her wild black hair held back with a hairband. Like a missionary, her cousins will say, like one of those Peace Corps girls who have let themselves go so as to do dubious good in the world. (3–4)

Ortiz-Márquez does not cite this passage directly, but she refers to it, observing that "from the beginning of the novel we are introduced to a conflicting relations between the two locations [. . .] The opening scene [in the novel] is marked by Yolanda's subtle struggle to reject the norms established by her maternal family as proper 'woman's behavior' and her 'foreign' approach to issues such as clothes, makeup, traveling, and friends" (236). Although recognizing the implicit challenge to gender politics in the Dominican Republic embodied in Yolanda's protagonism in scenes such as this, Ortiz-Márquez is also careful to note an ambiguity here, acknowledging that "the relative freedom [Yolanda] enjoys in the

U.S. is clearly intertwined with the comfort she experiences in the familiarity of the surroundings in the Dominican Republic" (ibid.). Reading this "intertwining" as still another instance in which the boundaries of immigrant life tend to be blurred, the effect of this interpretive move here is to reproduce a perfectly clear and distinct opposition between the familiar, comfortable, but, in matters of gender politics, less than ideal Dominican Republic against the unfamiliar, uncomfortable, but relatively more free and gender-enlightened United States.

In the case of gender too, that is, the logic of dislocalism plays itself out: the initial gesture that affirms the blurring of the boundaries only makes it possible to preserve them all the better in the end. And it is this simultaneous "intertwining" and recuperation of boundaries that is read most pointedly here through women's practices. Take, for example, Ortiz-Márquez's claims that Yolanda's subjectivity is "torn between a corpus that was not quite inscribed in Spanish nor English" (233). For this the following textual evidence is adduced: "For the hundredth time [says Yolanda] I cursed my immigrant origins. If only I too had been born in Connecticut or Virginia, I too would understand the jokes everyone was making on the number 69 and I would say things like 'no shit' without feeling like I was imitating someone else'" (ibid.). The cursing of immigrant roots is very often depicted as a generational battle in immigrant narratives, and *The García Girls* is no exception here. The parents represent the old world and the girls the new, though as if caught between the new and the old. A similar line of interpretation is pursued by Newton as well, whose reading of Alvarez correctly observes the way in which gender norms from the Dominican Republic make their way into the U.S., altering the space of the latter. She cites passages from *The García Girls* in which, Carlos, the girls' father, is portrayed as too obstinate in his ways, imposing, in Newton's words, "inhibiting island rules that run counter to the ways of a contemporary U.S. society," mandating that his daughters "not interact with men in any questionable manner" (57). Like Ortiz-Márquez, Newton emphasizes the intertwining of gender practices and norms, the positioning of the girls in the liminal space between the patriarchal order that has traveled to the mainland from the island and the seemingly less restrictive relationships they have with their "monolingual husbands" in the U.S.—husbands who, however, do not understand the complexity of their identities (59). But despite the inevitability of this intertwining, the old, patriarchal world with its bad gender politics here continues to function as a foil from which to set the U.S. apart from its others, providing the critics themselves with a standpoint from which to affirm the U.S. as always already a place of better gender politics.

Here as well, then, *The García Girls* is read primarily within the terms of domestic race- and gender identity-negotiations, and made to bear the burden of representation that comes with such discussions. Although she wants to question what she calls the "ethnic reading" of the text and even suggests that a "Latino" ethnicity is imposed on Alvarez's characters as a result of immigration, Ortiz-Márquez nevertheless produces readings of the novels that are in keeping with the standard U.S. rhetoric of identity as something to be negotiated by the individual. She suggests that Alvarez's characters have taken on a fractured identity through mobility—but this in turn suggests that those not required to be "mobile" can somehow have *unfractured* identities. Though the essay acknowledges the struggle that Latina women in particular must wage in support of their own independent identities in *both* the U.S. and in their homelands, in the case of the García girls this struggle is also precisely what *gives* them their identity. This ironic valorization of prolonged identity "negotiation" as a kind of end in itself is also explicit in Newton's reading of the novel, which reassures us that, after first having trouble defining themselves in the U.S, the García girls ultimately "learn to cross cultures with greater ease" or become "transcultural" even if they fumble along the way (53). Implied in the latter concept here too is the logic according to which the struggle over identity must be prolonged indefinitely if one is not to risk losing that identity itself. In fact, this metanarrative in which displacement occurs alongside and continuously accompanies "struggle" is not necessarily a story of dispossession and can just as well be understood as a narrative of cosmopolitanism in which the characters are represented as possessing a desirable perspective that *could come only* from being displaced. Displacement in this sense is removed from the material realities of the lives of immigrants and becomes a kind of ethical privilege. In effect, identity- and gender-centered readings of *The García Girls* such as those under discussion here have already compensated for its categorization as a "marginal literature" counterposed to dominant literary categories by restricting it to the domestic and "resistant" category of a United States–Latina ethnicity.[24]

Of course, as mentioned earlier, certain aspects of the novel could be interpreted as reproducing the very same dominant ideologies that are tacitly left unchallenged in these readings. So for example, growing up in the U.S., the girls come to rebel against what they see as their old world parents, whom they experience as overbearing and overprotective. In an effort to preserve their Dominican cultural heritage, the parents send the girls to the Dominican Republic in the summers during their teenage years, something the girls themselves resist, resulting in constant domestic conflicts. The latter are described in the novel as follows: "It was a regular revolution: constant skirmishes. Until the time we took open aim and won, and our summers—if not our lives—became our own" (111). The fact that their skirmishes are described as a "revolution" does indeed resonate with the title of Ortiz-Márquez's essay, "From Third World Politics to First World Practices." It may seem a minor point of semantics here, but the slippage is worth considering: "revolution" in the Dominican Republic concerns the political circumstances that had implicated Carlos García (and by extension his family) in a failed insurrectionary plot to assassinate Trujillo, resulting in the Garcías' flight to the U.S. The "revolution" in the U.S. is fought over whether the girls are to be allowed to stay out late at night, go to school dances, and spend the summers in the United States. It is precisely these teenage "skirmishes," narrated within the context of the old/new world divide as the García girls try to figure out their places in their new "first world" environment, that become the focus of the literary scholarship under scrutiny here, centered on the questions of women's identity formation and their struggle for liberation, both from the *machista* culture of old world patriarchy and from new world sexism. And yet it is also via these scenes of adolescent rebellion that the urgency of cultural preservation—and the unspoken law requiring women to be bearers of this preservation–is staged. Of course, one could also read such an episode, conveyed tongue in cheek, as a commentary on a U.S., metropolitan form of life in which the right to stay out could be even thought of as a "revolution." And it is possible to read the novel as merely representing this contradiction. But the elision of this difference between the two "revolutions" in the critical discourse then helps on the one hand to advocate for the preservation of Latino culture and yet on the other to argue for women's need to find a place outside it. The attempted revolution against Trujillo in the Dominican Republic turns into the revolution, either of keeping one's cultural identity or of escaping traditional gender norms in New York. And it is the concept of immigration itself here that foregrounds the critical positioning of the novel in such a way as to leave behind old world politics just as immigrants, according to the standard Americanizing mythology, supposedly leave behind their homelands—and with them the dangers of the real—in their search of a better life in the United States. Yet once in the U.S. these same immigrants are also to be accorded the freedom to preserve old world cultural practices.[25]

Some Notes toward a Historical Reading

Dislocalizing readings of *The García Girls,* typified in the scholarship on the novel examined above, essentially appropriate the narrative's global frame of reference in order to make more credible and politically acceptable a localized situating of the novel as "U.S./American." Through still another move of displacement and consolidation, this is secured by reading the novel exclusively within the overarching framework of domestic multicultural and gender-identity issues. The resulting tendency is to preclude other, non–identity-based readings, including those that might connect immigration as well as domestic issues of racism/sexism to broader global socio-historical conditions. Such dislocalizing readings remain limited in exploring the potential capacity of the novel itself, in conversation with the (im)migration experience, to resist easy categorization within accepted U.S. literary paradigms of localized ethnic identity. I will analyze some of these potential aspects of the novel below. I stress that I do not wish to produce a comprehensive reading here but merely to point out ways of glimpsing this resistant aspect of Alvarez's narrative.

How the García Girls Lost Their Accents elides any immediate localization of ethnic identity at one level simply because its characters move back and forth so readily between Santo Domingo and the U.S. mainland. Their lives unfold in continuous contact with the lives of Dominicans on the island itself, revealing a complicated network of socio-historical relations between two national loci whose multiple intersections, framed by global historical developments, makes it harder, if not impossible to draw ideological lines between an ominous Dominican desert of the real and a U.S. oasis of freedom and security. Moreover, the novel complicates any move to posit the local or a localized ethnicity as a site of critical opposition not only because the characters themselves cannot be physically or spatially localized in this way, but also because the *local itself* varies in different contexts.

For a better sense of this, let us revisit the beginning of the novel. On the surface, Yolanda's visit to the Dominican Republic is the opportunity for various characters to stress the "localism" of Santo Domingo in relationship to the global U.S. Her aunts greet her by saying "welcome to your little island." The cousins join in a chorus for her, singing: "here she comes Miss America." Yolanda, by the mere fact that she has been living in the U.S., represents the States to her cousins. Her family encourages her to speak in Spanish, which she describes as her "native" tongue, thus choosing at least for the moment to assume an uncomplicated connection between herself, the Spanish language, and the Dominican Republic. But

beneath the surface these easy connections and the sense of an uncomplicated locality rapidly disintegrate. Recall the opening scene again:

> The old aunts lounge in the white wicker armchairs, flipping open their
> fans, snapping them shut . . . [T]he aunts seem little changed since five
> years ago when Yolanda was last on the Island. Sitting amongst the aunts
> in less comfortable dining chairs, the cousins are flashes of color in tur-
> quoise jumpsuits and tight jersey dresses . . . Before anyone has turned to
> greet her in the entryway, Yolanda sees herself as they will, shabby in a
> black cotton skirt and jersey top, sandals on her feet, her wild black hair
> held back with a hairband. Like a missionary, her cousins will say, like one
> of those Peace Corps girls who have let themselves go so as to do dubious
> good in the world. (3–4)

Here the novel clearly throws into relief the gap that has opened up,
in terms of behavior norms and even personal appearance, between the
immigrant Yolanda and her nonimmigrating family members on the
island—something discussed by Ortiz-Márquez in her essay. But, this
passage also casts an oblique light on the terms that are often mobilized
by the field of immigrant and ethnic literary studies in response to the
pressure to globalize. The passage, for one thing, emphasizes that the
precise context in which the U.S. is seen as "global" is the socio-economic and historical conjuncture that has produced U.S. intervention and
domination of the Caribbean, in all its various forms. One of these is the
Peace Corps. The reference here to the latter's "dubious good," even if
embedded within the indirect discourse through which Yolanda imagines
how her more "localized" and gender-conservative aunts and cousins are
likely to judge her appearance, should not be overlooked. Created along
with Alliance for Progress in the early 1960s, the Peace Corps obeyed the
same Cold War logic that led, in the Caribbean, to even more "dubious"
ventures such as the Bay of Pigs invasion of Cuba and the 1965 armed
intervention in Santo Domingo to overthrow the popular and progressive
Juan Bosch government. The old aunts and the flashily dressed cousins
inclined to view Yolanda's "Peace Corp"–like (North Americanized)
appearance as "dubious" in this context is something not emphasized in
readings of *The García Girls* that understand the global within the limits
of cultural and gender-based identity politics of recognition.

Note here as well that, while those in the Dominican Republic come,
for the moment, to occupy the local position (the aunts who "seem
little changed") and the immigrant Yolanda the global, when she is in
the States, Yolanda is perceived as part of a different kind of local iden-

tity, that of a Hispanic woman or Latina. In addition, if in one context the local represents accumulated cultural practices in the Dominican Republic, how then do we account for Americanizing influences on the island that cannot be reduced to support for the Trujillo dictatorship, to the 1965 invasion, or to the statistics representing the numbers of Dominican displaced as a result? The latter, as immigrants to the U.S., in some sense arrive having already *been* Americanized. By the same logic, if we designate the category of "Latina" in the U.S. to be the site of the local then how do we account for differences of class structure within this category, not to mention the differences of race/gender/language that assign people within these categories varied access to the dominant sphere? Since the U.S. can claim (localized) Latino/a cultural practices as, in one sense, located securely within its borders, it posits itself as both a local and a global nation containing diversity while at the same time banishing—or at least attempting to keep out—the "real" dangers posed by the foreign.

The point of view according to which localized cultural practices provide both a refuge from and a standpoint from which to oppose globalization becomes extremely complicated and problematic when we consider it in relationship to *The García Girls*—as, indeed, to immigrant literatures generally. This being so, the question persists here of how to read those aspects of the novel that complicate the equation, as interpreted by some identity-based readings, of the local with an ethnically marginal position? Aside from telling the story of how its main characters become Americanized subjects, complete with phases of teenage rebellion, *The García Girls* narrates the process of globalized immigration in a way that, if critically reconsidered, undermines as readily as it lends support to any straightforward separation of the local from the global. The local, as implicitly constructed in Alvarez's novel, is too ambiguous to rely on when it comes to representing ethnic or identity-based critical resistance to dominant cultures—or to keeping the U.S. safe from the real.

For, to return once again to the point made above, Dominican immigrants to the U.S, like those from many other parts of the world, have in most cases already had encounters with America, Americans, and Americanization well before physically immigrating. Consider again, in this light, the specific circumstances that force the Garcías to flee their country for the U.S.: the fact that Carlos García falls under suspicion for his part in what had initially been a U.S.-backed plot to kill Trujillo. Here the novel reflects quite closely the actual record of historical events surrounding the attempted assassination—and, presumably, the actual experiences of some in the Dominican Republic in the early 1960s. Although invoked in some of the scholarship I have analyzed above in a nominal way, the historical backdrop generally comes into play only when discussing the novel's auto-biographical aspects, with generally no or only minimal references made to the U.S. role in events themselves—and more significantly, to how the novel *itself* is shaped by this specific historical conjuncture. In the novel, we learn that Carlos is being investigated through the point of view of the girls. Yolanda, for example, is described seeing her father hide in a closet from the SIM (Servicio Inteligencia Militar) agents who have come to question him. Her mother and the servant Cucha manage to distract them and prevent Carlos's arrest, but the impact of this experience on the girls persists and reflects the dreadful memories of the "trujillato" reported by many Dominicans who lived through it. The girls, in fact, have been told that the SIM is everywhere, watching to catch them if do anything wrong (195–98). Moreover, the novel makes very clear the Garcías' forced emigration and U.S. involvement in the failed assassination. In fact it is an official U.S. agent that literally makes the secret travel arrangements for them. Carlos, we learn, has been working all along with the U.S. State Department presence in the Dominican Republic in his organizing efforts against Trujillo. It is Victor Hubbard, officially the U.S. consul in Santo Domingo, but in actuality a C.I.A. agent and Carlos's American contact, who saves the family from certain, violent retribution. Known as "Tio Vic" to the girls, Hubbard has instructed them to call him at the first sign of trouble, and to use the (appropriately American-sounding) code phrase "tennis shoes." Hubbard is presented in the novel as an honest middleman, good on his word to help the Dominicans recruited by the C.I.A. to escape in case the plot should go awry. "It wasn't his fault," the novel informs us, "that the State Department chickened out of the plot they had him organize" (202). His "orders changed midstream from orga-nize the underground and get that SOB out to hold your horses, let's take a second look around and see what's best for us" (211).

That is, caught in the turmoil of rapidly changing political environment, the García family is sketched against a backdrop of a complex account in which the histories of the Dominican Republic and the United States are already deeply intertwined. But in much of the scholarship on the novel this history, if discussed, is effectively relegated to the realm of the real. Perhaps inadvertently, this reflects what is often the downplaying of such intervention in much of the historiography produced about the Trujillo period, which, in a reflection of the lurid figure of Trujillo himself as evil incarnate, has tended to represent the actions of the U.S. (which installed Trujillo himself in the 1930s) as exceptional, a necessary depar-ture from the supposedly more benign parameters of the Good Neighbor Policy or the Alliance for Progress.[26] It is true, of course, as already mentioned, that political events—especially the U.S. military invasion of the country in 1965 to overthrow the left-leaning Juan Bosch government and restore military rule—were the impetus for the first large waves of Dominican emigration to the U.S. But, although the phenomenon of (im)migration from the Dominican Republic and from the Caribbean in general cannot be adequately represented without an understanding of this kind of political chronology, the latter also runs the risk of obscuring the larger phenomenon of mobility in the context of the globalization of the region itself. I cannot adequately summarize here the breadth of the historical and economic research into the structural causes of the Dominican exodus to the U.S. But work by scholars such as James Ferguson, Eric Williams, Tom Barry, Peggy Levitt, Greg Grandin, Sherri Grasmuck, and Patricia Pessar allows us to see how the larger history of (im)migration from the island can be traced to the very socio-economic conditions that have themselves given rise to the history of U.S. occupation and intervention.[27] A careful study of the history of what has been, since the end of the ironically more nationalist and protectionist regime under Trujillo, the ever more merciless yoking of Dominican society to the needs of international (largely U.S.) capital, whether via IMF austerity programs or the forced conversion of the Dominican Republic into a tourism-based economy that has left the better part of the local population with little choice except to emigrate, helps to correct the picture here. This is a picture of suffering and hardship that is the unexceptional equivalent of the "exceptional" torture and brutality inflicted by Trujillo and by U.S. neocolonial aggression—and that Dominicans must contend with whether they leave the island or not.

While in some ways limited, too, by a more dramatic, "political" understanding of the causes of Dominican emigration, Alvarez's novel nevertheless allows us to see not only the political role of the U.S. in forcing the Garcías to flee the island, but also how their plight is symptomatic of the matrix of economic, political, and cultural factors that result in the too readily overgeneralized phenomenon of (im)migration to the U.S.—and how these factors also affect those who will, in fact, never (im)migrate. It is worth recalling again, in this context, that the relatively prominent and comfortable García family travels to and from New York at regular intervals. The girls' grandparents, we recall, already live in New York thanks to the grandfather's posting to the United Nations. But they also spend large amounts of time in the Dominican Republic, always arriving laden with gifts for their grandchildren. Thus, even before their own physical immigration, the girls have been well supplied with images and tokens of the purportedly glittering metropolis that lies across the horizon from their island hometown. Even after the entire family emigrates to New York, they make regular return trips to the Dominican Republic.[28] In this context, it may indeed seem only natural that the García family, given that it already has the money, the class status, and the family connections required to be quasi-"Americanized" before emigrating, will do the logical thing and emigrate.

However, even those who cannot and will never leave home are also formed by this same kind of experience. The American magazines and television programs available in the Dominican Republic translate into Americanized cultural practices not only for the members of the prominent García family, but also for the poorer Dominicans who work for them as servants. The latter, as the novel makes clear enough, must also negotiate their own identity in relationship to the U.S.—a relationship that, although it may display elements of critical resistance, is no less characterized by a desire to be part of the dominant. Carla, the oldest sister, retells, for example, a story told by her mother Laura about Gladys, one of their servants: "[she] was only a country girl who didn't know any better than to sing popular tunes in the house and wear her kinky hair in rollers all week long, then comb it out for Sunday mass in hairdos copied from American magazines my mother had thrown out" (258). Gladys, according to the novel, also dreams, no less than her daughters, of going to New York someday: "'I wonder where I'll be in thirty two-years,' Gladys mused. A glazed look came across her face; she smiled. 'New York,' she said dreamily and began to sing the refrain from the popular New York merengue that was on the radio night and day" (260). That is, Gladys is already practicing to be in New York before she gets there, and in some sense it does not really matter whether she ever gets there. Her desires, too, are formed by the particular environment of transnational migration.

In sum: the García family's (im)migration, as portrayed by Alvarez, is clearly a byproduct both of U.S. political intervention in Santo Domingo and of the more general economic, social, and cultural impact of global capital on the Caribbean as well as across the global South. There is little in the novel, despite its currently predominant mode of interpretation, to support an unambiguous account of immigration as fleeing bad gender politics or poverty of the island to the shores of the United States. By effectively consigning such historical contingencies to the realm of the real and reading the novel—and immigration itself—largely in terms of the categories of a decontextualized, racialized, and gendered identity, scholarship places itself in the position of appearing, at least, to regard the material conditions determining the experience of (im)migration itself as secondary to a U.S. multiculturalist/identity-political framework.

VI. ARAB-AMERICAN LITERATURE AND U.S. MULTICULTURALISM IN A GLOBAL AGE

Diana Abu-Jaber's *Crescent*

As noted in the introduction to this chapter, what has become the more and more widely embraced project of delinking American literary studies from older nationalist paradigms has produced scholarship "centering," so to speak, on figures of displacement and de-centering. Within this general move to shift the standpoint of Americanism as a disciplinary formation outside national frameworks of whatever kind, a variety of strategies have come into play. I would like to take up one of these in what follows, namely how questions of Islam and of Muslim, Arab, and Arab-American cultures have come to work within American studies as a fulcrum of displacement—a trend that has become especially marked in the progressive Americanist literary academy in the wake of 9/11. Notable examples of the latter in recent Americanist scholarship include Susan Stanford Friedman's "Unthinking Manifest Destiny," John Carlos Rowe's "Reading *Reading Lolita in Tehran* in Idaho," Brian Edwards's *Morocco Bound: Disorienting America's Maghreb, from Casablanca to the Marrakesh Express,* and Melanie McAlister's *Epic Encounters: Culture, Media, and U.S. Interests in the Middle East since 1945.* Such work has helped to undo some of the more parochially nationalist frameworks and also helped to move American studies in a more global direction. In addition to providing historical analysis of American policy, the Middle East, and questions of religion, this scholarship has provided interesting and useful models for American studies to displace itself and reposition itself as part of global discourse.

But this attempt at displacement has produced dislocalist practices as well that point to the problems as the field globalizes itself. Consider for example, Wai Chee Dimock's "Deep Time: American Literature and World History" that analyzes the influence of Islam on writers such as Emerson and is consistent with Dimock's larger project of unfixing the category of American literature by reading it as a subset of world literature. In her book-length study, *Through Other Continents: American Literature Across Deep Time,* Dimock produces readings of, in addition to Emerson, writers such as Thoreau, Margaret Fuller, Gary Snyder, and Leslie Silko by connecting them to and resituating them within the longer traditions of Africa, Egypt, and Mesopotamia—traditions that both predate but also transcend, on the categorical level, the existence of the U.S. as a nation-state. In this effort, the theory of "deep time" invokes the "hemispheric proportions" and "multilingual" and "multijurisdictional" reach of Islam. About Emerson, in "Deep Time," Dimock writes: "What impressed him about Islam (and world religions in general) was what would later impress Malcolm X: the scope, the long duration, the ability to bind people across space and time." To an Emerson who, she claims, had found it impossible to accept Christianity as an absolute, Islamic poetry—written in this case in Persian, accessed by him only through German translations and "burdened by no undue piety toward the Koran"—would speak "as a poetry uniquely vital" (766). Situating Emerson within a larger, "deeper" global dimension, as Dimock does here via Islam, does indeed allow us to read him in a new light, but it also erases historical specificities of the interactions of the world's geopolitical forces.

Reflecting, on one level, the same disciplinary as well as historical, cultural, and political pressures, Arab-American literature and culture have also become the subject of increasing interest and attention within Americanist frameworks. It is within the accepted intellectual paradigms—of immigrant/ethnic literature—that literary works labeled as Arab-American are being taught and studied. A substantial effort has been underway to shape Arab-American literature as a field in its own right comparable to African-American or Latino/a literature.

But the contradictions of the contemporary globalized context emerge in a somewhat different way in relationship to Arab-American literature and its particular curricular/scholarly locus. At one level, the focus on Arab-American cultural production is understood as crucial to the project of globalizing American literature, especially given its connection to Islam as well as the fact that it has until recently remained—and in some ways perhaps still remains—outside the nationally drawn boundaries of the field. Yet, in contrast to the projects of Dimock or Susan Stanford Friedman, which have attempted to forge an outward-looking, effectively transnational connection to the history of Islam and its cultural practices, critics working in immigrant/ethnic literary studies have tended to see it as their task to guarantee the inclusion of U.S. Arabs and Muslims as legitimately "American" and to ensure a stable presence of Arab/Muslim writing within the canon of American ethnic literature. At the center of this contradiction are some particularly fraught and potentially illuminating questions of immigrant/ethnic identity—questions I want to explore in what follows.

If we accept for the moment that Arab-American literature legitimately belongs within the category of immigrant/ethnic literature, this raises the question of why Arab-American literature cannot be taught under the aegis of other categories such as, say, African-American or Asian-American. Indeed, this question, if further pursued, would lead to the problematizing of *all* categories within ethnic literature and also the entire discipline. In *Unthinking Eurocentrism*, for example, Ella Shohat and Robert Stam argue against maintaining the existing separation between the various ethnically delimited areas of study in favor of a more interconnected methodology. And one also thinks here of warnings raised by many critics, among them Lisa Lowe, Shirley Goek-Lin Lim, and Amy Ling, regarding the arbitrariness of existing, institutionalized categories of immigrant/ethnic literature and, for instance, in the case of Asian-American literature, the risk of homogenizing the vast differences between the Asian national origins of Asian-American immigrants, not to mention the huge variety of languages spoken among them. Such categories are anything but culturally spontaneous or neutral, and reflect the colonial past and its carving up of the Asian continent into regions such as the Middle East, South and South East, and the Far East—divisions largely determined by global geopolitical economic and military interests, including those of the United States. As Lisa Majaj has noted, the differing national or cultural affiliations adopted by immigrants are in many ways historically overdetermined by the political and economic conditions that lead to the act of immigration itself.[29] The common sense that pervades much of immigrant and ethnic literary studies, according to which the various immigrant groups line up as so many instances of ethnic identity, inverts and obscures what is, more fundamentally, a historically and politically conditioned difference to which the grid of the notion of difference is affixed, to a large extent, *a posteriori*.

This applies equally to the question of an Arab-American identity, and, in many ways, is more easily brought to light in this context. Although clearly a distortion and false generalization, any reference in today's political and intellectual climate to Arab-Americans is spontaneously understood as a reference to Islam, as a term interchangeable with the term Muslim. Given the global political realities of the U.S.-led "war on terror" and its effective self-understanding as a "clash of civilizations" in which the "West" confronts an Islamic "other," the category of Arab-American cannot, for better or worse, evade its own immediately political, global contextualizations. Thus, as part of the creating and shaping of an Arab/Muslim identity, the people assigned to that identity are *already*, in effect, denationalized.[30]

In this political context, Arab-American literature has not been fully integrated as an object of sustained reading within U.S. nationalist disciplinary paradigms, at least in comparison to Asian-American or Latino/a literature. It remains a kind of liminal, less-defined area of ethnic literary studies, lacking, as yet at least, its own stable canon. It is therefore in some ways easier to observe the globalization-driven dislocalizing of nationalist paradigms of ethnic identity at work in the scholarship devoted to Arab-American literature.

To see more concretely how this is so, I turn in what follows, to criticism focusing primarily on the fictional work of the Arab-American writer Diana Abu-Jaber. Abu-Jaber has written a number of works including *Arabian Jazz* (1993), *Crescent* (2003), *The Language of Baklava* (2005), and most recently the mystery-suspense novel *Origin* (2007). I limit my analysis here to *Crescent*, a novel that has been gaining attention from readers and critics for a variety of reasons. Featuring Iraqi main characters, it was published after 9/11—though completed before the WTC explosions according to the author herself. Abu-Jaber's work also offers a look at the world of Arabs living in the U.S. quite different from what has become standard in popular media. And, as critics have observed, the very fact that her chosen medium is the novel also makes her somewhat different among Arab-American authors, for whom poetry has tended to be the genre of choice.

Crescent revolves around the stories of an Iraqi exile, Hanif (Han), and an Iraqi-American cook, Sirine. Han, a professor of American literature in Los Angeles, had left Iraq as a teenager to study in Egypt. Sirine, the U.S.-born child of an Iraqi father and an American mother, both of whom died when she was young, has been raised by and lives in LA with her uncle, also an Iraqi immigrant to the U.S. Through her relationship to Han as well as her job as a cook at a Lebanese café in the section of Los Angeles called Teherangeles, she is able to blend into the world of Arab émigrés and exiles. The novel tells the story of love between Sirine and Han that develops in Los Angeles. Han at one point decides to return to Iraq. There he is captured by Hussein's men and as a result loses touch with Sirine. But by the end of novel, he has managed to escape and is on his way back to LA. The story prompts a reflection of the ways in which the characters of Sirine and Han are produced by the historical connections between the U.S. and the Middle East.

Scholarship on Abu-Jaber's work, though not copious, has been growing in step with the general increase of interest in Arab-American writing, especially since 9/11. Much of it, as in the case of scholarship on Alvarez's writings, focuses on questions of identity and the politics of representation. In the critical analysis to follow, I will take up recent work on Abu-Jaber and specifically that of Carol Fadda-Conrey because she has written one of the few analyses on *Crescent* and whose work is representative of the ways in which the critical reception of Abu-Jaber's work (and Arab-American writing in general) is following familiar trends in ethnic/immigrant literary studies as a whole.[31] But before I analyze the dislocalist practices in the critical work, any critique must take into account the present conditions within and the outside of the United States for academics who work in areas of Middle East, Arab, or Muslim-related issues. To take just a few examples, Rashid Khalidi, Joseph Massad, and Norman Finkelstein, who regularly critique U.S. and Israeli policies, have been subject to harassment, investigated on various charges, taken out of consideration for jobs, and sometimes removed from their positions. Their scholarship and teaching have been dismissed as a "political agenda." Such practices are indicative of a larger environment that has seen increased assault on academics, academic knowledge production, and any kind of critical dissenting voice in general. In this context, publication of Arab-American literature and its place in literary studies is particularly vexed. My critique is mindful of this context and attempts to contribute in a small way to an understanding of what appears to be the early stages of the development of Arab-American literary studies.

My approach here is similar to the one followed in relationship to Alvarez: I first identify and trace patterns of dislocalism in the critical scholarship on Arab-American writing and Abu-Jaber and then suggest ways in which the novel resists being categorized within nationalist paradigms.

Steven Salaita in "Sand Niggers, Small Shops, and Uncle Sam," raises the issue already broached above, namely, how, assuming it to be possible at all, to define the category of Arab-American literature when the "ethnicity" of the literature itself often cannot be inferred from that of its authors. "A good amount of work written and received as Arab-American," Salaita notes, is in fact, "produced by authors with no Arab background" (424). As an example, he cites Joanna Kadi's anthology *Food for Our Grandmothers: Writings by Arab-American and Arab-Canadian Feminists,* a volume that includes selections from many non-Arabs, among them the Armenian writers "Zabelle" and Martha Ani Boudakian, the Iranian writer Bookda Gheisar, and the Jewish writer Lilith Finkler. Moreover, he goes on to point out, "many non-Arab authors—including American Lisa Gizzi, editor of the Arab-American arts journal *Mizna,* and British poet Anna Reckin—produce work with Arab themes received in an Arab-American context" (425). This, according to Salaita, considerably complicates the claim, made by some, that "since Arab-American authors are descendants of peoples from the Arab world, the proper way to contextualize them is within the tradition of Arabic literature, which dates to the pre-Islamic era" (425). Even when identity is predicated upon ethnic origin, further complexities arise: "some writers who have been counted as Arab-Americans have one Arab grandparent, while others who publish in Arab-American forums were born and live in the Middle East" (425). Language is also a complicating factor in this regard, since, as Salaita argues, "many authors write in English, sometimes out of necessity, and yet others write in Arabic in Arabic language publications in the United States" (ibid).

Salaita appropriately acknowledges and emphasizes the role of global patterns of mobility in complicating any attempt to ground the identity of an Arab-American literature, or indeed of any ethnically identified literature, on the author's cultural origins. But at the same time he does not fully develop the theoretical importance of this complicating factor, arguing that critics of Arab-American literature are "squabbling over terminology and intellectual credibility, at the expense of the literature itself" (425). Yet while this criticism is very important, it does not consider that the debate over the meaning and even the possibility of the category of Arab-American literature are symptomatic and reflective of the way in which the literature *itself* is being read. Salaita attempts to solve this problem by making a generic distinction, arguing that although poetry may be said to be "linked to various Arabic traditions, the Arabic novel was, and in many ways continues to be, heavily influenced by Europe. Arab-American fiction [. . .] is ultimately a decidedly American enterprise" (426). It would require a stretch to "rationalize Arab-American letters as directly connected to Arabic literature" (426). "A more useful methodology," according to Salaita, would "place Arab-American writing in its American context but locate Arab themes that distinguish it from other ethnic American literary movements" (426).

While aptly acknowledging the global dimensions of Arab-American literary production, Salaita nevertheless proceeds, at least in the case of this particular novel,[32] to delink it from its global or international connections and resituate it within the boundaries of "other ethnic American literary movements." Thus we are, it would appear, back in the familiar territory already mapped out above in the case of Alvarez and her critics: the cultural and historical complexities and specificities associated with the literary narratives of immigrant groups are bracketed off in favor of establishing an ethnic identity so as to facilitate their inclusion within an American literary canon and curriculum.[33] Arab-American literature comes to serve, for some of its readers at least, as merely one of the remaining pieces of unfinished business for U.S. multiculturalism. And yet it is evident at the same time that the still relatively small amount of critical scholarship devoted to Arab-American literature also invests its subject with an aura of alterity and an outsider status that set the latter apart from other immigrant/ethnic literatures. The immigrant status of this literature, as is the case with U.S. Latino literature and a text such as *The García Girls,* continues to supply its critics with a locus from which to critique dominant practices, outside as well as within ethnic literary studies. Nevertheless, the specific relationship to globalization of the Arab in Arab-American—especially when equated with Islam—adds to this locus an additional layer of complexity.

Such complexity becomes particularly visible if we consider the role the idea of testimonio plays here and how it differs, in subtle but important ways, from the one we have seen in operation in the case of Alvarez and her critics. Again, Salaita's arguments are telling here. Abu-Jaber, he writes, "recoils at the idea that Arab-American writing should be limited to the political arena or immigrant testimony. . . ." And he cites a remark by the author on this point: "'I've always had the sense that both poetry and belles lettres are somehow more accessible to Arab-American writers because of their 'testimonial' quality. It's as if we're somehow still at the stage where it's ok to write from lived experience but there's a perceived audaciousness about crafting or constructing a 'story.'" (433). Both Salaita and Abu-Jaber herself thus allow that much Arab-American writing functions and can be read as testimonio, but they caution against reducing the Arab-American novel to its testimonial function. Unlike a direct and immediate "writing from lived experience," the novel is, in this view, needed in order to give the Arab-American writer the fullest possible range of freedom to represent the complexity of Arab-American life—a complexity at constant risk of being reduced to stereotypical representation in post-9/11 America. The specific realities of globalization when it comes to the "global war on terror" and the rise of anti-Islamic demagogy make the conventional claims for testimonial immediacy, as exemplified above in the case of the readings of *The García Girls,* too potentially risky when it comes to depicting the lives of Arab-Americans—or so it is implied here. The realm of the real in the case of Arab-Americans cannot be safely quarantined outside U.S. borders, making a domestic testimonio as the genre best equipped, ironically, to keep the "real" at bay, a less viable option.

And yet at the same time the present political climate does not seem to permit that the Arab-American novel *not* be read as a testimonial. For one thing, even if the reduction of the Arab-American novel to its testimonial dimension is resisted, the implicit requirement that the authors of such novels themselves be Arab-Americans is not itself subject to any real question here. The urgency and authenticity of the ethnic/immigrant experience, if not vested in the form or genre of writing, must still be vested in the writer. This becomes if anything even more of a necessity when, as in the case of Abu-Jaber, the author is not herself an immigrant. Moreover, the U.S.-born Abu-Jaber, child of a Jordanian father and an American mother, writes, in *Crescent,* about characters that are Lebanese and Iraqi. The fact that she spent a couple of years of her childhood living in Amman is often cited in discussions of her work, as if to compensate for what might seem—from a "testimonial" standpoint—the tenuousness of her own "lived and immediate" connection to what she writes about. In her interview with Abu-Jaber, published in the winter 2006 special issue of *MELUS* devoted to Arab-American literature, Robin E. Field is especially careful to emphasize the author's organic connection to the Arab world, asking her, for example, to compare her own experiences of food while growing up in an Arab-American household to the culinary world of the Iraqi and Lebanese immigrants depicted in *Crescent.*

An anecdote related by Abu-Jaber herself on her official website sheds an additional and even more penetrating light on this politically overde-termined compulsion to testimonialize Arab-American writing. She had received an e-mail from a teacher in Texas informing her that *Crescent* had been banned in the state because of sexual content in four paragraphs of the novel and asking permission to teach the book with the offending passages blacked out. Abu-Jaber responded by leaving the decision up to the teacher but also informing her that if she chose to teach the novel with censorship, the students could access the author's website and read the offending paragraphs on their own. But it is not the attempt to censor the novel's sexual content that disturbs Abu-Jaber so much as its possible political and ethnic implications. Abu-Jaber writes on her website "that a friend, upon hearing about this debate, postulated that the real reason the students' parents are upset is because the book gives a human face to Arab Muslim people." "That," she writes, "might be the part of this that unnerves me the most—and like so many forms of subtle discrimi-nation and racism, we'll never really know if that's the case or not. The people who want the book banned may not even be entirely conscious of it themselves" (www.dianaabujaber.com).

That is, Abu-Jaber's Texan would-be censors were, she speculates, tes-timonializing *Crescent* and—though this is my inference here, not neces-sarily hers—*didn't like what they found there when it didn't confirm their preconceived notions about Arabs and Muslims and "why it is that they hate us so much."* *Crescent* had evidently frustrated certain readers by frustrating their own *a priori* desire to use it as a way to look into the mind of the "enemy." But this in turn means that Abu-Jaber's own charge as a writer has, in a sense, already becomes, whether she likes it or not (and clearly she does not), to frustrate that desire. To this extent, the critical perspectives aligned with the *a priori,* political burden of representation placed on *Crescent* tend to frame the novel itself as testimonial *despite* simultaneous efforts to disavow such a framing. The very fact that the novel depicts the lives of Arab-Americans, no matter its fictional form, already casts it as a testimonio given its testimony to the humanity and complexity denied to Arab-Americans by the anti-Arab and anti-Islamic ideology and demagogy of the "war on terror."

Although not as wary of the spontaneous testimonializing of Arab-American fiction as Salaita or Abu-Jaber herself, Carol Fadda-Conrey's critical reading of *Crescent* in "Arab-American Literature in the Ethnic Borderland"—to which I now turn in some detail—is symptomatic of the tension I have been describing here between the drive to incorporate Arab-American writing into the canon of U.S. ethnic and immigrant literature and the political urgency of resisting the homogenization and reductive ethnicizing this incorporation also threatens to impose. This tension shows itself as a latent ambiguity in "Ethnic Borderland," which both notes with appropriate alarm the fact that Arab-Americans have fallen "under an interrogative and suspicious light that conceals the complex makeup of this diverse group," (190) but at the same time insists that "Arab Americans need to be acknowledged as important contributors to the nation's racial, ethnic, and literary cartography" (187). The question as to whether such "acknowledgment" as full-fledged national subjects, given the ideological make-up of the nation in question here, does not come at the price of the very ethnic homogenization that feeds into the "why do they hate us so much" pathology cannot, it seems, be posed here, at least not consciously. The dislocalism that predominates in U.S. ethnic and immigrant literary studies—one which adjusts to globalization by carefully projecting "the real" beyond U.S. borders—sets the tone in "Ethnic Borderland" as it does in the case of the scholarship on Alvarez analyzed above. This translates into a reading of *Crescent* that, as with *The García Girls,* reduces it to its testimonial function at just those moments when the "real" threatens to disrupt the multicultural Americanization of the literary writing itself. Yet the specific political realities that overdetermine this dislocalizing imperative in the case of Arab-Americans post-9/11 cannot be conjured away in the same way that, say, the U.S. connection to the Trujillo dictatorship is lost to view simply by being read into *The García Girls* as domesticated "trauma." Here the "real" must be managed in a different way.

This is accomplished in Fadda-Conrey's study of *Crescent,* I argue, through recourse to a concept and figure that effectively does the work of testimonio here, that of—as indicated in the title of the essay itself—the "ethnic borderland." Arab-American ethnicity can, it seems, both preserve its cultural identity and yet remain complex by resituating itself within such a "borderland," one in which "interethnic gaps" can be "bridged" (193). The latter metaphor automatically evokes the name of Gloria Anzaldúa, whose work, from which Fadda-Conrey explicitly adopts her own critical paradigms, is, not coincidentally, often invoked in intellectual celebrations of testimonial narratives.

Thus, for example, Fadda-Conrey cites *This Bridge Called My Back,* the widely known volume edited by Anzaldúa and Cherríe Moraga: "We do this bridging by naming ourselves and by telling our stories in our own words" (193).[34] Such stories told in "our own words" then become, in the context of Fadda-Conrey's approach to *Crescent* and to Arab-American narratives generally, testimonies to the cultural vitality and resistance of Arab-Americans within a generally suspicious and hostile U.S. society. Drawing upon Anzaldúa again, Fadda-Conrey positions *Crescent's* protagonist, Sirine, as a "Nepantlera" or the living incarnation of an "Unnatural Bridge" able to overcome "the gulf between realities, perspectives, ethnic communities, and racial categorizations"—a process of which the novel itself, in Fadda-Conrey's reading of it, becomes a kind of testimonial allegory (198). But this is achieved at what interpretive costs to the specificities of the text and of history itself? The essay appropriately includes some broad historical information about Arab immigration into the U.S. and can be helpful in providing a corrective to the negatives images of Arab-Americans. However, this history is subordinated to the task of dislocalizing nationalist paradigms and does not inform the reading of the novel itself.

Take the example of food, a prominent theme in the novel. Fadda-Conrey casts Sirine and the Middle Eastern food she cooks at Nadia's Café, the LA restaurant where she works, as "bridges" facilitating the boundary-traversing of characters from many different Arab countries who gather there (196). At Nadia's "Arab regulars open up to her how painful it is to be an immigrant and she becomes a bridge between lost or abandoned cultures on the one hand and adopted cultures on the other" (ibid.). The love affair between Sirine and Han, the novel's two main characters, is also, it is noted, negotiated through food. Their relationship, argues Fadda-Conrey, functions as a bridge to a different kind of life, one in which Sirine embodies "the place [Hanif] wants to be . . . the opposite of exile" (198). In Los Angeles which for him is such a place of exile, Sirine functions, we are told, as Hanif's "Nepantlera," helping, him to imagine a different world in which being an Iraqi does not automatically invite suspicions of terrorism and fanaticism.

There is nothing, prima facie, untrue in this reading. As a food narrative—about which, in relation to Abu-Jaber more below and more generally in relation to food narratives, in chapter 4—*Crescent* certainly does, like many earlier immigrant texts, utilize the relative universality and neutrality of cooking and eating to stage its border-crossing. However, the analysis here does not go far enough in showing how the space of Los Angeles is reconfigured by the experiences of immigrants that have taken place and continue to take place *outside* the spatial boundaries of the United States. The concept-metaphor of bridges or borderlands, even as it sets in relief the legitimate need on the part of immigrants for refashioning and reconnecting their lives, simultaneously becomes a rhetorical mechanism through which the essay in fact *reaffirms* the national space of the U.S. as set off from and situated in opposition to the space of other nations—particularly those in the "desert of the real."

Consider that the ability of Sirine as well as that of the other characters to cross "borders" is here largely based on their ethnicity. Fadda-Conrey states that it is Sirine's "potential space on the hyphen" [Iraqi father, American mother], her straddling of the space between Arab and American, that "propels her into a constant state of border-crossing" (198). However, border-crossing as a way of negotiating one's identity in relation to the world is not a process requiring one to be an immigrant or someone with immigrant parents. As we shall see below, the novel itself shows how Hanif, as a little boy in Iraq, is compelled to transform his identity well before he leaves his home country. Moreover, when Hanif does embark on a crossing of the Iraqi border, he does so at considerable danger to himself. Fadda-Conrey only alludes to this by citing Hanif's exile in juxtaposition to the voluntary immigration of Sirine's uncle and father, something which, in her essay, is meant to serve as an example of diversity among the Iraqi characters in the novel. She posits border-crossing as entirely positive, an enabling experience for immigrants desirous of telling stories in their "own words," a telling taking place only once they are in the U.S. In effect, the circumstantial fact that Sirine should come to represent the opposite of exile to Hanif is made to serve as an instance of life in the "ethnic borderlands" here without a theory or narrative of what produces that exile in the first place. By furnishing such a "borderland," Los Angeles (and, by extension, the U.S.) is transformed from a place of exile to a place where exiles can find refuge. No doubt some exiles do find such places of refuge, but there is nothing privileged about LA or the U.S. in this respect, nor must such a refuge necessarily be found in an interethnic "borderland." (Think of Sweden, for example, home to many Iraqis exiled by the U.S. invasion and resulting war.) Not to mention the fact that, in Fadda-Conrey's reading of *Crescent,* at least, nothing is said about the role of U.S. policies in creating these exilic conditions. Los Angeles and the U.S. become one more version of that dislocalizing, "global yet local" place, mapped by a cosmopolitan narrative emphasizing mobility's positive attributes as opposed to those of uprooting and dispossession. In this framework, LA might indeed persist as a painful place for immigrants, but with the implicit understanding that more painful still is what the immigrants have left behind in their "homelands."

Such dislocalism becomes especially clear in Fadda-Conrey's reading of the following episode of *Crescent:* at one point Han decides to return from LA to Iraq to see his family, but at what he assumes will be great danger to himself, thinking it likely he will be killed there—this is pre-2003—by Saddam Hussein's agents. Although he eventually manages to escape and come back safely, Sirine, who has never been outside of the U.S., finds it hard to imagine the world that Han has left behind and is consumed with worry about what will happen to him. She considers talking to Cristóbal, one of her co-workers in the kitchen at Nadia's Café, and a refugee who escaped from his native El Salvador after losing his entire family in a death-squad firebombing, thinking that he would somehow be more likely to know what might happen to Han (196). The essay presents this as a further example of Sirine's role as "bridge," and of how Abu-Jaber's novel, by "blurring" the ethnic distinctions between Cristóbal and Han, also "changes the internal makeup of the ethnic borderland by bridging boundaries between different ethnicities residing within it" (ibid.). Here the essay distinctly contrasts places like Iraq and El Salvador with the U.S. as a place in which immigrants are potentially free to change their lives. According to this view, though life in the U.S. may be an unhappy one in which immigrants must face ethnic stereotyping, once they cross its borders and begin telling their stories, giving testimony to the horrors they have left behind, the U.S., as "ethnic borderland," becomes the place of healing.

This move is clearly intended to counter monolithic representations in which immigrants, especially Arabs and Muslims, are all seen as religious fundamentalists and potential terrorists or political extremists. And although the essay contains some historical facts about Arab immigration, the effect here is to deemphasize, if not render invisible, the role of the U.S. in supporting and carrying out terror in places like Iraq and El

Salvador. Rather than explore the connection made in the novel between the Middle East and Central America in historical terms, this reading not only overlooks history, but, as in the case of the above-examined readings of *The García Girls,* cultivates a deliberate ambiguity regarding history. Fadda-Conrey cites Anzaldúa in this context, according to whom "bridges become thresholds to other realities, archetypal, primal symbols of shifting consciousness" (192). But such "bridges" here seem to be lifted out of their material-historical conditions, reducing history itself to the real (190). The threat of being killed by military death squads in El Salvador or by Saddam Hussein's agents is securely situated outside U.S. borders, leaving the space within it free to become one in which the bridging and blurring of ethnic boundaries can occur at will, a local but global place, existentially "other" to an Iraq or El Salvador. The figure of the immigrant here, while delivered from the "desert of the real" in which it is situated by mainstream media and political discourse in the U.S, trades this deliverance for a less obvious configuration in which it is history itself that is relegated to the real, on the global peripheries of the U.S. Life in the "ethnic borderlands" is still a life lived in- and outside historical and political borders, even if the emphasis on ethnicity and cultural identity and hybridity has made them less visible.

This underlying structure of analysis and reading—a kind of ethnic/politico-historical economy—repeatedly foregrounds the cultural similarities and differences subsisting among the various characters in the novel. Fadda-Conrey points, for example, to the fact that the Arab students in the novel, from places as different as Egypt and Kuwait, "manage to negotiate the barriers" by "partaking in the kitschy Arab culture provided at the café, and through television in the medley of 'news from Qatar . . . endless Egyptian movies, Bedouin soap operas in Arabic and American soap operas with Arabic subtitles'" (195). But note here again how the space of the U.S. has already been posited as one in which the Arabs and Muslim who gather at Nadia's can negotiate their differences and partake in a global media culture. Moreover, the mixing and melding of popular cultures here becomes like the mixing and melding of ingredients in food preparation—the latter being, as already observed, a key and, so to speak, neutralizing metaphor in Fadda-Conrey's reading for the mixing of ethnic and cultural differences without loss of diversity. One particularly good example of this is her reading of the "Arabic Thanksgiving" scene in the novel, in which Sirine invites everyone to her home for a Thanksgiving meal. Fadda-Conrey suggests that the dinner scene highlights both the differences among the various guests but also the fact that these can be overcome by using food as a "major tool of communication" (202). During the meal, Gharab, a student from Egypt, says that his background dictates that men and women eat separately. This statement in the novel is met with a variety of reactions. Um-Nadia says that in her native Beirut it's boy–girl while the Iraqis in the group explain that in their experience men and women are separated only at large functions. For Fadda-Conrey, such a "mixing together of interethnic ingredients and identities ultimately sets the stage for new identities to emerge," making possible "new grounds for communication between different minorities" (202). The reading of food and dinner table conversation on Thanksgiving as a recipe for increased intercultural, even inter-Arabic awareness becomes a way of celebrating this scenario made possible in an American setting. This allegorizing reading of the scene sacrifices awareness of the novel's own very specifically cosmopolitan-Los Angeles setting, becoming, by default, its celebration. Nor does the essay problematize the politics and the sheer *availability* of food in metropolitan Southern California for those who can afford it. Such specificities can, it seems, disappear so long as food narratives stand in for stories of ethnic and national antagonism and the setting is a historyless "borderland."

Some Notes toward a Historical Reading

Meanwhile, Abu-Jaber's novel itself, while it certainly focuses a certain amount of attention on issues of immigrant/ethnic identity, cannot be so easily situated within the categories of U.S. multiculturalism and identity politics. The very least that can be said is that it furnishes us with the opportunity to think more specifically about American involvement in the Middle East and the interconnections between the U.S. and other parts of the world that propel global migration. As we have seen already, it also helps to shed a critical light on categories of analysis such as borderlands and border-crossing—categories that have become a kind of common sense in thinking about immigrant/ethnic fiction. As in the case of Alvarez and *The García Girls*, it is not my intention here to provide a comprehensive reading of *Crescent* but only to point out some aspects of the novel that run counter to the dislocalizing project of what is in effect a domestic nationalizing of Arab-American literature.

From the outset, the novel frames itself against a complex and shifting network of geopolitical and economic interests connecting the nations in the Middle East and the United States. The novel begins with a vivid description of a night in Baghdad, lit up by exploding rockets. But this is the 1970s, not the 1990s or the 2000s, and the rockets are not (yet) directly launched from U.S. planes or warships but "from the other side of an invisible border, from another ancient country called Iran" (13). This is experienced through the eyes of Han, a young man at the time of the Iran-Iraq war, seeing his "sister's face glow like yellow blossoms" in the light of the explosions and already dreaming of escape to some place where "his mouth will not taste like iron" (14). As the story unfolds we learn how, as a teenage boy in the early 1970s, Han had been hanging around the Eastern Hotel in Baghdad and had met Janet, the wife of an American diplomat. Janet asks Han to teach her Arabic, and they have a brief affair. But at one point she finds her way to Han's house in the city and convinces his family to send him out of the country, having become privy to the knowledge that Saddam Hussein would soon openly seize power. Janet offers to pay for Han's education, and his family decides to send him to school in Cairo for a few years. When he returns to Baghdad he gets involved in anti-government politics and writes diatribes against Hussein under a pseudonym. Ironically, it is his brother who is accused of writing them and is arrested under charges of being a CIA informant, while Han, under the protection of his family, is able to escape detection. After remaining in hiding for a time, Han is able to make a difficult escape from Iraq and go to England. There he eventually earns a PhD in literature from Cambridge, and, after a post-doc at Yale, he ends up as a university professor in Los Angeles.

In mapping out this personal trajectory, the novel draws us into a complex history, not of an "ethnic borderlands," but one involving a variety of nation-states such as Iraq, Iran, Kuwait, Israel, the United Arab Emirates, Egypt, Syria, the United States, and the United Kingdom—a political history of crisis and instability that has resulted, among other things, in an increased flow of (im)migrants both out of and into the Middle East. *Crescent,* that is, leaves the reader in no doubt that Han's flight from Iraq is directly connected to the U.S. involvement in the region. Abu-Jaber's depiction makes a clear connection not only between regional warfare as an impetus for the forced movement of peoples across and out of the Middle East but between both of these and the economic control sought by ruling local and imperial interests. The border-crossing narrative in the novel is not merely a story of Americanization but of movement along and across many regional and national dividing lines. The social and cultural realities normally associated with the life on the borderlands are depicted here in a narrative context of aggressive, directly economic, and political forces.

And the individualized details of Han's journey only serve to concretize this complex, global narrative context even further. Han, for example, tells the story of his own education as one of cooptation into a liberal form of Americanized consciousness. "I left when I was too young," he tells Sirine. "When I grew older, some of my school friends started saying that America was the great traitor, consuming goods and resources and never giving anything back but baubles, cheap entertainment . . . I began to understand" (292). But he acknowledges that his Americanization is, in many ways, not something that can be reversed: "America," he continues, "had also sent me to my new life and I couldn't imagine turning back from that. I wanted to be a writer, like Hemingway" (292). As a university student, Han has specialized in American literature—American transcendentalism, in particular—and has translated Whitman, Poe, Dickinson, and Hemingway into Arabic (30). (Han's departure from Iraq for Cairo, long a center of American intellectual and academic influence in the Middle East, and his eventual decision to study American literature could—though Abu-Jaber does not explicitly discuss this in *Crescent*—not unreasonably be inferred as something directly linked to American foreign policy, given the U.S. State Department's long history of funding American studies programs around the world and supplying these programs with publications that frame American literature as one great espousing of universal values.) Han's character serves as a particularly good example of the various ways in which the U.S. has produced consent and alignment with its policies, not least via the cultural exports (music, film, and television) that have played so powerful a role in advertising the American way of life. Only retrospectively does Han become aware of the degree of American influence and penetration of Iraq. He tells Sirine that "even after [she] spent so much money on me, I'd never learnt Janet's last name or what she and her husband were doing in my country. But she knew that Saddam Hussein was coming to power" (293). In these ways, the novel explores the contradictory conditions that have become part of his intellectual training and produced his thinking as a whole. Han eventually comes to understand how even the fact that he has been unable to contact his family back in Iraq, as well as the killing of his brother and ultimately his sister Leila are a part of this same history, inseparable from the same American influence over Iraq that has shaped his own life in seemingly more innocent and beneficial ways. Such aspects of *Crescent* ask us to tread with caution in thinking about borders and border-crossings as experiences whose impact and meaning are by nature progressive or emancipatory. Han's border-crossing has been brought about by the same kinds of policies and politics that have killed his family as well as resulted in the voluntary immigration of Sirine's father and uncle.

But just as significant here is *Crescent*'s ability to make us see how the experiences of Arab characters can have a profound, if hidden, effect within the domestic space of the U.S. itself, regardless of whether such characters make their way across its borders or not. The interconnections between the Middle East and the history of U.S. intervention in the region seem here to permeate the very space of Los Angeles, where most of the story takes place. *Crescent*'s other main character, Sirine, for example has never known anyplace outside of LA. But, even though she is part Iraqi herself, she seems at times susceptible to U.S. mainstream media narratives about Arabs and Muslims. This already adds a degree of ambiguity and tension to the experience of LA as an interethnic, Arab-American borderland. Sirine is initially suspicious of Han, not just out of conventionally jealous inhibitions when it comes to trusting a new lover but, as can be discerned, due to a preexisting climate of suspicion in the U.S surrounding Arabs and Muslims. This is abetted and complicated by the fact that Sirine's private, affective and associative links to the Arab world are second-generation and familial, and tend to make her feel inadequate next to Han and his Saudi student Rana, or even to the U.S.-born Nathan, who has been to Iraq and who seems to have a much better comprehension than does Sirine of the politics of the Middle East. Sirine anxiously imagines that Han would be more attracted to a foreign-born sophisticate like Rana and even worries that he might have a woman back home in Iraq. Her jealousies are spurred by an unknown woman's photo in Han's apartment (whom she later finds out is his sister) and further fueled by Um-Nadia's story of her own husband who had secretly kept another family back in Lebanon. But a good deal of this mistrust simply comes from the fact that, although she is Iraqi-American, she knows little about life in Iraq itself. And Hollywood, meanwhile, has done its share hereto in dissemination of an image of Arab and Muslim men as universally regressive when it comes to gender politics. Even though with each conversation with Han, Sirine's suspicions are proven wrong, it is still difficult for her to shed these doubts. On one foggy LA evening, while walking down the street, she thinks that she sees Han walking a few blocks in front of her with a woman, perhaps Rana. She hurries to his apartment expecting to confirm her suspicions by not finding him there, but she does, and he denies being the man she thinks she has seen. But clearly one could read the atmospheric fog here as itself akin to symbolic haze over LA, one in which the historical and political realities of the Arab world outside the U.S. loom in and out of sight.

Considered from this angle, the moments in the novel cited by Fadda-Conrey as examples of Sirine as "Nepantlera" facilitating the boundary-crossings of other characters take on a different dimension. Consider

again the part of the novel in which Sirine thinks that she might consult her Salvadorean co-worker Victor, hoping his own experiences of
resistance and repression might help her cope with her anxieties about
the dangers she imagines Han must be facing during his return to Iraq.
Sirine's thoughts, presented casually in the novel, invoke a history in
which U.S. imperial aims connect up regions as geographically distant as
Central America and the Middle East in a dangerous politics of guns and
oil. (Think only here of the Iran-Contra scandal of the Reagan years.)
While Sirine herself does not make these connections explicit, *Crescent*
itself certainly gestures at this, and her development as a character coin-
cides in part with her effort to penetrate the ideological and mainstream
media "fog" that obscures the deeper reality of empire. At the very least
she begins to understand how few reliable sources there are to help her to
make sense of the world that flashes before her eyes on television. Thus
the connection between El Salvador and Iraq casually invoked via Sirine's
uncertainties seems less a sign of the novel's concern with borderlands or
the blurring of interethnic differences than it is an attempt to map out
the narrative and subjective contours of an underlying, border-crossing
global system of oppression and exploitation. As much as it complicates
an essentializing system of separable ethnic identities, *Crescent* can be
read as moving both its protagonists and its readers away from an exclusively event-based history in which lurid figures such as Saddam Hussein
and indeed entire sections of the world are rendered as the real. It is in
the context of this alternative historical insight that the deeper realities
behind migration into the U.S.—also indirectly but vividly disclosed to us
in Abu-Jaber's novel—themselves escape the ideological "passion for the
real," revealing how national and historical borders in fact persist, even
after the American border itself has been crossed.

Experiences of food in the novel, while accorded a definite prominence,
are similarly recalcitrant to readings such as Fadda-Conrey's, in which
the mixing of cuisines becomes tantamount to an interethnic bridge. Such
mixing is not presented entirely affirmatively or without question in *Crescent*. Sirine, it is true, finds a certain satisfaction in making Arabic food
since she feels that it brings her closer to a sense of Arab identity that has
never been entirely accessible to her. But there is a politics to food here as
well, namely the question of where the ingredients themselves come from,
and to whom they are available in the first place. Consider once more
the Arabic Thanksgiving scene in *Crescent*, read by Fadda-Conrey as a
kind of culinary allegory of ethnic border-crossing. For this meal, Sirine,
set on preparing the kind of meal Han would have eaten as a child, has
researched Iraqi recipes. She has no problem finding the ingredients at

the Arabic shops in LA, but this is contrasted in the novel with the scenes in which Han thinks back to the way people in his village produced and sorted food. For example, Han recalls how the "women in his village were constantly at work clearing rice, threshing wheat, sweeping the floors" (218). And after age twelve the boys in the village were expected to work in the olive orchards, and Han would have had to do the same had he not been tutoring Janet. This juxtaposition of the work of growing, harvesting, and refining food alongside images of Sirine's experiences in her kitchen is instructive. Sirine "winds the bread dough in and out of itself, spins cabbage leaves, fat and silky, around rice and currents. She puts new ingredients in a salad, a frill of nuts, fresh herbs, dried fruit. Um-Nadia samples her salad, which tastes of ocean and beach grass, and she seems startled. "'It's good,' she murmurs" (131). Yet, as opposed to the women in the Iraqi village of Han's childhood, Sirine can play the privileged role of the tastemaker here, selecting her ingredients from the markets of a metropolitan cornucopia and experimenting with her own combinations of tastes and textures. Consider as well here the way in which, against the grain of a "culinary borderlands" reading of it, the dinner table scene here references the extreme conditions that effectively enforce the separation of the production and consumption of food. Gharab speaks about the growth of starvation in Iraq along with crime and prostitution, while Nathan elaborates, saying that "Iraq is suffering prefamine conditions and is still being regularly bombed by America" (219). Hearing this, "all get quiet and stare at their plates" (ibid.) "The real irony of today," he continues, "is that this kind of all-American feasting and gorging is going on when back home they're starving" (197). Here the consumption of food in the U.S. is directly linked to the starvation of others.[35] Nathan's comment in the novel can be read as an implicit criticism of the view that celebrating food as a medium for bridge-building and forging hybrid identities presupposes the seemingly limitless availability of food in the U.S. (and elsewhere) for those who can afford it. The availability of food to some is linked in our economy to its unavailability to others, especially to those who work to produce it.[36]

Even the romantic moments that Sirine and Han mediate with food are not immune from this critical awareness. A scene in which they share the same cup of Lipton tea prompts Han to observe the tea bag's colonial history: "a brown tea bag upon which great white empires are built" (79). Apart from drawing attention to the colonial networks through which food is produced and sold, this moment in the novel is also calling attention to the ways in which colonialism has brought the two of them together in Los Angeles. Projecting onto the latter the colors of a "borderland" where diverse people can meet and blend, while not false per se, too easily paints over the reality of LA as a space where people intersect because of the man-made disasters globalization has unleashed on people around the world.

In sum: celebrating the border-crossings in *Crescent* under the sign of a seemingly transnational, ethnic borderlands threatens to obscure a historical consideration of what is more often than not the fact that border-crossings are coerced. Representing the U.S. as a cosmopolitan and diverse place where ethnicities shed their distinct boundaries underplays the marginality and the extreme exploitation characterizing the really existing political and historical "borderlands" of this world, as places that exclude, repel, and decimate as many if not far more people than they bring together. And, as Abu-Jaber's novel itself, if read carefully, can tell us, even the most innocent portrayal of the U.S. as a "borderland" risks making invisible those who have crossed borders, and experienced the more sinister side of America, long before physically reaching the U.S. itself—if they ever do.

CHAPTER 3

American Sojourns

I. THE END OF TRAVEL?

"When travelers, old and young, get together and talk turns to their journeys, there is usually an argument put forward by the older ones that there was a time in the past—fifty, sixty years ago, though some say less—when this planet was ripe for travel. Then, the world was innocent, undiscovered and full of possibility," remarks Paul Theroux in his 1976 essay "Strangers on a Train" (130). This lament, a seeming constant in travel writing, a genre in which writers are given license to flaunt their journeys to the remotest places, expresses nostalgia for a bygone era when the elite traveler apparently enjoyed greater privileges. But it is a lament that seems to speak more loudly than ever to a globalized world of "time-space compression." David Harvey characterizes the latter as a condition produced by "the differential powers of geographical mobility, for capital and labour have not remained constant over time" (*Condition of Postmodernity*, 234). "Space," he goes on to say, "appears to shrink to a 'global village' of telecommunication and a 'spaceship earth' of economic and ecological interdependencies. . . . We have to learn how to cope with an overwhelming sense of compression of our spatial and temporal worlds" (240). The spreading dominance of capital reduces the spatial barriers erected between different parts of the world and shrinks the time it takes to get from one place to another. This has profound implications for travel writing. So, for example, descriptions of space in older travel narratives in which voyages were made by sea came alive when travelers reached their destinations and related the exotic scenes and peoples they beheld. But with the reduction of travel time, the risks of the voyage itself diminish and exotic destinations can no longer be magnified by the uncertainties and tedium of travel. Meanwhile, as a result of time-space compression, middle-class mobility expands enormously, making it seemingly impossible for travel writers to "report" new places, people, and cultures as, purportedly, their earlier counterparts had done.

Writing in 1976, Theroux was already clearly troubled by this drying up of travel, and had set about trying to resuscitate "every traveler's wish to see his route as pure, unique, and impossible for anyone else to recover" ("Strangers on a Train," 130). Some twenty-five years later, this lament over the end of travel is even more pronounced. In his introduction to the *Best American Travel Writing* collection for 2001 Theroux concedes that "it is not hyperbole to say there are no Edens anymore: we live on a violated planet" (xvii). Even the remotest corners of the world seem to have turned into tourist resorts.[1] Yet along with this truism, there also persists the need to affirm that, despite it all, if not travel then travel *writing* must still be possible. So, for example, in *Dark Star Safari* (2003), Theroux writes of a journey from Cairo to Cape Town saying that he wanted to see the "hinterland rather than flitting from capital to capital being greeted by unctuous tour guides" (3). But in his search for whatever remains of the "interior of Africa" as a "dark" place still concealing mysteries and intrigues there is a palpable sense, not only of imperial Victorian pastiche but of a nostalgia for the lost Eden of travel writing itself—especially for an American tradition which, only about half a century before, had been the province of authors such as Paul Bowles in *The Sheltering Sky* (1949) or *Their Heads Are Green and Their Hands Are Blue* (1963) and Saul Bellow in *Henderson the Rain King,* (1959).

But does the anxiety over a "planet . . . not ripe for travel" in fact contradict the continued possibility, even the success of travel writing?[2] While it is true that a genre that has historically taken upon itself the depiction of faraway worlds for the benefit of domestic audiences can no longer depend on the existence of these worlds in the same way, travel writing responds by engaging in a dislocalism all its own: here, the travel writer invokes the notion of the end of travel precisely as a way of preserving the genre itself. Thus it is that, in 2001, Theroux finds himself less concerned with the hope that real travel could be resuscitated (as he was in 1976) than with propping up the genre of travel *writing* itself. The latter, according to him, has now in fact become "a label for many different sorts of narrative" (*Best American,* xix). Travel writing is not the story of "a first-class seat on an airplane, nor a week of wine tasting on the Rhine" but of a "journey of discovery that is frequently risky" and "often pure horror" (xix).

The redirecting of Theroux's recuperative gesture toward the direct reconsolidation of the *genre* of travel writing rather than the activity itself is an expression, I propose, of a more general rhetoric of dislocalism pervasive within the genre as a whole. I will show how, much as in the case of the other genres that I have already discussed, travel writing has always produced a national imaginary of displacement with respect to the "global." But as travel writers contend with issues of globalization—in what is, for them, its most obvious manifestation, the pervasiveness of tourism—they increasingly become anxious over the loss of both the concept and the genre of travel itself. So travel writing must articulate ways in which travel can continue to furnish a viable form of knowledge in the context of globalization. In so doing, it dislocalizes its own practices while producing and contributing to the rhetoric of globalization. I will explore the way this dislocalism takes specific shape in three travel narratives. Two of them—Robert Kaplan's *The Ends of the Earth: A Journey at the Dawn of the 21st Century* (1996) and Mary Morris's *Nothing to Declare: Memoirs of a Woman Traveling Alone* (1989)—are nominally nonfictional works that report the writer's own journeys. The third, Paul Theroux's *Hotel Honolulu* (2001), is a novel—a less typical narrative form within the genre of travel writing, but notable titles include the aforementioned *The Sheltering Sky*, say, or Saul Bellow's *Henderson the Rain King*, or even Theroux's own novels such as the *The Mosquito Coast* (1981) and *Blinding Light* (2005). I will show, however, that Theroux employs the genre of the novel as itself a strategy of dislocalism to preserve the travel-writing genre in the wake of the so-called end of travel. I have chosen to analyze these particular works for a variety of reasons, among them because they capture the changes and accompanying anxieties not only of global capitalism but also of the more nuanced shifts that have occurred within the latter in the transition from the twentieth century to the twenty-first.[3]

But before addressing this, it should be noted here that the "end of travel" lament has long been a fixture in travel writing, taking on a variety of forms over time. Historically, the notion of travel is replete with nostalgia and what Ali Behdad calls belatedness. In *Belated Travelers* (1994), Behdad shows that the discursive practices of Orientalism were a significant aspect of the European travel writing of the nineteenth century. He argues that since the "European colonial power structure and the rise of tourism had transformed the exotic referent into the familiar sign of Western hegemony" travel writers exhibited nostalgia for the loss of an "authentic other," thinking they had arrived "belatedly" (13). Behdad points out that the "belated Orientalism of travelers such as Nerval,

Flaubert, Loti, and Eberhardt vacillated between an insatiable search for a counter experience in the Orient and the melancholic discovery of its impossibility" (15). Mary Louise Pratt further argues in *Imperial Eyes* (1992) that early European travel writers were in effect tools of colonialism. Even though they cast themselves as innocuous observers, they were part of the system of colonization and helped to produce a view of an "other" world that was easily dominated. So on the one hand, while furthering the aims of imperialism, they are nostalgic for a lost world that imperialism itself has worked to alter. Renato Rosaldo, in *Culture & Truth* (1989), speaks in this context of an "imperialist nostalgia" that "uses a pose of 'innocent yearning' both to capture people's imaginations and to conceal its complicity with often brutal domination" (70).

American travel narratives in the nineteenth century used the pose of "innocent yearning" in a slightly different way. Americans who wrote about their journeys abroad took on the project of producing Americanness and American identity not only in relationship to the exotic other but also against the "evil" powers of Europe, casting the American in an innocent position as against the European and thinking of themselves as a benign presence. For example, in *Typee,* Herman Melville describes the "natives" using familiar tropes of simplicity, purity, and the "savagery" associated with closeness to nature. But such images of nature and paradise are then counterposed to the French fleets that are, for Melville, symbols of colonization in the Marquesas. If the seeming impossibility of travel in the nineteenth and even the early part of the twentieth century could, as Pratt and Behdad suggest, be attributed to European colonization, then an analogous sense of impossibility in the neoliberal context can be said to result from the forces of globalization set in motion by a new, more all-embracing mode of economic and political hegemony that has come to be seen as synonymous with Americanization. American travel writing must then, inevitably, be read as marked by this phenomenon. To be sure, in many of Bowles's writings there are already narrative moments that call attention to the penetration of capital in the form of encroaching industrialization into the coastal towns of North Africa. But for Bowles, it was still possible to imagine an interior of Africa as yet relatively unpenetrated by capital. In *Their Heads are Green and their Arms are Blue,* for example Bowles writes about difficulties securing even the most rudimentary sleeping quarters at the more remote destinations to which he travels. *The Sheltering Sky,* made famous by Bernardo Bertolucci's 1990 film adaptation, tells a story of completely foreign experience, in which, for example, the protagonist Kit finds herself becoming, virtually by force, the fourth wife of a Berber, Belquassim. And her eventual escape back to Oran reads, unavoidably, as the return from a still-faraway world. However, by the time of Theroux's earlier writings such as *The Great Railway Bazaar* (1975), *The Old Patagonia Express* (1979), and *The Mosquito Coast* (1981) it has already become impossible to sustain the idea of such an interior. The first two works are dominated by a sense of disappointment as Theroux repeatedly fails to find any interior destinations that have escaped the spreading tentacles of tourism. In *The Mosquito Coast,* the protagonist Allie Fox goes to Central America and tries to develop "Geronimo," a utopian society "outside" of the U.S., which has lost its identity for him as it moves production offshore in pursuit of cheap labor. Fox, who has come to Central America embittered by what he sees as the flooding of a once "made in the USA" national market with foreign goods, is disheartened to find American multinationals such as Dole already there exploiting child labor for canning fruit. The fact that Fox's experimental society fails to immunize itself against a spreading corruption that has already stolen a march on travel clearly shows that for Theroux the idea that, with the globalization of capital, nothing counts as remote has already come home.

Critical studies on American travel writing have made much about the adventuresome nature of Americans. Ihab Hassan in *Selves at Risk* for example, considers travel writers to be questers looking to connect spiritually with things and people in the outside world. Others, including Justin Edwards (*Exotic Journeys*) and Terry Caesar (*Forgiving the Boundaries*) have argued that metaphors of travel and mobility remain crucial to the notion of American identity. I have already discussed such identity formation in relationship to the concept of immigration, something that could, in some sense, be loosely categorized as travel. In his introduction to *The Immigration Reader,* for example, David Jacobson argues that the (often proudly proclaimed) immigrant origins of Americans makes their rootedness in the land a more nuanced one, more akin to that of a traveler. Whereas for most other nations, travel is a transitory phase, for Jacobson, America never really exits this phase, and is better thought of as a state of constant "becoming" rather than of static "being."

But a form of travel that connotes a Euro-American, male, upper-class subject as its agent can also be thought of as the flip side of immigration, as its privileged and aristocratic form.[4] More importantly, if literary critics conceive of immigration as a voyage into the U.S. establishing a new national identity, travel writers use the concept of travel as a voyage *out* of the nation in order to do some of the same work. In this sense, dis-localist practices in the genre of travel writing are far more pronounced than in the genre of immigrant fiction. As I have shown in the previous chapter, the category of immigration ironically serves to shore up the discipline of American literature by dislocalizing it. Travel writers, however, appear much more invested in preserving the category of travel writing than their immigrant writer counterparts, if only because immigrant writing must follow on the act of immigration, whereas, in most cases, travel writers travel *in order* to write. Hence the quasi-autobiographical aspect present in both genres assumes much greater importance in travel writing and is in a certain way inseparable from the genre itself. Though criticism can point to a canon of immigrant fiction that is largely written by immigrants themselves, it is possible to write about others' immigrant experiences and still participate in the genre of immigration narrative. But it seems that one must write about one's own travel experiences rather than those of other people in order to remain a bona fide travel writer. Even if travel writers write fictions, it is their reputation as authors of nonfictional reportage that bestows the status of "travel writer." Consequently the anxiety of travel writers about the end or impossibility of travel has become far more pronounced, since it threatens the existence of the genre and its corresponding writerly subject position.

I argue, in fact, that because great distances increasingly need not be traversed and national borders need not be crossed in order to see something "different," travel writers must try to recreate that sense of distance or risk in order to reproduce what we might simply term the heroic narrative of travel. In other words, if the nineteenth century travelers traveled long distances in order to see the "other," late twentieth century travelers must travel in order to produce the perception that the very space that has been progressively annihilated through time/space compression still exists. The production of this respatialization counts as an especially pronounced instance of dislocalism, since not only travel itself, but an important site for the construction of an American identity, is at stake. Maintaining the distance between the U.S. and its "abroad" are reduced to the gesture of defending and redeploying the genre of travel writing itself.

I now turn directly to the three works of travel writing mentioned above: Kaplan's *The Ends of the Earth,* Morris's *Nothing to Declare,* and Theroux's *Hotel Honolulu.* In all of these narratives, dislocalism takes the following shape: intervening directly on behalf of what is in effect their own literary niche, these narratives proceed on the assumption that since American travel writing has always defined itself in relationship to the rest of the world, it is now in an especially good position to mediate this relationship in the context of globalization. In so doing, travel writing not only makes a case for its own viability as a global form of producing knowledge, but also, as part of the same rhetorical move, counteracts the threat of its own obsolescence as a genre.

II. ACTUAL TRAVELS AND FIRST-HAND ACCOUNTS
Robert D. Kaplan's *The Ends of the Earth: Journey at the Dawn of the Twenty-First Century*

In *The Ends of the Earth,* the narrative of a journey through Africa and Asia, Robert D. Kaplan, a widely known writer on foreign affairs as well as travel—and a favorite of American neoconservatives—claims that his objective is simply to document how the processes of globalization affect different parts of the world. Globalization, we are given to understand, is still an uneven process and only seeing its realities up close can make it something fully palpable. Along the way, between pausing to berate the unheroic behavior of tourists, Kaplan, like Theroux, evokes the notion of the "end of travel"—but in a distinct and decidedly more politicized context.

Yet I will argue that travel for Kaplan, even on these grounds, is not really necessary to his "ends," since, without real exception, his "first hand" experiences turn out to be perfectly congruent with the thinking of elite policy makers in the U.S., merely reiterating the already existing and dominant views about the places he visits. And in this process *The Ends of the Earth* speaks, more than to the "earth" itself, to a preexisting ideological drive to shore up the national boundaries of the U.S. by reexperiencing its national "others" as so many attempts, many of them doomed, to enter the U.S-dominated global order. Since travel writing as a genre has traditionally been premised upon travel from one nation into another, reporting the adventures experienced along the way as well as at the point of arrival itself, Kaplan stresses the continued importance of national boundaries so as to preserve the space of heroic travel and thereby the genre of travel writing as a whole. The difference between *The Ends of the Earth* and the genre with which it seeks to identify itself, however, is that its reported border-crossings are like visits to quarantined patients in a hospital, many of whom are not expected to survive. The "end of travel" is averted by traveling to witness what are, in more than just a geographical sense, "ends."

Acknowledging one of the major claims of the discourse of globalization, that nation-states are weakening and breaking down, Kaplan proclaims as his purpose the direct verification of this theory. The "first act of geography," he proclaims, "is measurement" (6). "I have tried," adds Kaplan, "to learn by actual travel and experience just how far places are from each other, where the borders actually are and where they aren't, where the real terra incognita is" (6). Of course, thanks to the first travelers, there are now maps that tell us perfectly well where the borders are, but maps themselves do not preserve the real sensations of distance, especially when these borders may be about to disappear. And so they must, it seems, periodically be tested by further, "real" travel.

In part, of course, Kaplan's travels are motivated by fear that what is happening around the world may have also begun to happen in the United States. "Many of the problems I saw around the world—poverty, the collapse of cities, porous borders, cultural and racial strife, growing economic disparities, weakening nation-states—are problems for Americans to think about. I thought of America everywhere I looked. We cannot escape from a more populous, interconnected world of crumbling borders" (6). Thus he makes much of the fact that two of the poorest sections of Abidjan, Ivory Coast, are named after American cities, "Washington" and "Chicago." Abidjan's Chicago is a "patchwork of corrugated zinc roofs" and cardboard walls where hotel rooms are "crawling with foot-long lizards" (19). But as the distance between the domestic and the African "Chicago" is reaffirmed, the effect is to remind us that the lines between poverty and wealth can just as easily be drawn between various parts of the U.S., as they can between, say, Washington, DC, and Abidjan.

Thus, crossing boundaries for the purposes of travel writing becomes more complex than simply going from one nation to another. So for example, about Pakistan, Kaplan writes that the country has a "growing middle class that increasingly has more in common with its American and European counterparts" than it does with the rest of the Pakistani population (326). While clearly aware that negative effects of globalization such as capital flight are not limited to places falling outside of U.S. borders, Kaplan's travels seem to project and spatialize a desire to keep such effects at a safe distance, seeking reassurance that, even though parts of the world such as Ivory Coast and Pakistan may have something in common with the U.S., they, unlike the latter, exist outside the magic zone in which (as the wishful thinking goes) economic collapse is unthinkable. Kaplan's becomes, in a sense, a journey aimed at exorcizing the demons of capitalist crisis from the U.S. and banishing them, as convincingly as possible, to other parts of the world. In *The Ends of the Earth*, dislocalism thus also takes the form of consolidating "crumbling borders" *through* the act of traveling. Travel thus becomes the privileged term here, preferable to other forms of mobility such as immigration, exile, or pilgrimage because it connotes a temporary state, a leaving one's home only in order to return to it. And indeed for Kaplan this return to the U.S., or in more general terms securing of U.S. boundaries against the ills of the world, is what has become the new—perhaps the last—purpose of travel. The metaphors of travel and mobility themselves become ways of upholding the identity of America according to its own official self-image—and to the ideology of its policymakers.[5]

In order to accomplish this, Kaplan (drawing upon the work of nineteenth century theorists such as that the German geographer Karl Ritter) employs the old notion of geographical destiny, that is, the theory that it is nature and geography that determine the destinies of nation-states. Those countries able to best control geographical and natural disasters, such as the U.S., stand a chance of remaining viable. And by extension those nations that have perfected American ways and know-how will fare far better than those that have not—which will therefore not survive. Geography allows Kaplan to adduce local reasons for the failures of nation-states.

> No longer a victim of slavers, Sierra Leone now became a victim of its location—a backwater attracting only dregs and mediocrities from Europe . . . The Atlantic that had once brought slavers and a rudimentary measure of contact with the Western World now brought almost nothing. Sierra Leone was a metaphor for geographical destiny. Sierra Leone helped [him] to feel what it is *like to be cut off*. (48)

For Kaplan *any* contact with Europe, even if it was the slave trade that had once made Sierra Leone's Freetown "a center of human activity," is far better than being "cut off." "The slave coast in Africa was ready to be re-colonized, if only the Portuguese, the Dutch, and the English would agree to come back with their money" (80). But being "cut off" is attributed entirely to a "geographical destiny" and a pernicious locality. For Kaplan locality (whether cultural or geographical) in Africa offers no respite against domination, nor it is a repository for ideas that might change the inequities of the world. If globalization is to take effect then this will require in principle that all remnants of locality be done away with, if "geographical destiny" should demand this. The only locality that is worth globalizing is that of the U.S. itself, since, according to Kaplan, it is the adaptation of American-style business systems and work habits that has led to the success of national economies in parts of Asia.

And yet Kaplan's travel narrative remains invested in the local in seemingly doomed places such as Sierra Leone because, as noted above, there is a simultaneous ideological need to vaccinate the U.S. against effects of globalization that threaten to make parts of it own local territory resemble Freetown. Though at times Kaplan seems to chime in with the standard neoliberal wisdom that attracting foreign investment is the only salvation for regions such as sub-Saharan Africa, the reduction of the local to the determinism of the geographical already implies the point-lessness of resisting the negative effects of globalization. But then, if the U.S. is threatened with a creeping "Africanization," as Kaplan at times warns his readers, might not this too be a question of "geographical des-tiny"? To evade such a logic, and to uphold neoliberalism's providential narrative of globalization against what is unequivocally the latter's dark side in places such as Africa, Kaplan must resort to a dislocated form of travel: only a traveler's eye-witness knowledge of the faraway and the "geographical" could hope to "prove" the abstractions of dominant neo-liberal policies without raising the question of the latter's responsibility for poverty and inequality *everywhere,* whether in Chicago, Abidjan, or Chicago, Illinois. One has to travel to *see* geographical destiny erasing national borders in order, in the end, to secure, ideologically, the one border that really matters: that of the U.S.

But there are intermediate zones between Africa and the Euro-Amer-ican West. Again offering first-hand eyewitness accounts, Kaplan cites developments in parts of Asia as proof that, due to their adaptability to and a willingness to learn from the West, they have won the position of active participants in global economic developments. As in other Asian tiger economies such as Singapore and Hong Kong, Kaplan observes the effects of rapid development in Thailand. Taking a walk in Bangkok he is "struck by the noise: the grinding, piercing high-pitched racket of power drills and jackhammers, along with churning ignitions of the three-wheeled tuk-tuks" (373). Bangkok's "twenty-four-hour-a-day activity" is a sign of how "many years of fast economic growth rates and cor-respondingly low birthrates . . . have worked to liberate Thailand from the horrors [Kaplan has] witnessed elsewhere" (373). By "elsewhere" he means, by and large, Africa. And he attributes this success to the fact that in Thailand "Western know-how was welcomed and then improved upon" (378). Similarly, a country such as Pakistan—where he sees a rela-tively sizeable middle-class and a market for foreign goods—serves as protection against African "horrors." But what, then, has become of the vaunted law of "geographical destiny" in these faraway places? Does the mere influx of money work in some "geographies" and not others? And why travel to them, if first-hand accounts only confirm what global finance-capital already presumably knows?

The answer, according to Kaplan, is that people in Asia possess far more intellect and ingenuity and are better able to control their geography than the apparently also culturally disadvantaged inhabitants of Africa. Not only, according to Kaplan, are Asians—unlike Africans—willing to Americanize themselves, but in most of Asia Kaplan finds people who are using what he terms "local ingenuity," a quality he attributes in turn to Asia's ancient, civilized past and its written languages. On his tour of the Rishi Valley in India, Kaplan claims to observe a form of illiteracy qualitatively different from illiteracy in Africa. He supports this with the frankly preposterous notion that since oral stories in India are based on written epics "thousands of years old" this "allows illiterate villagers [to] tap into a well developed, literate cultural environment, whereas in much of sub-Saharan Africa, local languages have been written down only in the last century" (365). But assigning a qualitative value to literacy does nothing for those who do not and cannot have access to a literate environment if they cannot read. In fact, even if a traditional literary culture exists within certain national boundaries, this works only to emphasize the barred access of the illiterate to a literate environment.

And in any case, even if we are to believe that ancient languages and civilizations, and the "local ingenuity" they purportedly give rise to are what is going to save Asia, this hardly supports the view—one Kaplan also claims to advance—that the only way to economic stability is through capital investment. His tour of Asia, and the Rishi Valley in particular, seems to have as its central ideological purpose allowing Kaplan to affirm that a still tribalized Africa is simply not worthy of such investment. Reverting back to his geographical and environmental determinism, Kaplan writes the following of his trip through civil war torn Liberia:

> Though I had seen no soldiers, let alone any atrocities or juju spirits, an indefinable wildness had set in. It occurred to me that the forest had made the war in Liberia. I have no factual basis for this, merely a traveler's intuition. The forest was partly to blame . . . teenage soldiers [broke] into bridal shops of Monrovia, dressing up like women-cum-juju spirits, and going on rampages that ended in ritual killings. (27)

In claiming to find a causality linking the forest, rampages, ritual killings, and the war, Kaplan takes an imaginative leap that effectively allows him to refer to without having to state the blatantly racist idea that Africa is simply too uncivilized. An "indefinable wildness" seems, on the one hand, purposefully ambiguous—is it the forest or the Liberians, or both, that are wild?—but in the end it simply renders Liberia as helpless against a geography and nature which can hardly be blamed on past colonization or present-day exploitation by global capital. The operant rule for the traveler/writer here seems to be: where global finance and its state policy makers have already determined investment to be warranted (Asia) culture (in the guise of "ancient languages and civilizations") becomes something the traveler can claim to witness "first hand"; where such investment has been essentially ruled out (Africa), nature (in the guise of geography and the environment) takes over. Africa may be, for Kaplan, "the inescapable center"(5) of humanity—in a purely paleontological sense—but he travels there only so as to find ample reasons to continue to consider Africa as socially peripheral.

Kaplan states that his goal in the travels recorded in *The Ends of the Earth* "was to see humanity in each locale as literally an outgrowth of the terrain and climate in which it was fated to live" (7). But, as I have tried to show, the idea of the local means many, often-contradictory things for Kaplan. Locality can be the wrong kind of locality, as in the case of Africa, where it works to repel capital, or it can be the right kind, as in the case of Asia, where it works in the opposite way. Moreover, the evocation of the local—in the case of Africa, probably (as Kaplan sees it) beyond saving—allows Kaplan to warn the U.S. against "Africanization" (the turning of Washington, DC, into Washington, Abidjan) without pointing to the connections between the U.S. and global capital generally and conditions in Africa. Kaplan's travel narrative works to separate the world from Africa, implying that cultural values separate Africans from Asians as well as from Americans. In this regard, Kaplan has only to draw on the familiar domestic discourse that attempts to pin much of the ills of the underdeveloped parts of the U.S. on African-Americans, and presents Asian-Americans, on the other hand, as model minorities, willing to work in desperate conditions for low wages. Implied as well here is the idea that the culture of the U.S. would never let conditions deteriorate to the African levels. In an insidious sense, Kaplan travels to Africa, not, as travel writing has traditionally done, to encourage others to follow in his footsteps (even if only in fantasy) but so that the rest of us can be spared this experience. He goes, so to speak, for the last time, but go he must—showing how the "end of travel" itself requires a form of travel.

It is interesting to note, in this connection, that Kaplan refers to the experiences that produce his "first hand accounts" (upon which rest the entire credibility of his book) as "actual" travel. Globalization, and the ideological task of keeping Washington, Abidjan, safely distant from Washington, DC, now require not only that travel in the traditional sense be possible—so as to continue to locate an exotic other to help secure the national identity formations of a continuously expanding U.S. global presence—but that it continue to involve adventure and risk. Without these, the "first-hand accounts" themselves lose value. Crossing national boundaries to see and document "novel" things is not enough. Kaplan must go about crossing different kinds of borders, while also insisting that older political borders still matter, in order to create this sense of adventure and thus to preserve the heroic form of travel. This requires that he take a jab at how others travel. He says that one does not learn much traveling in an "air-conditioned four-wheel drive Toyota Land Cruiser" which, he says, is the "medium through which senior diplomats and top Western relief officials often encounter Africa," as though "suspended high above the road and looking out through closed windows you may [actually] learn something about Africa" (25). He goes on to say that in a "public bus, flesh pressed upon wet, sour flesh, you learn more"; and in a "bush taxi" or "mammy wagon," one may learn even more, but it is on foot that one learns the most. For here, he writes, "you are on the ground on the same level with Africans rather than looking down at them. You are no longer protected by speed or air-conditioning or thick glass. The sweat pours from you, and your shirt sticks to your body. This is how you learn" (25). In other words, "actual travel," the kind from which one "learns," requires some risk and discomfort. Or stated yet more precisely: adding discomfort and risk—and therefore credibility—to an account of Africa that in no way otherwise differs from what the "senior diplomats and top Western relief officials" themselves have to offer requires a kind of retro-fiction called "actual travel."

Those who eschew this risk and discomfort and thus refuse to "learn" what official ideology already tells them are mere "tourists." With undercutting commentary, Kaplan describes Anatolia, the Caucasus, and other stops on his own end-of-travel tour, as "toxic holiday camp[s] for the working class on seven-day package tours" (147). But Kaplan is not averse to the idea that "actual travel" might also afford a kind of excitement and self-fulfillment. And, though the possibilities of finding such fulfillment in Asia and Africa are far greater than in the U.S. or Europe, even parts of Africa and Asia can no longer continue to afford this, so he must find places that he considers even more remote—as well as look and act the part. As Kaplan observes in his "marble-and-glass 'efficiency' hotel" in Bangkok: "I crowded into the elevator with several men in expensive lightweight suits. One held a Compaq Contura in his hand . . . With only my backpack and batch of blank notebooks and Bic pens, I suddenly felt antiquated" (371). Again, Bangkok, for all its economic progress—lauded by Kaplan when it is a question of abandoning Africa to its "geographical destiny"—has lost something for him, specifically the traditional privileges of "actual" travelers. Kaplan admits that "the poorer and more violent the country, the greater the social status enjoyed by a foreign correspondent. In Bangkok, a journalist was nothing compared to an investment banker" (371–2). Thus he offhandedly concedes that the distinction between travel and tourism has more to do with the will to take risks, suffer discomfort, and "learn"; the economic progress, development, and investment, of which the marble hotel is indicative, cheapens his own travel experience. Since Bangkok does not afford him an "actual" enough experience, Kaplan must in fact travel to places that seem to have been left out of the processes of globalization—but where, unlike Africa, the human catastrophe for the moment does not interfere with a strictly nonpolitical form of risk. Witness Kaplan, then, in the Hunza Valley (under the control of the Pakistani government), where he takes an immediate liking to a traveling couple, Dave and Lynn. The latter have come here after unsatisfying experiences in Kuala Lumpur, where, Kaplan tells us, they saw about "a hundred cranes" outside their window. In India they saw haze over the Taj Mahal, and "they told sad tales of deforestation in Nepal" (320). The Hunza Valley, even if it benefits from "irrigation and reforestation programs," shows none of the signs of the development that elsewhere win Asia praise from Kaplan (320). Here, in fact, we have an especially poignant form of dislocalism: Kaplan must travel to—and write about—the Hunza Valley so as to endow his frankly neoliberal views of Africa and Asia generally with the heroic, first-hand "actual" aura of the true traveler. He approvingly quotes Dave as saying "it's dangerous but what the hell . . . I'd rather die on a glacier than be mugged in a western city or be killed in a suburban car accident" (319). Kaplan goes on to relate that "Dave and Lynn were getting the equivalent of a classical education free-of-charge simply by traveling and studying the ancient spoken languages in these valleys" (320). He is "delighted" by their "stories of being awakened in the middle of the night by yaks outside their tent in Tibet, and feels like hugging [Lynn]" when she tells him that she writes her free-lance stories on note-pads rather than bringing a laptop, which in any case probably would not work in places like Hunza Valley. Kaplan himself says that he has stopped bringing a computer on his trips and that the result is "liberating" (320). That is, the lack of technology, which, in other parts of the book, he presents as detrimental to development, nevertheless becomes "liberating" for him.

The same dislocalizing logic occasionally even informs what is otherwise Kaplan's grim, quasi-Malthusian African narrative. In Freetown,

Kaplan stays with a friend, Michelle, who works as a diplomat in a foreign mission. He describes Michelle's life in Sierra Leone with a twinge of envy, terming a dinner party she hosts as "charming" because, he says, "here was a diplomat who, neither an ambassador nor even a chargé d'affaires, was nevertheless able to attract some of the most important people in the nation to her house where a fine meal was prepared with the assistance of a housekeeper" (55). "The style in which Michelle was able to live in Freetown and the rank of officials she was able to attract were," he concedes, "indicative of the gap between a wealthy Western land and a poor African one" (55). However, the very gap that makes Michelle's dinner party "charming" for Kaplan, is elsewhere charged with having made even old-style colonialism essentially too good for Africa. The one redeeming feature of "ends of the earth" such as Sierra Leone is that they afford the possibility of self-fulfillment for Western travelers and diplomat-adventurers such as Michelle: "To most people, especially to Washington careerists, the idea of being a middle- or low-ranking diplomat in a place like Sierra Leone would represent the ultimate in underachievement, unless it came very early in one's career" (57). But Michelle is to be envied for having a job "far more stimulating intellectually than almost any job a capital like Washington or London had to offer" (57). Here the "learning" that distinguishes the tourist from the traveler takes an insidious form indeed. Kaplan quotes his diplomatic friend approvingly: "Waking up each morning in a place that's on the verge of anarchy provides a unique insight into humanity. There are never any lulls" (57).

Here we appear to have "traveled" a long way from Kaplan's notion of crumbling borders and the experience of seeing America everywhere. But keeping to the official creed of neoliberal globalization is only half of Kaplan's mission in *The Ends of the Earth*. The sameness and sanctity of "America" must, as in virtually all American travel writing, be reaffirmed, and thus there must always be created a clear dividing line between the U.S. and the rest of the world. It is this ideology and accompanying narrative structure that allows Kaplan to look with a certain favor on the idea of keeping some nations on the "verge of anarchy" because, thanks to U.S.-led global capital, it is only that way that they can provide a stimulating education for the likes of American "actual travelers" such as Kaplan. Kaplan reproduces a worldview in which the only answer to poverty and inequality is the influx of capital and then, in a typically dislocalizing move, goes on to invoke the notion of local culture and geography—the *sine qua non* of "actual travel"—as placing severe limits on the usability of that capital. It is just in this way that the real forces of globalization threaten to undermine the genre of travel writing, while the *ideology* of globalization requires the genre's perpetual continuation. Dislocalism is called forth to solve the contradictory task of proclaiming the crumbling of borders while simultaneously reconsolidating them through the act and the discourse of travel. Without the risk of poverty and even anarchy, the risk of travel itself cannot be safeguarded, a risk without which, in turn, a certain deeper risk to the integrity of American identity formation is brought into play—a dislocalizing set of moves that, as I shall show, unfolds in a different way in Mary Morris's memoirs, *Nothing to Declare*.

III. INTERRUPTING DOMESTICITY
Mary Morris's *Nothing to Declare*

Women travel writers have long contended with the fact that that travel has traditionally been and remains a primarily male genre. For example, Flora Tristan (*Voyage to Brazil*, 1824), Maria Graham (*Letters from India*, 1824), and Mary Elizabeth Crouse (*Algiers*, 1906) write at some length about how travel for women poses special problems. The genre of women's travel writing, as Mary Louise Pratt has argued, both duplicates and interrupts the various strategies that male travel writers deploy.

Mary Morris, in keeping with this long tradition, attempts, like male travel writers, to reproduce a sense of risk in her writing. Yet, ironically, as a woman she is in some ways better able to exploit the sense of danger and fear so valued by her male counterparts in the genre, simply by tapping in to the common belief that women are at far more risk while traveling than men. But since time-space compression and the corresponding industrializing and globalizing of travel have made it a relatively risk-free activity, Morris, like Kaplan, finds herself in the paradoxically dislocalized position of having to reinsert a risk factor in order to reproduce the genre of travel writing itself. The title of her book—*Nothing to Declare: Memoirs of a Woman Traveling Alone*—already points to this quite blatantly with its reference to a solitary woman abroad and the evocation of going through customs at a border crossing, always an experience fraught with a certain tension and anxiety.

At the same time, like other contemporary travel writers in the U.S. faced with the effects of globalization, Morris comes under ideological pressures not only to resuscitate "travel" in its heroic form but to maintain the kind of neat and clean separation between "here" and "there"— in this case the U.S. and Mexico—that has traditionally made travel narratives an effective dislocalizing medium for reproducing and redrawing discourses of national identity. As I will show, Morris accomplishes this in large part by redeploying some of the more conventional moves in women's travel writing.

Specifically, I will show that, for Morris, a rather old theme in women's travel writing—the interruption of the narrative of domesticity—becomes a way to reaffirm national boundaries. More precisely, I will demonstrate that, while, for women, international travel typically signifies an escape from home and domesticity, in *Nothing to Declare,* it is the same inter-ruption-of-domesticity narrative that furnishes a way of *rearticulating* a U.S. nationalist framework. If Kaplan travels in order to articulate the perniciousness of various national localities as a result of their adherence to non-Western ways, for Morris, the locality of Mexico is, on the surface of things, a refuge from a life grown weary in the hyper-Westernized, overcivilized setting of contemporary New York City. In search of respite from a "terrible feeling of isolation and a growing belief that America had become a foreign land" Morris goes in "search of a place where the land and the people and the time in which they lived were somehow connected" (11). Reading the word "foreign" here as connoting simply the effects of loneliness and alienation, one finds oneself on the familiar ground of a kind of pastoral, with Mexico and its "land and people" standing in as the warm and welcoming peasants and shepherds. But "foreign" also must clearly be read as referring to the perceived denation-alizing of New York and the U.S. in general, thanks to immigration and other effects of increased globalization. In this sense, Morris's narrative suggests other than merely pastoral motives: home has become "foreign," therefore it has become necessary to travel to something even more "for-eign" so as to redomesticate and safeguard the homeland.

Morris, her locus of narration already Mexico, tells us that in her apart-ment in New York she is surrounded with "familiar things"—"mementos from friends," and pictures of her grandmother's family and of her par-ents (41–42). But, she relates, "all of this is my memory now . . . I have brought nothing to recall my former life, none of the smells or textures or tastes or faces or roads or landscapes I have known before" (42). In other words, Morris declares herself committed not only to interrupting a familiar domestic narrative but also to making sure there is a definite break between her life in the U.S. and in Mexico, including geographical differences. All of this, as we might suspect, is a prelude to the confes-sion of another kind of domestic estrangement: "there was a man named Daniel who had left me the year before. . . . He was one of the reasons for my going to Mexico" (50). We also find out that she has had another lover in New York who hit and abused her. Though seeking the risks and adventures of a "woman traveling alone," it emerges that home in New York for Morris has become a danger zone of another kind. She is trying to heal from failed and abusive relationships and she imagines Mexico to be the place that can help her realize this.

Thus—and here again she is initially unlike the declaredly dystopian Kaplan—Morris imagines Mexico, at the beginning of her journey, as a faraway place where unfamiliarity and foreign ways can work to restore the sense of domestic happiness and security. But to make a new home in a strange, distant place requires, for the pastoral traveler just as much as for Kaplan the cynical voyager through the underworld, that the stigma of tourism be carefully avoided. Here Morris makes the anti-tourism moves familiar in travel literature. So, for example, she chooses not to stay in Mexico City because it is too overrun by tourists and settles for a supposedly less globalized (but, as any traveler to Mexico will know, also heavily populated by U.S. travelers and visitors) San Miguel de Allende. She finds a place to live in a neighborhood called San Antonio where very few Americans lived because it was "too far from the center of things" (8). So, though in a less pronounced way than Kaplan, Morris finds that simply crossing national borders is not enough to feel that she has traveled and that her life in the U.S. is safely far away.[6]

Though Morris tells the reader that she desires to go to Mexico for its supposed power to heal her alienated self, she immediately begins to underscore her fears of the place as well. Thus, "San Miguel de Allende is not a dangerous place, not a threatening place," she insists, but even while adding that she had "never been more afraid in [her] life than [she] was in San Miguel" (25). For Mexico, while a setting for a pastoral idyll, is also a land of predatory men for Morris. There are numerous points in the book at which Morris imagines being pursued by unknown male assailants. For example, while taking a swim at night, she suspects she is being pursued by two men. She thinks to herself that it "would be easy for them to pluck [her] from the sea" (102). She decides to swim "into the darkest water of all" and stays there "until they were gone" (102). These kinds of fantasies likely strike a chord with those of her readers who have already been caught up in the narrative imagining of Mexico as a dangerous place, especially for women. Again, as with Kaplan, this element of fear and risk is somehow required to certify that it is travel, not merely tourism, that is the subject of her story. Citing Camus, Morris claims that "what gives value to travel is fear" (25). But more than simply valorizing Morris's travel narrative, the surplus fear and danger available to women travelers are extracted from the U.S. and placed safely within the borders of Mexico. Morris recounts her romantic past in New York while she is in Mexico as if she is trying to remember a dream: "Sometimes at night I lie awake and try to remember a certain person's features. Or his scent . . . And I try to piece him together, like a jigsaw, but I cannot find his substance" (42). And yet, these sorts of recollections seem almost outside the substance of her book if only because, as she says, she is making an effort to forget that life. What amounts to her domestic misadventure in New York manifests itself only at the margins of her Mexican solo quest as what she calls her "ghosts." But these ghosts soon become pronounced in the story in unanticipated ways.

Morris's effort to leave behind her broken relationships increasingly breaks down because she must confront them again in the course of her relationship with a Mexican woman named Lupe. Lupe, with whom Morris forms her closest relationship in San Miguel, lives near her house, running errands for her and taking care of other domestic chores. "I went to Lupe," writes Morris, "for things I needed. For washing clothes I could not get clean, for cooking rice" (27). Lupe herself, meanwhile, has been in a relationship with a man, José Luís, whom she rarely sees. She has seven children, and one of her daughters, it turns out, is expecting a child with a man who is also an absentee father. Morris's living situation assumes, then, representational shape as the direct contrast to Lupe. Morris rents a house that "has a living room, kitchen, and small patio" in addition to two bedrooms and a balcony. (8). Lupe on the other hand, lives in a small place with several children, a place "infested with flies" and with no place to wash and clean. Though neither Morris nor Lupe has a stable love life, Morris portrays Lupe's state of abandonment as the consequence of her own looseness in relations with men. Lupe, it turns out, was married before she met José Luís, and has children both from him and from her former husband. José Luís, while still paying Lupe occasional visits, sees another woman as well. In fact, it is unclear exactly how many children Lupe has by each man. At one point teary-eyed Lupe tells Morris that José Luis's other "señora" is having another child, but follows this with the rueful observation that "a man isn't worth crying over" (127).

Aware that Lupe (at least in Morris's depiction of her) fits into widely held North American views regarding the gender relations of Latin American men and women in general, Morris writes that she found herself "wondering if [she] felt judgmental" (33). But Lupe is disturbing to Morris's Mexican interlude in a still more profound way, for, by bringing into sharper focus those troubling aspects of domesticity that Morris would rather keep relegated to a ghostly netherworld, Lupe also makes it harder for Morris to draw a clear borderline between her lives in the U.S. and Mexico. Here the dislocalizing impulse of *Nothing to Declare* emerges into fuller view: the escape from the domestic misadventure in New York into the hoped-for self-reintegration of her Mexican solitaire only confronts Morris with a domestic scene that suggests how lucky she has been all along. The stage is now set for shunning Lupe's world and returning to the relative haven of superior gender politics and domestic possibility in New York—for women like Morris, that is. Leaving "home" is merely a way of securing it more firmly against the possibility of real dislocation and critique. But in the age of globalization and time/space compression, the fiction of "travel" becomes more and more necessary to this domestic restoration.

It is true that, on its surface, the relationship that Morris shares with Lupe appears to make a case for bridging the differences between two women who do, after all, share similar experiences with men. Perhaps Mexico is not so "far" from the U.S. after all. For example, Lupe finds Morris crying and, with sisterly concern, chides her gently with her refrain that "it was no good to cry over a man" (19). Later, while attending the celebrations for the Mexican Day of the Dead, Morris asks Lupe to bury her in the Mexican part of cemetery since the part where the Americans were buried was "all fenced in, well gardened and kept up, but with no visitors and no one bringing flowers" (187). But though Morris here seemingly desires a connection with Mexico, on a more fundamental plane she continues trying to rebuild that fence. Here the reader is reminded of Morris's depiction of a hole in a city wall through which poor people were crossing into more well-off areas and which had been cemented closed with "shards of U.S. soda pop bottles . . . to keep the poor people away" (89).

It is through Lupe that Morris confronts the ghosts of her own past relationships with men, suggesting, perhaps, that Morris did have to leave home in order to rediscover it. She confesses to Lupe that she would like to have both a husband and children. Lupe jolts Morris out of her ghostly relation to her own domestic troubles. But there is a subtle move to exclude and separate the two worlds at work here, outside the sisterly bond. Lupe's woes—broken relationships, little money, more children than she can take care of, a house hardly adequate for living—are all symptomatic of the condition of poor and working women generally under the globalized, neoliberal regime that has more and more placed the boundaries of nations in question. Lupe, for example, tells Morris: "José Luis gives me fifty pesos a day to feed my children. It is not enough. I barely make do. That is why I work for the señora of the Blue Door

Bakery" (33). It is precisely this kind of low-wage work, routinely performed by women in the informal sector, that has made their exploitation even greater than in their work as part of a formal workforce. Historically, even in the formal sector, women have performed temporary and low-wage labor. Furthermore, Mexican women perform this kind of informal labor even in the U.S., often in the employ of women like Morris. But these forces do not enter into Morris's imaginary, Lupe's exploitation here being linked largely to gender and to her experience with Mexican men. This is because, if they did enter into the equation, they would complicate the dislocalized arrangement that restricts them safely to the Mexican side of the border, where the well-intentioned feminist traveler from the north can regard them from a safe distance.

In effect, the character of Lupe makes it possible for Morris to attribute a national and cultural character to conditions for women that are class-based. "It is difficult for men and women to get along," says Lupe, with an ethnographized naivety that more easily shrugs this all off as a simple fact of (Mexican) life (33). "Mexican men," proclaims Lupe, "are either too serious and no fun or fun and lighthearted and not to be trusted" (128). And Morris needn't tell the reader whether she agrees with this native wisdom in order for the global conditions of gender and class to be safely recontained across the border.

Morris's impetus to project bad gender politics onto Mexico also takes other forms in her narrative. For example, she finds herself getting bored in a relationship she initiates with a Mexican man, Alejandro. He seems to be the opposite of José Luís in terms of his relationship to domesticity. Alejandro largely takes care of the domestic chores and even proposes marriage to the author. But Morris writes that she grew bored with his domestic solicitude: "I had been with men where I had to do all the work and I had hated that. . . . But the opposite wasn't satisfying either, and I felt in my relationship with him more like a man than a woman" (179). Leaving aside for the moment the possibility of reading this relationship in terms of the politics of racial hierarchies, this episode suggests that, while Lupe's relationships with men are framed within *machismo*, Alejandro (North-)Americanizes Morris's desire to be "more like . . . a woman." Is there a possibility given these parameters to imagine Morris having the same opportunity of domestic happiness in New York?

Lupe's role as foil to Morris's dislocalized domesticity works in other ways as well. If Lupe brings her to the realization that she wants a husband and kids and at least the part-time duties of a housewife, this hardly enforces on the author/narrator a deeper understanding of the latter category. In a discussion about the effects of machinery on the worker in the first volume of *Capital*, Marx explains how machinery was "transformed into a means of increasing the number of wage laborers by enrolling . . . every member of the worker's family without distinction of age or sex" into the workforce (517). This meant the usurpation of the free domestic labor of the women, a cost that would otherwise have to be covered by capitalists. It is this particular relationship of women to domesticity (where their labor is considered a natural resource) that Morris wants to interrupt through her Mexican sojourn. And yet this interruption is *itself* dependent on Lupe's labor, who, like many women, while working for free in her own household is also driven by her economic circumstances to do odd jobs for Morris and take care of Morris's apartment while she is away touring the rest of Mexico. The conditions that force women to work as domestic servants hardly leave room for the kind of familial environment so desired by both Lupe and Morris.

This is a set of conditions that *Nothing to Declare* cannot confront and so displaces through a cultural-essentializing that in turn masks itself behind an abstract gender politics. Again, by implying that Lupe's situation is the result of the *machismo* of Mexican men—after all, Morris pays Lupe for her work, while José Luís merely takes from her—Morris can reproduce the distance between the U.S. and Mexico, interrupting the domestic misadventure that haunts her wherever she goes. In this context, a fantasy Morris has in which she imagines herself as a bird that flies to her grandmother's Ukrainian village is worth quoting at some length:

> I perch above the house. I drink black tea, suck sugar in my beak, and munch on dried bread, and when it is time for them to leave for America, I follow. I fly. I must go and build my nest . . . A male finds me and we mate, almost in midair. He hovers over my back and our wings enfold . . . I am an eagle woman, a builder now, layer of eggs, perched on high, a woman of both heights and heart. I lay two perfect eggs . . . My mate disappears, but for forty-two days I sit and wait, and then they hatch. I care for these young until the fledglings go. And then I am free to fly to new places. (245)

The eagle seems to be a reference to Quetzalcoatl, an Aztec god who, according to legends, created life and would one day return to reclaim the lost empire—and a symbol evoked by a range of emancipatory movements in Mexico and elsewhere.[7] This fantasy, occurring to Morris as her departure back to the U.S. is imminent, is one of freedom in domesticity and also reasserts her view of Mexico as an ancient and legendary place that has helped her to heal. In its structure, it shares certain similarities with Lupe's life: men appear to produce children but then disappear.

But this fantasy is unavailable to Lupe for she is unable to fly free. Her children and the barely tolerable living conditions in which she has had to make her home bind her to Mexico. And it is precisely because of her specific condition that she can support Morris's fantasy but not her own, even if both share the same desire for a rewarding domestic life. Having safely shunned her ghosts within the boundaries of Mexico, Morris returns to the U.S., where the rhetoric of a more enlightened gender politics redeems and liberates a narrative of domesticity now safely restored to its place within national borders.

IV. THE POLITICS OF FICTION
Paul Theroux's *Hotel Honolulu*

It is useful to recall at this point Paul Theroux's lament in the Introduction to *The Best American Travel Writing* that there are no Edens anymore, and that "the world has turned . . . Just about the entire earth has been visited and re-visited" (xvii). As I have shown in relationship to Kaplan and Morris, it is this anxiety about the end of travel that drives travel writers to focus on preserving the genre itself and, through this dislocalizing detour, the notion of a distinctive American identity. Theroux's novel, *Hotel Honolulu* (2001), a work of outright fiction at one level at least, resonates strongly with his lament that there are no more Edens. As the setting in a novel about the excesses of tourism, Honolulu itself emphasizes the compression of space through time and highlights the "end of Edens" anxiety by taking as its point of departure not only the turning of exotic destinations into tourist resorts of the most mundane kind but the fact that one need not even travel outside the U.S. to get to these places.

The narrator is himself a writer who claims to have given up writing. He takes a job in the seedy motel from which the novel takes its title. As the novel begins, we hear the voice of the narrator: "nothing to me is so erotic as a hotel room" (1). So from the very beginning of the narrative we find ourselves already in a touristic world, far removed from Theroux's privileged and anti-touristic world of real, but bygone travel. The narrator, like Theroux, has written about thirty books and claims that he is trying to start his life over at the age of forty-nine, after having lost money and houses and gone through a divorce. He confesses that in his new occupation as the manager of Hotel Honolulu, he is taking refuge from his writerly life: "I needed a rest from everything imaginary, and felt that settling in Hawaii, and not writing, I was returning to the world" (7). The fiction openly proposes the idea that tourism has so pervaded the planet that there is nothing more for a travel writer to write about, nothing to do but to start working in the tourist industry. The narrator/ protagonist is frequently thankful for his job. "My career as a writer," he confesses, "had not trained me for anything practical. . . . I had no marketable skill. . . . I was grateful to my employees for their work. They ran the hotel and they knew it" (52). There is essentially nothing for him to do. What better job for a failed writer? As he states: "I had gotten to these green mute islands, humbled and broke again, my brain blocked" (52). The novel thus makes a direct link between the blocked brain of the writer and the need to work in tourism for money. The block itself afflicts the protagonist while still living, and trying to write travel narratives, on the mainland. Thus it is the (fictionally) declared end of travel and the exhaustion of travel writing (or what passes for it) that endangers the narrator's way of making a living and sends him "traveling," so to speak, into the dark heart of tourism itself.[8]

The setting of Honolulu gestures in several different directions in the novel. As I have already pointed out, it emphasizes the fact that one need not travel outside the U.S. to experience the exotic locales so desired by travelers and tourists alike and that it helps travel writers such as Theroux to circulate the notion that travel is threatened. But more importantly, Hawaii as a setting facilitates the drive of travel writers such as Theroux to dislocalize their own writerly practices. In some sense, Honolulu has become emblematic of the fact that, with the "end of travel," what passes for the exotic may as well be sought within the U.S. itself, and nowhere more successfully than in cities that depend upon tourist dollars, such as New York, San Francisco, Orlando, or Honolulu.

And yet Honolulu is not quite like other cities. It is not American in quite the same way as the others. As part of the Asia Pacific Rim, Hawaii is a politically American destination able to represent itself as a place in which pleasurable excesses of a different sort than those in New York are available for the tourists. The narrator and Theroux himself as author, draw upon this perception so as to help shore up the increasingly globalized imaginary borders of the U.S.: whatever excesses of tourism found within the borders of the U.S. can be contained within the only quasi-American periphery of Hawaii. I will argue in what follows that *Hotel Honolulu*, perhaps even more emphatically than nonfictional travel writing, implicitly reaffirms the hegemonic imaginary of the U.S. as the *mainland,* to be cautiously kept apart from the more peripheral states, territories, and military bases in places such as Hawaii, Puerto Rico, and

Guam. I will also show that, for Theroux, the very fictional form of the novel itself functions dislocally as a way to preserve the genre of travel narrative and the notion of a distinctly American (or this case mainland, continental) cultural identity.

Theroux, in fact, gives some hint of this specific utility of fiction in his aforementioned introduction to the edited collection *Best American Travel Writing*. Here, in addition to criticizing dismissively much of the travel writing being done today and lamenting the "end of Edens," he holds out a reprieve for the genre: the literary notion of point of view. People, he says, do not read his books to learn, say, about China but rather to gain *his perspective* on China. This move clearly opens a path to the travel novel, and travel fiction in general—a category to which Theroux's own writing has substantially contributed—a medium in which the author need not be responsible for reporting facts and in which the idea of their perspective correspondingly gains in value. Indeed, the concept of point of view or perspective is given special emphasis in *Hotel Honolulu*, whose very abstract form *as* a novel positions it, in a sense, to play the role of a meta–travel narrative. The fictional narrator of *Hotel Honolulu* both rationalizes his life in Hawaii and yet sees it as an ill fit for his pre-existing self-image. Within this particular negotiation, the narrator thus dramatizes in relation to himself the ambiguity noted earlier in the physical setting of Hawaii: far enough away to be imagined as exotic and yet close enough to become merely the sad emblem of the domestic excesses of tourism to be found anywhere within the U.S.[9]

What is distinctive about *Hotel Honolulu,* however, is that it (loosely) fictionalizes even the ambivalences and possible exhaustion of the travel writing genre itself, taking the impulse to rescue the genre through the foregrounding of "perspective" still one step further. For Theroux, the novel offers a way of taking even further license with the genre of travel writing than its general rules and conventions.

By making fictionalization a means to what is also the metanarrativizing of travel, Theroux can not only claim the ultimate value and authority of his own "perspective"—not just the real "China" but *his* China—but also create an extra space within which to distance himself from this perspective when the need arises. His "point of view" regarding Hawaii is licensed as the invention of Hawaii. Here we have dislocalism at full throttle: thematizing the "end of travel" allows not just for the continuation but for the *proliferation* of writing about travel. The specific mechanisms of this dislocalist metanarrativizing in *Hotel Honolulu* are as follows: 1) the narrator/author can represent his own (travel) writer's block and resulting abandonment of his career in travel writing precisely so as to convey the ironic result that he will always be a writer; and 2) despite, and precisely because of his (fictionalized) belief that life as a quasi-phony hotel manager in Honolulu is all that he is fit for now, he engineers the implication that in fact he will be always be different simply because he is still the genuine article: a writer from the mainland.

The narrator in *Hotel Honolulu* might in some ways be described as "going native." He marries a woman named Sweetie, who, along with her mother Paumana, has worked most of her life in the hotel. He has a child with her, who, like her mother also grows up in the hotel. But in effect, he preserves a more distant relationship with most of the people around him. His invariably bungled and ironized attempts to be like the Hawaiians he lives and works with merely furnish him with further opportunities for marking his distance from them and for condescending to them. He tells us that the owner of the hotel Buddy Hamstra, "always introduced me by saying, 'Hey, he wrote a book!' I hated that" (7). Buddy's new manager knows right away, and lets us know, that his boss is almost illiterate and that that perhaps that was the real reason why Buddy hired him—out of respect for someone who wrote books. Or consider, for example, the protagonist's confessed response to people whenever they asked him what he did for a living. He tells us: "I never said 'I am a writer'—they would not have known my books—but rather, 'I run the Hotel Honolulu.' That gave me a life and, among the rascals, a certain status" (7). The narrator of *Hotel Honolulu* does not want to admit he is—or was—a writer, not so much because he has left his career behind as he claims to have done (or to have wanted to do) but because he would not be recognized. Hawaii, after all, is not, for him, the sort of place that is much concerned with reading and writing. For him, writing about Hawaii is one thing; but to be a Hawaiian writer—if such a thing could in fact exist—is something else entirely.

For the narrator, writing, even when it is blocked and fails, is still the mark of a superior mind. The protagonist complains, for example, of a group of "visiting journalists, brazenly demanding a week of freebies in exchange for a few paragraphs in a colorful puff piece . . ." (308). "These potential guests always asked to see me, and they'd announce 'I am a travel writer.' I associated this term with people who recounted their experiences in . . . glossy in-flight magazines. . . . 'Travel at its best,' one of them wrote about the Hotel Honolulu" (308). It's almost as if the protagonist had come to the Hotel Honolulu for no other reason but to be able to sneer back at these would-be imitators and debasers of travel writing. In the very next line he seeks to rescue the genre by confiding to the reader his own conviction—a refrain already familiar here in both

Kaplan and Morris—that "travel at its best, in my experience, was often a horror and always a nuisance, but that was not the writer's point" (308). The resonance with much of Theroux's other fictional writings about the state of travel writing today is here unmistakable.

No matter here that the narrator cannot write or the fact that he is now a hotel manager in Honolulu, and no matter how much he claims he is at home on the island: he takes great pains to establish that he will never be like the Hawaiians. It is not so much that he will always be an outsider, but that they, even on their own turf, will never be insiders. Once a writer, always a writer, especially since it is, after all, not the object written about but the perspective that really matters. To be a writer becomes, in Theroux's version of the "ends of the earth," purely a passive mark of identity and distinction. Sneaking looks at other people's mail, the protagonist readily excuses himself: "this, I told myself, was part of my job, my exploratory life as a writer" (86).

Writing—even if nothing is written—and point of view—even if it is only that of a motel manager—are intimately connected in the novel. From his position at the front desk, that is, squarely in the center of a touristic-industrial "heart of darkness," the narrator nevertheless gains a point-of-view that is far more credible than anyone else's in the novel. Theroux's often expressed claims that that he, as a writer, must be accorded the right to be an unreliable narrator ring a bit false here.[10] "Unreliability" apparently rests on a privileged kind of surveillance with which the locals themselves could not be trusted. A place to sneak looks at people's mail, the Hotel Honolulu is also a place for secret sexual adventures, and here too, the front desk is the best place for the non-writing writer to be perched. Here he has only to consult the other hotel employees, especially the workers who clean the bathrooms, and he will become privy to these secrets. In fact the details of his own adoptive family life as a transplanted mainlander supposedly contain such a secret, one of major proportions. Rumor has it that the narrator's wife Sweetie was born out of a sexual liaison between her mother Paumana and a visiting John F. Kennedy. But Paumana, it seems, never knew and remains ignorant of the identity of her one-night stand. Her own "point of view" as a local vouchsafes her nothing. This is something for the protagonist to know: he names his daughter (by Sweetie) Rose and explains that it is after her great grandmother. Secrets become, for the narrator, the place-holders of writerly privilege and self-image, even when writing itself has to be given up. Secrets, even if known by the locals, would be wasted on them, for precisely because of their proximity to things, they could not remain distant enough to be able to write about them. They may live the stuff of secrets, like Paumana, but they still have no knowledge of it. Having sacrificed travel, and even writing itself, the protagonist of *Hotel Honolulu* would seem to conserve in every other respect the Western, imperializing epistemological authority analyzed and critiqued by Pratt, Rosaldo, Clifford, and others.

This dislocalizing move—traveling "there" precisely so as to remain where and what one is—extends to Hawaii/Honolulu itself as setting. It becomes a repository for what has come to be identified as the excesses of tourism: sexual exploits, affairs, even murders. And as semiperiphery, Hawaii is also sensed as containing the secrets of an even more dangerous and sinister nature, notably those of Pearl Harbor and the island's violent, colonial history. Though not explicitly mentioned in *Hotel Honolulu,* the novel is clearly informed by these historical ghosts.

But the narrator makes it plain that he is a poor fit for the tourist-minded Honolulu society. His mainland identity must be maintained. He considers that he has gotten the hotel manager job largely because he is a "haole"—a white mainlander—a point he particularly insists upon (7). While feeling like an outsider at a family dinner at the Honolulu Elk's lodge, the narrator finds himself asking questions like "Where am I?" and "Who am I?" (206, 7). At one point during the dinner he goes outside and joins a man who turns out to be Leon Edel, the biographer of Henry James. The narrator takes an immediate liking to him because he uses what the narrator considers eloquent language describing the sun as "rubious," "effulgent," and "tessellated" on top of the distant sea waves (209). This meeting and his subsequent conversations with Edel drive home the fact that the narrator had never considered himself as part of his adopted Hawaiian surroundings. "I stared at him as though at a brave brother voyager from our old planet" he says after first meeting Edel, thus widening to cosmic dimensions the gulf between Hawaii and the mainland. When at one point Edel says to him that he "had no idea you were here too" this makes the narrator confide to the reader: "That 'too' was nice and made me feel I mattered" (211). When Edel inquires about his present writing projects, he says nothing about his supposed decision to stop writing and responds that he is "thinking of a book, titled Who I Was" (211). Suddenly the protagonist seems less settled with the idea of who he has become—a hotel manager. Luckily for him, as he notes, Leon is tactful enough not to inquire too much about that. Further conversations with Edel show that the protagonist is also less than comfortable with the idea of having Sweetie as a wife. With Edel, he refers to her as a "coconut princess" and a "little provincial" (211). He feels his wife has never understood him. When this line of thought seems about to go too

far, however, he grows more philosophical about it, even trying to rationalize it, with the support of Edel, by supposing that someone like Henry
James would have approved of them living in Hawaii. Edel reassures him:
"Henry James would love Hawaii because we do" (212). "We mused
without regret," says the narrator, "knowing that we really belonged back
there but that we had succeeded in slipping away" (213). Enlisting James
as someone who would approve of their slipping away since he spent
much of his own life in Europe, especially England, they happily fantasize
a "Henry James in a billowing aloha shirt approach[ing] as Leon spoke,
seeming to conspire, speculating about another inhabitant of our world"
(212). This momentary image of James, far from his East Coast/European
milieu, evokes for the marooned narrator a kind of compensatory image
of exiled, mainland sophistication. But soon he wonders: "how much
of this description fitted me and my living here. James with plump sun-
burned jowls, in island attire . . . big busy bum . . . indicating throngs of
tourists" (212).

This attachment to Leon Edel (and through him, to the real trove of
cultural capital, Henry James) is a near perfect emblem of the narrator's
fear of taking on the persona of a tourist. The knowing confabulation
with Edel and their desire to create an enclosed world for themselves—a
kind of island-mainland within Hawaii—works to seal off any solidarity
with the rest of the real island itself. Edel—the successful, if slightly over-
shadowed writer-biographer who will never have to fear the eclipse of
his effectively immortal and inviolable subject—is the perfect foil against
which to put in proper perspective the hero's condescending relations with
the rest of the local characters, with perhaps the exception of Rose. His
response to Buddy's request to get Edel to write a blurb about the hotel in
the local newspaper is quite telling: "The very idea that the eighty-nine-
year-old biographer of Henry James and chronicler of Bloomsbury would
write a squib for the local paper about his liking for Hotel Honolulu was
so innocent in its ignorance that I laughed out loud" (387). Only to such
"innocent," unknowing, and intellectually clueless types—"lovable," of
course, for those very reasons—would it occur to propose such a thing.
But, then, only in the Hotel Honolulu would the self-reassuring and self-
restoring gesture of a metropolitan/mainlander's laughter at the ignorance
of the natives perform its real, dislocalizing work of reproducing the distance between the mainland and Hawaii. Everything, even the slightest
idea that might call the essential borders into question, is placed back
within safe bounds.

By the novel's end, it becomes very clear that, though the narrator has
come to Hawaii to make his peace with his life, he will never be at peace

in it. He weeps incessantly at the news of Edel's death. Toward the end of the book, when Sweetie shares with him that she has become privy to another secret—John F. Kennedy Jr. will be visiting Hawaii—she learns that he already knows about this secret news. But, we are told, Sweetie refuses to believe him when he explains to her that he discovered this secret because Jacqueline Kennedy herself had called to tell him of her son's visit. He wonders whether his wife knew him at all. Ruefully, the narrator concludes that his wife is a hopeless naïf, and that he has much more in common with his daughter Rose, who can still be rescued from the islander's provincialism and who might, after all, come to appreciate her fortuitous if distant connection to the Kennedys, represented here as the paragons of East Coast aristocracy and refinement. Theroux's time/space compression is momentarily defeated and the wide and safe gulf between mainland and island, the nation and its dangerously ambiguous semiperiphery, traveler and tourist, opens reassuringly before him.

There is no return home in this novel, but none is needed. Though the narrator throughout the book claims that he has left his writing career behind, the ending of *Hotel Honolulu* reveals this to be false. He has, as might have been expected, been writing the book we read, a book he calls a "book of corpses" (424). But the narrator has apparently been resurrected—assuming he was ever in any real danger. Writing about travel is still possible after all: all that is necessary is to locate its "end" somewhere far away, at the "ends of the earth."

CHAPTER 4

The Global Palate

I. RESCUING TOURISM

This chapter further extends my discussion, begun in chapters 2 and 3, regarding metaphors of mobility. In chapter 3 I analyzed the ways in which the rhetoric of the end of travel works "dislocally" precisely so as to preserve and consolidate the genre of travel writing, and reinscribe its nonidentity with tourism. But what of the latter category itself, and the narratives through which it is reproduced?

Tourism—the structure that would describe much of leisure travel today—has been maligned in popular discourse for so long that even tourists themselves do not like to identify themselves as belonging to this group. Tourists are often seen as people who go elsewhere only to do what they would do at home, thereby obliging entire nations to change themselves according to their demands. As per usual, Theroux's lament about tourists is quite typical of this pejorative image. He makes a point to note that travel writing is "not about vacation or holidays." Nor is it about "a survey of expensive brunch menus, a search for the perfect Margarita, or a roundtrip of the best health spas in the Southwest"; it is indeed "seldom about pleasure" (*Best American Travel Writing*, xix). For him Lago Agrio, "hideous oil boomtown in northeast Ecuador," would make the "perfect subject" of travel writing because it is so inhospitable to tourism (xviii, xix). What Theroux seems to overlook here, however, is that tourism as a marketable "experience" has become more and more dependent on ideas such as newness, adventure, the exotic—that is, precisely the kinds of experiences Theroux reserves for the traveler like himself. For some time now, tourism has had to resuscitate itself by appearing to be travel. Thus, for example, the numerous guides for the average tourist often construct their readers as heroic travelers and include information about places and foods that are labeled as "off the beaten path." *Lonely Planet,* a popular Australian series of tourist guide-books that began publication in the early 1980s and subsequently came to have a major web presence, has been marketing itself to "adventurous travelers" who want to "explore and better understand the world" (6). The British *Time Out* series includes articles on culture, dining, and history. These and other tourist guides must in some way acknowledge that there are fewer and fewer new places to see, and yet must, at the same time, provide the tourist with precisely such new places to see—along with places to dine and sleep. The project of rescuing tourism in the face of the globalized erosion of precisely those dwindling pockets of exotic difference (and the seemingly ever present world on the World Wide Web and other media) that make it possible, involves capital investments in the billions, on the part of airlines, travel agencies, credit card companies, the travel/tourism magazine industry, food industries, and even entire national economies. All to some degree come to rely upon narrative strategies for representing as new and different places that are increasingly no longer new or different.

As noted in the previous chapter, travel writing often acts to rescue itself from what seems the impending "end of travel" by making itself out to be a form of narrative that carries otherwise inaccessible knowledge about culture, people, and places. (For Kaplan this is a "first hand" knowledge that augments the abstraction of foreign policy reports; for Morris, knowledge of gender and self "outside" the domestic sphere; for Theroux, the sheer metaknowing of the writer's own "perspective"). Tourism, however, although it can often claim to have the added attraction of being a learning experience, remains, initially, ludic in form. Tourism cannot be work. But because of the bad name it has acquired as sheer recreation, it cannot be mere fun or play either. It therefore redeploys itself, on the narrative and symbolic level, somewhere between these two extremes, as what might be termed a form of pure, sensory *experience* as such: the aesthetic experience, through mobility and displacement, of the new.

But this is precisely the shrinking quality that travel once claimed to provide. How is tourism, as narrative, to do any better? For one thing, it can, partially because of its partial exemption from travel narrative's moral imperative to learn, reaestheticize itself in a variety of ways, fantasizing the new and untried in the folds of "experience," even those of an experience as routinized as the ones Theroux describes above.

One of the most promising of these folds, I argue, is food, and the experience of eating—as well as, in a certain context, that of preparing it. The fact that food can be eaten and prepared in seemingly endless combinations is more and more that which provides tourism—that is, touring the same places over and over again—with a new slant. Food infuses newness into what has become, as movement through space, the often totally predictable trajectory of tourists. It may not be necessary to travel in order to eat, and eating itself is stationary, even sedentary. But eating, and food in general, are sensory experiences to which there can be added a seeming infinity of nuances, narratives, and fantasies. Therefore the experience of food, once one *has* traveled, can work retrospectively to add newness to the tour itself.

Food tourism and its narratives, moreover, play what I will show to be a subtle but nevertheless influential role in reproducing a dominant American identity-formation and adapting the latter to globalized conditions. Precisely because of what can be argued to be the nonexistence or at least noncohesion of a U.S. national cuisine, U.S.-based food tourism and food narratives generally become highly adaptable and mutable symbolic staging areas for the dislocal reproduction of nationalist paradigms.

I will look specifically in this context at *Endless Feasts* (2001) an edited collection of writing from the archives of *Gourmet* magazine[1]; at the magazine *Food & Wine* (issues ranging from 1998 to 2008) as a prime example of a medium that combines food narratives with how-to techniques for the home chef; and at the cable-television program that began airing in 2002, *A Cook's Tour,* produced by the Food Network, starring the chef-author Anthony Bourdain.[2] I will examine the way in which these three cultural productions participate in globalism by attempting to position themselves as both local/national and global through ideas such as fusion cuisine, adventure, newness, fantasy, and exotic locales/cultures. It should also be noted here that these narratives are largely written for and marketed to a white middle/upper-class audience and both presuppose and reproduce the notion of America as synonymous with such a demographic.

Food description in the context of travel/tourism is not new. Nineteenth century travel narratives often commented on the ways food was prepared and consumed. But these commentaries were often framed by notions of risk and health that were part of a larger symbolic construction of faraway places and peoples as strange, different, and potentially dangerous. Mark Twain, for example, is famous for fasting and describing the nature of eating on board ships during periods of food scarcity. In "My Debut as a Literary Person" (first published in 1899), he described

sailors as going to bed hungry and eating such things as leather boot-
straps and whatever salvageable bits of food were around. He and his
shipmates arrive starved in Hawaii, having had to survive on ten days
of food rations during forty-three days of sailing. Yet despite the gru-
eling situation at sea, one does not get what today would be the expected
account of savory and exotic food experiences once the remote destination is reached. Although at times described as delicious, food away from
home simply does not have this kind of narrative, or aesthetic value. (In
Roughing It, Twain, in Honolulu, speaks of some delicious fruits; but
after eating tamarind we get a description of how he suffered as a result of
problems with his teeth). Melville's *Typee* is also replete with examples of
the many times the narrator and his companions had to survive without
food and had to make do with whatever they had. And even accounts of
food that the narrator describes as not "disagreeable to the palate of a
European" and sometimes delicious—such as the breadfruit poee-poee
he eats at a reception where he fails to observe normal customs—are
often accompanied by statements of his own state of starvation (70–73).[3]
Framed by a narrative of risk and danger, of starvation, and even of can-
nibalism, the food descriptions of nineteenth-century American travelers
often reported about foods not only that their readers would never get to
taste but that they might not want or dare to taste.

Since then, this identification of the pleasures of travel with the pleasures of eating has over the last century become so intimate an aspect
of contemporary mass-media-produced narratives that it readily becomes
the food experience that foregrounds the travel experience, rather than
vice-versa. Even more significantly, the contemporary food narratives
generated in unprecedented quantities by a mass-media enterprise comprising magazines, newspaper articles, food television programming,
Internet and even cookbooks evoke a food experience that is completely
aestheticized.[4] In a way that nineteenth-century travelers could scarcely
have imagined, the narratives of modern food tourism not only graduate
from the alimentary to the strictly culinary, but, in assuming that food is
always already provided, no longer serve as a prelude to eating itself—as,
for instance, in the reading of restaurant menus. Even the menus in many
restaurants are written to narrativize the various food items on it to the
degree that reading the menu itself may be an aesthetic experience albeit
designed to produce a desire to eat them. Similar points can be made
about the ways in which searching the various restaurant websites prior
to visiting them can produce visual and narrative pleasures that are part
of the experience of anticipating food in a way that would have been
unimaginable not too long ago.

At the same time, this apparent disappearance of hunger and the general functionality of food from travel/tourist narratives produce certain shifts in the relationship of food to national identity. Near-starvation on a long sea voyage to the South Pacific could only have produced a culinary fantasy reduced to its bare minimum: longing for food of any kind, but preferably one's customary local or domestic diet. The nation becomes a place in which, even if hunger is not uncommon, its assuaging requires no added estrangement. But a contemporary vacation to Hawaii or Bali, by contrast, already obeys a radically altered mode of culinary fantasy: one in which satiety replaces hunger but also one in which cuisine itself displaces the merely alimentary, thus highlighting the perceived absence of the former in the United States. And here it becomes precisely the felt lack of a national cuisine or positive food identity in the U.S. that calls forth a new—sharply dislocalized—class of food adventure stories in which, as I will show, national borders are redrawn yet again, and an American way of eating is constructed on a seemingly global terrain. But before we look at the way in which these contemporary narratives redraw (and thus shore up) national borders, it becomes important to consider how and why the notion of the threatening erasure of these borders itself takes shape.

II. AUTHENTICITY
The Anxiety of Disappearance and Domestic Space

A large part of what makes food, together with travel and tourism, the subject of far-ranging cultural analysis and critique is its vulnerability to standardization. U.S. fast-food companies such as McDonald's have indeed made huge amounts of money by consistently producing homogeneous and standardized food experiences. Alan Bryman in "Theme Parks and McDonaldization" has argued that "McDonaldization" as both a paradigm and a metaphor for food standardization can be extended as a term to the sphere of equally standardized tourism experiences, such as those of Disney Parks. In their essay "'McDisneyization' and Post-Tourism'" George Ritzer and Allan Liska, for example, take issue with John Urry, who questions the McDonaldization argument and suggests that standardized items such as package-tours might be on the decline. "Raised in McDonaldized systems, accustomed to a daily life in those systems, most people not only accept," they argue, "but embrace those systems" (100). Though Ritzer and Liska raise this issue primarily as a way to intervene in the conversations about tourists seeking "new experiences," the fact that much of the activity of tourism takes the form of organized and prepackaged systems has also come to permeate popular discourse on tourism.

In analogous ways, the export by U.S. companies of standardized food production is a topic of much contention within the debates about globalization, and has been a chief concern in World Trade Organization meetings. Among the important issues in these debates are U.S. (as well as European) trade policies, the new role of biotechnology firms in the food industry, government, agribusiness, and the standardized methods of farming required for the production of genetically modified food around the world.[5] The popular books, film, and news media in recent decades have begun paying increased attention to the new levels being reached by food standardization. Eric Schlosser's *Fast Food Nation* (2001), made into a feature film in 2006, Morgan Spurlock's documentary film *Super Size Me* (2004), and Robert Kenner's *Food Inc.* (2008) chronicle, for large audiences, the ills of fast food production/consumption. But even more mainstream media have periodically taken up the question. In September 2002, for example, ABC aired a multi-part series "In Search of America," hosted by Peter Jennings. The series—which also resulted in a book of the same name, cowritten by Jennings and Todd Brewster—shows the Frito Lay Company expanding into Europe and Asia, employing local people as managers and buying and maintaining farms to produce a standardized potato for the company. Company executives openly maintained in the series that their goal was to turn the world population into consumers of Frito Lay potato chips. So blatant is the Frito Lay strategy that even a mainstream network like ABC evokes some skepticism, as Jennings asks people in China if they would really give up their normal snacking habits of eating nuts and dried fruit to eat potato chips. He finds some skeptics and some enthusiasts. As a U.S. company in search of ever-bigger chunks of market share and earnings, Frito Lay, a division of PepsiCo, obviously is not an isolated case. U.S. or U.S.-style food is already firmly established on the streets of Shanghai, Kuala Lumpur, Bangkok, and many other parts of the world where, until recently, eating habits and life-styles were relatively unaffected by U.S.-led food standardization that not only has changed consumption habits but has massively shifted the production of food as well as land ownership and allocation, subjecting farming communities to extreme subjugation.[6] But even setting aside the increasingly critical alarms being raised in popular media, the news itself, whether of salmonella ridden tomatoes from Mexico or of Mad Cow Disease itself, already makes an implicit argument for better controls of the drive to standardize all aspects of U.S. food production and distribution.

It is significant, however, that even in the above cases, the identification of a standardized U.S. food product with the idea of a U.S. national cuisine remains fraught and ambiguous. Though U.S. food companies such as Kentucky Fried Chicken, Pizza Hut, and TGIF can be found across the globe, the idea of a U.S. national cuisine is, in fact, much contested. For example, the prominent U.S. anthropologist Sidney Mintz relates in his book *Tasting Food, Tasting Freedom* that the idea of American cuisine is, at the very least, suspect. He tells us how his statement that the U.S. does not have a national cuisine, delivered during a class lecture, generated responses to the effect that the idea of being able to eat Thai one night and Chinese another could be considered American cuisine (107). Mintz argues that the idea of cuisine in other nations is more connected to seasonal foods and reflects a closer relationship between growers and eaters than exists in the United States. At best, the U.S. has some regional cuisine and any "local variation in cuisine is under continuous pressure from commercial enterprise aimed at profiting by turning into a national fad every localized taste opportunity" (114). Products that don't travel well, according to Mintz, are altered in order to be made "available elsewhere, even if they no longer are (or taste like) what they were at home" (114). In Mintz's account, this empty domestic space, ready to be filled—but only with marketing opportunities, not with food experiences—is only one of the many explanations for the lack of a genuine national culinary tradition in the United States.

In reference to other instances of dislocalism discussed in previous chapters, I have tried to show how various institutional and literary practices, such as American immigrant literature or American travel writing, contribute to preserving (even if loosely) defined and already existing national boundaries. But the case of food and cuisine is unusual in this context, since, as Mintz (and others) points out, food as a domestic, American space appears to be largely an empty one. Not only has the domestic space of the United States in relationship to food lacked the kind of cohesiveness found in food traditions of other nations such as Italy, France, Thailand, Indonesia, and Mexico. The American (largely white middle-/upper-class) palate itself has often been perceived to be a kind of *tabula rasa* onto which the grafting of other food traditions has consequently become a relatively easy task. The very sense of a lack seems to make possible the idea that eating, as one chooses, Thai, Chinese, or Italian food is *itself* American in form.

What I intend to show here, vis-à-vis food and dislocalism, is how food tourism narratives seek to construct via and project onto this empty space an imagined national food tradition but also take peculiar advantage of this empty space so as to adapt and affirm new forms of American identity as simultaneously global and local. However, such attempts at establishing a kind of local food identity in terms of the food traditions of the U.S. present particular problems, since it must also contend with the widespread perception of the U.S. as producer of standardized, mediocre food experiences in stark opposition to local and "authentic" food cultures or new food experiences.

It should be noted that the opposition to the "inauthentic" food cultures of the U.S. comes in good measure from those who champion the preservation, and lament the erasure, of certain food traditions. The search for food authenticity in direct relation to nationalist paradigms seems, in a world where things are not only standardized but also mixed (for example, Korean-Japanese-Italian fusion cuisine more readily available in centers such as New York, San Francisco, Chicago), to be a way to infuse newness and variety. The concept of authenticity has often seemed essential in distinguishing one food experience from another: whatever an American cuisine or palate may or may not be, it is not what one consumes in Chinese restaurants. And national-cultural traditions are seen as unquestionable receptacles of such authenticity—as if nations themselves had a taste. Given this, the food tourism narratives that I will examine seem to perform a multifold task: they establish themselves as against the standardization narrative, looking for reaffirmation of American identity and newness through both authentic and hybridized food experiences. They present globalization as a structure that produces sameness and yet at the same time makes variety, difference, and authenticity possible. It is as if the idea of an American cuisine, even though seeming to lack any referent, could, merely by being placed in a relationship to the myriad of national and local culinary authenticities, persuade us of its possibility, that it is something searchable.

III. FILLING THE GAP OR NARRATING THE NATION
Ruth Reichl's *Endless Feasts*

Ruth Reichl's collection *Endless Feasts: Sixty Years of Writing from Gourmet* (appearing in 2002 through Condé Nast Publications Inc.— also the publishers for the magazine that ran from 1941 to 2009), part of the series of "The Modern Library of the World's Best Books," was published on the occasion of *Gourmet* magazine's sixtieth anniversary. *Endless Feasts* features writing from such authors as Edna O'Brien, Madhur

Jaffrey, Ray Bradbury, and Paul Theroux, comprising a collection that Reichl refers to in her introduction to the volume as "sample tidbits of the many riches still hidden in the archives of the magazine." About Earle MacAusland, the founder of *Gourmet,* she writes: "In conceiving America's first epicurean magazine, he thought big. In a time when food was not considered big, he believed it was the only one" (x).

Published for a class of reader whom it referred to as the "sophisticated epicurean," *Gourmet* harkens back to definitions not unlike that of Brillat-Savarin regarding a related term: "Gourmandism is an act of judgment, by which we give preference to those things which are agreeable to our taste over those which are not" *(The Philosopher in the Kitchen).* But *Gourmet* seems to have lost the exclusivity of being *the* discerning magazine for an elite audience. In *Endless Feasts,* Reichl describes it as a magazine that "roamed the world long before it had been shrunk to its current size by the speed of jets" and whose writers were asked to "venture far and send back reports from the front" (x). Interestingly, in reporting the Condé Nast decision to discontinue the print publication, various news outlets claim that the decision was based on the perception that *Gourmet'*s readership was too restrictively exclusive for the magazine to have a continued financial viability. Playing up the "end" of *Gourmet* more so than the ways in which the brand will continue to exist through television and the Internet, as well as book publications, the *New York Times* states that the decision "reflected a bigger shift both inside and outside the company: influence, and spending power, now lies with the middle class."[7] The very elitism that Reichl seems to suggest is lost is then cited as a reason for the closing of the paper-print form of *Gourmet.* *Endless Feasts* as a volume then makes an interesting case study for its dislocal attempt to refashion the magazine and to reassert its status as a pioneer of sorts. But in presenting *Gourmet* as a forerunner, already long ago doing what is considered new today, *Endless Feasts* must also deal with the fact that not only the size of the world but the size of *Gourmet'*s share of the food publication market has shrunk. From being the only publication of its kind sixty years ago (looking back in 2002), *Gourmet* has become only a part of a myriad of how-to magazines, cookbooks, and television shows that feature everything from recipes to articles and programming about the contemporary fusion of flavors, the excitement of discovering trendy and elegant restaurants in one's neighborhoods, and the exotic ingredients found in local grocery stores.

Endless Feasts, however, is hardly concerned with providing how-to knowledge about cuisine. As Reichl states, "In later years, the food magazines would come to rely on recipes, but in [founder] MacAusland's

Gourmet they did not hold pride of place" (x). Instead, "in looking back, what stands out is the breadth of the coverage and the quality of writing" (x). Given the fact that *Gourmet's* articles are marketed to readers who can, it is claimed, "use the magazine to live a destination, becoming part of the local culture by following in the writer's footsteps" (Amazon. com magazine subscriptions: *Gourmet*), it is all the more interesting that *Endless Feasts* promotes itself in opposition to the how-to aspect of the magazine, almost as if it were establishing a new, *"Gourmet"* genre, a writing about food that is also quasi-travel writing, quasi-literary, and fictional. On the inside of the dust jacket appears a list of other works in the Modern Library series, most of them literary "classics": Joseph Conrad's *Heart of Darkness,* Charlotte Brontë's *Jane Eyre,* Mark Twain's *Adventures of Huckleberry Finn,* and many more. The established repu-tation and canonical imprimatur of the Modern Library collection—a veritable menu for the seasoned literary "gourmet"—helps consolidate the identity of *Gourmet* with its declared affinity for Brillat-Savarin's definition of gourmandism, an identity now threatened by the onset of the mass-media food narratives. But in order to differentiate *Gourmet* from other such publications, *Endless Feasts* must try to bestow a literary quality on a rather vexed project: establishing a U.S. culinary history, or what Reichl refers to as an "ongoing history of our national adventures at the table" (xi). Reichl suggests a history that is in flux by stating that "American food is a constantly changing representation of who we are" but, overdetermined as it is by the effort to canonize *Gourmet,* the effect is to render history as something static, a sort of food-inflected version of an "invented tradition."

In a world of food magazines to suit "every taste," and with fusion cui-sine seeming to making it harder to narrate food within nationalist para-digms at all, *Endless Feasts*' narratives are placed exclusively within such paradigms. The narratives themselves, dating from the 1930s to 2000, are categorized into a number of sections. The one entitled "Gourmet Travels" primarily contains stories written by Americans about food experiences they have had abroad. The "American Scene" is comprised of narratives about U.S. regional food culture. "Personalities of Gourmets" focuses on figures such as MFK Fisher and James Beard as American icons. "Matters of Taste" and "On Foods and Cooking" house narra-tives that relate varied experiences about cooking and ingredients in the U.S. While gesturing toward the gourmand's cosmopolitan enjoyment of food around the globe, *Endless Feasts* insinuates that the U.S. is much like European, Asian, or Latin American countries, in the sense that it has a history of its own particular cuisine and is just another part of the globe in questions of food production and preparation. Here we find the familiar attempt to consolidate national boundaries and at the same time promote newness and variety. In travel stories such as those by Ruth Harkness and MFK Fisher, food experiences in Mexico and Switzerland both presuppose the existence of national characteristics and yet must work to (re)produce the U.S. as a distinct nation. Meanwhile, the various stories in *Endless Feasts* focusing on American regional foods clearly purport to be about an American cuisine but tend to reinforce the image of the U.S. as a nation with diverse food preparation and consumption patterns, lacking a national-culinary common denominator. Both categories of food narratives, whether foreign or U.S.-regional in theme, are joined together by an emphasis on quasi-literary writing framed by travel and mobility and obey a dislocalizing strategy whereby the seemingly innocent recounting of stories of food from any and every part of the world works, at the same time, to fortify the borders separating the U.S. from other nations.

The quasi-fictional project of narrating U.S. culinary history benefits greatly here by deploying the popularized notion of literature as something timeless.[8] The cliché that suggests that discerning readers prefer older fictional works by writers such as Twain, Brontë, and Conrad, once ahead of their time but of course still relevant as ever, works to the advantage of *Endless Feasts* by helping to flatten out historical time periods that have themselves produced changes in food practices and on *Gourmet* over the years. Rather than submit to historicization, national and regional boundaries are treated as something *a priori*, placing *Gourmet* in a privileged position as narrator of a U.S. food history. By deploying the cliché of timeless literature, Reichl's introduction seems able to bestow a timeless quality on *Gourmet* magazine itself, one that protects it from historical change even if one of the stated goals is to provide a historical overview of it. The cover of the book itself is an example of the way in which style and visual narrative achieve this effect. In an understated beige background with an off-white, dark shadow-casting plate, the visual effect here is quite different from that employed in most contemporary cookbooks or magazine covers, with their sleek designs and colorful and artful presentations of food. The rusty looking fork on the plate, also with its accompanying shadow, works together with the rest of the color scheme to produce a faintly nostalgic effect, the effect of a distant but still intimate past. Here the link between discerning readers of literature and discerning gourmets is given a directly visual-narrative form. The entries contained within the covers have the original date of publication appended at the end of each one of them. And, rather than appearing chronologically, they are interspersed through the various sections. While this strategy, in which a story written in 1992 appears in the same section as one written in 1941, could be very helpful in tracing the shifts that have taken place in the magazine, here they seem to obfuscate them. While some stories more clearly register their socio-historical context than others, by and large the quality of the writing of most of the selected stories for this volume emphasize reminiscing about and romanticizing food and food memories, creating a sense of a timeless passage of time.

Let me offer a quick example. Madhur Jaffrey, who writes in 1974 about food memories using phrases such as "when I was a little girl" or Laurie Colwin, who in 1992 shares what she cooked "when [she] was a young bride," both employ the storytelling strategy of "once upon a time." As the date of original publication is provided, one can guess what time period they are talking about. And though one is about India and the other about the U.S., and those details are not interchangeable, the notion of time in the stories is treated as if something unaffected by history. This strategy in general works to secure *Gourmet* as a register of U.S. national culinary "adventures." The decades stretching from the 1930s to 2000 have seen major shifts in the history of the U.S. emerging in relationship to, say, the Depression, the World War II period, the postwar boom, the Civil Rights era, immigration reforms, and so on. And more directly on the plane of food, the twentieth century saw major changes in the production, consumption, preparation, and availability of food. To the extent to which the writing in *Endless Feasts* does narrate the context of food, it effectively produces a historyless history of the U.S. national "adventures at the table" as a continuous and cohesive tradition.

A close analysis of the various narratives shows how *Gourmet,* and its ideal exclusive/elite reader, can observe/remark about the changes—registering the *differences* between U.S. and other cuisines, and remembering them with nostalgia, but remaining unaffected by them.

For the purposes of exploring the dislocalist strategies at work in *Endless Feasts,* I begin by examining specific narratives in the collection written in the 1940s, and move to look at those written during or about the long 1970s (late 1960s to early 1980s), and finally those written after the mid-1980s.

Unlike earlier nineteenth-century travel writings by Twain or Melville, *Endless Feasts'* entries from the 1940s and the 1950s—such as MFK Fisher's "Three Swiss Inns" (1941) and Ruth Harkness's "In a Tibetan Lamasery" (1944) and "Mexican Morning" (1947)—all describe food as pleasurable and one of the primary reasons for travel. Reading these stories one would not know they were written for an audience living in the U.S., where many people (like those in other parts of the world) were dealing with food shortages and rationing during World War II and immediately afterwards, highlighting the elite readership of the magazine. These authors narrate their food and travel experiences within the framework of adventure, mystery, and intrigue and rely on some of the strategies of narration typical of the travel writing at the time in constructing a faraway world of food cultures. And since their readers would likely never get to taste such foods themselves, their narrative quality, utilizing aspects of the genre of fiction, becomes extremely crucial.

Ruth Harkness's story "Mexican Morning" relates her experience in the kitchen of an inn she stays at in the village of Tamazanchales: "when I became sufficiently familiar with the inn to be accepted by its Oriental mistress, the Indian cook, and barefoot, brown-skinned girls who pat-patted the tortillas in the dim Mexican kitchen, I was permitted to witness the mysteries and rites that produced the tongue-tingling *salsas de chile* to which our commercial chili sauce is a very pale cousin" (23). While producing credibility for herself by suggesting that she had to *earn* her entry into the kitchen, much as ethnographers must do in order to be able to observe the culture they are studying, Harkness simultaneously adopts an outsider's lens in order to be credible with her U.S. readers. The description combines elements of fiction and ethnography in the juxtaposing of the Oriental mistress, the Indian cook, and the barefoot, brown-skinned girls as co-initiates in an exotic ritual. It not only allows her to represent them from a distance but also produces a sense of intrigue. The mildly glib reference to the "mysteries and rites" of the local salsa, "cousin" to its "pale" counterpart on the supermarket shelves in the U.S., not only works to reproduce the difference between the U.S. and Mexico but also places commercialized food in opposition to the concept of authenticity that in fact must remain "mysterious" if one is to be able to narrate such food experiences within these frames. Elements of classic ethnographic reporting with their underlying representation of cultures that are contained within themselves, appear in an indiscriminate manner to emphasize locality while at the same time giving Harkness a narrative alibi for actual travel in order to witness the rites. And despite the fact that Fifth Avenue shops in New York were full of "Mexican embroideries" and "pottery"—in fact one "heard and saw nothing but Mexico" in New York—one must nevertheless go to Mexico for authenticity. The ethnographized travel narrative is necessary to produce the effect of history, a history that in turn seals up this narrative within itself as an experience not only unavailable to people who do not travel to Mexico but also, potentially, unavailable to those who do. And the fictional aspect of this narrative, presented as being as much about travel as about food, guarantees the fact that even if the reader traces Harkness's trajectory, in an effort to emulate a gourmet, s/he is not guaranteed the same experiences. Harkness's other travel story, "In a Tibetan Lamasery," though written in 1944 is an account of travel in 1939. It relates the rituals of tea and food in another "faraway" location and is delivered in much the same way, as a product, almost, of chance. Some tourists are mentioned. But tourism is easily dismissed because it would tend to negate the idea of an experience essentially unavailable to the reader. The story mentions the war but only as a personal inconvenience of sorts when she could not find anyone but her "former Chinese cook to accompany [her] to Tibet." The date at the end of this narrative, as in the case of the others, gestures toward locking the story within a timeless past, yet it simultaneously bestows a historical quality on it, in keeping with the heroic genealogy of *Gourmet* and American literary-culinary genius under construction in *Endless Feasts*.

Fisher's "Three Swiss Inns" (1941) works in a similar manner, highlighting the magical quality of her food experiences in Switzerland. She relates the experience of eating a pea dish claiming that all she can "remember now is hot unsalted butter"—notwithstanding which she "can almost see it, smell it taste it now" (6). She, too, renders this experience unrepeatable and unavailable to anyone else, here by saying that she could "never copy it, nor could anyone alive, probably" (6). This kind of exclusivity in which one can focus on taste adventures and remain detached from the war is perhaps more possible within the politically "neutral" national boundaries of Switzerland. In 2002, the same detachment would help *Endless Feasts* dislocalize the idea of an American gourmet tradition.

The readers of *Gourmet* likely did not need convincing that there are novel culinary experiences to be had outside the U.S., but the writers for the magazine featured in *Endless Feasts* clearly knew that their audience would need to be shown that the U.S. was also a place for authentic, gourmet food experiences. While food experiences outside of the U.S. could fairly easily and believably be attributed to a distinct national character, however, this attribution evidently was to prove more refractory in the case of the U.S.[9] Here *Endless Feasts* secures national boundaries through stories of diverse regional foods.

The entries by Frank Schoonmaker, on California wines, and by Robert Coffin, on food in Maine, suggest, as we shall see shortly in more detail, that this required a kind of synecdoche—a narrativizing of the regional—in which local cuisines and food experiences could stand in for the (missing) whole.

Setting itself the task of putting the U.S. on the map of cuisine, Schoonmaker's "The Vine Dies Hard" (1941) provides an almost historical account of the California wine industry. The tone here is strictly *Gourmet*—discerning and cosmopolitan—but unapologetic, optimistic, and gingerly patriotic. "Since 1936 and 1937," writes Schoonmaker, "the situation [for California wines] has changed remarkably and for the better. [. . .] This country for just and valid reasons condemned the California wines that were being marketed in 1934 and 1935. For no less just and valid reasons we should now welcome with open arms the California wines which are being produced today" (108). Words such as "just and valid reasons" and "should" seem curiously out of place in the lexicon of gourmandism—almost as if one had the duty to partake of food and drink one already knew to be superior. Wine-drinking readers of *Gourmet* are being gently lectured here to be more open-minded about a non-European vintage when it happens to spring from the native soil itself.[10] In Schoonmaker's narrative California—a mediational place name that stands mid-way between Mexico or Tibet and, say, a suburban American supermarket—works much better, exploiting a subtle form of dislocalism that continues to function to this day.

But not all the featured narratives in *Endless Feasts* are so overt in cajoling and coaxing readers into leaving aside conventional ideas about American food and conceding that a familiar, domestic environment could make for good culinary experiences. Consider the following passage from Coffin's "Night of Lobster" (1946): "The pail boiled over fiercely for the third time. This time the lobsterman let it boil. Then he poured the lobsters out bright red in the glow of what coals were left. He kicked on a whole new heap of brush. The fire danced up, sprinkling the night with wild stars. It was light as day (113)." The strategy here is evidently to exoticize a local, domestic food by slightly defamiliarizing and, in effect, overnarrativizing the *site* of the culinary experience. Maine becomes a place like Mexico, Tibet, or Switzerland not just because lobsters are caught, cooked, and eaten there, but because these activities become, literally, part of a ritualistic pyrotechnic exercise. In what seems almost an unwitting pastiche of surrealism, lobsters become a starry night. While for the contemporary reader a title such as "Night of Lobster" might suggest a grade B horror movie or a Stephen King short story, for Coffin lobster at night is an epiphany, almost supernatural: "It was a night like a night of marriage. I shall remember it all my days. I hope I shall remember it, too, beyond even those" (114).

One would think, from reading *Endless Feasts*, that lobster, prior to *Gourmet*'s discovery of it, had been a well-kept culinary secret of the remote New England coast. But in fact, prior to becoming the delicacy it is considered today, Maine lobster was anything but an exotic food commodity, often purchased in cans (Burnham & Morrill Company, a cannery in Maine, was beginning to can lobster meat as early as the 1830s) and commonly eaten as a protein substitute during World War II, when it was one of the few nonrationed meats. (Consumption of lobster after the war actually dropped because of this, although it rose again soon afterwards.) Moreover, its initial appearance on the U.S. market outside its local fishing waters coincided with the early history of food standardization in the U.S. in which the canned and packaged foods produced by companies such as Heinz, Armour, Swift, Kellogg, and Post were shipped all over the country by rail and sold in massive quantities.[11] In addition, as George Lewis states in "The Maine Lobster as Regional Icon," a wealthy new national elite in the 1800s that began to buy "land in order to establish summer homes in coastal places such as Bar Harbor, Boothbay, Kennebunkport and Camden" could buy lobsters from local fisherman and eat it fresh boiled instead of from a can—something available only to summer vacationers. Thus lobster in this context is seen as the food of both the "poor Maine local" and a "wealthy summer resident" (66). However, in Coffin's account, the references to starry nights and boyhood speak only to the upper-class association with lobster. The especially curious and suggestive thing here is that, in order to coax it into being an American tradition of authentic cuisine, a food that was also once regarded as inferior with a history of industrial packaging and mass distribution must have this history erased and a quasi-fictional style adopted to produce an aesthetically credible once-in-a-lifetime experience of eating a "meat as hot as a spruce bonfire and as sweet as a boy's first love" (113). Lobster as food then must undergo a kind of relocalizing and hyper-aestheticizing in order to take its place on the menu of national delicacies and authentic, nonstandardized food experiences.

Nowhere is the attempt to render the passage of time as timeless clearer than in the entries that either are written during the long 1970s or are accounts of this time period. In Reichl's own words: "In the later years the magazine would give Laurie Colwin a place to write about the pleasures of home cooking and would encourage writers like Madhur Jaffrey, Anita Loos, and Claudia Roden to look back at the way they once were (xi)." This is all Reichl has to say directly about the change. But these narratives by Jaffrey, Loos, Roden, and Colwin all in some way register post-1960s, discursive shifts in the relationship to immigrant/ethnic identity and the changing role of women, as well as of gender/sexuality—and some even include recipes. But as I have briefly alluded to earlier, these stories become a way of modernizing but at the same time consolidating tradition in the magazine.

Anita Loos, in "Cocktail Parties of the Twenties" (1970), nostalgically relates cocktail parties of the 1920s frequented by James Cagney and Bogart as "marked by an ambience of great virility." Referring to her own novel-turned-into-film *Gentleman Prefer Blondes,* she bemoans that "gentlemen have begun to prefer gentlemen" because "ladies no longer dress as incentive to romance" (157–58). While the past is something to long for in Loos, in other stories it must be utilized to both extol the changes that are occurring in society as well as to provide a buffer from them.

Laurie Colwin's piece, entitled "A Harried Cook's Guide to Some Fast Food," (1992), begins by stating: "Sometime ago, when I was a young bride, I had endless time to cook" (319). Although she doesn't say when the "sometime ago" was, it can be ascertained that it was sometime in the late 1970s and early 1980s. The story relates how Colwin could not continue to cook leisurely meals after her daughter was born and came up with some fast-food recipes that she calls the "cooking of the refined slob" (320). Including recipes for scalloped potatoes and brownies, this story is prompted in obvious ways by questions of professional or career women in the kitchen and the changing character of domestic labor. But even as the story revolves around how cooking for Colwin cannot continue in the same way as it used to, it becomes a tale about how food preparation can continue just as before only with some tricks, such as not peeling potatoes or making salad dressing in advance. As I have remarked earlier, her use of the phrase "some time ago" to tell the story bestows a sense of mythic time which can be equated with having "endless time" to cook things like "lemon mousse" and "chocolate cake." And after the birth of her daughter, though this mythic time becomes harried, it is not lost and can be recreated by cooking in slightly different ways.

The notion of mythic time is also at work in Claudia Roden's "An Arabian Picnic" (1978) and in Madhur Jaffrey's "An Indian Reminiscence" (1974). Roden, an immigrant from Egypt to the UK, reminisces about such foods as falafel and pilav, stating that her "favorite picnic as a child in Egypt was on the dunes of Agami in Alexandria" (67). Roden's piece along with that of Madhur Jaffrey's (1974) (immigrant to the U.S.) about her childhood food contain recipes of what has come to be known in the U.S. as Egyptian and Indian food. If for Colwin the recipes help to create a sense that endless feasting is still possible even if endless time may not be, Roden's and Jaffrey's stories suggest that while their childhood memories/foods cannot be recreated, nevertheless some essence of them can be tasted in the U.S. by following their recipes. So even if *Gourmet* is concerned more about food experiences than recipes, in the above stories they become an integral part of the former.

If *Endless Feasts* must attempt to represent what could be argued as a post 1960s sea-change in a North American middle-class palate, due to importation of newer food ingredients and techniques from elsewhere, it is very much invested in the idea of homegrown U.S. national even if regional cuisine. James Villas, in "Down in the Low Country" (1973) writes about the 275-mile coastal region that extends from Wilmington, North Carolina, to Savannah, Georgia. Unlike, Colwin, Jaffrey, or Roden, Villas includes some historical information of the development of the cotton industry and of rice cultivation in the region, along with ethnographic nuggets about the inhabitants' food consumption patterns. But he goes to lengths to give this region of the country an aura of the remote but at the same time of the local, identifying it as "one of the nation's most remote and mysterious areas" (168). It is, for Villas (much like Maine is for Coffin) a place that "evokes vivid childhood memories," thus both distancing in relation to a biographical time, sealing it within the intimate localism of childhood (168). The story highlights the availability of fresh seafood and includes recipes for items such as oyster stew, barbequed spare-ribs, and low-country shrimp pilau that do emphasize regional patterns of cooking and eating, but it does not include the histories of, say, migration and farming that are inextricably linked to food in this region. History, in this narrative thus becomes merely decorative and keeps the romanticized notion of U.S. coastal food intact.

Providing still further instances of a pseudo-historicizing narrative strategy that might be termed the reproduction of the past in the present, the entries dating from the mid-to-late 1980s in *Endless Feasts* also plot food within structures of romance and intrigue. Here, however, the dislocalism of the collection, in which the juxtaposing on the same discursive plane of foreign national food experiences with ethnographized accounts of regional cuisine in the U.S. serves to nationalize the latter, becomes even more acute. For, given that the ever-greater globalization of the world capitalist economy has diffused "local" foods of the most diverse kind throughout metropolitan spaces in the U.S., it becomes correspondingly more difficult to narrate the more pronounced fusion of food along national/regional lines. Even such natural determinants of distinct national and regional cuisines as the local food-growing environment and growing seasons come to influence less and less what local ingredients are available to consumers—at least in the wealthiest parts of the world, where publications such as *Gourmet* have found readers. Nevertheless, the impulse to construct and reproduce a U.S. national identity formation through food remains as strong as—if not stronger than—ever.

Irene Corbally Kuhn's story, "Shanghai: The Vintage Years," originally published in *Gourmet* in 1986, serves as a particularly interesting example of the way in which *Endless Feasts* reproduces the past in the present. At first, it would seem, Kuhn moves against the grain of the older narratives of *Endless Feasts* on the "then" and the "now." She starts her story by arguing that Shanghai, once known as the "Paris of the Orient," now exists only in the Western imagination as "the essence of exoticism, excitement, color and vitality persisting through wars, revolutions, and decades of isolation" (74). "Vintage Shanghai," the city that epitomized these qualities, "actually existed," she reminds us, for only a very short period of time, "during the years between the end of World I and the capture of the Chinese part of the city by the Japanese in 1937" (74).

But note here that, underneath its evidently more cautious form of periodization, the once vibrant milieu of Shanghai is not to be derived for Kuhn from fusion cuisine or the mixing of ethnicities and nationalities—the current meaning of the exotic in much new-wave popular food discourse—but rather from a kind of imperialist nostalgia for the days when a Westerner was "once privileged to call himself a Shanghailander," when the British presence produced a "police force of tall, straight-spined turbaned Sikhs," and when there was a "dazzling array of choices, for restaurants abounded and ranged from the elegant formality of the St. Petersburg, owned and managed by a former white Russian cavalry officer, to the small dark, steamy noodle shops of the old Chinese walled city" (77). Kuhn's "vintage" years were the ones during which a (Western) foreigner could count on segregated dining spaces to which Chinese were denied entry, while still partaking of the mystery and intrigue of the noodle houses. "There was," she declares with open admiration, "an easy mixing among the nationalities composing the foreign population" (76). Her rueful acknowledgment that "even as we lived those days, somewhere deep below our consciousness we sensed that this was a life that would never exist again" declares the past to be past, but only so as to denigrate the present (81). Nowhere does "Shanghai: the Vintage Years" so much as gesture toward what has replaced this life. (As I will show a bit later, at least in terms of cuisine, the streets of Shanghai have been experimenting with food just as much as those of any other big city.) Although perhaps from Kuhn's point of view the foreign population, in the form of businessmen with investment prospects in a modernizing China of the 1980s, does not enjoy the luxury of segregated restaurants and nightclubs. Kuhn, in effect accepts, with one hand, the more contemporary food mixing and the corresponding diffusion of national cuisines, while, with the other, she projects it back into a nostalgic past in which the exotic blend was a privilege set aside for the Western gourmands and colonials who could call themselves, to repeat here that strangely appropriate linguistic hybrid, "Shanghailanders." The idea, as important to *Gourmet* as ever, of a "true" national cuisine able to heal the wounded sensibilities of Yankee gourmets begins to look less like a foray to Maine, New Orleans, Savannah, or the Napa Valley and more like a domestic colonial enclave, with walls to keep it from being "shanghai-ed" by the immigrant hordes crowding into the land with their strange looks and ways. It's one thing to eat their food, another to have to sit next to them.

Pat Conroy's "The Roman of Umbria" (1992) dislocalizes the threatening nonidentity of American food in still a different, though more familiar way. His story is about taking his wife on a honeymoon to Umbria. She occupies the role of the "provincial" American—a kind of food virgin—while he, a man of the world, leads her into faraway gardens of earthly delights: "It amazed me," he relates that "though, she traveled to London twice, [she] had never drifted over to continental Europe, where our language is put out to pasture. Not to have traveled widely seemed unlucky to me, but not to have seen Italy seemed heartbreaking and unimaginable" (84). In this narrative, knowing Italy is also knowing food. But while Umbria inspires him to speak of "albino-faced cauliflowers," "porcini mushrooms," "fennels," and similar foodstuffs, the more cautious reader notes that, in 1992, these are ingredients that are no longer unfamiliar to the middle and upper middle class (the likely readers of *Gourmet*) who largely live in, and even never leave the U.S. Have, in some ways as a result of global food—and human—traffic, parts of the U.S. become Italy? In a far less obvious, less conscious sense, that, too, would be "heartbreaking and unimaginable." But by framing this as a tale of romance and the beginning of a new life together, new love becomes new food, and thus, through this scarcely noticeable displacement, keeps Italy and the U.S. at a safe distance from each other. Conroy's story here seems to have far more in common with Coffin's story about the romance of lobsters in Maine in the 1940s than with the trendy cuisine of the 1990s—in which, for example, one might discover recipes combining Maine lobster and Italian herbs. Both indirectly eroticize food as a way of distracting attention from its increasing obsolescence as a vehicle for cultural-nationalist experience. Placed in the same volume, they suggest a world in which eating (like sex) seems to take place outside the history that includes such things as immigration and famines, but safely inside national borders.

The narratives about the U.S. in the 1990s are written in much the same vein. And quasi-fictional aspects of these narratives here too become an important device for seeing routine experiences in a new, "national-izable" light. Many of them offer an East Coast perspective on various regions of the U.S. far enough away to require travel. In "All Aboard! Crossing the Rockies in Style" (1995), our old friend Paul Theroux is once again on a train, *The Los Angeles,* heading west on a coast-to-coast trip to LA. Along the way we hear quaint information about the various places that he passes through: Princeton, Illinois is the "pig capital of the world" and Galesburg, Illinois, is the place "where popcorn was invented by Olmstead Ferris" (185–86). Implying his own traveler's extra-territo-riality, Theroux likens the Midwest to another, legendary setting for long train trips: "I was put in the mind of Russia, of long journeys through forests and prairies . . . It was like that, the size of the landscape, and the snow and the darkness, and the starry nights over Iowa" (185–86). While he mentions local towns with filling stations, or a bowling alley particular to a Midwestern city, these places nevertheless seem as far-flung to him as Siberian villages. He later asks Christopher Kyte, the owner of the restaurant aboard *The Los Angeles,* about his oddest customers. Their conversation turns from the odd dining habits of a person who showed up without clothes for breakfast to another man who, sedate during the day, drank too much at night, when he wore wigs and did cartwheels. Listening in on these droll anecdotes about people's dining habits, set against the backdrop of "small nameless towns" across the U.S., one gets a sense of watching them unfold in an unfamiliar terrain. And Theroux's description of the food on the train as "Southern cooking with a differ-ence" and "traditional dishes" that are "served with a flourish" further infuses the bland backdrop of nameless towns with an aesthetic aura of newness (189).

Such dislocalizing through defamiliarization, achieved in much the same way that older narratives presented the U.S. with a "new look" that nev-ertheless left many new conditions out of the picture, here requires some revisiting. I have already discussed this form of dislocalism in relationship to Theroux's emphasis on train travel as a kind of planned obsolescence that diminishes the hyper-velocity of tourist traffic and allows the aesthetic dimension of travel, supposedly, to be resuscitated. But the metaphor of mobility has renewed its importance in a different context in part due to its relationship to food narratives. By adding food—as already observed, an aesthetic (or at least aestheticizable) medium offering almost infinite variability—the notion that there are places still to be discovered or at least seen from a different perspective appears to gain a new lease on life.

Jane and Michael Stern bring this home in "Two for the Road: Havana, North Dakota" (1997). The mention of North Dakota does not readily conjure up images of sought-after food experiences. But here, as one might put it, even the gustatory dimension of food is almost separated from its subtly defamiliarizing narrative properties. The Sterns tell the story of a restaurant, The Farmer's Inn, located in the remote small town named in the title of the narrative: a "valued gathering place for locals and a farm food oasis for hungry travelers" (191). First opened in 1913 as the Havana Café, it closed in 1984, succumbing to decades of depopulation due to the decline of the local farming community. Realizing that a "restaurant in so remote a location had no chance of success if someone tried to operate it as a profit-making business, the members of the community decided to reopen the café on their own" (192). The story of the café frames itself within the much-romanticized idea of a community-gathering, one that could just as easily have occurred a century earlier. With customers helping themselves to coffee and "high school girls that get paid a $10.00 honorarium per day" working as waitresses, The Farmer's Inn is hardly a place to make a living. But of what fundamental interest is this to the discourse of gourmet travel, for which the experience of eating is effectively represented as retroactively transcending time and place? It is true that the social realities of food, usually reduced to the folkloric in *Endless Feasts,* are here given more than their usual share of attention. The clientele of The Farmer's Inn travel sometimes huge distances, less for the food itself than for the pleasant stimulation of a "small town café [. . .] so conducive to a relaxed exchange of news and opinions," and people say that the Inn "holds their community together" (192, 195). But for the Sterns, who are clearly enchanted and intrigued by the homespun, mildly retro, Norman Rockwell–ish Americana of the scene, the novelty of The Farmer's Inn is not so much its communal, anti-commercial spirit but its marked contrast to the standardized, corporate anti-aesthetic of restaurant-industry giants such as McDonald's, Starbucks, and TGIF, purveyors of American food experiences. What is needed, for ideological, dislocalizing purposes here, is an "oasis" of cultural novelty and authenticity in the desert of standardized American food experience, even if the food itself does not taste all that different than it would elsewhere. Although the authors "pitch in" by providing recipes from The Farmer's Inn, what *Endless Feasts* celebrates here is not the taste of the food but the taste of its American heartland location and its ethnographized, communal mode of preparation and consumption. In this instance of dislocalism, we are invited, so to speak, to imagine eating the restaurant itself.

The presence of so many narratives in *Endless Feasts* striving to keep up the search for traditional and culturally authentic food in new ways— whether as novelty in the past or as a novelty searched for in the present— is an attempt to hold onto the idea of national, regional, and local cuisine at a time when the concept of the gourmet itself, as defined by *Gourmet,* appears to require the impossibility of the former.

IV. FUSION
Food & Wine

Unlike *Gourmet,* and its literary monumentalization in *Endless Feasts,* the widely read magazine *Food & Wine,* which began publication thirty years ago, appears to care very little about the national identity crisis of American gourmets. Its emphasis is clearly on combining ingredients and flavors from around the world without particular regard for national boundaries, the process now well-known to New Age gourmets and mass consumers alike as "fusion." In "The Art of Fusion" (published in *Food & Wine*'s September, 1998 issue) Jeff Weinstein, a fine arts editor and a food columnist at *The Philadelphia Enquirer,* offers a standard definition of fusion as a cooking that "combines ingredients from dramatically dissimilar cuisines or cultures. Typically that means recipes in which Asian ingredients are used to shock French or American standards out of their complacency." He goes on to say that more recently "fusion has gone further, incorporating ingredients and methods from the Middle East, the Caribbean and Central and South America into menus that, when they're successful, begin to lose their national identity and become something like the diet for a culinary One World "(*Food & Wine*/The Art of Fusion). But, according to Weinstein, fusion is actually more than the mixing of national cuisines since they too are in flux. "'Fusion,' he writes, "is a particular historical circumstance having to do with late-20th-century chefs and their urge to create" (*Food & Wine*/The Art of Fusion). Fusion "dishes are usually variations (often wonderful variations) on standard themes—southwestern American, northern African, bistro French" (*Food & Wine*/The Art of Fusion). Paying homage to premier chefs who espouse the concept of fusion, he credits Wolfgang Puck with being the first "postmodern" chef, whose restaurants "were the first to acknowledge that the world's appetites have become nomadic, touristic, ready to throw any and all ingredients into a carry-on and take off" (*Food & Wine*/The Art of Fusion). Presented as a jet-setting, touristic, adventuresome experience in which national traditions matter only for the inspiration they provide to creative chefs (not just the celebrities but also home-based amateurs), Weinstein's version of fusion seems to need national boundaries only in order to dispense with them.

The possible hyperbole of Weinstein's paean aside, it seems clear that fusion reflects significantly changed middle-class American eating habits and an increased overall awareness of food and food traditions around the globe. Fusion cuisine, roughly the culinary equivalent of globalization (at least for those who are able to reap the latter's benefits as consumers), seems to be about the opening of national borders to global flavors in such a way as to render any sort of national identity based on food tradition much harder to narrate.

Food & Wine includes features on exotic ingredients that can be found in local grocery stores, articles on best restaurants, and recipes for the home-cook. It openly proclaims its mission to cater to the culinary tastes of the economic elite. And more significantly, it is published by American Express Inc., the company that, according to David Harvey, first popularized the term globalization in an advertisement for its credit cards.[12] Thus, it seems only appropriate that American Express should sell a guide to the myriad of food and wine choices that are now available to elites—and not just in the U.S—as a result of the liberation of markets from state control.

But is fusion simply, as its celebrants in venues such as *Food & Wine* claim for it, a culinary free trader's liberation from the protected enclaves of national cuisines? Is it, in fact, the brave new food of the global citizen? Or might it, in ways far removed from the old-money penchants of *Gourmet* and *Endless Feasts,* be a food for a new kind of American national-imaginary?

The best clue to the nationalist fantasy mechanisms of fusion, I suggest, lies as it does in the case of *Endless Feasts,* in its connections to metaphors of mobility and displacement. For what fusion offers to the consumer looking for newness and variety in his or her daily consumption of food is not, as in *Gourmet,* the aperitif of traveling to exotic food destinations, but the pure fantasy of travel. The discerning diner no longer needs to go out into the world; the world itself now travels to his/her plate. Remembering our earlier stipulation about tourism as the industrialized, but also purely aestheticized form of travel, it might be said that *Food & Wine* fusion narratives present the domestic national space as something renewed and ripe for tourism. This is especially true of metropolitan centers such as New York and San Francisco, where one can eat one's way through endless combinations of food—say, for example, Japanese-Italian-French fused together in some form—without having to leave the United States. And as for those who don't live in these areas, the recipes published in *Food & Wine* will help them achieve the same fantasy. Although the idea of actual travel and mobility is indeed important to *Food & Wine*, what it sells is a kind of ultimate world tour in which the destinations themselves have been detached from their spatial location, becoming fantasies in the form of pure flavors, smells, and colors. As a guide to the sophisticated palate, *Food & Wine* has done the traveling for the consumer, and what we get is a diffused expertise of cooks, writers, and advertisers that provides how-to knowledge for the magazine's elite and wealthy subscribers. The infusion of newness into food experiences requires nothing, in principle, beyond the extension of free markets and trade routes into every corner of the culinary world, the knowledge (resulting partially from the exploits of the early food-travelers, now more widely disseminated than ever) of how to prepare and combine the imported culinary goods, and the money to buy them.

But I will show that, notwithstanding its fantasy-driven mobilization of culinary experiences without regard to borders, fusion cuisine, far from erasing the desire for narratives of food within nationalist paradigms, dislocalizes this desire in such a way as to reassert food experience as American. It very well exemplifies Immanuel Wallerstein's argument that narratives of homogeneity are invariably accompanied by narratives of newness and diversity.[13] And it is precisely this newness that is claimed as American. Fusion food—to abbreviate and anticipate my argument below—works by leaving the domestic space formerly to be filled by a putative national cuisine empty and transferring the cultural identification power of cuisine from the food on the plate to the act, and the performance, of consuming it—from the eaten, to the eating.

Not all of this necessarily rests on fantasy. Fusion cuisine as displayed in *Food & Wine* reflects the recent American "discovery" of new foods that have helped to change American eating habits and to achieve new food goals, such as weight loss or the learning of new ways of preparing familiar ingredients. Fusion reflects an increased awareness of food and food cultures around the world, and it instructs Americans (especially, but not exclusively, the elite) not only in how to partake of elegant food but in how to perform refinement and elegance through and food and wine choices, whether it be eating in a restaurant or preparing it at home. It has allowed Americans to take up food as a noble pursuit and has helped in some respects to decode food choices and cooking practices.

But fusion retains the form of dislocalism precisely by representing the empty space that comes to be saturated with global food as a domestic one. After all, even if one can eat anything, from anywhere, at any time, one cannot *do* this anywhere. Fusion is not something for, say, working-class people or those who live in rural areas whether in the U.S. or elsewhere. As seems to be the case with most narratives of globalization, the real point from which one imagines the "one world" remains fixed, national, and—largely—the urbanized/gentrified United States.

That is, unlike *Endless Feasts,* the fusion cuisine promoted by *Food & Wine* is not constrained to narrate the nation as one containing food experiences equivalent to those of other nations, but rather wants to maintain the gap so that the space is available for fusion to take place continuously, providing newness through pure fantasy. It is newness and not authenticity that *Food & Wine* wants to provide to its customers. The magazine is invested in maintaining an empty domestic space because it is precisely such emptiness that allows the flavors from outside the nation, whether they have been localized or not, to continue to infuse newness. Emptiness can be filled only with pure fantasy in order to inject newness into daily experiences. An American identity marked by a lack must be maintained so that fantasy about travel, other national traditions, and the mixing of new flavors can continuously reaestheticize American food experiences as in themselves performances. For foods from other nations to serve as objects upon which to perform an American food identity, the stage itself must remain stationary and vacant. This performance is essentially that of consumption. Asian flavor and European sophistication are not able to change the structure of American identity so long as participating in these food cultures remains an act of sheer consumption. Thus it is the structure of fantasy itself, not any particular fantasy over others, that permits *Food & Wine* to dislocalize, allowing all tastes and flavors to permeate food experiences without regard to borders, but at the same time reaffirming an American identity (effectively marked as upper class) as the only one that is perfectly open to these experiences.

Pursuit of Refinement

The pursuit of upper-class refinement in dining experiences through borrowing from food traditions of other countries is not a new phenomenon. So, for example, Wolfgang Schivelbusch in *Tastes of Paradise* (1992) explains the medieval European penchant for Asian spices not as a consequence of the desire for new food preparation and preservation techniques but rather of the desire of "refined people" to imagine them-selves differently through new flavors from an imagined "elsewhere." He writes: "The aroma of spices was believed to be a breath wafted from Paradise over the human world. Medieval writers could not envision Paradise without the smell or taste of spices" (6). It was not until the seventeenth century that spices lost their supremacy, because they began to glut the market and thus became more commonplace. And "with the French leading the way, European cuisine had evolved to become very much like the one we know today, more moderate in its use of spices" (14). Similarly, in relationship to the U.S. elite, Harvey Levenstein writes as follows in *Revolution at the Table:* "By 1880, upper class Americans along with their British counterparts, had discovered the delights of fare more sophisticated than their national cuisine" (10). After the Civil War many more Americans became wealthy and "awash in wealth the new upper class inaugurated a new 'Age of Elegance'" (10). Levenstein goes on to say that though the American culinary heritage may have been one of abundance, it had little in the way of elegance to offer, so Americans turned to Europe, in particular to the cuisine and manners of France (10).

This tradition continues in the late twentieth and twenty-first cen-turies, but in the form of fusion. For example, the July 2007 issue of *Food & Wine* (invariably bound to be patriotic) features a report by Kate Krader on America's "Best New Chefs" and declares Gavin Kaysen of San Diego as one of them because he is "amazingly adept at taking serious French cooking techniques he mastered in Europe and turning them into playful dishes" (259). But here instead of turning to France to copy its dining habits and manners, it is Kaysen's mixing of flavors and techniques—French ones prominent among them—that constitutes the pursuit of elegance. While Europe continues to inspire form, elegance, and structure, *Food & Wine* persuades consumers to become attuned to different flavors, such as those brought over by immigrant populations from the global South, and to non-Euro-American cuisine in general. But since many of the food choices available from the various non-European traditions (such as Chinese, Thai, or Mexican) are too widely available and have been relatively inexpensive (for those with money) to be consid-ered elegant, *Food & Wine* moves away from localized ethnic cuisine into that of fusion, which has as much or more to do with the form in which food is presented as with the combination of flavors and ingredients.

In his classic sociological study *Distinction*, Pierre Bourdieu differen-tiates between the notion of taste as refinement and taste as a property of food, arguing that for the French class of *nouveaux riches*, whose habits he examined, taste as refinement occupies the center of the dining experience because only thus can such diners remove themselves from the "crude necessity of eating." While the peasantry might also evolve a style of eating distinct from "crude necessity" itself—hearty meals in large family groups at which one doesn't necessarily pay attention to table manners—the *nouveau riche* stylizes his eating so as to distance it as much as possible from the corporeal, cultivating light and nonfattening foods and tastes, such as fish.

Bourdieu's account of taste as a class-marking food code in which eating and mere consumption are counterposed also describes, to a degree, American eating habits. But *Food & Wine* encodes food differently for its American readers. The magazine does not so much strive to divert attention from the crude act of eating as it turns consumption itself, with eating as one of its subsets, into a form of art—even implying that consumption is a moral and ethical duty. Eating is here refined—rescued from its immediately physiological reality—by being integrated into a whole chain of consuming performances, including buying and consuming the products advertised in the magazine and even buying the magazine itself. American Express's mission statement explicitly links consumption itself with refinement:

> American Express Publishing's mission to reach affluent consumers with publications that address their greatest passions is a natural extension of the 151 year-old American Express Company. Generations of people who have the means to indulge themselves with travel and good living have turned to American Express. Thirty years ago, American Express began providing these high-income consumers with some of America's finest lifestyle publications, creating a tradition of affluent lifestyle marketing that continues to expand under American Express Publishing (Amex Custom Publishing Company).

This seems, on the surface, to be a strange mode of refinement, given how readily the act of consuming can carry a taint of unreflective decadence. In the American context, it is hard to resist the further equation of globalized consumption with global cultural domination and imperialism. As with the "ugly American tourist," the American consumer has come to possess an unflattering image. But underlying this image is the idea of consumption as sheer appetite, as nondiscriminating. This, as I have shown in chapter 3, is the stigma that pushes contemporary U.S. travel writing to seek ever new and different ways to make travel out to be productive and value-creating, unlike the commodity that tourism is seen to have become. The American Express mission articulated above and in the pages of *Food & Wine,* however, does not evade consumption but rather seeks directly to generalize and repackage it as refinement. According to American Express Publishing, "*Food & Wine* delivers a perfect balance of travel, drinks and cooking—the lifestyle that defines today's taste makers. Each page seduces readers with attitude and elegance, which turn aspiration into inspiration. With a circulation of nearly 900,000, *Food & Wine* reaches America's most discriminating epicurean market" (Amex Custom Publishing Company). The emphasis on taste and elegance works not so much to divert attention from the perception of self-indulgent and exorbitant U.S. spending (in the form, say, of both rich, high-calorie foods and weight-loss products, as set against widespread hunger and malnutrition in the world), as to balance the various objects of consumption, and, jettisoning an older, class-neutral construction of America, openly equate spending with cultivation: whence the barely disguised linguistic grotesquerie of a "discriminating, epicurean market." Despite the fact that *Food & Wine* is a largely commercial endeavor on the part of American Express Inc, with sometimes over half of the total pages devoted to advertisement, and with the recipes and articles on the remaining pages scarcely distinguishable themselves from forms of advertising, the magazine presents food experiences as something that nevertheless bypass commercialism by packaging those marketed experiences in a "discriminating" and refined way and thus, ideally, providing them with cultural capital. Borrowing from others even when they look toward any one national food tradition, *Food & Wine's* narratives are turned into *narratives of consumption* themselves, and more often than not delve into other national traditions only to be able to pick and choose from the ingredients and flavors already at the disposal of the consumer. Here again we see how the culinary lack at the center of the U.S. as a domestic space is turned to advantage by becoming the site of consumption as sheer performance—a performance of class that is at the same time essentially American.

Advertising Elegance and Fusion, Tradition and Fantasy

Dislocalism—a simultaneous flight to the global and investment in the local—is especially acute in the way *Food & Wine* (like many other kinds of specialty product magazines and shopping catalogues) does the work of turning consumption into refinement by blurring the lines to a considerable degree between feature articles, recipes, and paid commercial messages. For example, among the numerous pages given over to advertisements in the July 2007 issue, there is an ad for Holland America Line Cruises on a page that is partly folded over. Turning to this page one sees a picture of an elegant yellow pear that takes up most of a black background. Next to the pear is the word "sublime." As one scans to the bottom left of the page, one sees a very small picture of a cruise liner in gray. The link between the elegant pear and the cruise liner is made in the inner part of the fold, which when lifted greets the reader with the words "intrigue your senses" (33). The inside of the fold also reveals three small pictures, one of a couple, the other of a cruise-line employee, and the third of a berry dessert. A short narrative tells the reader that his/her senses are in for a treat, her palate as well as her eyes. But since the only prominent picture is that of the pear (reinforced by that of the berry dessert), this ad effectively brackets all other supposed sensual delights by those of food. The images here are a near perfect visual analog or metaphor for the dislocalizing of tourism through cuisine: tourism, even if—as on cruise ships—it cannot finally aspire to become legitimate travel, achieves what is, at least, a refinement through fine dining.

Feature articles follow this structure as well. Emphasis on consumption not only as the national pastime but also as almost a moral and civic obligation, can be observed in a feature article in the July 2003 issue of *Food & Wine* (published just three months after the U.S. invasion of Iraq), "A Banner Day," by Kate Krader. The article, about Fourth-of-July picnics and cookouts, features suggestions from Los Angeles chefs Suzanne Goin and David Lentz, who describe the techniques and styles used in their restaurants. Recipes are also provided for those wanting to recreate that experience for themselves. The recipes themselves, however, go beyond a simple listing of ingredients and techniques. One of them, entitled "Lemony Halibut Skewers with Charmoula," prefaces the list of ingredients as follows: "These skewers are based on one of Goin's favorite dishes at her wine bar A.O.C.—grilled yellowtail with Meyer lemon and charmoula, a cilantro-based Moroccan marinade and condiment traditionally served with fish" (168). While the ingredients of this marinade have become very recognizable in some areas of domestic food experiences—cilantro, parsley, bay—the mention of its traditional Moroccan provenance seems at first to create a kind of dissonance. Moroccan (read, Arab and perhaps Islamic) flavors on the Fourth of July? Yet this is not a Moroccan dish but rather fusion, seen here as a tacitly American mode of consumption. Moreover, Morocco itself, a close American ally and standard and safe destination in travel and food tourism stories, is not Libya, Syria, Iraq, or Palestine. Morocco can be safely consumed on the Fourth, and consumption, in turn, can be American and comfortably perform Morocco. Furthermore, the mention that this dish is Goin's favorite at her wine bar A.O.C. makes for a neat and patriotic plug for Goin as chef as well as for her wine bar. Highlighting the way in which the pages of many publications negotiate relationship with corporate sponsors, *Food & Wine* maintains consumption itself as the site of legitimated identity, refinement, and style. Whether A.O.C. compensated *Food & Wine* for this plug, likely a matter of closed record, seems beside the point. It is clear, despite its minimalism, that this is not a narrative in which Moroccans are likely to be eating hot dogs on their own national holiday. Although taste in this sense does not free itself completely from the narrative of national tradition, it ceases to be merely synechdochic in its relation to the latter and acquires a degree of autonomy for the U.S. global consumer/reader of *Food & Wine*. In many ways fusion food creates an international context for consumption and dispenses with it for the all-important act of consuming, an act that in turn works as a space-clearing gesture in which the domestic space remains marked as a lack.

To complement further what was evidently its annual "patriotic" issue, *Food & Wine* features an article by Peter Wells, "A Chef at Peace," which tells the story of John Besh, a cook who had almost completed his diploma at the Culinary Institute of America when he was called up for the first Gulf War. Wells tell us how Besh kept a professional diary during the conflict that outlined menu items he wanted to create once the war was over. Born and raised in Louisiana before going to New York to attend CIA, Besh at war found his imagination more occupied by the local foods of Louisiana than by New York's trendy ethnic-nouvelle cuisine primarily because it became a way of remembering home while far away in Kuwait. Wells quotes him as follows: "I figured out it's not all about what they're doing in New York or Los Angeles. . . . It's about learning what we had back in Louisiana. That woke me up—that I miss Mom and Dad, I miss the food, I miss all the things that gave me comfort" (78). While in the Gulf, Besh even drafted what he termed a "mission statement" for a hypothetical restaurant called the New American in which "everything down to the coffee, would be made in America" (78). "No longer," Besh's manifesto further states, "would America's cuisine be looked down on by other nations. [. . .] It's time for America's cuisine to reflect its people and personality" (78).

With the second U.S. war on Iraq and a bloody and dangerous U.S. military occupation of the country underway in July 2003, it certainly seems legitimate to read Wells's piece as a cautious and line-toeing epicurean salute to the flag. Here the fusion food narrative gives way to what also seems a more traditional culinary nationalism, in the manner of

Endless Feasts. The familiar synechdochic relation—Louisiana's regional authenticity and originality *is* American cuisine—appears to be back in force. But, while reverting to a culinary nationalism resting on the eaten rather than the eating, "A Chef at Peace," more carefully considered, turns out to be the exception that proves the (fusion/consumption nationalist) rule. For this is not primarily a food-experience narrative at all. There are no descriptions of food here, or recipes, such that food itself becomes a screen upon which to project fantasies. It is a story about war in what is not only a literal but also a kind of food desert: Kuwait, Iraq, KP rations, or otherwise militarily standardized food. Homesick fantasies about a "New American" restaurant/cuisine in which even the "coffee" (not something, by the way, that can be cultivated anywhere in the U.S., with the exception of Hawaii, for he does not specify whether the coffee bean, distributor, or style would be American) is home-grown are the predictable results when a food expert like Besh must be removed from the site of both cooking and consumption. Though toward the end of the article, Wells informs the reader that not every single ingredient in his restaurant is American (since national boundaries in relationship to food would be impossible to achieve), the article emphasizes his patriotism in stating that Besh "traveled all the way around the globe" and "discovered" his home. Now "a chef at peace"—presumably inner as well as outer—Besh, having found (in a dislocal fashion) his home away from it, can fulfill his dream of getting back to his culinary roots without having to do battle with foreign ingredients and flavors.

As I argued at the beginning of this section, *Food & Wine*, together with its fusion food aesthetic, differs from earlier genres of food tourism narratives by transforming travel into its pure, fantasy form and incorporating the linguistic and visual markers of such fantasies directly into food descriptions, recipes, and advertisements. But this does not mean that travel itself is missing entirely from the narrative culture of the magazine. For example, *Food & Wine* regularly features "global superchef" Jean-Georges Vongerichten, famous for mixing French with Asian flavors and ingredients in dishes featured on the menus of the dozen or so restaurants he owns around the world, including Manhattan and Hong Kong. Along with selections of his recipes, these articles often combine the imagined, food-travel of the fusion dishes themselves with literal travel. A May 2007 article on the chef, "Jean-Georges Bora Bora" written by Tom Gilling, reports on Vongerichten's trip to Bora-Bora as the chef gets ready to open his restaurant, Lagoon, at an expensive resort on the French Polynesian island. Gilling follows Vongerichten as he fishes in the ocean and scouts for Polynesian ingredients in the local markets, looking for inspiration for his French/Polynesian fusion menu (43). Here, as in the cruise ship ad analyzed above, the exotic setting and the food that "fuses" its cuisine or ingredients invert what, in more traditional, *Gourmet*-style food and travel narratives, is the customary hierarchy. Place belongs to, and is posited by, food, and not vice versa.

Such food/travel journalistic fusion is even more emphatic in a July 2003 article by Jane Sigal, a contributing editor at *Food & Wine* (and who also writes for the *New York Times, Wall Street Journal,* and *Time Out New York).* Titled "Jean-Georges's Asian Accent," the article features Vongerichten and his Manhattan restaurant, named 66. The layout of the first page of the story places the following subheading at the top of the page: "Having a meal at superchef Jean-Georges Vongerichten's new restaurant 66 is like traveling to Shanghai without leaving New York City. An admirer attempts to eat her way to an understanding of his intensely personal cuisine" (149). This is positioned above a photograph of a white bowl of cabbage resting on a yellow base with green asparagus peeking out of the broth. With a black mat as background, the visual oozes contemporary design. The photographer's name appears on the bottom right hand corner, emphasizing the artful dimension of the food photograph, here and throughout the pages of the magazine. A mere glance at the article, with its reference to fusion, Shanghai-in-New-York, a chef with a French-German name, and an international visual design flavor in which the taste of the food and taste in the sense of refinement and visual sophistication effectively merge, already tells the reader that travel to far flung lands is no longer necessary if American cuisine is to come of age and into its own. The world has now beaten a path to America's door; there's nothing left to do but discriminate— and consume.

Vongerichten's cuisine is, however, reconnected to travel in at least two, nonimaginary senses. First, there are his restaurants. Sigal tells us that Vongerichten "grafts Asian flavors onto French techniques at both Jean Georges' in New York and at Vong, which has outposts in Hong Kong, Chicago, and Manhattan" (150). These outposts in fact serve as perfect culinary examples of Saskia Sassen's thesis that the major city-centers in the world are economically linked with each other far more than with their own national economies. Still, though his food reaches beyond U.S. boundaries (he is opening a restaurant in Shanghai as well), the U.S., especially New York, is constructed as the vanguard of fusion cuisine, the place where the melding of different flavors finds its optimal space, as there is no strong, uniform domestic tradition to stand in its way. Travel here starts at the place where, fundamentally, travel is no longer necessary.[14]

Yet there are still ways to infuse newness into the New York food scene. "After a few trips to Shanghai," reports Sigal, Vongerichten has reversed the direction of the graft and started to bring "French ingredients into Asian dishes" (150). Evidently there are still invigorating things to be learned from travel and study outside the American metropolis. After dining at 66, Sigal has a number of questions for the super-chef: why, for example, does tuna tartar appear on a Chinese menu? Might the lacquered pork with scallions and ginger be a "nod to his roots in Alsace" rather than something discovered in, or inspired by Shanghai? Vongerichten's only reply to her is that she must to go to Shanghai and find the answers there. Further travel so to speak, into the heart of the menu must have the way prepared by travel across the globe.

Sigal complies. Upon reaching Shanghai, she writes that some of her "first impressions" were "expected," but the city turns out to be far more "cosmopolitan" than she had imagined. There are still food experiences waiting to be discovered by the traveler. Adopting a quasi-ethnographic style, Sigal reports that "although the food was recognizably Chinese" she "had never seen most of the dishes before" (151). The menu at Bua Lao's "is a thick manual on how to build your own harpsichord" and it "features a long list of cold marinated dishes, including smoked fish, bean-curd skin, jelly fish, drunken crab. . . ." To partake of the latter, you "pick out the bits of shell and cartilage with chopsticks to get at the creamy roe and sweet flesh" (151). Such details may not be important to the people who go out to eat at 66 but the article specifically aims to provide information that will better enable them not only to know something about what they're consuming but also to travel imaginatively from Shanghai back to the menu at 66. Sigal herself returns to 66 after her trip, where now, lo and behold, the lacquered pig reminds her of "China, not of France" (177). She in fact realizes that Vongerichten is right, and the "trip to Shanghai had given [her] all the answers" (177).

Could anything be more cosmopolitan and less Americanizing than this story of food travel (or perhaps better said, food-travel-food)—complete with Vongerischten's recipes and a section called "travel details" in which information about places to stay and eat in Shanghai are listed? Has not fusion here, in fact, truly become the food of the "global city"? It may appear so, but, though it is a subtle one, the fact remains here that international travel is no longer a means of discovering new or more authentic cuisines. It is in effect a mere appendage to a food experience complete in itself, or, at best, a means of deepening one's interpretation, or embellishing one's fantasy, of the tastes and combinations on the domestically located plate. And the place from which the taster interprets and further fantasizes is New York, not Shanghai, the place that lacks, and must therefore continuously be reinvested with meaning. Here food perfects its mediation of travel. Tourism can mean going or staying, so long as it takes the form of eating. Dislocalism functions regardless of whether travel is real or fantastic.

Such a domestic space of fusion also clearly requires that nothing stand as a barrier to the flow of goods/flavors, hence the liberation of all markets from state controls. This is especially acute in the case of China. In a "postmodern" version of *Endless Feasts'* celebration of Shanghai—that is, one without the weight of history—Sigal attributes Shanghai cosmopolitanism to the presence of "foreigners—Japanese, Koreans, Taiwanese, Europeans and Americans." She goes on to say that judging from the "billboards advertising everything" from KFC to "Thai-owned lotus supermarkets" the foreigners "are all here to do business" (150). Though the U.S. is presented as one of many foreign players in Shanghai, it is its presence, as, implicitly, the overseer and sponsor of globalization, as well as the principal market for Chinese exports, that makes the presence of the other "cosmopolitans" possible. And although the specter of an all out trade war with the Chinese is always hovering, China's apparently high growth rates are one of the few remaining international economic indicators of the conventionally measured health and sustainability of U.S.-led globalization. And all of this, in Sigal's as in the *Food & Wine* narrative generally, has its culinary analog: all tastes and ingredients come together into one fusion melting pot because the pot is American. China, once the evil, communist other par excellence, the barricaded and forbidden monolith, now, unlike the former USSR, succeeds at business like a more youthful U.S., and, in any case, reopens itself to the world like one giant and welcoming Chinese restaurant.[15]

V. THE END(S) OF CUISINE AND ANTHONY BOURDAIN'S *A COOK'S TOUR*

Dressed in a leather jacket and jeans, and radiating anti-institutional charm, Tony Bourdain, star of the Food Network series *A Cook's Tour*[16] looks like he belongs in the beat generation. For him "eating is a way of life." He goes "in search of food around the world." Still, when not on camera or on the road, a chef in the swanky New York restaurant Les Halles, who started as a dishwasher in a Provincetown restaurant, Bourdain is constructed by the show as someone who has seen—and eaten—it all. Bourdain's cool is reinforced even further by the fact that he has written a number of books, some of them novels. His search for "extreme" cuisine mostly takes Bourdain outside the U.S., although he has done shows in New Orleans, Minneapolis, and, most memorably, Los Angeles—where he eats in high-end restaurants as well as in hot dog joints. He generally accompanies his eating tours with a sarcastic commentary on people who eat trendy food, on the moralism of vegetarians, and even on the Food Network itself. No one, from the *nouveaux riches* to the poor, is exempt from his wit, something that provides him with credibility and helps him (as it does travel writers) to establish himself as an anti-institutional rebel and individual, separate from other tourists. The only thing that matters in the end is the food he eats. But this generates only the aesthetic effect of critique, and Bourdain's food commentaries, always presented within the frame of a tourism narrative, are kept carefully apolitical. Or, more precisely, as one might otherwise put it, politics are largely the politics of food as an aesthetic experience, and not so much, for example, a politics of food production or of hunger. Given this constraint, it is nevertheless explicit that Bourdain's search for extremes is a response to the abundance and wide availability of foods in a globalized U.S., albeit in endless combinations and suffused with flavors from all over the world. The U.S. is seen as a place over-saturated with food—an image reflected, positively and without the sarcasm, in magazines such as *Food & Wine*.

Holding out the possibility of some corner of the world of food experience that has not been discovered, *A Cook's Tour* sets out to find it. But these are not the national self-identity pilgrimages of *Endless Feasts*. Bourdain, by taking on the style and the persona of the fifties and sixties rebel, automatically conveys his contempt for this sort of culinary civic pride. No less than *Food & Wine*, *A Cook's Tour* starts out from the premise of a national cuisine as an empty space or a lack. And an American way of consumption as style and performance is, once again, the response, the mobilizing of the lack itself becoming the national identifying mark. But, unlike those of *Food & Wine*, Bourdain's food narratives relish the backdrop of consumption, turning the tour's destinations themselves into a kind of palate (as well as palette) upon which to experiment with food. As Bourdain repeats in the standard series intro, featuring him at work in Les Halles ("this is my world") overseeing the preparation of lamb chops, pepper steak, and a chocolate tart, even the wonderful worlds of fine eating leave a cook hungering for novelty, and so one must shock one's taste buds, and sensibility, back into life. ("Taste and smells are my memories. Now I am in search of new ones. So I am leaving New York to have a few epiphanies around the world.

I am looking for extremes in emotions, and I am willing to go to some lengths for it. I'll risk everything. I've got nothing to lose."). Not the lack of authentic domestic cuisine nor the ever more institutionalized routine and standardized menus of "ethnic" foods make Bourdain yearn to go in search of food extremes; rather it is the fact that eating, consumption itself, even when "fused," becomes too satisfied with itself, too well fed, and too risk free. The show presents the mobilization of the lack to be in danger of getting fat and sedentary if all it does is order from the menu and try faint-heartedly to stimulate itself at the price of the boredom and exploitation of the underpaid and usually immigrant kitchen crew. And so Bourdain, sporting a cigarette along with his jeans and leather, sets out to wrestle with his food, in a rebellious manner that is largely stylized, for he is often nervous about eating unfamiliar things.

In accordance with this defiant stance, his tours within the U.S. are more often than not mere spoofs. The opening of the LA show mocks Hollywood, and in New Orleans, Bourdain misbehaves in typical French Quarter tourist style—or rather pretends to—getting himself arrested. His fine is to be taken out to eat some decent food. At the Mall of America in Minnesota he does a riff on standardization and corporatization, eating deep-fried cheesecake and jokingly insisting that scenes of *A Cook's Tour* supposedly filmed in Cambodia and Vietnam were actually simulations shot at the mall. True, he discovers that there are a few oases in Minneapolis, where he samples tripe prepared by a French/New York expatriate, enjoys locally made sausages in a neighborhood bistro, and finds good Vietnamese food, noting that in thirty years the latter will have become as American as apple pie. But one senses that these scenes might have been inserted at the Food Network's insistence, since they have nothing at all "extreme" about them. In effect, while touring the domestic scene (although significantly, not New York) he takes the performance of taste beyond refinement to its logical conclusion, purifying it of what are still its aristocratic, gourmand pretensions even in the fusion aesthetic of *Food & Wine*. From the Cold War type democrats and food embassies of *Gourmet,* the yuppie shopping artists and fusing flavor collectors of *Food & Wine*—traveling to eat and eating as traveling—we arrive at the cook as bohemian and vagabond: eating travel.

Bourdain seems to become a culinary version of the travel narrators I have critiqued in chapter 3. Like them, he borrows a form of ethnographic narrative that is also quasi-fictional whose predictable drama and plot revolves around whether he is going to like what he tastes in different parts of the world. Mostly he does, but there are times where he does not like what his hosts have prepared for him. Bourdain's partly ethnographic and partly fictionalized narrative allows him to position himself against the average tourist, creating a sense of adventure, risk, and danger. The back cover of the series' companion book (authored by Bourdain and also entitled *A Cook's Tour*) states that it "chronicles the unpredictable adventures of America's boldest and bravest chef"—subtly taking it for granted that the bravery of a person has anything at all significant to do with his being a professional cook. All throughout Bourdain's adventures, both literary and televised, we are treated to nuggets of learning about the way that people eat. But since much of that is no longer so mysterious as it was even fifty years ago, Bourdain's ironic, undercutting narrative becomes all the more important. And, indeed, Bourdain's witty mannerisms and clownish behavior are entertaining enough to become the real law of narrative motion in *A Cook's Tour*. In other words, more than watching the show to see what food he eats, we watch to see how he reacts to it. Indeed, Bourdain seems, at times, to grow bored with his search, even, occasionally, almost angry with what the show's producers and director evidently force him to do—such as, for example, eating tamales laced with stewed iguana outside Oaxaca, Mexico. But it is clear that the series' own investment in looking for newness is so pronounced that the search for extreme cuisine must go on, even if the chef/hero must ironize the whole affair for effect.

One way or the other, however, Bourdain produces narratives about national cuisines effectively in keeping with accepted wisdom about them, even if he pokes fun at them. While the series and (much more so) his books reveal him as someone critically aware, the food narrative itself works to dissipate and neutralize any criticism of institutions, government policy, or accepted stereotypes. In an episode of the TV show that takes him to St. Petersburg, Bourdain is taken to eat reindeer, which prompts him to say on camera that he may decide to serve it himself at Les Halles, for the Christmas season, just to terrorize children. ("Mommy, did he cook Rudolph? Yes, Timmy, he cooked Rudolph.") Though the opening of the show has Bourdain noting that as a child of the Cold War—from whose official, American version he clearly distances himself—he would never have imagined himself someday coming to Russia, he promptly dissipates even this incipient criticism by playing spy with his food "informant," Samir, with whom he communicates in secret code. As we watch Tony sampling reindeer, or blinis, or drinking himself into oblivion on the local vodka, the American viewer cannot help summoning up media-circulated images of Russians whose food rations left them deprived during the Cold War. Presumably, no one ate well in the USSR. Only with the arrival of U.S.-led global capitalism, with Bourdain following in its wake, did "Russia" come to qualify as a food experience. The reality—that there is more hunger in today's Russia than twenty years ago under the Communists—is just too real, certainly for the Food Network, and even for Bourdain's caustic, off-beat New Yorker's skepticism. Even Bourdain's complaints dissipate critique, as when he tells us that he gave in and wore a huge fur cap for the Russia show although he had specified "no funny hats."

In *A Cook's Tour*, Europe is largely reproduced as a purveyor of tradition and history. For example, on his visit to Portugal with José, his (Portuguese) boss from Les Halles, Bourdain sounds like any tourist guide as he tells us that "Portugal is a step back in time" and still "very much like it was 100–200 years ago." His trip to France, where he had spent childhood summers with his father, is laced with nostalgia. With his brother, he eats the vichyssoise soup and oysters he says he remembers from years ago. But even as he cooks French brasserie food at Les Halles, the nostalgia for childhood summers still gives the familiar food something that, for Bourdain, food in the U.S. does not have. Here the spoofing is toned down, and as is generally the case when he is in Europe, Bourdain's personal and professional familiarity with European cooking, ingredients, and habits put the "extremes" on the back burner.

For the world's "extreme cuisine," he must seek out the peasants and the poor in countries such as Cambodia, Thailand, Morocco, and Mexico—according to Bourdain, the real food innovators, because driven by tradition but also by scarcity and necessity. The critical force of the latter fact, though given more consideration in Bourdain's writings, is muted on the series by a careful practice of always showing even the humblest people in these settings to be eating. "Extremes" pertain to taste, and to the personal quests for "epiphanies"—not to hunger and exploitation on the land.

Bourdain certainly makes no secret of his admiration for third world peasants, especially when they become immigrants to the U.S., bringing their culinary ingenuities with them. On the top of his list are the mostly Mexican sous-chefs who work for him in the kitchen at Les Halles, and one of whom acts as his guide on a food tour of Mexico. Here, of course, the specter of third world hunger can be more easily shooed away, even while its ironic benefits to cuisine in the U.S., by driving the world's best cooks to live and work there, are openly acknowledged. Here we find *A Cook's Tour* producing its particular variation on dislocalism: the lack is simultaneously filled and maintained by tracing the true culinary artistry of peasant innovators from their "extreme" locations at the "ends of the earth" back to the domestic enclosure of the U.S., where they can be fully aestheticized, but with a better conscience than what is on offer in *Gourmet* or *Food & Wine*. The only catch is that, because even this food will soon become "American as apple pie," the identity-producing lack can be maintained only if Bourdain continues to travel in search of still greater "extremes." Having become saturated not only with standardized food but with immigrant foods as well, what Bourdain must find in order to secure newness and extremity are the poor and immobile, those left out of the discourses on global cuisines, whom even Vongerichten's French/Chinese/New York/Shanghai fusions are too faint-hearted to discover. But note that by going in search of this food, Bourdain simultaneously appears all the more American, while Vongerichten, 66, and writers for *Food & Wine* all look like "rootless cosmopolitans" by comparison.

As noted previously, the book, *A Cook's Tour,* contains critical comments evidently too dangerous for the television series. For example, Bourdain writes that "once you've been to Cambodia, you'll never stop wanting to beat Henry Kissinger to death with your bare hands" (162). Calling Kissinger a "murderous scumbag," Bourdain continues: "while Henry continues to eat nori rolls and remaki at A-list parties, Cambodia, the country he secretly and illegally bombed, invaded, undermined, and then threw to the dogs is still trying to raise itself up on its one leg" (162). We also hear that one in eight Cambodians—as many as 2 million people—were killed during the Khmer Rouge's campaign to eradicate their country's history (162). With such comments rare anywhere in print in the U.S., much less in food narratives, Bourdain notes the "killing fields" of Cambodia as a tragedy prepared by U.S. carpet bombing and the resulting threat of famine.[17]

Still, even these critical and historical asides are kept within narrow bounds that tend, even in the more uncensored book version of *A Cook's Tour,* to dissipate their force. First there is the fact that they are delivered within the familiar format of an amateur ethnography, of going to see the "abject squalor" for oneself. Even if the critique is occasionally on target, this is a narrative strategy more concerned with warding off the stigma of tourism—that is, with being "critical" of the "ugly American" on a package tour—than with questions of power and oppression. Even more crucially, however, this is still a narrative that, in the end, is about enjoying food, and nothing can be permitted to stand in the way of that. On this score, book and TV series are one.

A further barrier against critique—against the real extremes one finds on the peripheries of global capital—is simply the quality of Bourdain's voice and mannerisms. Although he personally goes places and does things beyond the experience of the typical viewer, his on-camera persona is clearly designed to make all this seem familiar to his audience. For example, when he eats a raw and still beating snake's heart in Cambodia, the shock of the spectacle is guided back by Bourdain's commentary into the standard U.S. sense of Cambodia as a place of violence and lawlessness. We hear him say that this is a place where tourists come to "behave badly," thereby positioning himself both as a part of such bad behavior and yet outside of it—a fairly conventional ethnographic move in which the ethnographer gains close grounds yet somehow maintains a critical distance. Continuously striking the attitude of the rebel, Bourdain avoids the hotel lobbies and enlists the help of local translators and "informants" who show him around and take him to eat what the "people" eat, allowing him to maintain a simultaneously humble and cynical pose. In this same Cambodia show, we see Bourdain going down the Mekong River on a boat with another of his bosses at Les Halles, a Frenchman named Philippe. They see a poor woman cooking on a dismal-looking houseboat and ask her if they can taste the food, all the while protesting that they don't want to deprive her or her family of their sustenance. The woman seems doubtful a first, but, of course, consents, and the two of them are given generous helpings. Immediately, the focus is on the moment of tasting, and, despite the care taken by the pair of adventurer gourmets to show sensitivity to the poverty of their "informant," the narrative of scarcity and hunger, with its strong ethical underpinnings, is instantly evaporated. Tasting, and the heaping of praise on the clearly overwhelmed and gratified boat woman, who smiles broadly, are what conclude the narrative. Where did the woman get this food? What did she have to do to get it? Is this how she and her family eat everyday, or was this an unusual occasion? What will become of her? These are questions nervously set aside as Bourdain and Phillipe are boated away, congratulating themselves on a once-in-a-lifetime experience. And though in both book and the TV show there is reference to the fact that the woman was washing her pans in dirty water, this only attempts to produce the stylized pose of Bourdain as a risk taker as he quips: "How do you say e-coli in French?" Though U.S. media projects images of the world's poor on a regular basis, what is produced here as "new" is the "fact," represented with an almost ethnographic detail, that these people do sometimes eat, and, even if they have little food, they certainly know what to do with it. It is as if good cookery could somehow always prevail and save the day, even in the absence of anything to eat. The idea is that there are gems in the dirt, starkly positioned against the nothingness of cuisine in the U.S., despite its abundance.

A scene in Bourdain's tour of Thailand in which he is shown eating a durian further typifies the series' theme of finding the good things amidst the rot of the world. The durian fruit emits an intense, rotting-like aroma but has a taste described as heavenly by those who eat it. A veritable forbidden fruit, it remains generally unknown and unavailable in the U.S., where it had once been illegal to import. Even in Thailand and other parts of tropical Asia eating durian is often prohibited in public places. Bourdain's ritualized eating of the durian—outdoors, but respectfully distant from the public—nicely condenses all the edges of his narrative strategy: food as novelty, as danger, as something stripped of the snobbery of Western gourmets, as a form of communion with the culinary genius of poor peasants, the good "rot" of the tropics positioned against the bad, tasteless rot of junk and standardized food in the United States. Though the book version of the episode contains more critical commentary, it also strips down the narrative into one of good taste amidst the muck. "It was fantastic," he reports. "Cheesy, fruity, rich, with a slightly smoky background. Imagine a mix of Camembert cheese, avocado, and smoked Gouda. Ok don't. [. . .] Tasting the stuff one struggles with words. . . . Durian was one of the first truly 'new' flavors I'd encountered." Note the rhetorical ploy of making a comparison to standard gourmet flavors and ingredients in the U.S., followed by the sudden, ironic abandonment of the trope ("OK don't.") as if to familiarize and defamiliarize in the same stroke. And we read that he sat there "licking the delightful gleet off my blade": an almost reassuring gesture amidst his nervous anxiety about the sanitary condition of the food he is about to consume (170–71).

One of Bourdain's favorite targets of playful ridicule is the Food Network itself, which obviously is not threatened by any of it and sanctions it within the frame of this particular show. He is often shown taking pot shots at the big chefs of the Food Network: Emeril Lagasse, who at this time has probably more airtime than any other TV chef; or Bobby Flay, who also has more than one show and gets daily airtime; or Rachel Ray, who has become a star in her own right. (Bourdain continues this mock food rebellion in No Reservations.) In these comments, Bourdain presents Emeril and company as not daring enough to go where he goes or to perhaps eat durian or a raw snake's heart. Back at the Mall of America we see Bourdain at one point observing a salesman demonstrate a mechanical vegetable chopper. He makes snide remarks about it, saying that with one of these he could fire most of his staff back at Les Halles, since the chopper is so efficient. He walks away muttering that he ought to get several as presents for Emeril, Bobby Flay, and Martha Stewart.[18] Of course one has to laugh. The regular viewer/reader of Bourdain knows that he appreciates and admires his kitchen staff, most of them Mexican immigrants. In a show referred to earlier, he travels with his sous-chef Eddie to the small town in Mexico where Eddie—and other cooks on his staff—came from and where many of their family members still live. The episode begins with Bourdain bantering with his staff: "I want your Mom, somebody's Mom to cook for me." And what the boss wants the boss gets, as a whole assembly of mothers and other family members turn out to produce a feast of delicious Mexican peasant fare for a grateful Bourdain. Now he realizes where his cooks learned their skills.

As with the incident on the river in Cambodia, Bourdain's populist willingness to fly in the face of gourmet snobbery and rub elbows with his Mexican cooks and their families gestures at genuine social critique— evoking a Jack Kerouac-like narrative of a hip-plebeian American identity—only to dissolve it in the supposedly neutral ideological substance of good food, eaten in common. Spiced and flavored with Bourdain's folksy and (within the limits of the occasion) gracious ways, the fact that neither Eddie nor the other cooks at Les Halles whose faces Bourdain recognizes in those of their mothers can afford to either bring their families with them to New York or visit them with any frequency back in their village in Mexico is not something the Food Network, for all its occasional munificence, is willing to have its viewers consume.

Once again, the book version sheds some critical light on what went on behind the scenes. It is here that we learn that the Food Network paid for the food at the feast in honor of Bourdain's visit, the cost of which would otherwise have been prohibitive for Eddie's and the other sous-chefs' families. And Bourdain professes his own reluctance to join in with the staging. "I'd had a grim duty to perform. Yet another forced march to television entertainment. 'Tony . . . Tony . . . listen. It's a food show. It's going to be on the Food Network. We need some variety! We can't just show you hanging around in Puebla, getting drunk with your sous chef!'" (205). But the less-censored literary version of the narrative doesn't stray too far from the general, dislocalizing constraints of the food narrative as genre. The book tells in great detail the story of Eddie's beginnings as an undocumented worker in the U.S., but sweetens the sauce by emphasizing Eddie's success (legal, a good job in the kitchen at Les Halles) and pushing its exceptionalism off the table. Eddie, says Bourdain (something repeated on television), is his role model, and he feels privileged to know him. The Food Network gets lightly bashed for scripting the trip to Mexico and keeping Bourdain from simply relating to Eddie off the job and man-to-man. Still, Bourdain cannot resist letting slip another key ingredient of his affection for his sous-chef here, and one more akin to his sarcastic remark about the virtues of the mechanical vegetable chopper at the Mall of America: he especially likes working with Eddie, and undocumented and immigrant workers from places like Mexico and Ecuador, because they are grateful for what little they have and will do what he says—unlike French or Italian chefs, who, he tells us in his book, have too many ideas of their own.

Eddie and the other sous-chefs at Les Halles are, after all, the ones who have to continue reproducing Bourdain's recipes while he travels the world in search of extremes and epiphanies. His mobility is the antithesis of theirs. They move toward work, if they can find it. He moves away from it, tired of its alienating routine and its gradual sapping of his culinary imagination. The peasant innovators he goes in search of, such as the boat woman in Cambodia, are, after all, just like Eddie's mother: those left behind in the great forced labor migrations of our time, so that their knowledge can find its way to the tables of Les Halles or 66 or the pages of *Food & Wine,* while their children chop the vegetables for a song, allowing the televised master chef, but not them, to travel and thereby appear to reverse the motion of the whole.

As a form of the exotic that can be reproduced anywhere and is seemingly innocent of the excesses of tourism, food has become a site of tourism in itself. Food tourism narratives in *Food & Wine, Gourmet,* and *A Cook's Tour* are even produced as "morally" better alternatives to "fast" or standardized food. While the search outside of national boundaries for food experiences is framed in these narratives with an almost-moral "must-do" rhetoric of newness and adventure, eating the foods of immigrants in the U.S. is presented as an ethical duty. Yet ironically, because the search for newer foods is presented as desirable and even moral in itself, food tourist narrators find themselves under subtle pressure to maintain the domestic space as one marked by a lack of food experiences. Through complex dislocal strategies, such narrators not only champion a rhetoric of adventure but also conserve or restore strict boundaries between the U.S. and the rest of the world, leaving both available to them as spaces of creativity, pleasure, and new experiences.

CONCLUSION

The "Turn to Fiction"—and "Fictional Capital"—Revisited

The introduction to *Dislocalism* closes with a brief remark on a "general facet of dislocalism that has particular implications for the humanities and especially for literary/cultural studies" which I refer to as the "turn to fiction," The latter, as very briefly outlined and previewed there, appears, with greater or lesser emphasis, as a recurrent conceptual and analytical theme throughout all four chapters of the book. But I want to devote this concluding chapter to some further reflections on the turn to fiction insofar as it represents a possible direction and focus for future work. This is both because of what I see in general as the significance of the turn to fiction in relation to globalization and its accompanying crises and because the turn to fiction is relevant to those working with fictional narratives and imaginative texts (across a range of disciplines in the humanities) not only in writing but in the many newer forms of mass, electronic, digital, and visual media. Lastly, there is also the question of the turn to fiction as a dislocalizing strategy in its own right, a way of fending off globalization's rhetoric of obsolescence.

But I conclude with the turn to fiction also because it gives me the immediate opportunity to return, in a more detailed if still necessarily speculative way, to what I see as a key moment in the theoretical argument developed in chapter 1 as concerns the critical analysis of U.S. management theory and corporate culture more generally. This is the question of the connection between 1) the latter's dislocalizing resort to fictional narratives themselves as well as to *theories* of narrative and fiction for purposes of theorizing globalized corporate organizations and 2) the un- or semiconscious dilemma posed to management by "fictitious," or, as modern critiques of political economy more often term it, "fictional capital." "Fictional capital" is, as far as I know, not literally part of the conceptual language of management theory. Nor is the connection between the literal "turn to fiction" in U.S. management theory and the turn to something approximating "fictional *capital*" in its present form within a heavily financialized global capitalism (to be explained in some detail below) explicitly posited—much less able to pass through management's own ideological filters.

To refer, selectively, to the pertinent section of the first chapter: having explained how, for management theory, "[a]longside helping to guide managers in their organizational decision making by providing ethical templates and by furnishing simple and compelling behavioral models capable of reflecting complex situations, fiction itself becomes a blueprint for organization," chapter 1 continues:

> [I]t is hard to avoid the speculative conclusion here that, however unwittingly, unsystematically, and, so to speak, facing backwards, management theory [has] been driven to formulate or at least to imagine something like the Marxian category of . . . fictional capital. [. . .] [O]ne does not have to be knowledgeable on this point of Marxian critical political-economy to have more than an inkling that, as increasing masses of fictional capital remain unrealized, as more and more "good" money is thrown after "bad," a "tipping point" will be reached beyond which capital itself must come to function more as a "fiction," a financial *fictio juris*, than as anything with a *real* basis in production. If, however, for ideological reasons, "theory" is prevented from entertaining the thought that such "hyper-fictionalization" calls into question the continued viability of global capitalism itself, then, as bizarre as this undoubtedly may appear, it is hard to see what alternative remains but to complete the ideological inversion itself and conclude that the whole business is a fiction anyway, and the sooner one realizes this, and sets about the task of selecting the fictions best-suited to getting the job done, the better. (53, 54)

The concluding sentence in the above self-citation, especially in the absence of further argument, leaves the hypothesis of a hyper-fictionalization in a still somewhat precarious position. While I think it is virtually self-evident that a discipline such as management theory cannot, without calling its own *raison d'être* into question, *literally* "question the continued viability of global capitalism," to conclude that the only way it *could* accommodate the thought of *non*viability would be through thinking not only corporate organization but capitalism itself as fictional leaves out a number of other possibilities. Perhaps, for instance, the very thought of capitalism's nonviability is not considered for far more elemental reasons than those having to do with disciplinarity. (Although, of course, that does not mean that management theorists may not have sensed quite acutely the fact that crises, even severe ones, have been in the offing.)[1] But, then, how to explain both the continuous alarm-sounding and the continued popularity of corporate lecture-circuit gurus such as Tom Peters and others who employ much the same rhetoric of "now or never"? Perhaps, after all, it is quite possible to be a fervent adherent of a postmodern, myth-empowered "liberation management" or of Drucker's views on the primacy of the *culture* of the organization *and* an unrepentant neoliberal or neo-Keynesian when it comes to charting U.S. capitalism's sure course into the future. And yet, granting any one of these hypothetical possibilities, the existence of something like a "political unconscious" when it comes to management theory's need to steer clear of a Lacanian "real" that is, in this case, not only the darker side of globalization but its specific role in fueling, accelerating, and increasing to an almost fantastic degree the volcanic explosiveness of global financialization and hence of capital's hyper-fictionalization can still be counted as *no less plausible* than are the above mentioned counterpossibilities. Management theory's "turn to fiction" still requires *some* explanation, and even if the references to fiction in volume 3 of *Capital* and in, say, Sandra Sucher's Harvard Business School teaching guide *Teaching the Moral Leader* are as fortuitous and unrelated as the fact that Marx and Sucher have both read *Macbeth,* management theory's linking of "fiction" to capital, whatever the context, suggests that the hypothesis advanced rather brusquely in the above passage from chapter 1 opens more doors than it closes.

But if only so as to be able to advance further down the road toward future projects involving critiques of globalization from within (and from the standpoint of) cultural studies, I see it as necessary to clarify further than I have in my brief aside in chapter 1 what is meant by the hyper-fictionalization of capital.[2] This is especially important, given what has become the vastly increased role of finance and financialization in all areas of global social and economic policy, in both rescuing and reimagining the nation itself, in promoting debt as the continued social remedy for everyone and everything from consumers, homeowners, and students to universities and municipalities in the "developed world" and in the widespread emphasis on institutions offering "micro-credit" as a supposed remedy for poverty in the poorest parts of the "underdeveloped" capitalist periphery. All of these social and political ramifications of finance-capital have, obviously, enormous implications for changes in the sphere of the cultural as well, both in practice and in theory. This is something *Dislocalism* has analyzed in depth in the case of management theory. And it has shown how the turn to fiction in relationship to corporate practices, immigration, travel, and food (in addition to being a conservative strategy for fending off the threat of obsolescence) can be read as symptomatic of the fictionalization of the economy itself (in ways that we shall discuss in more detail below). Given a context in which the humanities suffer from a sense of increasing irrelevance both within and outside the academy, this trend of turning to fiction, stories, and cultural theory at large cannot be ignored and suggests the need for an analysis that connects the questions of politics, economics, and socio-historical contexts to the study of cultural and literary texts. Indeed, the work of critics such as Masao Miyoshi, Lisa Lowe, Cedric Robinson, Fredric Jameson, and others has taken important steps in this direction. In order to progress within this mode of analysis, I will attempt to work out the forms of mediation between the turn to fiction and an increasingly "fictionalized" economy.

Therefore, I will begin with some thoughts on what is meant by the hyper-fictionalization of capital itself, both via a review of the—for our purposes—more pertinent aspects of the concept of (as it is customarily translated) "fictitious capital" in *Capital,* volume 3 and of some of the current theories of the phenomenon in light of the recurrent and, as some would claim, downward spiraling crises of post-Fordism. I will follow these sections with a brief review of one important section of Georg Lukács's *History and Class Consciousness* on the relationship between reified consciousness, theory, totality, and capitalist crisis. From here, for illustrative purposes that I trust will have become clear, I shift to an abbreviated analysis of the work of management theorist Stephen Denning, author of numerous publications on the role of storytelling in corporate and financial organizations, particularly at the World Bank, where he was a high-ranking official during the mid- to late-1990s; and, finally, again for purposes of illustrating, a critical reading (in relationship to the notion of hyper-fictionalized capital) of Stephen Best and Sharon Marcus's introduction ("Surface Reading") to "How We Read Now," a special 2009 issue of the theoretical and literary/cultural journal, *Representations.*

I want to make it absolutely clear here that my purpose, as throughout the text of *Dislocalism,* in juxtaposing the approach of management theory to narrative, fiction, and culture to that of literary and cultural studies is not to conclude that such convergence is proof that narrative, fiction, and culture have therefore lost all oppositional value and that the work of cultural and literary studies should be limited to social and economic theory and critique. While there is no doubt that the latter should indeed be a central part of the work of cultural studies, the point of analyzing this convergence has been to demonstrate the historically specific manner, across disciplinary and intellectual boundaries, in which the hyper-fictionalizing of capital has determined dislocalism's turn to fiction in the neoliberal period.

I. MARX'S CONCEPT OF "FICTITIOUS CAPITAL"

The concept of "fictitious capital" ("fiktives Kapital" in the original German) does not make its appearance in Marx's major work until well into its third and final volume, left unfinished and published posthumously in 1894 after undergoing considerable editing at the hands of Engels. It is mentioned repeatedly but sporadically in part five of *Capital*, volume 3, "The Division of Profit into Interest and Profit of Enterprise," and, as shall be noted momentarily, using a variety of more or less synonymous terms. Marx first refers to it in chapter 25, entitled simply "Credit and Fictitious Capital," where it functions, as it often does in *Capital*, as another term for credit itself, specifying one sense in which the latter can be identified in its relation to—or as itself a paradoxical form of—capital.[3]

In the subsequent chapters that make up part five of volume 3, Marx also uses, more or less interchangeably, other terms such as "illusory" and "illusion"; "paper duplicates"; "non-existent"; "imaginary"; and even "insane."[4] What makes them interchangeable is, as even a perusal of the chapter titles of part five makes clear, their shared opposition to "*real* capital," that is, capital, whether in the form of commodities, money, or means of production, that represents a definite quantum of value in the form of objectified or "dead" labor and that can, via the absorption of additional "living labor" in the form of labor-power, valorize itself yet again and thereby commence or continue to accumulate.

Two further points need to be emphasized here. The first is that, writing at what was still, relative to the present, a phase of overall expansion and growth, here of capitalism's "first industrial revolution," Marx clearly perceived the contradictions and crisis-potential latent in "fictitious" or "illusory" capital. But he regarded the latter as an inevitable and in this sense perfectly nonillusory aspect of credit itself, a necessary facet of the turnover of industrial capital if it was to continue to expand. The *potential* for what I have termed, with more than strictly economic realities in mind, hyper-fictionalization—here the failure to convert fictional *back* into real capital, about which more, and with reference to more authoritative theories of such failure and its potentially huge contemporary repercussions to follow shortly—is certainly glimpsed by Marx (and Engels). The effects of the great crisis of 1857 can clearly be read in Marx's caustic references to the illusory and even the insane.

But there are *suggestions* in volume 3 of *Capital*—and this is my second point—that Marx attached greater significance to the concept of fictitious or illusory capital than is conveyed by the more or less straightforward concept of credit. These make their appearance in chapter 27, "The Role of Credit in Capitalist Production," in connection with a series of remarks on credit as a precondition for the formation of joint-stock companies.[5] Just after the passage on the transition of the joint-stock company to the form of the cartel or monopoly ("*one* big joint-stock company with a unified management") added, presumably, some three decades later by Engels (see note 5) Marx writes:

> This is the abolition of the capitalist mode of production within the capitalist mode of production itself, and hence a self-abolishing contradiction, which presents itself *prima facie* as a mere point of transition to a new form of production. *It presents itself as such a contradiction even in appearance.* [. . .] It is private production unchecked by private ownership. (569; my emphasis)

It is exceedingly difficult to connect what Marx is saying here to anything more concrete or conjunctural vis-à-vis its own mid-nineteenth century historical frame of reference, much less our own contemporary moment. But without claiming any special, hidden affinity here between, say, 1857 and 2008, it would also be hard to top the first and last sentences in the above-cited passage as dialectical crystallizations of the panic in the fall of 2008 after the decision to let Lehman Brothers go down and the ensuing decision, in the midst of the Bush–Obama regime change, to nationalize whatever still appeared to be standing on Wall Street—or was it rather to complete the process of letting the big banks inch ever closer to declaring *themselves* the agents of nationalization, at least when it came to the public coffers? Both sentences can be read both ways. And either way, the contradiction "abolishes" itself by making no effort to present itself *as* anything else, by merging with its own *prima facie* appearance—this being the price of now being enabled, if nothing else, to wait things out, to buy time. But to wait for what? No one, as we shall see shortly in the section to follow, really seemed to know. Officially sanctioned economic theory, in the wake of master theorist Greenspan's remarkable confes-sion and abdication, also declares itself, in effect, at an end.[6] Recall once more Marx's words in the passage cited above: that "the abolition of the capitalist mode of production within the capitalist mode of production" is a contradiction "that presents itself as such a contradiction even in appearance." Here then we have a contradiction between the reality of "abolition" (panic, meltdown, crisis) and the reality that capitalism somehow continues to be capitalism even when it "abolishes" itself by socializing huge volumes of private capital. "Even in appearance": is not that as good as if to say that the contradiction here is also, unabashedly, that between the reality of abolition and the abolition of reality? Capitalism becomes, that is, a kind of *fiction*—but not as opposed to its reality; rather, a fiction that is intrinsically an essential *part* of that reality, as a *real* fiction.

II. "HYPER-FICTIONALIZATION," OR *REAL* FICTIONAL CAPITAL

If, by now, all of this is itself beginning to sound too abstract, then consider the following brief analysis, excerpted from a longer piece written by the Marxist economist (as well as art critic and historian) Paul Mattick Jr.[7] in October, 2008 for the *Brooklyn Rail*. Writing just before the passage of the second version of the so-called TARP ("Troubled Asset Relief Program") bill, initially voted down by the U.S. House of Representatives in September 2008, Mattick writes that if the House does finally approve spending the "trillion dollars or so that you might have fantasized would some day pay for new schools, healthcare, or even just bridges that don't fall down" then

> [t]his will be money spent not for things or services but simply to replace some other money, now departed from this world of woe. *Or, more accurately, money that people thought was real has turned out to be imaginary; to deal with this, more imaginary money—money that future economic activity is supposed to generate—will take its place. Such a radical detachment of money from anything but itself may be hard to grasp, but it's the key to understanding what's going on.*[8] [my emphasis]

Although Mattick refers to "imaginary money" rather than to "fictional capital," it is clear from the logic of his argument here—and in the three following pieces for the *Brooklyn Rail*[9]—that this is synonymous with the elaboration of Marx's theory of fictitious capital that I have referred to as hyper-fictionalization. The latter, to repeat, refers to a threshold of capitalist crisis that, having been reached, makes it impossible to reconvert fictional back into real capital through the accumulation of new masses of surplus value. Existing stocks of fictional capital, in whatever form (for stocks and other forms of financialized goods such as securities, credit default swaps, etc., *can* still, up to point, be sold and converted back into money or means of production, or even reinvested) face the imminent threat of devalorization. As Mattick puts it in the conclusion to "Up in Smoke":

> What will the financiers invest in, if they become solvent again? This is the big question that is neither asked nor answered. It's just assumed that the natural course of prosperous events will resume. If debt expansion could bring prosperity, however, we'd already be living in a golden age. The problem is that all the money that has sloshed around the world for the last thirty years [i.e., since the crisis and collapse of Fordism] has led less to growth in what economists, in times like these, like to call "the real economy"—the economy of production, distribution, and consumption of actual goods and services—than to the expansion of the imaginary economy whose *real* nature is currently becoming visible. (4; my emphasis)

Hyper-fictionalization also reveals itself in the numbers themselves. See, for example, the original English version (2009) of economist Robert Brenner's prologue to the Spanish translation of his 2006 book *The Economics of Global Turbulence*.[10] In a section of this study entitled—appropriately enough, given our general focus here on fictional capital—"Speculation Dependent Accumulation," Brenner recounts what very nearly became, in 1998–2000, a crisis of the proportions of 2008, when the fallout of the Southeast Asian collapse of 1997–98 hit the U.S. economy. Revisiting the government bailout of the gigantic hedge fund, Long Term Credit Management, Brenner writes: "What happened next . . . could not have revealed more graphically and definitively the extraordinary degree to which an increasingly enfeebled real economy had come to depend on waves of runaway speculation, consciously nurtured by US economic authorities" (27). Brenner details the succession of measures, including successive reductions of the Federal Funds rate and even (shades of things to come) inducements to the "Government Sponsored Entities" Fannie Mae and Freddie Mac to increase their loans to U.S. homebuyers by enormous amounts. "In view of such powerful and blatant official support for the stock market—and the implicit assurances that lay behind it," Brenner continues:

[I]t should have surprised no one that share prices took off *as they had not done since the 1920s, severing all connection with the real economy, its actual growth and profitability.* In the brief period between the Fed's interest rate reductions of autumn 1998 and spring 2000, the S&P 500 share index recovered the ground it had lost since the previous summer and shot up by a further 30 per cent, *its price-earnings ratio reaching 35:1, the highest in all of US history.* By the first quarter of 2000, the total value of the equities of US non-financial corporations, their market capitalization, had reached $15.6 trillion, more than triple its level of $4.8 trillion in 1994, with the consequence that, *in that brief interval, the ratio between the market capitalization of non-financial corporations and non-financial corporate GDP leaped from 1.3:1 to 3:1, more than 75 per cent above the highest level previously reached during the post-war period (1.7:1 in 1968).* This was so, despite the fact that, in that six-year period, after tax non-financial corporate profits (net of interest) had risen by only 41.2 per cent. By contrast, it had taken fourteen years, from 1980 to 1994, for the ratio of non-financial corporate market capitalization to GDP to increase from 0.9:1 to 1.3, even though non-financial corporate profits had risen by 160 per cent in the intervening period. [my emphasis]

Can one, in the end, make real sense of figures such as these and not at least begin to reflect again, even if from an angle not precisely articulated by its author, on what is meant by "the abolition of the capitalist mode of production within the capitalist mode of production itself"?

Hyper-fictionalized capital has other critical analysts as well that, were a review of this concept within contemporary critical theory our central purpose here, would certainly have to be mentioned and carefully assessed: from David Harvey, who, for example, in his 2010 address to the World Social Forum[11] makes repeated mention of the "fictions" that have "characterized asset market and financial affairs over the last two decades" (1) to the concise but theoretically rigorous exposition of fictional capital's central and unprecedented role and effects within the current crisis in Norbert Trenkle's 2008 "Tremors on the Global Market."[12] As Trenkle as well as Brenner and Mattick is careful to remind us, no matter how crucial financialization and its ever more self-endangering resort to the hyper-fictionalization of capital become in the drive to reinflate "bubblenomics" (Brenner) each time one of its speculative balloons (third world debt, informational technology's "new economy," real estate) bursts, we are still left with the question of what enabled the crisis to be evaded so effectively for most of what is now the thirty year interregnum called post-Fordism? And this is not, moreover, only a question of economics—which brings us back now to the turn to fiction once more and how fiction, in keeping with the specific ideological structures of dislocalism, comes, as one might say, to coincide with the real for *want* of the real.

III. CRISIS AS FICTION, OR, FROM REIFICATION TO STORYTELLING AT THE WORLD BANK

In *History and Class Consciousness,* written in the early 1920s in the wake of the First World War, Georg Lukács observes as follows:

> The superior strength of true, practical class consciousness lies in the ability to look beyond the divisive symptoms of the economic process to the unity of the total social system underlying it. In the age of capitalism it is not possible for the total system to become directly visible in external phenomena. For instance, the economic basis of a world crisis is undoubtedly unified and its coherence can be understood. But its actual appearance in time and space will take the form of a disparate succession of events in different countries at different times. . . .[13]

Lukács's reference to the appearance of the "disparate" brings up the theoretical concept for which *History and Class Consciousness* is best known, namely that of "reification": the necessary fragmentation, isolation, and alienating objectification of reality as perceived by the social consciousness of bourgeois society, extrapolated by Lukács from Marx's theory of the fetishism of the commodities. The connection drawn by Lukács here between reification, totality, and crisis turns out, as I think can be demonstrated in shorthand here, to be a key, but thus far neglected link between fictional capital in its crisis form (hyper-fictionalization) and the turn to fiction—as well as between both of these and dislocalism itself.[14] "The further the economic crisis of capitalism advances," Lukács continues a few lines further on:

> the more clearly this unity in the economic process becomes *comprehensible to practice.* It was there, of course, in so-called periods of normalcy, too, and was therefore visible from the class stand-point of the proletariat, but the gap between appearance and ultimate reality was too great for that unity to have any practical consequences for proletarian action.
>
> *In periods of crisis the position is quite different. The unity of the economic process now moves within reach. So much so that even capital-*

ist theory cannot remain wholly untouched by it, though it can never fully adjust to it. (74–75; my emphasis in second paragraph)

Lukács might very well have had someone like Max Weber or Georg Simmel, or—leaping ahead, anachronistically, a decade and some—someone like Keynes in mind here when speaking of "capitalist theory." But in what sense could it be said—if at all—that "unity . . . now moves within reach" vis-à-vis "capitalist theory," in the case of the long crisis of post-Fordism and the increasing domination of financialization and of hyper-fictionalized capital within it? Here, keeping in mind the sheer impenetrability and hyper-complexity of a financialized capitalism that leads capitalist theory in the case of management into its turn to fiction, might we not attribute to the dominant, conscious social representatives of capital what is rather a tendency toward the *total abdication* of theory as such? *Is* there any longer a capitalist *theory* properly speaking except the one that *must* "remain wholly untouched" by a global crisis as it has evolved and matured within the specific dynamics of post-Fordism? A crisis that can only give way to a "speculation dependent accumulation" (in Brenner's understated expression), that is, more precisely, to a fully realized "abolition of the capitalist mode of production within the capitalist mode of production" (Marx). And would this amount to anything more than a consciousness of the crisis of hyper-fictionalized capital, reified in the sense of remaining "wholly untouched" by theory itself and putting in the latter's place what has been reduced, finally, to nothing more than the *conscious forms or mediations of hyper-fictionalized capital*—that is, to *fictions* themselves?

Of course, such thinking must remain entirely hypothetical, at this point. With it, however, we come back around full circle to dislocalism in its various manifestations—first and most obviously to management theory again, but with, I think, a more mediated explanation for the turn to fiction—this genre's dislocalizing form of "spatial fix"—as inseparable from the hyper-fictionalization of capital in the epoch of globalization.

So as to illustrate, in passing and symptomatically, the idea that the turn to fiction in management theory is also a turn to fiction as a surrogate *for theory*, I want to make a few observations here concerning the work of Stephen Denning, an author, lecturer, and management consultant, whose books include *The Springboard* (2000), *The Leader's Guide to Storytelling* (2005), and *The Leader's Guide to Radical Management* (forthcoming) as well as a novel and a book of poetry. A high-ranking official for years at the World Bank, and at one point its program director for Africa from 1996 to 2000, Denning directed the Bank's program in

"Knowledge Management." In a 2005 publication, *Storytelling in Organizations: How Storytelling is Transforming 21st Century Organizations and Management*,[15] edited and co-authored by Denning together with, inter alia, Laurence Prusak, former high-ranking executive at IBM, and John Seely Brown, former chief scientist at Xerox, Denning tells how, beginning in the mid-1990s when the fortunes of the World Bank, a notoriously "change-resistant" organization, were in rapid decline, he was given the supposedly broom-closet type assignment of doing something about "information management" at the Bank. He says: "The scene had changed. Now private banks had emerged and they were lending far more to developing countries than the World Bank could ever lend. And they were doing it faster and cheaper and with less conditionality than the World Bank" (102). He goes on to say, "There was even a worldwide campaign to close the World Bank down. There was a political slogan chanted by protesters, 'Fifty years is enough!' So our future as a lending organization was in question. Simply becoming more efficient wasn't going to solve our problems" (102). He began to test his idea that the Bank should not remain a straight lending institution but become an institution of knowledge management. Denning reports that he tried "rational" arguments but they were not working and no one was listening to him.

But a series of happy accidents led him eventually to the idea of storytelling as a highly efficient mode both of storing and transmitting information and knowledge and of bringing about institution-wide change.[16] By 2000, the year he left the Bank for better things, it had a "Knowledge Management" division in place, and even the Bank's president lost no opportunity to tell the various change-catalyzing, so-called springboard stories (among them the "Zambia," the "Madagascar" and the "Pakistani Highway" anecdotes). The story that began to change the minds of the World Bank executives was the Zambia story:

> In June 1995 a health worker in a tiny town of Zambia logged on to the website for the Centers for Disease Control and Prevention in Atlanta, Georgia, and got the answer to a question on how to treat malaria. (Now, this in 1995 in a tiny town not the capital. Zambia was one the poorest countries in the world.) But the most important part of this picture for us in the World Bank is this: that World Bank is not in the picture. We don't have a know-how organized so we could share our knowledge with the millions of people in the world who make decisions about poverty. (104)

With this story, there began, to hear Denning tell it, the shift in the World Bank that reshaped the institution. To hear Denning tell it, the World Bank's *esprit de corps* had undergone a complete overhaul, and storytelling had everything to do with it.

But storytelling has an implied other here. In a section of Denning's chapter in *Storytelling in Organizations* ("Using Narrative as a Tool for Change") subtitled "Unlearning What I Knew about Storytelling" Denning starts by confessing to surprise at

> telling you about it [storytelling] at all. That's because 5 years ago, when I stumbled upon this, I knew that knowledge was solid and objective and abstract and analytic. And I knew that something like storytelling was nebulous and ephemeral and subjective and unscientific. I knew that all of these qualities of knowledge—solid, objective, abstract, analytic—were the good qualities. And I knew that all of the qualities of storytelling— nebulous and ephemeral and subjective and unscientific—were very bad. Over the next couple of years I learned how wrong I was. In effect, I had to unlearn a great deal of what I thought I knew about organization and storytelling. (99)

Could it be, in fact, that Denning had to "unlearn" the assumption that storytelling was, in fact, "subjective and unscientific"—and that, like "knowledge," it too had its "solid and objective" aspect? Not at all. "From a strictly rationalist perspective," he writes on the following page about attempting to convince the World Bank to adopt knowledge management, "the situation [in 1996] was hopeless. But a strictly rationalist perspective is an inadequate way of understanding organizational realities" (100).

One must remind oneself that this is a (former) high-ranking official of the World Bank. Of course, not all "rationalist perspective" is to be dropped in favor of the "subjective and the unscientific." In the Preface to *Storytelling in Organizations,* Denning, here writing more self-consciously on behalf of the other contributors to the volume (included among whom is the mathematician and computer scientist John Seely Brown), writes that "in promoting the cause of narrative, we're obviously not opposed to science. Nor are we proposing to abandon analysis. Where science and analysis can make progress and make a useful contribution, we should use them. Where they can't or don't, they should step aside and let narrative contribute" (xii). But, to hear Denning tell it, "science and analysis" apparently had to step aside in the mid to late 1990s to pull the Bank out of its doldrums. The concluding chapter to the volume, also authored by Denning ("The Role of Narrative in Organizations") goes so far as to draw up a warning against the "enemies of storytelling": none other than Plato, Aristotle (who, we are told, "helped implement much of the intellectual agenda of *The Republic*"), and Descartes, the originator of "Scientism."[17]

It would be a fallacy, of course, to regard Denning's outright call for storytelling to replace or at least take priority over objectivity and analysis as typical of capitalist theory in the age of bubblenomics. Recall, however, that, at least as concerns management theory, this privileging of narrative and fiction has solid academic credentials. (Curiously, Denning, unlike Peters and the various management theorists cited and discussed in chapter 1, insists that to accomplish their task, stories must both be "true" and have "happy endings" [121–23]). But, while outwardly a caricature, given what counts as respectable, credentialed capitalist theory, whether in economics departments or in the pages of the *Wall Street Journal,* the *New York Times,* and the *Financial Times,* and the general inability—or refusal—to explain, for example, how it is that the world of international finance could have accorded to Alan Greenspan an unquestionable theoretical authority, Denning's outright case for storytelling over theory is more like a collective *self*-caricature. It is as sure a symptom as any other of how the quest to theorize hyper-fictionalized capital without posing the question of the whole, now more plainly exposed than ever by the evolving crisis of post-Fordism, ends, whether explicitly or not, by theorizing nothing but the reality of the fictional.

IV. THE WAY WE REIFY NOW

But what, then of the theory of fiction in the hermeneutic sense—necessarily inclusive here of the many cultural genres of fiction as something read or simply interpreted—given what is, as I have speculated, the pressure to abandon theory itself, leaving only fiction in its place? Let us, for the sake of maximum clarification here, quickly retrace our steps to my hypothesis regarding what has, in the post-Fordist historical context that has generated dislocalism per se, become the specific dynamic interrelation linking systemic crisis, capitalism as social totality, and reification. *History and Class Consciousness,* to repeat, observes that under the exceptional conditions of capitalist crisis, the tendency of consciousness in its scientific, theoretical form (initially independent of the class-belonging of its subject) to remain effectively blind to the whole of society and to focus on the isolated facts and experiences that make up the multiple branches of knowledge and their many corresponding theories is interrupted. By placing in question, inescapably, the continued existence and survival of the "economic process" of capitalism, the "unity of the latter moves within reach," both to practice and in theory—so much so that capitalist theory cannot remain untouched by it, thereby becoming forced, if only momentarily, to confront its fragmented, reified configuration. This assumes, however—correctly for the historical period in which Lukács formulated the theory of reification—that crisis itself, as a crisis of the reproduction of capital as the dominant relation of society, is temporary. Society then resumes its normal mode of self-reproduction as do the reified forms of consciousness that are an essential part of such reproduction.

But the turn, by fairly wide consensus, to a financialized, speculation-dominated form of capitalism after the end of the Fordist boom and the onset of a long period of decline in the real economy accompanied by the periodic rises and falls of "bubblenomics" creates the conditions for a crisis, or a series of crises, of a new type. With globalization now a virtual *fait accompli* and the hyper-fictionalization of capital becoming, progressively, the *only* remaining means for prolonging any semblance of continuous self-reproduction, crisis is never fully overcome. It remains periodic only in appearance, and looking transparently—to those willing or able to see—like the "abolition of the capitalist means of production within the capitalist means of production" the hyper-fictionalization of capital is bound to reach the point at which the social whole that is constituted and reproduced through capital assumes necessarily the appearance *either* of the totality that it is or—as its dislocalized form of reification—a *real* fiction.

Thus far I have developed the turn to fiction concerning hyper-fictionalization in relationship to management theory, and were it my purpose now to continue rethinking the other chapters of *Dislocalism* from this same vantage point, I would be drawn to reflect again, most immediately, on the question of "testimonio" as "real fiction" in the prelude to the analysis of dislocalizing readings of immigrant fictions in chapter 2, and perhaps subsequently to the problem of uncertain boundaries between the real and the fictional in the dislocalized travel writings that are the subject of chapter 3. And in the case of chapter 4, I would refocus on the "real fiction" that now, in certain mediatized contexts, has become the recipe itself as a form of reading/watching for dislocalized gourmets.

But, taking the final pages of this conclusion as an opportunity for surveying the possible ramifications of fiction in the theoretical context

I have tried to map out here—very freely and still *in*conclusively—for the critical analysis of literary/cultural fictions, I have decided to venture some critical observations on "The Way We Read Now," a recent special issue of the journal *Representations*.[18] Clearly intended as a manifesto of sorts, the issue consists of seven articles, including a programmatic introduction by editors Stephen Best and Sharon Marcus. "The Way We Read Now" generated considerable notoriety and controversy by framing itself as simultaneously an ironic sort of commemoration of and simultaneously an organized, deliberate repudiation of Fredric Jameson's *The Political Unconscious* and the method of "symptomatic reading" as purportedly codified by Jameson's book, first published roughly a generation prior to "The Way We Read Now."

Best and Marcus entitle their introduction "Surface Reading," a practice they openly counterpose to Jamesonian symptomatic reading and to the influence of the two theoretical discourses that epitomize the idea and practice of depth-based interpretation and, as they say, "hermeneutics of suspicion": Marxism and Freudian psychoanalysis.

What, then, apart from the self-proclaimed nemesis of symptomatic, depth-based readings, is surface reading? According to a rapid survey of Best and Marcus's quite lucid overture, surface reading is "looking at rather than seeing through," surface itself being "neither hidden [n]or hiding" (9). Paraphrasing contributor Anne Anlin Cheng—who writes about architectural "surfaces"—they write that "underneath surface there is only more surface" (8–9). "Attention to surface" is equated with a "practice of critical description," according to which "what . . . theory brings to texts (form, structure, meaning) is already present in them (11). "The purpose of criticism is thus a relatively modest one: to indicate what the text says about itself" (ibid.) For Marcus herself, writing in her 2007 book *Between Women*, surface reading is termed "just [that is, "only"] reading." "Just reading," write Best and Marcus, "sees ghosts as presences, not absences, and lets ghosts be ghosts, instead of saying what they are ghosts *of*" (13). Best and Marcus strike a kind of alliance at one point—one may well wonder whether reciprocated—with the so-called "New Formalism," and its ideal, according to Marjorie Levinson's review of the trend in a recent issue of *PMLA*,[19] of "learned submission" to the text, a "bathing" in the "artwork's disinterested purposelessness" (Best and Marcus, 14). Best and Marcus make the invocation of Levinson's work an entrée of sorts for invoking the authority of Adorno, especially the essays from *Notes to Literature*, "Commitment" and "The Essay as Form." Citing the latter—"thought's depth depends on how deeply it penetrates its object, not on the extent to which it reduces it to something else"—becomes a justification for affirming Adorno's advocacy of "an immersive mode of reading that does not need to assert its distance and difference from its object" (ibid.). Adorno, that is, becomes here the champion of "surface" and an ally in the abandonment of the Jamesonian interpretive model with its Marxian and psychoanalytical "depth" hermeneutics.[20]

And so on. I have (so far) purposefully left out of this abbreviated remapping of "Surface Reading" Best and Marcus's more explicit references to politics, ideology, and even capital itself so as not to clutter unnecessarily here what is already quite a distinct picture—a picture, namely, of what reading, or a theory of reading would become if all connections between what is read and what is not literally present in what is read could somehow be erased. "Surface" here wastes no time at all in becoming a tautology, but with a twist: it becomes what we would read if reading were all there were, as though one could read without thinking. It is, in the world of "Surface Reading," as though reading, even "just reading," were not *already* premised on depth, if only in the sense of distinguishing between *representans* and *representandum*. For we certainly cannot read without posing the question of the possibility of difference from what is—from the "surface" as that which is not read. We cannot read, that is, without repeatedly posing the question, the possibility of the *negative*.

But what, for me, makes "Surface Reading"—and "The Way We Read Now" *in toto*, as, I think, quite well captured in Best and Marcus's introduction—so redolent, indeed so *symptomatic* of the new ideological inflection of "real fiction" as reification itself in the moment of hyper-fictionalized capital fully comes into view only when the authors themselves characterize the "now" in the title of their collective project. The reader will, I hope, forgive a citation in full of the pertinent passage:

> In the last decade or so, we have been drawn to modes of reading that attend to the surfaces of texts rather than plumb their depths. Perhaps this is because, at the end of the first decade of the twenty-first century, so much seems to be on the surface. "If everything were transparent, then no ideology would be possible, and no domination either," wrote Fredric Jameson in 1981, explaining why interpretation could never operate on the assumption that "the text means just what it says." The assumption that domination can do its work when only veiled, which may have once sounded almost paranoid, now has a nostalgic, even utopian ring to it. Those of us who cut our intellectual teeth on deconstruction, ideology critique, and the hermeneutics of suspicion have often found those demys-

tifying protocols superfluous in an era when images of torture at Abu Ghraib and elsewhere were immediately circulated on the internet; the real-time coverage of Hurricane Katrina showed in ways that required little explication the state's abandonment of its African American citizens; and many people instantly recognized as lies political statements such as "mission accomplished." Eight years of the Bush regime may have hammered home the point that not all situations require the subtle ingenuity associated with symptomatic reading, and they may also have inspired us to imagine that alongside nascent fascism there might be better ways of thinking and being simply there for the taking, in both the past and the present. We find ourselves the heirs of Michel Foucault, skeptical about the very possibility of radical freedom and dubious that literature or its criticism can explain our oppression or provide the keys to our liberation. Where it had become common for literary scholars to equate their work with political activism, the disasters and triumphs of the last decade have shown that literary criticism alone is not sufficient to effect change. This is in turn raises the question of why literary criticism matters if it is not political activism by another name. . . ." (1–2)

The logic of what is being said here, unless I am mistaken, boils down to this: Everything *is* transparent after all, right there on the "surface." What is transparent *is* sheer domination and lies, making the very theory of ideology—another "depth" hermeneutic after all—superfluous, and along with it, the critique of ideology as well, to which Best and Marcus appear, in some idiosyncratic way to have equated "literary criticism." As "heirs of Foucault," they/we must be "skeptical of the possibility of radical freedom" (2) (This same admission is repeated is less equivocal terms on p. 16: As they say: "We also detect in current criticism a skepticism about the very project of freedom, or about any kind of transcendental value we might use to justify intellectual work.") They ask why then does "literary criticism matter if it is not political activism by another name"? Here too the answer comes only toward the end of "Surface Reading":

> Surface reading, which strives to describe texts accurately, might easily be dismissed as politically quietist, too willing to accept things as they are. We want to reclaim from this tradition the accent on immersion in texts (without paranoia or suspicion about their merit or value) for we understand that attentiveness to the artwork is itself a kind of freedom. [. . .] Criticism that valorizes the freedom of the critic has often assumed that an adversarial relation to the object of criticism is the only way for the critic to free himself from the text's deceptive, ideological surface and uncover

the truth that the text conceals. We want to suggest that, in relinquishing the freedom dream that accompanies the work of demystification, we might be groping toward some equally valuable, if less glamorous, states of mind. (16–17)

There is scant indication anywhere in "Surface Reading"—or in the essays that make up "The Way We Read Now"—of much concern for a theory of the deeper, social and economic realities that might explain why it is that "at the end of the first decade of the twenty-first century, so much seems to be on the surface." For that, if one's field is literary and cultural criticism, one would have to turn to critics such as Fredric Jameson among others. Although they do not say so outright, theory itself, along with the "freedom dream" and uncovering "the truth that the text conceals" if it happens to require an "adversarial relation" on the part of the critic would be yet another casualty of "surface reading." Or rather, theory, to find its way into the "way we read now" according to Best, Marcus and co., would need to have already found a place for itself on the surface—as a part of the reified, post-Fordist, dislocalized landscape where, alongside hyper-fictionalized capital itself and the society that rests on it, it too would line up with its putative objects as nothing more than a real fiction.

NOTES

Introduction

1. See *The Work of Nations: Preparing Ourselves for 21st Century Capitalism* (New York: Vintage, 1992).

2. See *The Lexus and the Olive Tree* (New York: Anchor, 2000) and *The World Is Flat: a Brief History of the 21st Century* (New York: Farrar, Straus and Giroux, 2005).

3. "The problems which had dominated the critique of capitalism before the war, and which the Golden Age [from World War II to 1973, not the beginnings but the apogee of Fordism] had largely eliminated for a generation—'poverty, mass unemployment, squalor, instability'—reappeared after 1973. Growth was, once again, interrupted by severe slumps, as distinct from 'minor recessions,' in 1974–75, 1980–82, and at the end of the 1980s." Eric Hobsbawm, *The Age of Extremes* (New York: Vintage, 1996), 406. Meanwhile, the financial crisis that began in 2007 with the massive default on subprime mortgages, threatening a genuinely global collapse of banking with the bankruptcy of Lehman Brothers in September 2008, certainly has appeared, despite state-funded rescue packages, to leave the world's political and business elites without a clue as to how to avert a *truly* global crisis of unprecedented severity. This has, to say the least, made the real contradictions of globalization far more difficult to conceal. Indeed, as this crisis has unfolded, the slogans and official truths of neoliberalism, globalization chief among them, became, at one point almost overnight, the targets of officially sanctioned skepticism and anger. One must be extremely cautious, even and especially when day-to-day events appear to warrant them, not to deliver eulogies that may turn out to be premature. Nor must one lose sight of the fact that, in the view of many economists, not all of them on the left, the crisis at one point dubbed The Great Recession has its roots in the breakup of Fordism more than a generation ago, and in the transition to the finance-driven economy that *itself* gave us neoliberalism and ushered in what passes for the heroic age of globalization. The point, for purposes of the present work, is to analyze—with an eye to critique—cultural and intellectual phenomena beginning in the 1980s, in which globalization, as measured against the needs of shoring up Americanism, has exerted the latent force

of a crisis all along. What is certain about the chain of events beginning in 2007 is, in a sense, how powerfully they corroborate the "globalization anxiety" of dislocalism. The utopian universalism heralded by the neoliberal prophets of globalization beginning nearly three decades ago certainly now reveals more of its sinister and dystopian side than most could then have imagined. Globalization itself, it seems, has run the risk of becoming a casualty of its own master-narrative: has not it too appeared to be threatened with obsolescence?

4. See *Spaces of Hope* (Berkeley: University of California Press, 2000), 13.

5. Other authors and works important to my thinking include Arturo Escobar, *Encountering Development: The Making and Unmaking of the Third World* (Princeton, NJ: Princeton University Press, 1995); Manning Marable, *The Great Wells of Democracy: The Meaning of Race in American Life* (New York: Basic Books, 1993) and "9/11: Racism in a Time of Terror," *Souls* 4 (2002); Maria Mies, *Patriarchy and Accumulation on a World Scale: Women in the International Division of Labour* (London: Palgrave, 1998); Silvia Federici, *Caliban and the Witch* (New York: Autonomedia, 2004); and Cedric Robinson, *Black Marxism: The Making of the Black Radical Tradition* (Raleigh: North Carolina University Press, 2000).

6. I should also mention here that my work differs from scholarship on globalization that attempts a critical understanding of globalization as a process and that nevertheless regards that process as a *fait accompli* and then proceeds to map its *effects* on culture and its other quotidian realities. Here I have in mind especially work by critics such as Mike Featherstone, though many others could be mentioned. See, for example, John Tomlinson, *Globalization and Culture* (Chicago: University of Chicago Press, 1999) and *Cultural Imperialism: An Introduction* (London: Continuum, 2001); and Jan Nederveen Pieterse, *Globalization and Culture: Global Melange* (Lanham, MD: Rowman Littlefield, 2009).

7. Not least—if not only—because of the hyperabstraction and strangely neutralizing physicalism of the term "globalization" itself. As Justin Rosenberg writes: "The word 'globalization' is a geographical term, denoting a process over time of spatial change—the process of becoming worldwide. Twist and turn this word as you will, space, time and a reference to the shape of the planet are its only intrinsic concerns. *Prima facie*, it contains nothing else which can be drawn upon in order to explain any real-world phenomena it is used to describe." "Globalization Theory: A Post Mortem," *International Politics* 42 (2005): 11.

8. Studies of globalization have come to house discussions of contemporary politics, economics, culture, finance, technology, and so forth, with an increased emphasis on the "corporatization" of institutions. The term "global" thus comes to describe those institutions and institutional practices—such as global corporations—that stretch beyond the limits of a bounded national space. The term "transnational" functions in a similar way. "Global" is also sometimes used interchangeably with the term "cosmopolitan," especially when qualifying groups of people. In "The Vanguard of Globalization," James Hunter and Joshua Yates describe as "cosmopolitan" those elites that "travel the world . . . and see themselves as 'global citizens' who happen to carry an American passport" rather than as "U.S. citizens who happen to work in a global organization" (355–56). Timothy Brennan explains that in "marked contrast to the past, the term ["cosmopolitan"] has become less an analytical category than a normative projection complementing at once celebratory claims and despairing rec-

ognitions: the death of the nation-state, transculturation (rather than a merely one-sided assimilation), cultural hybridity (rather than a simplistic contrast between the foreign and the indigenous)" (*At Home in the World*, 2). Another closely related term is "glocal." Used in different contexts, it generally refers to the way that local places are affected by global policies. Thus, cultural studies of local communities become a way of measuring how the global influences them. In "Glocal Knowledges: Agency and Place in Literary Studies" Robert Eric Livingston writes that understanding the "scenarios of globalization . . . requires resisting the impulse to set global and local into immediate opposition. Their intertwining may be more helpfully understood by what Japanese marketing consultants have termed *dochakula*, "glocalization" (148). Livingston argues that as opposed to the terms global and local, glocal emphasizes "constant, often conflictual, working and reworking of practices" (149).

9. Think here, for example, of the incorporation of the former Soviet bloc into a globalized, "free-market" economy, and the resulting collapse, especially in the Balkans, into civil war, "ethnic cleansing," and the formation of microstates.

10. See *The Follies of Globalisation Theory* (London: Verso, 2001).

11. See *Modernity at Large: Cultural Questions of Globalization* (Minneapolis: University of Minnesota Press, 1996), 19.

12. See Anderson, *Imagined Communities* (London: Verso, 1991); Gellner, *Nations and Nationalism* (Ithaca, NY: Cornell University Press, 1983); Hobsbawm, *Nations and Nationalism since 1780* (Cambridge, UK: Cambridge University Press, 1992); Amin, *Class and Nation, Historically and in the Current Crisis* (New York: Monthly Review Press, 1981); Mann, *Incoherent Empire* (London: Verso, 2005); Schwarz, *Misplaced Ideas: Essays on Brazilian Culture* (London: Verso, 1996); Ahmad, *In Theory: Nations, Classes, Literatures* (London: Verso, 2008); and Escobar, *Globalistan* (Ann Arbor, MI: Nimble Books, 2006).

13. See, for an elaboration of this, Bob Jessop, "Post-Fordism and the State," in *Post-Fordism: A Reader*, ed. Ash Amin (1994), 251–79.

14. Questions such as who and what "Americans" and "America" are have never been simple. Benedict Anderson, in *Imagined Communities* (1983), has already shown the problems in designating the U.S. as "America." Anderson argues that the geographical closeness between the centers of the original thirteen colonies, along with their tight-knit connections via print and commerce, allowed the U.S. to establish a version of nationalism different from that of South America. This also helped the U.S. to "eventually [succeed] in appropriating the title of 'Americans'" (64). Anderson further shows that despite the tight connections between the centers, the "non-absorption" of Canada along with the "rapid expansion of the western frontier" serve as reminders that nationalism in the U.S., or what can be termed the project of "Americanization," was never completed (64).

15. Yet, as David Harvey has noted, the U.S. "would not have been able to impose the forms of globalization that have come down to us without abundant support from a wide variety of quarters and places." He nevertheless maintains that "globalization is undoubtedly the outcome of a geopolitical crusade waged largely by the U.S." *Spaces of Hope*, 69, 68.

16. "Re-thinking 'American Studies after US Exceptionalism,'" *American Literary History* 21, no. 1 (Spring 2009): 19–27.

17. See, for example, Bauman's *Liquid Modernity* (London: Polity, 2000).

18. See, for example, *Spaces of Capital: Towards a Critical Geography* (London: Routledge, 2001), part two, chapter 14.

19. This seemingly *sui generis* anxiety of obsolescence clearly has its extrinsic, fully objective basis, given the ways administrative budget cuts and restructuring have increasingly shifted priorities toward nonhumanistic disciplines such as business and the sciences. So, for example, in the words of Grant Farred, "the susceptibility [of the humanities] to corporatization includes . . . not only the 'streamlining' or 'upgrading' of academic or bureaucratic functions in the university but the 'restructuring of academic curricula' themselves." Here of course such restructuring is, rightly, regarded as something that the humanities must resist.

20. The best-known instance of this trend is *Cultures of Globalization,* ed. Fredric Jameson and Masao Miyoshi (Durham: Duke University Press, 1998).

21. See here again the previously cited work by American studies critics such as Rowe, Kaplan, and Pease.

22. Brazil, Russia, India, and China.

23. The title of Kaplan's widely read 1994 *Atlantic Monthly* article (and, subsequently, a book of essays), which became a manifesto of sorts for neoconservatives such as Samuel Huntington and Francis Fukuyama.

24. For a discussion of how the proliferation of images in the new media shapes our understanding of and relationship to the world, see Douglass Kellner's *Media Spectacle and the Crisis of Democracy: Terrorism, War, and Election Battles* (Boulder: Paradigm Publishers 2005); Jay Bolter and Richard Grusin's *Remediation* (Cambridge: MIT Press, 2000); Terry Flew's *New Media: An Introduction* (London: Oxford University Press, 2002).

Chapter 1

1. Accounts of globalization, whether subscribed to by university administrations or by the humanities themselves, essentially function as narratives of obsolescence. In the Introduction, I have cited Evan Watkins, who in his *Throwaways* (1993) explains how the concept of the "obsolete" is itself the necessary creation of the discourse of the "new." The rhetoric of obsolescence suggests that entire institutions can be rendered ineffective if they do not produce work useful in the context of globalization.

2. See, for example, Ross's *Fast Boat to China* (2006), *Low Pay, High Profile* (2004), and *No-Collar: The Humane Workplace and Its Hidden Costs,* (2002); Brecher and Costello's *Global Village or Global Pillage?* (1998); and During's *Cultural Studies: A Critical Introduction* (2005).

3. At the same time, it is also important to note here that this inverse mirroring of business and the humanities is an uneven one. While, spurred on by globalization, management theorists are turning to scholarship by critics such as Jameson, Derrida, and Lyotard, we have yet to see major literary and cultural theorists taking a serious interest in management theory *qua* theory. And as literary/cultural theorists engage with issues of economics and business, their work essentially retains a focus on culture and the cultural.

4. Though Tom Peters has some detractors in management circles, his ideas have influence and are in perfect congruity with the ways that organization studies and

management theory in general has seen a turn to issues of culture and postmodernism.

5. This comment appears in Tom Peters's biography on his website and in virtually every biographical blurb publicizing his books and speaking engagements. http://www.tompeters.com/toms_world/press_kit/who_is.php.

6. The comparison is made by Peters's mentor, Warren Bennis, professor of Business Administration at the University of Southern California. Bennis is cited in "Now That We Live in a Tom Peters World . . . Has Tom Peters Gone Crazy?" by Mark Gimein published in *Fortune*, November 13, 2000.

7. See especially Tom Peters's *Liberation Management* (1992) and *The Circle of Innovation* (1997).

8. For a lengthier discussion of the origins of management see Harry Braverman's *Labor and Monopoly Capital: The Degradation of Work in the Twentieth Century* (New York: Monthly Review Press, 1974).

9. See, for example, the *Harper Encyclopedia of the Modern World: A Concise Reference History from 1760 to the Present*, ed. Richard Brandon Morris and Graham W. Irwin (New York: Harper & Row, 1970).

10. Here, of course, I can only touch on a question too complex and wide-ranging for me to do full justice to in this space. See, foremost in this respect, the well-known arguments concerning globalization, capital, and space in the works of David Harvey, especially *The Limits to Capital* (1982/2006); *The Condition of Postmodernity* (1989); *Spaces of Capital: Towards a Critical Geography* (2001); and *A Brief History of Neoliberalism* (2005). See also, for an analysis that, although its terminology is not mine here, closely parallels and argues in much greater detail for the theory sketched out above, Bob Jessop's "What Follows Neo-liberalism? The Deepening Contradictions of US Domination and the Struggle for a New Global Order," chapter 4 in *Political Economy and Global Capitalism: The 21st Century, Present and Future*, ed. Robert Albritton, Bob Jessop, and Richard Westra (London: Anthem Press, 2007). See especially the section of this chapter entitled "The Ecological Dominance of Capitalism vis-à-vis World Society," where Jessop writes as follows: "one could argue that the ecological dominance of capitalism is closely related to the extent to which its internal competition, internal complexity and loose coupling, capacity for reflexive self-organization, scope for time-space distantiation and compression, externalization of problems, and hegemonic capacities can be freed from confinement within limited ecological spaces policed by another system (such as a political system segmented into mutually exclusive sovereign territories). This is where globalization, especially in its neo-liberal form, promotes the relative ecological dominance of the capitalist economic system by expanding the scope for accumulation to escape such political constraints. Neo-liberalism promotes the opening of the world-market and reduces the frictions introduced by national 'power containers'" (81). See also, for a fuller elaboration of this theoretical argument, Jessop's *The Future of the Capitalist State* (Cambridge: Polity Press, 2002.) On a more general plane see also Zygmunt Bauman's many writings on globalization, including *Globalization: The Human Consequences* (Cambridge: Polity, 1998), especially chapter 3, "After the Nation-State—What?" (55–76), in which he develops the theoretical distinction between universalization and globalization, given what he terms the "extraterritoriality of capital." "The very distinction between the internal and global market, or more generally between the 'inside' and the 'outside' of the state," writes Bauman, "is exceedingly difficult to maintain in any but

the most narrow, 'territory and population policing' sense" (65). He continues: "Due to the unqualified and unstoppable spread of free trade rules, above all the free movement of capital and finances, the 'economy' is progressively exempt from political control . . ." (66).

11. "Thus, while capital must on one side strive to tear down every spatial barrier to intercourse, i.e., to exchange, and conquer the whole earth, it strives on the other side to annihilate this space with time, i.e., to reduce to a minimum the time spent in motion from one place to another. The more developed the capital, therefore, the more extensive the market over which it circulates, which forms the spatial orbit of its circulation, the more does its strive simultaneously for an even greater extension of the market and for greater annihilation of space by time." *Grundrisse,* 539

12. This was noted as long ago as the 1940s by Theodor Adorno and Max Horkheimer in *The Dialectic of Enlightenment.*

13. See, for example, Charles Hampden-Turner and Fons Trompenaars, "Cultural Intelligence," *Group & Organization Management* 31, no. 1: 56–63 (2006).

14. Boston College School of Management offers a PhD degree in Organization Studies. See http://www.bc.edu/schools/csom/graduate/phdprograms/phdos.html.

15. Note that a desire for a simpler version of culture is also a theme in cultural anthropological writings. Take for example, Claude Lévi-Strauss (*Tristes Tropiques,* 1955), Ruth Benedict (*Patterns of Culture,* 1934), and Mary Douglass (*Purity and Danger: An Analysis of Concepts of Pollution and Taboo,* 1966), all of whom studied non-Western groups of people in order to produce simpler, more diagrammatic patterns of culture. Their assumption was that Western societies were too complex to study and studying non-Western societies would be helpful in producing simpler patterns of culture. For a good analysis of the notion of culture for anthropologists, see Susan Hegeman's *Patterns for America,* 1999. Business theorists have routinely borrowed anthropological notions of culture for their own purposes.

16. See, for example, the edited volume *International Management and International Relations: A Critical Perspective from Latin America,* ed. Ana Guedes and Alex Faria (New York: Routledge, 2010).

17. See p. 144, *Classic Drucker* (2006), a volume of Drucker's writing taken from the *Harvard Business Review* and published by the Harvard Business School Press with an introduction by Thomas Stewart. The "New Society of Organizations" was originally published in 1992.

18. The course's original creator is Robert Coles, a psychiatrist who was a longtime professor for both the Harvard Law and Business schools. He published an edited volume with coeditor Albert LaFarge in 2008 titled *Minding the Store: Great Writing about Business from Tolstoy to Now* (New York: The New Press).

Sandra J. Sucher, one of the instructors of this course, published a teaching guide for others. *Teaching the Moral Leader: A Literature-Based Leadership Course* (New York: Routledge, 2007). Another instructor of this course, Joseph Badarraco Jr., published *Questions of Character: Illuminating the Heart of Leadership through Literature* (Boston: Harvard Business School Press, 2006).

19. Other examples of such management courses include "Managerial Ethics: Lessons from Literature and Film," listed in the catalogue at NYU's Stern School of Business. In the spring of 2006 this course required the students to read, *inter alia,* Sinclair Lewis's *If I Were Boss: The Early Business Stories* and Shakespeare's *Henry*

IV. Virginia Wesleyan College lists a course in its business catalog titled "Management in Literature," featuring a typical reading list that includes management standards such as Conrad's *Heart of Darkness* and *Henry IV,* along with the *Autobiography of Malcolm X* and writings by Mahatma Gandhi.

20. For example, the journal *Management Decision* recently published an article—Islam Gazi and Michael J. Zyphur's "The Sweetest Dreams That Labor Knows: Robert Frost and the Poetics of Work"—that analyzes Frost's poetry in order to understand how work can be a "personally liberating but also [a] culturally stifling" tool. "The relation of poetic knowing to more mainstream forms of theoretical knowledge," the writers argue, "is particularly poignant in the field of Management, where one of the greatest criticisms of organizational theories is that they do not resound with the everyday lived experiences of managers." Gazi and Zyphur further posit that "because of the emphasis in poetic works on understanding as it appears from within a person's own experience, the study of poetry is one way to integrate [management] theory with experience" (4–5).

21. See Marx, *Capital,* Vol. 3, especially chapters 25, 32, and 33, trans. David Fernbach (London: Penguin: 1991).

22. See also, on the subject of fictional or "fictitious" capital, David Harvey's *The Limits to Capital,* especially chapter 9. Here Harvey defines fictitious capital as the "money that is thrown into circulation as capital without any material basis in commodities or productive activity" (93). See also Harvey's discussion of the category at numerous points in *The Condition of Postmodernity* (1989) and in "The Geopolitics of Capitalism," in *Spaces of Capital: Toward a Critical Geography* (2001).

23. Here they draw upon the entry on fiction, written by D. Davies, for the 2001 edition of the *Routledge Companion to Aesthetics.*

24. For another example of how fictional works are employed in management theory, see E. M. Essex and C. Mainmelis, "Learning from an Artist about Organizations: The Poetry and Prose of David Whyte at Work," *Journal of Management Inquiry* (2002): 148–59.

25. See, for example, Peters, flamboyant and unabashed as always, in *Re-Imagine:* "Brits ruled the world, from a wee island, for hundreds of years. While I, an old Navy guy, admire the Royal Navy, I more admire the entrepreneurial British Trading Companies . . . that made it all possible . . . [and] funded the Royal Navy" (1). Heeding lessons learned from the old British Empire, American managers can build the "virtual" and "flexible" organizations that will deliver the world back to the U.S—a nostalgic replay of the days of Churchill and Roosevelt: "The Yanks tipped the balance in WWII . . . Greatest Weapons Producers . . . via the Greatest Economy? Yup" (ibid.).

26. This essay, published in the *Handbook of Globalization, Governance, and Public Administration* (ed. Ali Farazmand and Jack Pinkowski), is typical in the way that it attempts to take stock of the issues affecting development management. Jennifer Brinkerhoff is a faculty member at the Elliot School of International Affairs at George Washington University. Derick Brinkerhoff is a researcher at RTI International, a corporate research organization located in the Research Triangle in North Carolina.

27. See, for example, Anshuman Prasad, ed. *Postcolonial Theory and Organizational Analysis: A Critical Engagement* (New York: Palgrave Macmillan, 2003); and Campbell Jones, "Practical Deconstructivist Feminist Marxist Organization Theory: Gayatri Chakravorty Spivak," in *Contemporary Organization Theory,* ed. Campbell Jones and Rolland Monro (Malden, MA: Blackwell Wiley, 2005).

28. Many have critiqued theories of postmodernism for this reason. See, for example, Anthony Appiah's *In My Father's House;* Roberto Schwarz's *Misplaced Ideas;* Simon Gikandi's "Theory, Literature, and Moral Considerations," in *Research in African Literatures* 32, no. 4 (Winter 2001); and "Narration in the Post-Colonial Moment: Merle Hodge's *Crick Crack Monkey,*" in *Past the Last Post: Theorizing Post-Colonialism and Post-Modernism,* ed. I. Adam and H. Tiffin (Calgary: University of Calgary Press, 1990).

29. This motif of an automatic American self-distancing in relation to European colonialism is an old theme in American literature. See, for example, Herman Melville's *Typee* and Mark Twain's *Innocents Abroad.* Mary Louise Pratt, writing in *Imperial Eyes,* analyzes this gesture at length, observing the general tendency of travel writers to represent themselves as innocent of colonialism even as they are complicit with it. I will comment more on this aspect of travel writing in the third chapter.

30. The postcolonial scholarship that Catlin and White refer to parenthetically is as follows: Annette M. Jaimes, *The State of Native America: Genocide, Colonization, and Resistance* (Boston: South End Press, 1992); Chandra Talpade Mohanty, "Under Western Eyes: Feminist Scholarship and Colonial Discourses," in *Colonial Discourse and Postcolonial Theory: A Reader,* ed. Patrick Williams and Laura Chrisman (New York: Columbia University Press, 1994), 196–220; Marie Anna Jamies-Guerrero, "Civil Rights vs. Sovereignty: Native American Women in Life and Land Struggles," in *Feminist Genealogies, Colonial Legacies, Democratic Futures,* ed. M. Jaqui Alexander and Chandra Talpade Mohanty (New York: Routledge, 1997), 101–21.

Chapter 2

1. Janice Radway, in her 1998 Presidential Address to the American Studies Association, proposed changing the name of the Association and possibly dropping the term "American." While in the 1950 and 1960s critics such as Henry Nash Smith and Warren Sussman sought to give the interdisciplinary formation of American studies spanning the diverse disciplines of history, English, sociology, and anthropology a loose unity via the term American, scholars today are working hard to decenter the very term while attempting to maintain some semblance of a unitary field.

2. See, for example, Caroline Levander and Robert Levine, eds., *American Hemispheric Studies* (Newark: Rutgers University Press, 2008); John Carlos, *The New American Studies* (Minneapolis: University of Minnesota Press, 2002); and Donald Pease and Robyn Wiegman, eds., *The Futures of American Studies* (Durham: Duke University Press, 2002).

3. Jonathan Arac, "Global and Babel: Language and Planet in American Literature," in *Shades of the Planet: American Literature as World Literature,* ed. Wai Chee Dimock and Lawrence Buell (Princeton, NJ: Princeton University Press, 2007).

4. This strategy is a broader phenomenon in the field of literary studies. In a very different spirit from that of Arac, who is attempting to work out the issues relating to globalization by displacing Americanist paradigms, Marjorie Perloff's 2006 MLA Presidential Address makes a case for a return to aesthetics and the "merely literary," advocating single-author studies by positioning Samuel Beckett as a global writer because his work is globally read and celebrated. A further example of the attempt

to globalize nationalist paradigms can be found in Stephen Greenblatt's essay "Racial Memory and Literary History," published in the January 2001 special issue of the *PMLA* titled "Globalizing Literary Studies." Greenblatt makes an argument similar to Perloff's for Shakespeare as "always already" a global writer: "Shakespeare may never have left England, yet his work is already global in its representational range" (59). Arguing what is superficially true, namely, that Shakespeare's works are *read* globally, Greenblatt both makes room for the "global" and yet leaves the author's centrality in the canon intact.

5. For a lengthier discussion of this issue see Walter Benn Michael's *Our America* and Werner Sollers's *Beyond Ethnicity.*

6. Academic debates on the topic in sociology and economics range from considering whether immigration has an adverse affect on the U.S. economy or testing out the hypotheses that more investment in developing nations would curb immigration and that higher mobility and true globalization is not the answer to the problem of immigration. See, for example, George Borjas's "The Labor Market Impact of High Skill Immigration," *American Economic Review* 95, no. 2 (May 2005): 56–60. Also see Devesh Kapur and John McHale's "What Is Wrong with Plan B? International Migration as an Alternative to Development Assistance," in *Brookings Trade Forum—2006:* 137–72. Also see Richard C. Jones, "Multinational Investment and the Mobility Transition in Mexico and Ireland," *Latin American Politics & Society* 47, no. 2 (Summer 2005): 77–102. For an excellent examination of the notion of "illegal immigrants," see David Bacon's *Illegal People: How Globalization Creates Migration and Criminalizes Immigrants* (Boston: Beacon Press, 2008).

7. Inderpal Grewal has discussed this question at length in *Transnational America.*

8. Critics such as Immanuel Wallerstein and David Harvey have shown that, abstractly and formally speaking, the existence of economic interconnections between the various parts of the world is hardly anything new. Nevertheless, the present, globalized stage of capitalism does represent a qualitative change. Globalization entails the direct, immediate reproduction of capitalist relation of production on the level of the global, rather than, in composite fashion, on the level of the nation, as a "functional economic space."

9. See, for example, the work of E. San Juan Jr., Michael Omi, Howard Winant, and Paul Smith in Gordon Avery and Christopher Newfield's *Mapping Multiculturalism.*

10. Critiques of identity such as Lowe's have shown the problems that arise when positioning the categories of identity—easily appropriated by capital—as though they were themselves outside and critical of the dominant social relations. Such critiques distinguish between identity as a politics of recognition and representation and other ways of analyzing identity.

11. See, for example, Michael Hardt and Antonio Negri's *Empire* and a critical review of the book by Timothy Brennan, "Empire's New Clothes" published in *Critical Inquiry.*

12. A somewhat more nuanced version of this argument can be found in Stephen Greenblatt's essay "Racial Memory and Literary History," which I reference above.

13. One could add to this list the work of scholars whose work, now widely read within literary and cultural studies, reflects an even more immediate, activist engagement with the contemporary problems of globalization. See, *inter alia*, works such as Mike Davis's *Planet of Slums;* Andrew Ross's *Fast Boat to China* and *Low Pay, High Profile;* and Grace Chang's *Disposable Domestics.*

14. Take, as only one further example of this, the 2005 volume *Writing the World: On Globalization,* ed. David Rothenberg and Wandee J. Pryor, featuring contributions from writers such as Naomi Klein, Arundhati Roy, and Frederick Buell. In the Introduction, "The World as We Found It," the editors define the task of the book as the attempt to capture the world as it has changed with the onset of globalization. It claims to bracket off what it sees as familiar tales of exploitation and oppression, backed up by statistics or data, in favor of showing "how all of our lives are interconnected"—as though the real truth of globalization were hidden somewhere even beyond its immediately measurable or theorizable realities as typically understood (xiv). Much of the work in the book is in effect aimed at uncovering this hidden reality. Roy's piece, "Ladies Have Feelings, So . . . Shall We Leave It to the Experts?," argues that it is the elites that tend to buy into the "expert viewpoint" sympathetic to globalization projects such as dam building in India, while ignoring the reality of those adversely affected by such projects. This is, of course, perfectly true and politically crucial, but it implies that the deeper reality of those marginalized or disadvantaged by globalization resides beyond the reach of "experts," and hence, perhaps, also of intellectuals and of theory themselves. Roy herself is an interesting figure in this respect, as she became famous as a result of her novel *The God of Small Things* but since then has primarily dedicated herself to writing in nonfictional genres.

15. See http://www.cnn.com/US/dobbs.commentary/archive/index.html.

16. See, for example, "Truth, Fiction and Lou Dobbs" a report by David Leonhardt published in the *New York Times,* May 30, 2007.

17. I will elaborate on this matter later in the sections devoted to the criticism on Alvarez and Abu-Jaber.

18. One of many examples of this trend is the caption on the back cover of Jessica Hagedorn's *Dogeaters* (1990), which states: "Welcome to Manila in the turbulent period of the Philippines's late dictator. It is a world in which American pop culture and local Filipina tradition mix flamboyantly, and gossip, storytelling, and extravagant behavior thrive."

19. It is, Beverley claims, not any factual inaccuracy but "the Big Lie of racism, imperialism, inequality, class rule, genocide, torture, oppression . . . that is at stake in testimonio" (*Testimonio,* 3)—thereby disavowing any connection between facts and the latter.

20. See, for example, Julie Barak's "'Turning and Turning in the Widening Gyre': A Second Coming into Language in Alvarez's *How the García Girls Lost Their Accents*"; Loes Nas's "Border Crossings in Latina Narrative: Julia Alvarez's *How the García Girls Lost Their Accents*"; and Jennifer Bess's "Imploding the Miranda Complex in Julia Alvarez's *How the García Girls Lost Their Accents.*"

21. Newton's essay is part of her book-length work, *Transcultural Women of the Late-Twentieth Century U.S. American Literature,* a critical study of work by various women of color in the U.S in which she attempts to introduce concepts of globalization. Ortiz-Márquez's essay appears in *Interventions: Feminist Dialogues on Third World Women's Literature and Film,* ed. Bishnupriya Ghosh and Brinda Bose. In her Foreword to *Interventions,* Chandra Talpade Mohanty explicity cites "the need for feminist enagagement with global as well as local/situational, ideological, economic, and political process."

22. This move on the part of both Suárez and Newton is reminiscent of the argu-

ments—discussed above—that were made in defense of Rigoberta Menchú's renowned testimono when she was accused of having fictionalized key parts of her story. The basic move here is to pull back from all strong claims to veracity and emphasize the constructed, that is, fiction-like, character of truth itself—even, in the case of Arturo Arias's "Authorizing Ethnicized Subjects," asserting the "potential inability of Westerners to grasp a subaltern testimonio" (77).

23. According to Noam Chomsky and Edward Herman's *The Washington Connection and Third World Fascism* (Boston: South End Press, 1979), right-wing death squad activity during the period following the 1965 invasion, under the directly U.S.-backed Balaguer regime, well exceeded anything under Trujillo—a fact that the exceptionalizing "regime of terror" narrative would tend to obscure (243–44).

24. Other critical work on the *The García Girls,* such as Joan M. Hoffman's "She Wants to Be Called Yolanda Now," concentrates, as do many other readings of Latina texts, exclusively on how immigrant characters, in this case the Garcías, manage their lives in the United States. Hoffman writes: "All of these girls—Carla, Sandra, Yolanda and Sofia—do come to some trouble in the New World . . . As the title of the novel suggests, not only words but also the manner of speech is significant to the story of the García girls' coming-of-age in America. The struggle to master a second language is a constant reminder to these girls of their weakened position as strangers in a new land" (21–22). Thus, on the one hand, Hoffman acknowledges that the girls suffer from a weakened position as result of being immigrants. Yet, on the other hand, she champions that same identity. The article ends with the following remark about Yolanda: "As troubled as it may be—by memory or failed love or fragmented identity or that precarious tightrope that is the immigrant's life—Yolanda still has spirit in her, she still has her art, her writing, her refuge. With that she will always be able to invent what she needs to survive" (26). Hoffman makes a case for reading the novel almost exclusively along the lines of the U.S. rhetoric of individuality and individual immigrant spirit. She concentrates on what is most typical about immigrant struggles in the U.S. and ends with the suggestion that even though Yolanda is in a precarious position as an immigrant, she has become sufficiently Americanized to realize that she can "invent" her own life. Though Yolanda is neither Dominican nor U.S./American per se, the very fact that it is her "identity" that is foregrounded serves to keep the novel well within the horizons of a U.S. nationalist paradigm reproducing dominant ideologies.

25. This tendency to champion the tough, adaptive spirit of immigrants while defending their identity rights can be traced in socio-historical scholarship on (im) migration as well. For instance, Mary Chamberlain in her Introduction to the edited volume *Caribbean Migration,* a broad and instructive examination of the phenomenon of mobility from and through the Caribbean, states of the project that it "shifts the focus away from the causes of migration toward the nature and meaning of the migration experience, a shift that has radical implications for those concerned with the consequences of migration and its future." This shift results in a form of analysis that attempts to capture what she calls the "vibrant culture of transnational and circular migration, in the home and the host countries" (10). In this shift, the focus on migrant *culture* can become celebratory—as signaled in the terms "vibrancy of culture." Take here as another example Peggy Levitt's cultural profile of Dominican (im)migrants in her book *The Transnational Villagers.* While the latter situates its findings within a

global economic and social context, it nevertheless exhibits a tendency to rely on the descriptive language and metaphors of a more cosmopolitan narrative of (im)migration. Emphasizing the continuous contact between the residents of the Dominican city of Miraflores and Boston, she writes: "Though electricity goes off nightly for weeks at a stretch, nearly every household has a television, VCR, or compact disc player. And although it takes months to get a phone installed in Santo Domingo, the Dominican capital, Mirafloreños can get phone service in their homes almost immediately after they request it" (2). "Because someone is always traveling between Boston and the Island," she goes on to say, "there is a continuous, circular flow of goods, news, and information. As a result when someone is ill, cheating on his or her spouse, or finally granted a visa, the news spreads as quickly in Jamaica Plain as it does on the streets of Miraflores" (3). There are a couple of points here that are especially worth considering. While Levitt does not state this, the mainland-island networks through which flow the goods, news, and information mentioned above are not unlike the financial networks connecting cities such as New York, London, and Beijing—networks that appear to transcend unevenness within and across national boundaries so as to produce a culture of transnational cosmopolitanism. Invoking the gossip that travels faster between Boston and Miraflores than between Miraflores and Santo Domingo, even if unintentionally, feeds into this same cosmopolitan narrative of mobility. Emphasis is placed on cosmopolitan interconnectedness rather than, say, on the uneven distribution of electricity.

Nevertheless, such metanarratives of (im)migration are still highly instructive when placed next to the critical metanarratives informing the scholarship on *The García Girls*. The details provided by Levitt show the extent to which the lives of Dominican immigrants in Boston are lived in continuous contact with the lives of those who remain on the island—a reality elided in the fetishized, identity-based reading of immigrant culture and in narratives of assimilation within the United States. Chamberlain's edited volume, while tending to foreground the cultural with its focus on the "intergenerational transmission of culture," and its documenting of women's stories of adaptation and change in the face of an obligatory mobility," nevertheless opens up new ways to consider the "links between subjectivity and material life" (11). Take, for example, Elizabeth Thomas-Hope's contribution to the volume, "Globalization and the Development of Caribbean Migration," which situates the Caribbean colonies "from the outset as part of the wider global political economy." Thomas-Hope analyzes the way that mercantilism, the transatlantic slave trade, and the plantation were already signs of globalization. The essays in *Caribbean Migrations*, despite sharing with the identity-based work on U.S. (im)migrant literary fiction a focus on the *culture* of (im)migration, also help to bring to light the *connections* between the material and the cultural.

26. See, for example, Russell Crandell, *Gunboat Democracy: U.S. Interventions in the Dominican Republic, Grenada and Panama* (New York: Rowan and Littlefield, 2006).

27. Eric Williams, *From Columbus to Castro: The History of the Caribbean 1492–1969* (New York: Vintage, 1984); Sherri Grasmuck and Patricia Pessar, *Between Two Islands: Dominican International Migration* (Berkeley: University of California Press, 1991); Tom Barry and Beth Wood et al., eds., *The Other Side of Paradise* (New York: Grove Press, 1984); James Ferguson, *Far from Paradise: Introduction to the*

Caribbean Development (London: Latin America Bureau, 1990); and Greg Grandin, *Empire's Workshop: Latin America, the United States and the Rise of the New Imperialism* (New York: Metropolitan Books, 2006).

28. Although earlier immigrant narratives also frequently made reference to the way images and narratives of the U.S. were already a distinct presence in preimmigration homelands (the protagonist of Abraham Cahan's *The Rise of David Levinsky,* for example, says that in Russia he was told the standard tale of the U.S. as a land in which the streets were paved with gold), the actual passage to the U.S. in these narratives appears as absolute and final.

29. See Lisa Majaj's "Arab Americans and the Meaning of Race" published in *Postcolonial Theory and the United States,* ed. Amritjit Singh and Peter Schmidt.

30. Such denationalization has, of course, its sinister correlate in the treatment meted out to Arabs and Muslims by the U.S.-led war on terror, most notably in the case of the extrajudicial detention and torture of suspects at the U.S. base at Guantanamo and elsewhere in secret U.S. detention/torture centers. Often suspected of a loyalty to Islam that supersedes any loyalty as American citizens, Muslims living within the U.S., regardless of their legal status, are rhetorically denationalized, considered to be possible terrorists at worst and resident aliens at best, and the legitimate targets, as such thinking goes, of constant monitoring. In ideological terms, American nationalism balks at the inclusion of the figure of the Arab/Muslim in a way that it does not in the case of certain other minorities. (For an extended discussion of this point see Evelyn Alsultany's "Selling American Diversity and Muslim American Identity Through Non-Profit Advertising Post-911," *American Quarterly* 59, no. 3 [Fall 2007].) As embodiments of Žižek's "desert of the real," Arab-Muslim immigrants to the U.S. are rhetorically and ideologically outside the latter's borders even when they physically, and legally, reside within them.

31. See Steven Salaita, "Sand Niggers, Small Shops, and Uncle Sam: Cultural Negotiation in the Fiction of Joseph Geha and Diana Abu-Jaber," and Carol Fadda-Conrey, "Arab-American Literature in the Ethnic Borderland: Cultural Intersections in Diana Abu-Jaber's *Crescent.*" Fadda-Conrey's article is published in a special issue of the *MELUS (Multi-Ethnic Literatures of the U.S.)* journal devoted to Arab-American literature, edited by Salah D. Hassan and Marcy Jane Knopf-Newman. The issue also contains two other articles that touch on Abu-Jaber: Michelle Hartman's "This sweet/ sweet music': Jazz, Sam Cooke and Reading Arab American Literary Identities" and Pauline Kaldas's "Beyond Stereotypes: Representational Dilemmas in *Arabian Jazz.*" The issue also contains an interview with Abu-Jaber conducted by Robin E. Field.

32. Steven Salaita's work in general deals with crucial historical and political complexities relating to questions of nation-state, colonialism, and the construction of Arab and Muslim identity. See, for example, The *Uncultured Wars: Arabs, Muslims and the Poverty of Liberal Thought—New Essays* (London: Zed Books, 2009); *Anti-Arab Racism in the USA: Where It Comes From and What It means for Politics Today* (London: Pluto, 2006); and The *Holy Land in Transit: Colonialism and the Quest for Canaan* (Syracuse, NY: Syracuse University Press, 2006).

33. A very typical claim is expressed by Tanyss Ludeshcer in "From Nostalgia to Critique": "Arab American Literature is an understudied and undervalued area of *ethnic* literature" (95).

34. Fadda-Conrey also cites the edited volume *Bridge We Call Home: Radical*

Visions for Transformation, ed. Gloria Anzaldúa and AnaLouise Keating (New York: Routledge, 2002).

35. Writing in *Late Victorian Holocausts,* Mike Davis has made the point that there is no link between food availability and famine. It is the ability of people to buy the food that determines whether they can eat it. Davis documents how the British in the nineteenth century had interlinked world markets and how the building of railways—for example, in India—made it possible for grain to be produced and shipped out of the region and sold in the markets in Europe. Phyllis Bennis, in "'And They Called It Peace': U.S. Policy on Iraq," outlines how the U.N. sanctions against Iraq (since the early 1990s) that restricted the sale of oil made the country largely dependent on imports for food. And since then Iraq has become even more dependent on food from elsewhere.

36. For a thorough explanation of how corporate agribusiness, monocultural agriculture, is reducing the ability of farmers to feed themselves, see José Bové and François Dufour's *The World Is Not for Sale: Farmer's Against Junk Food* and *Food for the Future: Agriculture for a Global Age.*

Chapter 3

1. The fact that the remotest corners of the world have been turned into tourist resorts is, contrary to what might appear, not a reason to conclude, as Dean MacCannell speculated long ago, that modern consciousness is that of a tourist (*The Tourist,* 1976). When MacCannell aptly noted that the "empirical and ideological expansion of modern society [was] intimately linked in diverse ways to modern mass leisure, especially to international tourism and sightseeing," tourism was well on its way to creating a service economy and to becoming an integral part of the project to repair societies left devastated by the failure of development projects (3). Places like South Africa are a prime example of this attempted repair.

2. While travel writers such as Theroux regularly lament the succumbing of travel to pervasive global tourism, travel books continue to appear consistently on *The New York Times* bestseller lists. Nearly every major daily newspaper carries a section on travel. Numerous magazines such as *Travel and Leisure, Salon* contain feature articles by travel writers. The popularity of books by writers such as Bill Bryson and Theroux are only a few instances among many to indicate that travel writing, judged quantitatively, is anything but a dying genre.

3. All three authors continue to publish works that essentially deal with the same issues analyzed in detail here. See, for example, Kaplan's *Imperial Grunts* and *Hog Pilots, Blue Water Grunts;* Mary Morris's *The River Queen* (2007); and Paul Theroux's *Blinding Light* (2005).

4. I will discuss issues of gender and travel writing below in relationship to the work of Mary Morris.

5. The same is true of many of Kaplan's other writings as well, notably his two recent books recounting his travels with the U.S. military, *Imperial Grunts: On the Ground with the American Military, from Mongolia to the Philippines to Iraq and Beyond* (2006) and *Hog Pilots, Blue Water Grunts: The American Military in the Air, at Sea, and on the Ground* (2008). In the former he writes that "by the turn of

the twenty-first century the United States military had already appropriated the entire earth and was ready to flood the most obscure areas" (3). Kaplan, a consistent proponent of the 2003 invasion of Iraq, has become even more blatant in his view that the U.S. is a benevolent presence as against "native" governance structures around the world. The distortions here, even in comparison to those in *The Ends of Earth*, are extreme to the point of caricature, especially as concerns the Islamic Middle East, and at one point they reach the extreme of advocating war with China. But Kaplan also considers the American empire to be in need of serious overhauling. He uses the "travel" writing and firsthand accounts in *Imperial Grunts* and *Hog Pilots* as a purportedly more credible platform from which to "view at ground level what it was that the U.S. was up against" (*Imperial Grunts*, 3) and to recommend how empire can be better managed. "The drama of exotic new landscapes," he writes, "had always been central to the imperial experience." Thus, in his words, "a series of books about the empire—at least to some degree—had to be about travel" (14).

6. *Nothing to Declare* appeared just three years before the North American Free Trade Agreement (NAFTA) was signed in 1992, and several years before the treaty was implemented in 1994. The perception that Mexico is integrally connected to the U.S. is articulated by some of the language in the preamble to the NAFTA agreement:

> The Government of Canada, the Government of the United Mexican States and the Government of the United States of America, resolved to: STRENGTHEN the special bonds of friendship and cooperation among their nations; CONTRIBUTE to the harmonious development and expansion of world trade and provide a catalyst to broader international cooperation; CREATE an expanded and secure market for the goods and services produced in their territories. . . . (*NAFTA—Preamble*, Capital Letters Original)

While the NAFTA language gestured toward what was already happening—the creation of an expanded market and cooperation of trade between the three signatory nations—the impending agreement prompted public rearticulations of the anxiety over the coming erasure of the boundaries between the U.S. and Mexico. The media exacerbated fears that hordes of Mexicans would stream across U.S. borders, demanding undeserved rights to jobs and money. The inclusion of Mexico in NAFTA provoked a resurgence of racist stereotyping, constructing Mexico as yet again the dangerous Other in the national imaginary of the United States. Though Morris does not speak directly about these ideas, her book, reflecting the public conversations at the time, also works to construct Mexico as a place of danger.

7. For a more detailed discussion of Quetzalcoatl, see Davíd Carrasco's *Quetzalcoatl and the Irony of Empire* (2000).

8. Theroux's novel *Blinding Light* (2005) also tells the story of a blocked writer, Steadman, with one, twenty-year-old, bestselling book to his credit. He travels to Ecuador to secure a drug he hopes will unblock his brain, but instead it temporarily blinds him. Thus here too the act of writing is frustrated, and travel is the result.

9. The genre of the fictional meta–travel narrative bestows on Theroux a kind of authority in much the same way that the notion of the firsthand account does on Kaplan. But nonfictional firsthand accounts of Hawaii are countless. In foregrounding the concept of perspective, Theroux's book remains credible while still playing with

the boundary between fact and fiction. In fact, playing with the boundary between fact and fiction is precisely what critics of the genre of travel writing characterized it as doing. Much has been written about the way in which travel writers negotiate such boundaries, primarily as a way to caution against taking the often "firsthand" narratives of the travel books as "true." Critics such as Mary Louise Pratt, Paul Fussell, and Terry Caesar continue to stress the way in which travel writers invent the world they claim to see. James Clifford has pointed to the need of ethnography to make clear distinctions between the literary travel writers and ethnographers themselves, primarily because travel writers are largely considered unaccountable for the highly entertaining narratives they produce of the places they visit. But travel writers themselves, if only so as to hold fast to the generic identity they have selected for themselves, must also doggedly hold on to the notion of "real" reporting. As I have shown, both Kaplan and Morris rely heavily upon the claim to firsthand veracity. And to reiterate, even *The Sheltering Sky,* one of the better-known of the travel novels that Paul Bowles was producing as early as the 1940s, , transports the reader into imagining that there is an interior of Africa that exists outside of the book. Theroux's own earlier novel *The Mosquito Coast* (1982), the story of a utopian society project in Latin America that eventually goes sour, builds itself around a similarly constructed belief on the reader's part in the "there" of the fiction. Travel writing has also and long since discovered how to position itself close to the margins of the fictional when its claims to the veracity of the "firsthand" are endangered.

10. In an interview, with Barbara Lane for the Commonwealth Club of California, Theroux states: "it's a mistake to confuse the 'I' in a novel with the person writing the novel. Because writers are notoriously unreliable . . . the whole notion of writing— writing is invention, it's imagination. You improve things, or you might make it worse, but what you're doing is inventing the truth" (*Commonwealth Club of California*). And yet, embracing the confusion between him and his narrators, he says: "I can only write about a writer like myself, who has my habits. I can't imagine writing any other way except the way that I write. So when I think of a writer . . . my own experience is tried and true" (ibid.).

Chapter 4

1. The publication of *Gourmet* magazine ran from 1941 to 2009. The Gourmet brand continues to have a television and web presence.

2. All of these publications and programs have a presence through a variety of media. The magazines *Food & Wine* and *Gourmet* have a web presence. Anthony Bourdain's narratives find their expression on television shows, books, and the Internet.

3. Contemporary narratives about polar expeditions, such as Sarah Wheeler's *Terra Incognita: Travels in Antarctica* and David Campbell's *Crystal Desert: Summers in Antarctica,* still retain much of these risky and dangerous aspects, but even these lament the onset of tourism in polar zones. Campbell, for example, discusses the spoiling of natural surrounding by whaling and sealing. But for the most part, contemporary narratives do not chronicle tales of starvation or hunger for the narrator/ traveler/tourist, but some do introduce risk in consuming the food itself. One example

would be television shows such as *Bizarre Foods with Andrew Zimmern* where Zimmern eats a variety of "risky" food—worms in Mexico, cow's heart in Morocco, or lemon ants in Ecuador. Such media narratives take full advantage of the visual and audio technology to produce the riskiness associated with eating "bizarre" foods.

4. A comparison of food photographs in magazines such as *Redbook, McCall's,* or *The Saturday Evening Post* during the mid-twentieth-century to late-twentieth/early-twenty-first-century publications, as well as in a variety of mass/social media, makes this point.

5. For a lengthy discussion of genetically modified food and standardized farming see José Bové and François Defour's *The World Is Not For Sale: Farmers Against Junk Food* and Vandana Shiva's *Stolen Harvest.*

6. More research needs to be done on the consumption of U.S. food around the world. Many anecdotes suggest that such consumption can become a way establishing prestige and status by association with the U.S. And in nations where this is a recent phenomenon, such as China, it also consumed as a novelty, and sometimes as a snack for children while the "real" food is consumed at home.

7. Stewart Elliot and Kim Severson, "Condé Nast Closes *Gourmet* and 3 Other Magazines." http://www.nytimes.com/2009/10/06/business/media/06gourmet.html Aug. 1, 2010.

8. See chapter 1 for a discussion of how management theorists employ the idea of literature as timeless for dislocal purposes.

9. Though distinct historical forces have always produced regional foods, recently the ideas of regionality and locality have taken on a different sort of significance. Barbara and James Shortridge, in the Introduction to their edited collection, *The Taste of American Place,* attribute a renewed interest in what they call "neolocalism" to the fast-paced lifestyle that has eroded a sense of community and a "commitment to experiencing things close to home" (7). Contemporary regionalism and localism in relationship to food that emphasizes "local" ingredients is often politically positioned against the global trends of genetic modification, use of pesticides, and standardization. And "local" foods need not be produced "close to home." In fact, "local" foods are marketed and sold to consumers living far way from the "originary" site of harvest and preparation.

10. What is missing from this quasi-historical account (as well as from the historical perspective of *Endless Feasts* overall) is the effect of Prohibition on the California wine industry. Repairing the wine business after Prohibition was lifted would indeed require pleas to potential consumers. For more detailed histories of California wine industries see James T. Lapsley's *Bottled Poetry: Napa Winemaking from Prohibition to the Modern Era* (1996) and Thomas Pinney's *A History of Wine in America: From the Beginnings to Prohibition* (1989).

11. For a lengthier discussion of the history of food production companies, see Harvey Levenstein's *Revolution at the Table* (2003).

12. *In Spaces of Hope* (2001), Harvey explains that "'globalization' seems first to have acquired its prominence as American Express advertised the global reach of its credit card in the mid 1970s. The term spread like wildfire in the financial and business press, mainly as legitimation for deregulation of financial markets. It then helped make the diminution in state powers to regulate capital flows seem inevitable and became an extraordinary tool in disempowerment of national local working-class move-

ment . . . And by mid 1980s it helped create a heady atmosphere of entrepreneurial optimism around the theme of the liberation of markets from state control" (13).

13. Wallerstein, in theorizing the idea of a "world culture," points to the "dialectic of creating simultaneously a homogeneous world and distinctive national cultures within this world" and "the creating of simultaneously homogeneous national cultures and distinctive ethnic groups or minorities within these nation-states" ("The National and the Universal," 99).

14. So, for example, in the June 2008 issue Sigal tells us in her "The Chef, the Pig and the Perfect Summer Party" that the jet-setting chef has time to throw a sophisticated barbeque in his home outside of Manhattan. He serves "sweet-tangy carrots flavored with pink peppercorns and a silken pea puree sparked with jalapeños," and "spit-roasted meat" (23). The recipes are included for those wishing to try the food themselves, but because this is New York, fusion's "native" land, the food alone can tell of his travels.

15. An athletic analog to this same phenomenon can be cited as well: the recruitment by Houston's NBA franchise of Yao Ming, a Chinese basketball phenomenon over seven feet tall. This has as much to do with globalization as it does with winning games. Yao, as a mega-celebrity both in the U.S. and China, is clearly understood to be a gateway into China for companies that thereby help to sell not only Apple computers, credit cards, and Gatorade but also NBA paraphernalia to two billion Chinese. Of course, it is because Yao can play the game that he takes the court in Houston. The presence of international players in the NBA has become commonplace. But the game itself, more obviously than in the case of the space of culinary consumption, remains American.

16. *A Cook's Tour* began to air in 2002. There were around thirty-five original shows produced and aired regularly until 2005. Weekly reruns of the show continue on the Food Channel, but Bourdain now has a similar show entitled *No Reservations* on the Travel Channel. In these programs, Bourdain samples food while visiting places both within and outside the U.S. He has also published books under the same title as his television series and has written numerous others, including works of fiction that feature prominently the theme of food. I have chosen to analyze *A Cook's Tour*—with references to the book version as well—in part simply because it has been a relatively long running show and has made Bourdain into a well-known television personality. Food programming on television has come a long way since the PBS-based instructional cooking of Julia Child and Jeff Smith; it need not provide recipes for dishes and can function exclusively as a narrative.

17. Bourdain's later television series *No Reservations* aired an episode in 2008 in which he visits Laos and the home of someone who lost a limb as he accidentally dug up a bomb dropped in the 1970s by the U.S., a bomb that was aimed at neighboring Cambodia. His injury occurred four decades later, while he was cleaning up around his house. Bourdain is appropriately contrite and apologizes on behalf of the U.S. as he partakes in the little bit of food the impoverished family has.

18. The New Orleans episode shows him getting kicked out of Emeril's restaurant in New York, implying that it was for the unkind remarks he made about Emeril in his books—*The Kitchen Confidential* and *A Cook's Tour*. *A Cook's Tour* contains a section called "Full Disclosure" in which he says that he is uncomfortable doing *A Cook's Tour* series and being associated with the Food Network because he has always made fun of the cooks associated with the Food Network.

Conclusion

1. Or perhaps management academics, similarly to others, generally do not think outside the box of their own disciplines except when the continued existence of that discipline itself, and hence their future employment, is at stake.

2. See, in addition to what has already been cited above from chapter 1, this adjacent passage:

> In the third volume of *Capital,* Marx refers to the system of credit in general as "fictitious capital." So, for example, the buying and selling of shares on the stock market neither creates new value nor injects increased capital into the firm whose shares are being traded. "Fictitious capital" is different from the money originally supplied for use in production. It is an additional amount of money that simply allows for the *circulation* of income or profit. In fact, this circulation represents claims to future, still unrealized surplus value, making it appear that the amount of capital has increased. Thus the increase in the price of shares, to take the most obvious example of fictitious capital, creates the illusion—the stuff of everyday economic life on Wall Street—that the stock market itself is creating value. Essentially, fictitious capital refers to a form of financialization—the listing of a given amount of prospective money capital on the books—that makes a claim on the future generation of real, nonfictional profits or surplus value.
>
> None of this poses any real threat to the reproduction of capital as a whole as long as such claims themselves are eventually made good and fictional is converted into real capital. But what happens if—or when—a point is reached beyond which this realization (in more than one sense here) ceases to be possible, and, to avoid defaulting on the claims already lodged against fictional capital, still *more* fictional capital must be injected into circulation in the hopes of putting off the inevitable day of reckoning? Here one encounters what has become a major question in discussions of contemporary political economy, one to which I cannot do real justice here. The most recent U.S. financial crisis, triggered in 2007–8 by massive defaults on subprime home mortgages and the resulting deflation of what had been Wall Street's latest, real estate–based speculative bubble, is only the latest indication that such a point—what we might term "hyper-fictionalization"—may have been reached." (53, 54)

3. Here we also learn that, as is so often the case, terms later assumed to have been coined by Marx are in fact carried over into the conceptual system of Marx's critique of political economy from the language of, in most cases, the British political economists and capitalists of the late eighteenth and early to mid-nineteenth century whom he studied assiduously, from Adam Smith to, in this case, W. Leatham, a Yorkshire banker who spoke of "fictitious capital" in a pamphlet published in 1840. As Marx's brief citation of Leatham makes clear, the latter was referring to a fact that every banker knows: at any given moment a bank has more money-capital out on loan than it does on deposit, but this does not prevent the bank from listing its still-unpaid loans as assets, or from selling them as the commodities known, generally speaking, as "securities." What counts as fictitious for Leatham is the supposition that the debt

will, at some point in the future, be repaid.

4. See, for example, chapter 29: "the capital of the national debt remains purely *fictitious,* and the moment these promissory notes become unsaleable, the *illusion* of this capital disappears. Yet this *fictitious* capital has its characteristic movement for all that . . ."; "interest-bearing capital always being the mother of every *insane [verrückten]* form, so that debts, for example, can appear as commodities in the mind of the banker . . ." (596); "Even when the promissory note—the security—does not represent a purely *illusory* capital, as it does in the case of national debts, the capital value of the security is still pure *illusion*" (597). Also see chapter 30: "These promissory notes which were issued for a capital originally borrowed but long since spent, these paper duplicates of *annihilated capital,* function for their owners as capital in so far as they are saleable commodities and can therefore be transformed into capital." "But these titles similarly become *paper duplicates of the real capital,* as if a bill of lading simultaneously acquired a value alongside the cargo it refers to. They become *nominal representatives of non-existent capitals*" (608). "This kind of *imaginary money wealth* makes up a very considerable part not only of the money wealth of private individuals but also of banking capital, as already mentioned" (609) [my emphasis throughout].

5. To get at this deeper meaning would ultimately require, however, an attempt to come to terms with what will strike the contemporary reader of this particular section of volume 3 either as a case of inconsistent editing, or—more likely—as one of Marx's more erroneous moments in the theory of "the role of credit in capitalist production." Rather than take the time to map out this confusing problem here, however, I consign this task, for those who want the details, to this footnote and proceed directly in the body of the text to the one or two remarks which, if my own reading of Marx here is on the right track, are the clearest indications of this.

While observing, so far quite uncontroversially, that the formation of joint-stock companies results in "tremendous expansion in the scale of production" as well as the "transformation of the actual functioning capitalist into a mere manager, in charge of other people's capital" (567), Marx adds:

> Capital, which is inherently based on a social mode of production and presupposes a social concentration of means of production and labour-power, now receives the form of social capital (capital of directly associated individuals) in contrast to private capital, and its enterprises appear as social enterprises as opposed to private ones. This is the abolition of capital as private property within the confines of the capitalist mode of production itself. (ibid.)

This is followed, after a dense chain of reasoning that I cannot take the time to summarize here, by what seems an even more mystifying miscalculation on Marx's part in which it is claimed that the separation of capital's managerial function from capital ownership also becomes a point of transition in which labor itself is separated from capital as mere "money capital." Thus the "result of capitalist production in its highest development [the joint-stock company] is a necessary point of transition back into the property of the producers, though no longer as the private property of individual producers but rather as their property as associated producers, as directly social property" (568). At this point, Engels himself interjects a passage, perhaps meant to correct for Marx's error as concerns the future of the joint-stock company, a passage (familiar from Lenin's *Imperialism*) observing the real "point of transition" latent in the latter change in form of capitalist property: the creation of giant cartels and monopolies. And then—as if to compound the problem of what Marx ultimately saw as the historical possibilities latent in "fictitious capital"—the words are again Marx's, and, after being stated once again that "this [presumably still the credit-enabled joint-stock company] is the abolition of the capitalist mode of production within the capitalist mode of production itself" (569), a strikingly different picture of such a dialectic (and the one which is my chosen point of departure above) is drawn:

> It gives rise to monopoly in certain spheres and hence provokes state intervention. It reproduces a new financial aristocracy, a new kind of parasite in the guise of company promoters, speculators, and merely nominal directors; an entire system of swindling and cheating with respect to the promotion of companies, issue of shares and share dealings. It is private production unchecked by private ownership. (ibid.)

6. Edmund L. Andrews reported on Greenspan's congressional testimony on October 23, 2008 in the *New York Times,* wherein Greenspan conceded that he was at least partially wrong in opposing regulation. He states: "Those of us who have looked to the self-interest of lending institutions to protect shareholder's equity— myself especially—are in a state of shocked disbelief." When questioned about his free-market ideology, Greenspan said: "I have found a flaw. I don't know how significant or permanent it is. But I have been very distressed by that fact." http://www.nytimes.com/2008/10/24/business/economy/24panel.html.

National Public Radio reported some of conversation between Greenspan and Rep. Henry Waxman (D-CA). Waxman: "In other words, you found that your view of the world, your ideology, was not right, it was not working." Greenspan replied: "How it—precisely. That's precisely the reason I was shocked, because I've been going for 40 years or more with very considerable evidence that it was working exceptionally well." http://www.npr.org/templates/story/story.php?storyId=96070766.

7. Not to be confused with his father, Paul Mattick Sr. (1904–81), a well-known German theoretician of the "council communist" movement, who later emigrated to the United States.

8. Paul Mattick Jr., "Up in Smoke," *The Brooklyn Rail,* October, 2008, 2. http://www.brooklynrail.org/2008/10/express/up-in-smoke.

9. See: "Risky Business," *The Brooklyn Rail,* November 2008. http://brooklynrail.org/2008/11/express/risky-business; "Ups and Downs: The Economic Crisis (part 3)," *The Brooklyn Rail,* February 2009. http://brooklynrail.org/2009/02/express/ups-and-downs-the-ec; "What Is to Be Done?," *The Brooklyn Rail,* April 2009. http://www.brooklynrail.org/2009/04/express/what-is-to-be-done.

10. Robert Brenner, "What Is Good for Goldman Sachs Is Good for America: The Origins of the Present Crisis." UC Los Angeles: Center for Social Theory and Comparative History, 2009. http://escholarship.org/uc/item/0sg0782h.

11. See "Organizing for the Anti-Capitalist Transition." http://davidharvey.org/2009/12/organizing-for-the-anti-capitalist-transition/.

12. Translated from its German original by Josh Robinson. http://www.krisis.org/2009/tremors-on-the-global-market.

13. Georg Lukács, *History and Class Consciousness,* trans. Rodney Livingstone (Cambridge, MA: MIT Press, 1972), 74

14. In the context of globalization theories, an immediate tendency in response to the above might be to question whether (referring to the first citation from Lukács) "the ability to look beyond the divisive symptoms of the economic process to the unity of the total social system underlying it" is now made possible by the existence of globalization. Not to dismiss that there *might,* in the end, be something to this, depending on how the historical changes referred to as "globalization" are themselves theorized, but rather to confer on globalization, whether in theory or in practice, anything like the potential to overcome reified consciousness, is, at best, to beg that question. And it has been the objective of the theory of dislocalism to demystify such notions. That the "unity of the social system" has increased enormously in scope and depth since the 1920s is beyond dispute, but so, along with this, has the weight and penetration of reification, and now not only on the level of the "divisive symptoms" but of ideologies of the whole—for example, dislocalism—that, as stated in the Introduction, "make it appear as though [the] erasure of the local were itself the meaning and content of 'globalization.'"

15. John Seely Brown, Stephen Denning, Katalina Groh, and Laurence Prusak, *Storytelling in Organizations: Why Storytelling Is Transforming 21st Century Organizations and Management* (Oxford: Elsevier Butterworth-Henemann, 2005).

16. Bret Benjamin, in his book *Invested Interests,* has suggested that we think about the stories that World Bank published as those of success as literary fiction. Utilizing the term World Bank Literature from Amitava Kumar's edited volume of the same name, to which Benjamin also contributes, offers an interesting analysis of the ways in which we can understand the Bank as a social/cultural institution. My analysis looking directly at the material produced by management emphasizes the attempt to understand the ways in which the Bank (and management in general) itself understands what it is doing with storytelling.

17. He goes so far as to suggest the kind of stories that do the work. "As a storyteller who is aiming at eliciting organizational change through stories, one doesn't need to tell the story with the panache of a Charles Dickens or a Mark Twain. With such writers, the explicit voice of the narrator is so large and generous and conveys so much enthusiasm and gusto for life that the reader is often swept along by it, and the stories become as real if not more real than life itself. In our context, it is more relevant to think about the minimalist stories of Raymond Carver. Remember that we are aiming to leave lots of space for the listeners to invent their own stories, and to fill in the blanks" (*The Springboard: How Storytelling Ignites Action in Knowledge-Era Organizations,* 181).

18. Volume 108, no. 1 (Fall 2009).

19. "What Is the New Formalism," 122, no. 2 (March 2007): 558–69.

20. "Instead of 'reducing' cultural phenomena, the essay immerses itself in them as though in a second nature, a second immediacy, in order to *negate and transcend the illusion of immediacy through its perseverance.* It has no more illusions about the difference between culture and what lies beneath it than does the philosophy of origin. But for it *culture is not an epiphenomenon* that covers Being and should be destroyed; instead, *what lies beneath culture is itself thesis, something constructed, the false society.*" Adorno, "The Essay as Form," *Notes to Literature,* vol. 1, trans. Shierry Weber Nicholsen (New York: Columbia University Press, 1991), 19 (with the exception of "thesis," italicized in the original, my emphasis).

BIBLIOGRAPHY

Abu-Jaber. Diana. *Crescent*. New York: W. W. Norton, 2004.

———. Arabian Jazz. New York: New York: W. W. Norton, 2003.

———. "Letter to Teacher." October 2, 2007. *dianaabujaber.com*. http://www.dianaabujaber.com/banned.html. March 12, 2008.

Alsultany, Evelyn. "Selling American Diversity and Muslim American Identity Through Non-Profit Advertising Post-911." *American Quarterly* 59, no. 3 (2007).

Alvarez, Julia. *How the García Girls Lost Their Accents*. Chapel Hill, NC: Algonquin Books, 1991.

Amex Publishing Inc. "Company." *Amex Custom Publishing*. http://www.aecustpub.com/company.html. August 2, 2003.

Anderson, Benedict. *Imagined Communities: Reflection on the Origin and Spread of Nationalism*. London: Verso, 1983.

Andrews, Edmund L. "Greenspan Concedes Error on Regulation." October 23, 2008. http://www.nytimes.com/2008/10/24/business/economy/24panel.html. August 12, 2010.

Anzaldúa, Gloria. *Borderlands/La Frontera: The New Mestiza*. San Francisco: Spinsters/Aunt Lute, 1987.

——— and AnaLouise Keating. *This Bridge We Call Home: Radical Visions for Transformation*. New York: Routledge, 2002.

Appadurai, Arjun. "Patriotism and Its Futures." *Public Culture* (Spring 1993): 411–30.

———. *Modernity at Large: Cultural Dimensions of Globalization*. Minneapolis: University of Minnesota Press, 1996.

Arac, Jonathan. "Global and Babel: Language and Planet in American Literature." *Shades of the Planet: American Literature as World Literature*. Ed. Wai Chee Dimock and Lawrence Buell. Princeton, NJ: Princeton University Press, 2007, 19–38.

Arias, Arturo. "Authoring Ethnicized Subjects: Rigoberta Menchú and the Performative Production of the Subaltern. *PMLA* 116, no. 1 (January 2001): 75–88.

Arrighi, Giovanni. *The Long Twentieth Century: Money, Power, and the Origins of Our Times*. New York: Verso, 1994.

Bacon, David. *Illegal People: How Globalization Creates Migration and Criminalizes Immigrants*. Boston: Beacon Press, 2008.

Badarraco, Joseph Jr. *Questions of Character: Illuminating the Heart of Leadership Through Literature*. Boston: Harvard Business School Press, 2006.

Barak, Julie. "'Turning and Turning in the Widening Gyre': A Second Coming into Language in Julia Alvarez's *How the García Girls Lost Their Accents*." *MELUS* 23, no. 1 (Spring 1998): 159–76.

Barry, Tom, and Beth Wood et al., eds. *The Other Side of Paradise*. New York: Grove Press, 1984.

Bauman, Zygmunt. *Liquid Modernity*. New York: Polity, 2005.

Behdad, Ali. *Belated Travelers: Orientalism in the Age of Colonial Dissolution*. Durham, NC: Duke University Press, 1994.

Benjamin, Bret. *Invested Interests: Capital, Culture, and the World Bank*. Minneapolis: University of Minnesota Press, 2007.

Bennis, Phyllis. "'And They Called It Peace': U.S. Policy on Iraq." *Middle East Report,* July 2000.

Bess, Jennifer. "Imploding the Miranda Complex in Julia Alvarez's *How the García Girls Lost Their Accents*." *College Literature* 34, no. 1 (2007): 78–105.

Best, Stephen, and Sharon Marcus. "Surface Reading: An Introduction." Ed. Stephen Best and Sharon Marcus. Special Issue: "The Way We Read Now," *Representations* 108, no. 1 (Fall 2009): 1–21.

———, eds. Special Issue: "The Way We Read Now," *Representations* 108, no. 1 (Fall 2009).

Beverley, John. *Against Literature*. Minneapolis: University of Minnesota Press, 1993.

———. *Testimonio: On the Politics of Truth*. Minneapolis: University of Minnesota Press, 2004.

Blackburn, Robin. *Age Shock and Pension Power: How Finance Is Failing Us*. New York: Verso, 2006.

———. "Financialization and the Fourth Dimension." *New Left Review,* May–June 2006.

———. "The Subprime Crisis." *New Left Review,* March–April 2008.

Boltasnki, Luc, and Eve Chiapello. *The New Spirit of Capitalism*. London: Verso, 2005.

Bolter, Jay, and Richard Grusin. *Remediation*. Cambridge, MA: MIT Press, 2000.

Borjas, George. "The Impact of Immigrants on Employment Opportunities of the Natives." *The Immigration Reader: America in a Multidisciplinary Perspective*. Ed. David Jacobson. Oxford, UK: Wiley-Blackwell, 1998, 217–30.

Bourdain, Anthony. "Cobra Heart—Food That Makes You Manly." *A Cook's Tour*. Food Network. January 24, 2003. 9:30 P.M.

———. *A Cook's Tour*. New York: Ecco, 2001.

———. "The Cook Who Came In from the Cold." *A Cook's Tour*. Food Network. July 25, 2003. 9:30 P.M.

———. *Kitchen Confidential. Adventures in the Culinary Underbellly*. New York: Ecco, 2001.

———. "Los Angeles, My Own Heart of Darkness." *A Cook's Tour*. Food Network.

March 21, 2003. 9:30 P.M.

———. "No Beads, No Babes, No Bourbon Street." *A Cook's Tour*. Food Network. June 20, 2003. 9:30 P.M.

———. "Puebla, Where the Good Cooks Are From." *A Cook's Tour*. Food Network. February 28, 2003. 9:30 P.M.

———. "San Sebastian: A Food Lover's Town." *A Cook's Tour*. Food Network. April 25, 2003. 9:30 P.M.

———. "So Much Vodka, So Little Time." *A Cook's Tour*. Food Network. February 7, 2003. 9:30 P.M.

———. "The Struggle for the Soul of America." *A Cook's Tour*. Food Network. August 1, 2003. 9:30 P.M.

———. "Tamales and Iguana, Oaxacan Style." *A Cook's Tour*. Food Network. August 8, 2003. 9:30 P.M.

Bové, José, and François Dufour. *The World Is Not for Sale: Farmers Against Junk Food*. New York: Verso, 2001.

Bowles, Pauls. *Their Heads Are Green and Their Hands Are Blue: Scenes from the Non-Christian World*. New York: Harper Perennial, 2006 (1st ed. 1952).

———. *The Sheltering Sky*. New York: New Directions, 1949.

Brantlinger, Patrick. *Crusoe's Footprints: Cultural Studies in Britain and America*. New York: Routledge, 1990.

Brecher, Jeremy, and Tim Costello. *Global Village or Global Pillage: Economic Reconstruction from the Bottom Up*. Boston: South End Press, 1994.

Brennan, Timothy. *At Home in the World: Cosmopolitanism Now*. Cambridge, MA: Harvard University Press, 1997.

———. "The Empire's New Clothes." *Critical Inquiry* 29, no. 29 (2003).

Brenner, Robert. *The Boom and the Bubble: The US in the World Economy*. London: Verso, 2002.

———. "New Boom or New Bubble?" *New Left Review*, Second Series, no. 25 (January–February 2004).

———. What Is Good for Goldman Sachs Is Good for America: The Origin of the Present Crisis." UC Los Angeles: Center for Social Theory and Comparative History. April 18, 2009. http://escholarship.org/uc/item/0sg0782h. August 2, 2010.

Brett, Jeanne, Kristin Behfar, and Mary C. Kern. "Managing Multicultural Teams." *Harvard Business Review* 84, no. 11 (2006): 84–91.

Brillat-Savarin (Jean Anthelme). *The Physiology of Taste*. New York: Liveright, 1948.

Brinkerhoff, Derick W., and Jennifer Brinkerhoff. "International Development Management: Definitions, Debates, and Dilemmas." *Handbook of Globalization, Governance, and Public Administration*. Ed. Ali Farazmand and Jack Pinkowski. London: CRC Press, 2006, 821–40.

Brown, John Seely, Stephen Denning, Katalina Groh, and Laurence Prusak. *Storytelling in Organizations: How Storytelling Is Transforming Twenty First Century Organizations and Management*. Burlington: Elsevier Butterworth-Heinemann, 2005.

Bryman, Alan. "Theme Parks and McDonaldization." *Resisting McDonaldization*. Ed. B. Smart. York: Sage, 1999, 101–15.

Bryson, Bill, ed. *The Best American Travel Writing 2000*. Boston: Houghton Mifflin, 2000.

———. "Travel." *New York Times Book Review.* December 6, 1998. http://www. nytimes.com. September 9, 2003.

Buell, Frederick. *National Culture and the New Global System.* Baltimore: Johns Hopkins University Press, 1994.

Caesar, Terry. *Forgiving the Boundaries: Home as Abroad in American Travel Writing.* Athens: University of Georgia Press, 1995.

Cahan, Abraham. *The Rise of David Levinsky.* New York: Harper, 1966.

Cardoso, Fernando Henrique. *Charting a New Course: The Politics of Globalization and Social Transformation.* Lanham, MD: Rowman and Littlefield, 2001.

Casanova, Pascale. *The World Republic of Letters.* Trans. M. B. DeBevoise. Cambridge, MA: Harvard University Press, 2005.

Catlin, Linda B., and Thomas F. White. *International Business: Cultural Sourcebook and Case Studies.* Cincinnati, OH: Southwestern, 2001.

CBS. Com. "Marquesas Nuku Hiva." *CBS.com.* http://www.cbs.com/primetime/survivor4/marquesas/marquesas.php. August 15, 2003.

Chamberlain, Mary. *Carribbean Migration: Globalized Identities.* New York: Routledge, 1998.

Chang, Grace. *Disposable Domestics: Immigrant Women Workers in the Global Economy.* Boston: South End Press, 2000.

Chatterjee, Partha. *The Nation and Its Fragments: Colonial and Postcolonial Histories.* Princeton, NJ: Princeton University Press, 1993.

Chomsky, Noam, and Edward Herman. *The Washington Connection and Third World Fascism:* Boston: South End Press, 1979.

Clifford, James. *Routes: Travel and Translation in the Late Twentieth Century.* Cambridge, MA: Harvard University Press, 1997.

Coffin, Robert. "Night of Lobster." *Endless Feasts: Sixty Years of Writing from Gourmet.* Ed. Ruth Reichl. New York: Modern Library, 2002, 109–14.

Coles, Robert, and Albert LaFarge, eds. *Minding the Store: Great Writing about Business from Tolstoy to Now.* New York: New Press, 2008.

Commonwealth Club of California. "Good Lit: Paul Theroux in Conversation." *The Commonwealth Club of California/Event Archive: Paul Theroux.* http://www. commonwealthclub.org/archive/01/01-05theroux-speech.html. August 4, 2003.

Conroy, Pat. "The Romance of Umbria." *Endless Feasts: Sixty Years of Writing from Gourmet.* Ed. Ruth Reichl. New York: Modern Library, 2002, 82–89.

Cornell University. "Cultural Studies of International Financial Markets." *Anthropology Course 304, Topics in Anthropology.* Spring 2001. http://www.einaudi. cornell.edu/eastasia/courses/courseNew2001Spring(Miyazaki).htm. March 2, 2001.

Crandell, Russell. *Gunboat Democracy: U.S. Interventions in the Dominican Republic, Greneda, and Panama.* Lanham, MD: Rowman and Littlefield, 2006.

Crothers, Lane. *Globalization and American Popular Culture.* Lanham, MD: Rowman and Littlefield, 2007.

Cruz, John. "From Farce to Tragedy: Reflections on the Reification of Race at Century's End." *Mapping Multiculturalism.* Ed. Avery Gordon and Christopher Newfield. Minneapolis: University of Minnesota Press, 1996, 19–39.

Czinkota, Michael R., and Ilkka A. Ronkainen, eds. *Best Practices in International Business.* Fort Worth, TX: Harcourt College Publishers, 2001.

Davis, Mike. *Late Victorian Holocausts: El Niño Famines and the Making of the Third World.* New York: Verso, 2002.

———. *Planet of Slums.* New York: Verso, 2005.

Denning, Michael. *Culture in the Age of Three Worlds.* New York: Verso, 2004.

Denning, Stephen. *The Springboard: How Storytelling Ignites Action in Knowledge-Era Organizations.* Burlington, VT: Butterworth-Heinemann, 2001.

Dimock, Wai-chee. "Deep Time: American Literature and World History." *American Literary History* 13, no. 4 (Winter 2001): 755–75.

———. *Through Other Continents: American Literature across Deep Time.* Princeton, NJ: Princeton University Press, 2006.

———, and Lawrence Buell, eds. *Shades of the Planet: American Literature as World Literature.* Princeton, NJ: Princeton University Press, 2007.

Dixon, Maria A. "Transforming Power: Expanding the Inheritance of Michel Foucault in Organizational Studies." *Management Communication Quarterly: McQ.* (February 2007): 283–97.

Dobbs, Lou. "Lou Dobbs Tonight." January 12, 2008. *CNN.com.* http://loudobbs.tv.cnn.com/tv/.

Douglas, Mary. *Purity and Danger: An Analysis of Concepts of Pollution and Taboo.* London: Routledge and Kegan Paul, 1980 (1st ed. 1966).

Doyle, Jacqueline. "'A Love Letter to My Motherland': Maternal Discourses in Jessica Hagedorn's *Dogeaters.*" *Hitting Critical Mass: A Journal of Asian American Cultural Criticism* 4, no. 2 (Summer 1997): 1–25.

Drucker, Peter Ferdinand. *Classic Drucker: Essential Wisdom of Peter Drucker.* Boston: Harvard Business School Publishing, 1998.

———. *The Effective Executive.* New York: Harper & Row, 1967.

———. *The Ecological Vision: Reflections on the American Condition.* New Brunswick, NJ: Transaction Publishers, 1993.

———. *Management Challenges for the 21st Century.* New York: HarperBusiness, 2001.

D'Souza, Dinesh. *The End of Racism: Principles for a Multiracial Society.* New York: Free Press, 1995.

———. *Illiberal Education: The Politics of Race and Sex on Campus.* New York: Free Press, 1991.

During, Simon. "Introduction." *The Cultural Studies Reader.* Ed. Simon During. New York: Routledge, 1993.

———. *Cultural Studies: A Critical Introduction.* New York: Routledge, 2005.

———. "Popular Culture on a Global Scale: A Challenge for Cultural Studies?" *Critical Inquiry* 23, no. 4 (Summer 1997): 808–33.

Edwards, Brian. *Morocco Bound: Disorienting America's Maghreb, from Casablanca to the Marrakech Express.* Durham, NC: Duke University Press, 2005.

Edwards, Justin D. *Exotic Journeys: Exploring the Erotics of U.S. Travel Literature, 1840–1930.* Hanover: University of New Hampshire Press, 2001.

Elliot, Stewart, and Kim Severson. "Condé Nast Closes *Gourmet* and 3 Other Magazines." *NYTimes.com.* October 5 2009. http://www.nytimes.com/2009/10/06/business/media/06gourmet.html. August 12, 2010.

Escobar, Arturo. *Encountering Development: The Making and Unmaking of the Third World.* Princeton, NJ: Princeton University Press, 1995.

Essex, E. M., and Mainmelis, C. "Learning from an Artist about Organizations: The Poetry and Prose of David Whyte at Work." *Journal of Management Inquiry* 11, no. 2 (2002): 148–59.

Emerson, Ralph Waldo. *The American Scholar. Self-reliance. Compensation.* New York: American Book Co., 1893.

Fadda-Conrey, Carol. "Arab-American Literature in the Ethnic Borderland: Cultural Intersections in Diana Abu-Jaber's *Crescent.*" *MELUS*. Special issue on Arab American Literature. Ed. Salah D. Hassan and Marcy Jane Kopf-Newman, Winter 2006, 187–206.

Farred, Grant. "Reconfiguring the Humanities and the Social Sciences in the Age of the Global University." *Neplanta: Views from the South* 4, no. 1 (2003): 41–50.

Featherstone, Mike, ed. *Global Culture: Nationalism, Globalization and Modernity.* London: Sage, 1990.

Ferguson, James. *Far from Paradise: Introduction to the Caribbean Development.* London: Latin America Bureau, 1990.

Ferris, David. "Indiscipline." *Comparative Literature in an Age of Globalization.* Ed. Haun Saussy. Baltimore: Johns Hopkins University Press, 2006, 78–99.

Field, Robin E. "An Interview with Diana Abu-Jaber." *MELUS*. Special Issue on Arab American Literature. Ed. Salah D. Hassan and Marcy Jane Kopf-Newman, Winter 2006, 207–25.

Fisher, M. F. K. "Three Swiss Inns." *Endless Feasts: Sixty Years of Writing from Gourmet.* Ed. Ruth Reichl. New York: Modern Library, 2002, 3–11.

Flew, Terry. *New Media: An Introduction.* London: Oxford University Press, 2002.

Franklin, Benjamin. *Autobiography.* Ed. J. A. Leo Lemay and P. M. Zall. New York: W. W. Norton, 1986.

Frederici, Silvia. *Caliban and the Witch.* New York: Autonomedia, 2004.

Friedman, Susan Stanford. "Unthinking Manifest Destiny: Muslim Modernities on Three Continents." *Shades of the Planet: American Literature as World Literature.* Ed. Wai Chee Dimock and Lawrence Buell. Princeton, NJ: Princeton University Press, 2007, 62–99.

Friedman, Thomas. *The Lexus and the Olive Tree.* New York: Anchor Books, 1999.

———. *The World Is Flat.* New York: Farrar, Straus and Giroux, 2005.

Geertz, Clifford. *The Interpretation of Cultures.* New York: Basic Books, 1973.

Gellner, Ernest. *Nations and Nationalisms.* Cornell: Cornell University Press, 1983.

Geok-lin Lim, Shirley, and Amy Ling, eds. *Reading the Literatures of Asian America.* Philadelphia: Temple University Press, 1992.

Gilling, Tom. "Jean-Georges Bora Bora." May 2007. http://www.foodandwine.com/articles/jean-georges-bora-bora. April 5, 2008.

"Globalization, Culture, and Management: Managing across Cultures." *Elective Curriculum MBA Courses. General Management Course 1538.* Harvard Business School. Cambridge, MA. www.hbs.edu/mba/admin/acs/1538.html. April 30, 2006.

Gordon, Avery, and Christopher Newfield, eds. *Mapping Multiculturalism.* Minneapolis: University of Minnesota Press, 1996.

Graff, Gerald. *Beyond the Culture Wars: How Teaching the Conflicts Can Revitalize American Education.* New York: W. W. Norton, 1992.

Grandin, Greg. *Empire's Workshop: Latin America, the United States, and the Rise of the New Imperialism.* New York: Metropolitan Books, 2006.

Grandy, Gina, and Albert J. Mills. "Strategy as Simulacra? A Radical Reflexive Look at the Discipline and Practice of Strategy." *Journal of Management Studies* 41, no. 7 (November 2004): 1153–70.

Grasmuck, Sherri, and Patricia Pessar. *Between Two Islands: Dominican International Migration.* Berkeley: University of California Press, 1991.

Grewal, Inderpal. *Transnational America: Feminisms, Diasporas, Neoliberalisms.* Durham, NC: Duke University Press, 2005.

Guedes, Ana, and Alex Faria. *International Management and International Relations: A Critical Perspective from Latin America.* New York: Routledge, 2010.

Guillory, John. *Cultural Capital: The Problem of Literary Canon Formation.* Chicago: University of Chicago Press, 1993.

Gunn, Giles. "Introduction." Globalizing Literary Studies. *PMLA.* 2001, 1–18.

Hagedorn, Jessica. *Dogeaters.* New York: Pantheon Books, 1990.

Hansen, Hans, and Daved Barry et al. "Truth or Consequences: An Improvised Collective Story Construction." *Journal of Management Inquiry* 16, no. 2 (June 2007): 122–26.

Harkness, Ruth. "In a Tibetan Lamasery." *Endless Feasts: Sixty Years of Writing from* Gourmet. Ed. Ruth Reichl. New York: Modern Library 2002, 12–19.

———. "Mexican Mornings." *Endless Feasts: Sixty Years of Writing from* Gourmet. Ed. Ruth Reichl. New York: Modern Library, 2002, 20–28.

Hardt, Michael, and Antonio Negri. *Empire.* Cambridge, MA: Harvard University Press, 2001.

Harlow, Barbara. "Testimonio and Survival: Roque Dalton's *Miguel Mármol"* (1991). *The Real Thing: Testimonial Discourse and Latin America.* Ed. Georg Gugelberger. Durham, NC: Duke University Press, 1996, 70–83.

Harmon, Michael M., and Richard T. Mayer. *Organization Theory for Public Administration.* Boston: Little, Brown and Company, 1986.

Harrison, Phyllis A. *Behaving Brazilian: A Comparison of Brazilian and North American Social Behavior.* Rowley, MA: Newbury House Publishers, 1983.

Hartman, Michelle. "This 'sweet/sweet music': Jazz, Sam Cooke, and Reading Arab American Literary Identities." *MELUS.* Special Issue on Arab American Literature. Ed. Salah D. Hassan and Marcy Jane Kopf-Newman. Winter 2006, 145–66.

Harvey, David. *A Brief History of Neoliberalism.* New York: Oxford University Press, 2005.

———. *The Condition of Postmodernity: An Enquiry into the Origins of Cultural Change.* Cambridge, UK: Wiley-Blackwell, 1991.

———. *Limits to Capital.* New York: Verso, 2006.

———. "Organizing for the Anti-Capitalist Transition: A Talk Given at the World Social Forum 2010." *Reading Marx with David Harvey.* http://davidharvey. org/2009/12/organizing-for-the-anti-capitalist-transition. August 16, 2010.

———. *Spaces of Capital: Towards a Critical Geography.* London: Routledge, 2001.

———. *Spaces of Hope.* Berkeley: University of California Press, 2000.

Hassan, Ihab Habib. *Selves at Risk: Patterns of Quest in Contemporary American Letters.* Madison: University of Wisconsin Press, 1990.

Hassan, Salah D., and Marcy Jane Kopf-Newman, eds. *MELUS.* Special Issue on Arab American Literature. Winter 2006.

Hatch, Mary Jo. "The Role of the Researcher." *Journal of Management Inquiry* 5, no. 4 (December 1996): 359–74.

———. *Organization Theory: Modern, Symbolic, and Postmodern Perspectives.* Oxford, UK: Oxford University Press, 1997.

Hegeman, Susan. *Patterns for America.* Princeton, NJ: Princeton University Press, 1999.

Heller, Thomas. "Change and Convergence: Is American Immigration Still Exceptional?" *Citizenship in a Global World: Comparing Rights for Aliens.* Ed. Atsuchi Kondō. New York: Palgrave Macmillan, 2001, 196–222.

Hjorth, Daniel. "Organizational Entrepreneurship: With De Certeau on Creating Heterotopias (or Spaces for Play)." *Journal of Management Inquiry.* Thousand Oaks, CA. December 2005, 386–99

Hobsbawm, Eric. *The Age of Extremes: The Short Twentieth Century, 1914–1999.* New York: Vintage, 1996.

Hoffman, Joan M. "'She Wants to Be Called Yolanda Now': Identity, Language, and the Third Sister in *How the Garcia Girls Lost Their Accents.*" *Bilingual Review/ La Revista Bilingue.* January–April 1998, 21–27.

"Holland America Line." Advertisement. *Food & Wine.* July 2007, 33.

Holland, Patrick, and Graham Huggan. *Tourists with Typewriters: Critical Reflections on Contemporary Travel Writing.* Ann Arbor: University of Michigan Press, 1998.

hooks, bell. "Eating the Other: Desire and Resistance." *The Consumer Society Reader.* Ed. Juliet B. Schor and Douglas B. Holt. New York: New Press, 2000, 343–59.

Hunter, James, and Joshua Yates. "The Vanguard of Globalization." *Many Globalizations: Cultural Diversity in the Contemporary World.* Ed. Peter L. Berger and Samuel P. Huntington. Oxford, UK: Oxford University Press, 2002, 321–58.

Jacobson, David, ed. *The Immigration Reader: America in a Multidisciplinary Perspective.* Oxford, UK: Wiley-Blackwell. 1998.

Jaffrey, Madhur. "An Indian Reminiscence." *Endless Feasts: Sixty Years of Writing from* Gourmet. Ed. Ruth Reichl. New York: Modern Library, 2002, 52–64.

Jameson, Frederic. *The Cultural Turn: Selected Writings on the Postmodern, 1983–1998.* New York: Verso, 1998.

———. "Preface." *The Cultures of Globalization.* Ed. Fredric Jameson and Masao Miyoshi. Durham, NC: Duke University Press, 1998.

———. "Globalization as a Philosophical Issue." *The Cultures of Globalization.* Ed. Fredric Jameson and Masao Miyoshi. Durham, NC: Duke University Press, 1998.

———. *Postmodernism, or, the Logic of Late Capitalism.* Durham, NC: Duke University Press, 1991.

———, and Maso Miyoshi. *The Cultures of Globalization.* Ed. Fredric Jameson and Masao Miyoshi. Durham, NC: Duke University Press, 1998.

Jay, Gregory S. *American Literature and the Culture Wars.* Ithaca, NY: Cornell University Press, 1997.

Jennings, Peter. "Headquarters." *In Search of America.* ABC News. September 6, 2003. 10:00 P.M.

Jessop, Bob. "Post-Fordism and the State." *Post-Fordism: A Reader.* Ed. Ash Amin. Malden, MA: Wiley-Blackwell, 1994, 251–79.

Jones, Campbell. "Practical Deconstructivist Feminist Marxist Organization Theory: Gayatri Chakravorty Spivak." *Contemporary Organization Theory.* Ed. Campbell

Jones and Rolland Monro. London: Wiley-Blackwell, 2005.

Kaldas, Pauline. "Beyond Stereotypes: Representational Dilemmas Is Arabian Jazz." *MELUS*. Special Issue on Arab American Literature. Ed. Salah D. Hassan and Marcy Jane Kopf-Newman. Winter 2006, 167–86.

Kaplan, Robert D. "The Coming Anarchy." *Atlantic Monthy*. February 1994.

———. *The Ends of the Earth: A Journey at the Dawn of the 21st Century*. New York: Random House, 1996.

———. *Imperial Grunts: On the Ground with the American Military, from Mongolia to the Philippines to Iraq and Beyond*. New York: Vintage, 2006.

———. *Hog Pilots, Blue Water Grunts: The American Military in the Air, at Sea, and on the Ground*. New York: Random House, 2005.

Kellner, Douglass. *Media Spectacles and the Crisis of Democracy: Terrorism, War, and Election Battles*. Boulder, CO: Paradigm Press, 2005.

Keynes, John Maynard. *The General Theory of Employment, Interest, and Money*. Amherst, MA: Prometheus, 1997.

Kim, Elaine H. *Asian American Literature: An Introduction to the Writings and Their Social Context*. Philadelphia: Temple University Press, 1982

Klein, Julie Thompson. *Crossing Boundaries: Knowledge, Disciplinarities, and Inter-disciplinarities*. Charlottesville: University Press of Virginia, 1996.

Krader, Kate. "A Banner Day." *Food & Wine*. July 2003, 160–73.

———. "Best New Chefs." *Food & Wine*. July 2007, 251–67.

Kruks, Sonia. "The Politics of Recognition: Fanon, Sartre, and Identity Politics." *Retrieving Experience: Subjectivity and Recognition in Feminist Politics*. Ithaca, NY: Cornell University Press, 2001.

Kuhn, Irene Corbally. "Shanghai: The Vintage Years." *Endless Feasts: Sixty Years of Writing from* Gourmet. Ed. Ruth Reichl. New York: Modern Library, 2002, 73–81.

Kumar, Amitava, ed. *World Bank Literature*. Minneapolis: University of Minnesota Press, 2002.

Leonhardt, David. "Truth, Fiction, and Lou Dobbs." *New York Times*. May 30, 2007.

Levander, Carole, and Robert Levine, eds. *American Hemispheric Studies*. Newark, NJ: Rutgers University Press, 2008.

Levenstein, Harvey A. *Revolution at the Table: The Transformation of the American Diet*. New York: Oxford University Press, 1988.

Lévi-Strauss, Claude. *The Raw and the Cooked*. New York: Harper & Row, 1969.

Levitt, Peggy. *The Transnational Villagers*. Berkeley: University of California Press, 2001.

Lewis, George H. "The Maine Lobster as Regional Icon: Competing Images Over Time and Social Class." *Food and Foodways* 3, no. 4 (1989): 303–16.

Lind, Michael. *The Next American Nation: The New Nationalism and the Fourth American Revolution*. New York: Free Press, 1995.

Ling, Amy. *Between Worlds: Women Writers of Chinese Ancestry*. New York: Pergamon Press, 1990.

"Literature, Ethics, and Authority." *MIT OpenCourseWare*. Sloan School of Management, MIT, Cambridge, MA. http://dspace.mit.edu/html/1721.1/36889/15–269ASpring-2004/OcwWeb/Sloan-School-of-Management/15–269ALiterature-Ethics-and-AuthoritySpring2003/Readings/index.htm. May 5, 2007.

Livingston, Robert Eric. "Glocal Knowledges: Agency and Place in Literary Studies." *PMLA* 116, no. 1 (January 2001): 145–57.

Loos, Anita. "Cocktail Parties of the Twenties." *Endless Feasts: Sixty Years of Writing from Gourmet*. Ed. Ruth Reichl. New York: Modern Library, 2002, 154–58.

Lowe, Lisa. "Decolonization, Displacement, Disidentification: Asian American 'Novels' and the Question of History." *Cultural Institutions of the Novel*. Ed. Deidre Lynch and William B. Warner. Durham, NC: Duke University Press, 1996, 96–128.

———. *Immigrant Acts: On Asian American Cultural Politics*. Durham, NC: Duke University Press, 1996.

———. "Work, Immigration, Gender: New Subjects of Cultural Politics. *The Politics of Culture in the Shadow of Capital*. Ed. Lisa Lowe and David Lloyd. Durham, NC: Duke University Press, 1997, 354–74.

Ludescher, Tanyss. "From Nostalgia to Critique: An Overview of Arab American Literature." *MELUS*. Special Issue on Arab American Literature. Ed. Salah D. Hassan and Marcy Jane Kopf-Newman. Winter 2006, 93–114.

Luis, William. "A Search for Identity in Julia Alvarez's *How the García Girls Lost Their Accents*." *Callaloo: A Journal of African Diaspora Arts and Letters*. (Summer 2000): 839–49.

Lukács, Georg. *History and Class Consciousness: Studies in Marxist Dialectics*. Trans. Rodney Livingstone. Cambridge, MA: MIT Press, 1971.

Lutz, Helma. "The Legacy of Migration: Immigrant Mothers and Daughters and the Process of Intergenerational Transmission." *Carribbean Migration: Globalized Identities*. Ed. Mary Chamberlain. New York: Routledge, 1998, 95–108.

MacCannell, Dean. *The Tourist: A New Theory of the Leisure Class*. New York: Schocken Books, 1976.

Marable, Manning. "9/11: Racism in the Time of Terror." *Souls* 4, no. 1 (January 2002): 1–14.

———. *The Great Wells of Democracy: The Meaning of Race in American Life*. New York: Basic Books, 1993.

Maribel, Ortíz-Márquez. "From Third World Politics to First World Practices: Contemporary Latina Writers in the United States." *Interventions: Feminist Dialogues on Third World Women's Literature and Film*. Ed. Bishnupriya Ghosh and Brinda Bose. New York: Garland, 1999, 227–44.

Marx, Karl. *Capital Volumes 1, 2 and 3*. New York: Penguin, 1981.

———. *Grundrisse: Foundations of the Critique of Political Economy*. New York: Penguin, 1993.

Maryville College. "Management Through Literature." *Business/Management Course 346*. Spring 2005. http://www.maryvillecollege.edu/gallaghe/managementlit.htm. July 30, 2005.

Mattick, Paul. "Ups and Downs: Economic Crisis Part 3." *The Brooklyn Rail: Critical Perspectives on Arts, Politics, Culture*. February 2009. http://brooklynrail. org/2009/02/express/ups-and-downs-the-economic-crisis-pt-3. March 12, 2010.

———. "Risky Business." *The Brooklyn Rail: Critical Perspectives on Arts, Politics, Culture*. November 2008. http://brooklynrail.org/2008/11/express/risky-business. March 12, 2010.

———. "Up in Smoke." *The Brooklyn Rail: Critical Perspectives on Arts, Politics,*

Culture. October 2008. http://brooklynrail.org/2008/10/express/up-in-smoke. March 12, 2010.

———. "What Is to Be Done?" *The Brooklyn Rail: Critical Perspectives on Arts, Politics, Culture.* April 2009. http://www.brooklynrail.org/2009/04/express/what-is-to-be-done. March 12, 2010.

Mayock, Ellen C. "The Bicultural Construction of Self in Cisneros, Alvarez, and Santiago." *Bilingual Review/La Revista Bilingüe.* September–December 1998, 223–29.

McLaren, Deborah. *Rethinking Tourism and Ecotravel.* Bloomfield, CT: Kumarian Press, 2005.

McNeely, Connie L. *Constructing the Nation-State: International Organization and Prescriptive Action.* Westport, CT: Greenwood Press, 1995.

Melamed, Jodi. "The Spirit of Neoliberalism: From Racial Liberalism to Neoliberal Multiculturalism." *Social Text* 24, no. 4 (Winter 2006): 1–25.

Melville, Herman. *Typee: A Peep at Polynesian Life.* New York: Penguin Classics, 1996.

Michaels, Walter Benn. *Our America: Nativism, Modernism, and Pluralism.* Durham, NC: Duke University Press, 1995.

Mies, Maria. *Patriarchy and Accumulation on a World Scale: Women in the International Division of Labour.* London: Zed Books, 1986.

Mintz, Sidney. *Tasting Food, Tasting Freedom: Excursions into Eating, Culture, and the Past.* Boston: Beacon Press, 1996.

Miyoshi, Masao. "'Globalization,'" Culture, and the University." *The Cultures of Globalization.* Ed. Fredric Jameson and Masao Miyoshi. Durham, NC: Duke University Press, 1998.

———. "Turn to the Planet: Literature, Diversity, and Totality." *Comparative Literature* 53, no. 4 (Autumn 2001): 283–97.

Moraga, Cherríe, and Gloria Anzaldúa. *This Bridge Called My Back: Writings by Radical Women of Color.* New York: Kitchen Table: Women of Color Press, 1983.

"The Moral Leader." *Elective Curriculum MBA Courses.* General Management Course 1562. Harvard Business School. Fall 2008. http://www.hbs.edu/mba/admin/acs/1562.html. September 15, 2008.

Morris, Mary. *Nothing to Declare: Memoirs of a Woman Traveling Alone.* Boston: Houghton Mifflin, 1989.

———. *The River Queen.* New York: Picador, 2007.

Morris, Richard Brandon, and Graham W. Irwin, eds. *Harper Encyclopedia of the Modern World: A Concise Reference History from 1760 to the Present.* New York: Harper & Row, 1970.

"Napa Valley 2000 Merlot Sterling Vineyards." *Food & Wine.* July 2003. Classic Wines Advertisement, 56–57.

Nas, Loes. "Border Crossings in Latina Narrative: Julia Alvarez's *How the García Girls Lost Their Accents.*" *Journal of Literary Studies* 19, no. 2 (June 2003): 125–37.

Naylor, Brian. "Greenspan Admits Free Market Ideology False." Transcript, NPR, October 24, 2008. http://www.npr.org/templates/story/story.php?storyId=96070766. August 12, 2010.

Newfield, Christopher. *Ivy and Industry: Business and the Making of the American*

University, 1880–1980. Durham, NC: Duke University Press, 2003.

Newton, Pauline. *Transcultural Women of the Late-Twentieth-Century U.S. American Literature*. Burlington, VT: Ashgate, 2005.

Nichols, Kenneth. "Decoding Postmodernism for Busy Public Managers." *The Public Manager* 36, no.1 (Spring 2007): 60–63.

"North American Free Trade Agreement." *NAFTA—Preamble*. http://www.sice.oas. org/trade/nafta/preamble.asp. September 9, 2003.

Novick, Sheldon. *Henry James: The Young Master*. New York: Random House, 1996.

Ohmae, Kenichi. *The End of the Nation State: The Rise of Regional Economies*. New York: Free Press, 1995.

Omi, Michael. "Racialization in the Post Civil Rights Era." *Mapping Multiculturalism*. Ed. Avery Gordon and Christopher Newfield. Minneapolis: University of Minnesota Press, 1996, 178–86.

Ong, Aihwa. *Neoliberalism as Exception: Mutations in Citizenship and Sovereignty*. Durham, NC: Duke University Press, 2006.

Ortíz-Márquez, Maribel. "From Third World Politics to First World Practices: Contemporary Latina Writers in the United States." *Interventions: Feminist Dialogues on Third World Women's Literature and Film*. Ed. Bishnupriya Ghosh and Brinda Bose. New York: Garland, 1999, 227–44.

Perloff, Marjorie. "Presidential Address 2006: It Must Change." *PMLA* 122, no. 3 (May 2007): 652–62.

Peters, Tom. *Re-imagine! Business Excellence in a Disruptive Age*. London: Dorling Kindersley Books, 2003.

———. *The Circle of Innovation: You Can't Shrink Your Way to Greatness*. New York: Knopf, 1997.

———. *Liberation Management: Necessary Disorganization for the Nanosecond Nineties*. New York: Knopf, 1992.

———. *Talent*. New York: DK Adult, 2005.

———, and Robert H. Waterman. *In Search of Excellence: Lessons from America's Best-Run Companies*. New York: HarperCollins, 1982.

Pieterse, Jan Nederveen. *Globalization and Culture: Global Mélange*. Lanham, MD: Rowman and Littlefield, 2009.

Portes, Alejandro. "From South of the Border: Hispanic Minorities in the United States." *The Immigration Reader: America in a Multidisciplinary Perspective*. Ed. David Jacobson. Oxford, UK: Wiley-Blackwell, 1998, 113–43.

Pottier, Johan. *Anthropology of Food: The Social Dynamics of Food Security*. Malden, MA: Policy Press, 1999.

Prasad, Anshuman, ed. *Postcolonial Theory and Organizational Analysis: A Critical Engagement*. New York: Palgrave Macmillan, 2003.

Pratt, Mary Louise. *Imperial Eyes: Travel Writing and Transculturation*. New York: Routledge, 1992.

"Puliga prmitivo fuedo monaci." *Food & Wine*. July 2003. Classic Wines Advertisement, 22–23.

Reich, Robert. *The Work of Nations: Preparing Ourselves for 21st-Century Capitalism*. New York: Knopf, 1991.

Reichl, Ruth, ed. *Endless Feasts: Sixty Years of Writing from* Gourmet. New York: Modern Library, 2002.

Rhinesmith, Stephen H. *A Manager's Guide to Globalization: Six Keys to Success in a Changing World*. Homewood, IL: Business One Irwin, 1993.

Ritzer, George, and Allan Liska. "'McDisneyization' and 'Post-Tourism': Complementary Perspectives on Contemporary Tourism." *Touring Cultures: Transformations in Travel and Theory*. Ed. Chris Rojek and John Urry. London: Routledge, 1997, 96–109.

Robbins, Bruce. *Secular Vocations: Intellectuals, Professionalism, Culture*. New York: Verso, 1993.

Robinson, Cedric. *Black Marxism: The Making of the Black Radical Tradition*. Raleigh: University of North Carolina Press, 2000.

Roden, Claudia. "The Arabian Picnic." *Endless Feasts: Sixty Years of Writing from Gourmet*. Ed. Ruth Reichl. New York: Modern Library, 2002, 65–72.

Rosaldo, Renato. *Culture & Truth: The Remaking of Social Analysis*. Boston: Beacon Press, 1989.

Rosenberg, Justin. *Follies of Globalisation Theory*. London: Verso, 2001.

———. "Globalization Theory: A Post-Mortem." *International Politics* 42, no. 1 (2005): 2–74.

Ross, Andrew. *Fast Boat to China: Corporate Flight and the Consequences of Free Trade; Lessons from Shanghai*. New York: Pantheon, 2006.

———. *Low Pay, High Profile: The Global Push for Fair Labor*. New York: New Press, 2004.

———, ed. *No Sweat: Fashion, Free Trade, and the Rights of Garment Workers*. New York: Verso, 1997.

———. *No-Collar: The Humane Workplace and Its Hidden Costs*. New York: Basic Books, 2002.

Rothenberg, David, and Wandee J. Pryor. *Writing the World: On Globalization*. Cambridge, MA: MIT Press, 2005.

Rowe, John Carlos. *The New American Studies*. Minneapolis: University of Minnesota Press, 2002.

———. "Reading *Reading Lolita in Tehran* in Idaho." *American Quarterly* 59, no. 2 (June 2007): 253–75.

Rowlinson, Michael, and Stephen Procter "Organizational Culture and Business History." *Organization Studies* 20, no. 3 (1999): 369–96.

Roy, Arundhati. "The Ladies Have Feelings, So . . . Shall We Leave It to the Experts?" *Writing the World: On Globalization*. Ed. David Rothenberg and Wandee J. Pryor. Cambridge, MA: MIT Press, 2005.

———. *Post-Nationalist American Studies*. Ed. John Carlos Rowe. Berkeley: University of California Press, 2000.

Salaita, Steven George. *Anti-Arab Racism in the USA: Where It Comes From and What It Means for Politics Today*. London: Pluto, 2006.

———. *The Holy Land in Transit: Colonialism and the Quest for Canaan*. Syracuse, NY: Syracuse University Press, 2006.

———. "Sand Niggers, Small Shops, and Uncle Sam: Cultural Negotiation in the Fiction of Joseph Geha and Diana Abu-Jaber." *Criticism* 43, no. 4 (Fall 2001):, 423–44.

———. *The Uncultured Wars: Arabs, Muslims and the Poverty of Liberal Thought—New Essays*. London: Zed Books, 2009.

San Jose State University. "Asian American Literature." *Course Proposal.* http://www. sjsu.edu/faculty/awilliams/E196.html. September 2002.

Santiago, Esmeralda. *América's Dream.* London: Virago, 1998.

———. *When I Was Puerto Rican.* Reading, MA: Addison-Wesley, 1993

Sassen, Saskia. *Deciphering the Global: Its Spaces, Scales, and Subjects.* New York: Routledge, 2007.

———. "Foreign Investment: A Neglected Variable." *The Immigration Reader: America in a Multidisciplinary Perspective.* Ed. David Jacobson. Oxford, UK: Wiley-Blackwell, 1998, 217–30.

———. *Globalization and Its Discontents: Essays on the New Mobility of People and Money.* New York: New Press, 1999.

———. *The Mobility of Labor and Capital: A Study in International Investment and Labor Flow.* Cambridge, UK: Cambridge University Press, 1988.

Saussy, Haun, ed. *Comparative Literature in an Age of Globalization.* Baltimore: Johns Hopkins University Press, 2006.

———. "Exquisite Cadavers Stitched from Fresh Nightmares: Of Memes, Hives, and Selfish Genes." *Comparative Literature in an Age of Globalization.* Ed. Haun Sassy. Baltimore: Johns Hopkins University Press, 2006, 3–43.

Schivelbusch, Wolfgang. *Tastes of Paradise: A Social History of Spices, Stimulants, and Intoxicants.* New York: Vintage Books, 1993.

Schlesinger, Arthur Meier. *The Disuniting of America.* New York: W. W. Norton, 1992.

Schmidt, Wallace V., and Roger Conaway et al., eds. *Communicating Globally: Intercultural Communication and International Business.* New York: Sage Publications, 2007.

Schoonmaker, Frank. "The Vine Dies Hard." *Endless Feasts: Sixty Years of Writing from Gourmet.* Ed. Ruth Reichl. New York: Modern Library, 2002, 104–8.

Schor, Juliet B., and Douglas B. Holt, eds. *The Consumer Society Reader.* New York: New Press, 2000.

Schulte-Peevers, Andrea. *Buenos Aires.* Melbourne: Lonely Planet Publications, 2000.

Sennett, Richard. *The Culture of the New Capitalism,* New Haven, CT: Yale University Press, 2006.

Shohat , Ella, and Robert Stam. *Unthinking Eurocentrism: Multiculturalism and the Media.* New York: Routledge, 1994.

Shortridge, Barbara, and James Shortridge, eds. *The Taste of American Place: A Reader on Regional and Ethnic Foods.* Lanham, MD: Rowman and Littlefield, 1998.

Sigal, Jane. "Jean-Georges's Asian Accent." *Food & Wine.* July 2003, 148–54 and 173–77.

Simmel, Georg. *The Philosophy of Money.* New York: Routledge, 2004.

Singh, Amritjit, and Peter Schmidt, eds. *Postcolonial Theory and the United States: Race, Ethnicity, and Literature.* Jackson: University Press of Mississippi, 2000.

Sollors, Werner. *Beyond Ethnicity: Consent and Descent in American Culture.* New York: Oxford University Press, 1986.

Sommer, Doris. "No Secrets." (1995). *The Real Thing: Testimonial Discourse and Latin America.* Ed. Georg Gugelberger Durham, NC: Duke University Press, 1996, 130–60.

Sone, Monica Itoi. *Nisei Daughter.* Boston: Little, Brown and Company, 1953.

Stahl, Leslie. "Interview with Lou Dobbs." *Sixty Minutes.* CBS, May 6, 2007.

Stern, Jane, and Michael. "Two for the Road: Havana, North Dakota." *Endless Feasts: Sixty Years of Writing from* Gourmet. Ed. Ruth Reichl. New York: Modern Library, 2002, 191–200.

Suárez, Lucía M. "Julia Alvarez and the Anxiety of Latina Representation." *Meridians: Feminism, Race, Transnationalism* 5, no. 1 (2004): 117–45.

Sucher, Sandra J. *Teaching the Moral Leader: A Literature-Based Leadership Course.* New York: Routledge, 2007.

Szadziuk, Maria. "Culture as Transition: Becoming a Woman in Bi-Ethnic Space." *Mosaic: A Journal for the Interdisciplinary Study of Literature* 32, no, 3 (September 1999): 109–29.

Takaki, Ronald. *A Different Mirror: A History of Multicultural America.* Boston: Little, Brown and Company, 1993.

Theroux, Paul. "All Aboard! Crossing the Rockies in Style." *Endless Feasts: Sixty Years of Writing from* Gourmet. Ed. Ruth Reichl. New York: Modern Library, 2002, 184–90.

———. *Blinding Light,* Boston: Mariner Books, 2005.

———. *Dark Star Safari: Overland from Cairo to Cape Town.* Boston: Houghton Mifflin, 2003.

———. *Hotel Honolulu.* Boston: Houghton Mifflin, 2001.

———. "Introduction." *The Best American Travel Writing.* Ed. Paul Theroux. New York: Houghton Mifflin, 2011, xvii–xxii.

———. *The Mosquito Coast.* New York: Penguin Books, 1982.

———. *Sir Vidia's Shadow: A Friendship Across Five Continents.* Boston: Houghton Mifflin, 1998.

———. "Strangers on a Train." *Sunrise with Seamonsters: Travels & Discoveries, 1964–1984.* Boston: Houghton Mifflin, 1985, 126–33.

———. *Time Out Series.* London: Penguin, 2001.

Thomas-Hope, Elizabeth. "Globalization and the Development of a Carribbean Migration." *Carribbean Migration: Globalized Identities.* Ed. Mary Chamberlain. New York: Routledge, 1998, 188–99.

Tomlinson, John. *Cultural Imperialism: An Introduction.* London: Continuum, 2001.

———. *Globalization and Culture.* Chicago: University of Chicago Press, 1999.

Trenkle, Norbert. "Tremors on the Global Market." *Krisis.* 2009. http://www.krisis.org/2009/tremors-on-the-global-market. August 2, 2010.

Trompenaars, Alfons. *Riding the Waves of Culture: Understanding Cultural Diversity in Business.* London: Economist Books, 1993.

Twain, Mark. *My Début as a Literary Person and Other Essays and Stories.* Hartford, CT: American Publishing Co., 1903.

———. *Roughing It.* New York: Harper & Brothers, 1913.

Veseth, Michael. *Selling Globalization: The Myth of the Global Economy.* Boulder, CO: Lynne Rienner Publishers, 1998.

Villas, James. "Down in the Low Country." *Endless Feasts: Sixty Years of Writing from* Gourmet. Ed. Ruth Reichl. New York: Modern Library, 2002, 168–83.

Vollmann, William T. *An Afghanistan Picture Show, or, How I Saved the World.* New York: Farrar, Straus and Giroux, 1992.

Wade, Robert. "Financial Regime Change." *New Left Review*. September 2008.

Wallerstein, Immanuel. *Decline of American Power: The U.S. in a Chaotic World*. New York: New Press, 2003.

———. "The National and the Universal: Can There Be Such a Thing as World Culture?" *Culture, Globalization, and the World-System: Contemporary Conditions for the Representation of Identity*. Ed. Anthony D. King. Minneapolis: University of Minnesota Press, 1997, 93–102.

———. *World-Systems Analysis: An Introduction*. Durham, NC: Duke University Press, 2004.

Watkins, Evan. *Throwaways: Work Culture and Consumer Education*. Palo Alto, CA: Stanford University Press, 1993.

Weber, Max. *The Protestant Ethic and the Spirit of Capitalism*. Trans. Peter Baehr and Gordon C. Wells. New York: Penguin, 2002.

Weinstein, Jeff. "The Art of Fusion" *Food & Wine*. September, 1998. http://www.foodandwine.com. October, 2003.

Wells, Pete. "A Chef at Peace." *Food & Wine*. July 2003, 74–78.

White, Jay D. "Knowledge Development: Views from Postpositivism, Poststructuralism, and Postmodernism." *Public Management in an Interconnected World: Essays in the Minnowbrook Tradition*. Ed. Mary Timney Bailey and Richard T. Mayer. Westport, CT: Greenwood Press, 1992, 159–76.

———. *Taking Language Seriously: The Narrative Foundations of Public Administration Research*. Washington, DC: Georgetown University Press, 1999.

Williams, Eric. *From Columbus to Castro: The History of the Caribbean 1492–1969*. New York: Vintage, 1984.

Williams, William H. A. "Immigration as a Pattern in American Culture." *The Immigration Reader: America in a Multidisciplinary Perspective*. Ed. David Jacobson. Oxford, UK: Wiley-Blackwell, 1998, 19–28.

Wong, Jade Snow. *Fifth Chinese Daughter*. New York: Harper, 1950.

Yamashita, Karen Tei. *Through the Arc of the Rain Forest*. Minneapolis, MN: Coffee House Press, 1990.

Yan, Yungxian. "Managed Globalization." *Many Globalizations: Cultural Diversity in the Contemporary World*. Ed. Peter L. Berger and Samuel P. Huntington. Oxford, UK: Oxford University Press, 2002, 27–39.

Yezierska, Anzia. *Bread Givers*. Garden City, NY: Doubleday, Page and Company, 1925.

Yúdice, George. "Testimonio and Postmodernism." (1991). *The Real Thing: Testimonial Discourse and Latin America*. Ed. Georg Gugelberger. Durham, NC: Duke University Press, 1996, 42–57.

Žižek, Slavoj. *Welcome to the Desert of the Real: Five Essays on September 11 and Related Dates*. London: Verso, 2002.

INDEX